Practical

Chinese/English English/Chinese Dictionary (Revised Edition)

中英
英中
常用 中英 辭典
(修訂版)

Edited and Compiled by
Duen Rou Chen
&
Francis Saw

黃敦柔
蘇發興   合編

J&R Co.
13729 Capistrano Rd.,
La Mirada, CA 90638

J&R Co.
13729 Capistrano Rd.,
La Mirada, CA 90638

常用中英/英中辭典 (修訂版)
A Practical Chinese/English English/Chinese Dictionary
(Revised Edition)

目錄
Table of Contents

編輯前言

編輯辭典是一項吃力任重的工作。因爲中、英語文的差異，編輯中英／英中辭典更是倍感艱鉅。

這一本"常用中英英中辭典"編輯工作是由任教於洛杉磯唐尼學區葛費絲中學及喜瑞都中文學校的黃敦柔女士和美國海外廣播新聞處翻譯蘇發興先生擔任。編者費長時間在研究和教學中文中，完成這本辭典，中外學生學習中英文將獲益匪淺。

此辭典以適應國小至大學學生學習中英文及海外僑生、外籍人士學習中國語文爲主。因此辭典中有中、英文註解、舉例和索引，非常適合英文讀者學習中文，也可適應一般社會人士參考。

此辭典所收的3,519漢字是依漢語拼音排列，並旁加注音符號，繁體字及簡體字對照表，書尾有許多用辭典練習，很適合中文教學和自修，這是一部標準繁、簡中英英中辭典。

此辭典是以黃彰任博士所著"黃草字庫"爲準，再選加"常用國字標準字體表"中之常用國字爲編寫的原則，是文字白話口語化，內容實用生動化，和查字簡便易懂化。假如此辭典有些錯誤，希望讀者能給編者貢獻寶貴的建議。

謝謝黃彰任博士，陳南瑾博士和蘇阮曉婉女士的鼓勵和支持，陳婷筆劃校對，蘇琤琤封面設計，Kathy的打字，此書才順利出版。

如何使用查字表？

爲了方便中國大陸、台灣及海外學習中文的讀者，本辭典所收漢字是依漢語拼音排列，並旁加注音符號、繁體字、簡體字和中、英註解和舉例。

如已知讀音的字，可直接由拼音欄而查到所想找的繁、簡體字。已學注音號的讀者則可參考書最後一頁的"發音對照表"而知該字的漢語拼音，或採用拼音、注音音節索引而可查出所需之字。

對於無法判斷讀音的字，可用"總筆劃對照表"。該表按筆劃排列，同筆劃的字又以部首排列，可參看部首查字表順序。簡體字用者，可參看簡體繁體對照表"。

Editorial Note

Compiling a dictionary is an arduous task regardless of the language involved, but compiling an English/Chinese dictionary is even more difficult because of the vast differences in the two languages.

The *Practical Chinese-English and English-Chinese Dictionary (Revised Edition)* was compiled and edited by Mrs. Duen Rou Chen, who teaches at the Griffiths Middle School of Downey Unified School District in Los Angeles and the Cerritos Chinese School, and Mr. Francis Saw, a free-lance translator.

The *Dictionary* can be effectively used from primary grades through college. Anyone interested in language learning, including overseas Chinese and other nationals, will find this book helpful. Included in the *Dictionary* are explanations and examples in Chinese and English, as well as an index toward the end of the book. It is also a good reference guide for the general public.

The 3,519 Chinese characters contained in this *Dictionary* are arranged in the order of the Chinese Pin-Yin System with notations in phonetic symbols as well as the traditional and simplified forms of writing. This book is ideal for self-study or teaching the Chinese language. Practice sheets are provided at the end of the book for drilling.

This *Dictionary's* format is based on the following principles: Chinese characters were first selected from the *Common Words in Huang-style Cursive* published by Dr. C. J. Huang. Then the characters from the *Table of Standard Chinese Characters in Common Use* were added. Written in the vernacular form of the written script, this *Dictionary* is presented in living Chinese language for practical use and easy reference.

The editors would appreciate very much the readers' valuable comments and suggestions for inclusion in future versions of this *Dictionary*.

Special thanks to Dr. Chang-Jen Huang, Dr. Nan Jim Chen, and Teresa Saw for their encouragement and support, without which this *Dictionary* could not have existed. Christine Chen, Cheng Cheng Tan and Kathy should also be acknowledged for their efforts in the proofreading, cover design and typesetting of this *Dictionary*.

How to Use the Cross Reference Tables?

For the convenience of readers from Mainland China, Taiwan and other countries in learning the Chinese language, this *Dictionary* presents the Chinese characters in the order of the Pin-Yin System, while providing notations in phonetic symbols, English definitions, and actual uses of the characters in useful phrases.

If the pronunciation of a word is known, the reader can look up the word in the Pin-Yin column and scan across to see the word in traditional and simplified forms. Readers familiar with the phonetic symbols can turn to the "Cross Reference of Pronunciations" on the last page of this *Dictionary*, look up the Pin-Yin of a particular word, and then locate that word in the body. The "Total Strokes Table" can be used to find a hard-to-pronounce character by the number of strokes. Users of simplified characters can make use of the "Cross Reference of Simplified and Traditional Characters."

漢語拼音 注音音節索引(ABC 排列)

1. 爲了方便學習拼音和注音的人士使用本書，特採用拼音，注音雙重索引，並附有漢字。
2. 每一音節後舉一字爲例，包括四個聲調的字。
3. 例如：一聲　二聲　三聲　四聲　輕聲
   mā　má　mǎ　mà　ma
   媽　麻　馬　罵　嗎
4. 漢字右邊的數字指本書正文頁碼。5.本書正文採用繁、簡兩種字體。

	A	ㄚ			chao	ㄔㄠ	抄	24
a	ㄚ	阿	1		che	ㄔㄜ	車	25
ai	ㄞ	哀	1		chen	ㄔㄣ	嗔	25
an	ㄢ	安	2		cheng	ㄔㄥ	撐	27
ang	ㄤ	骯	3		chi	ㄔ	吃	28
ao	ㄠ	熬	2		chong	ㄔㄨㄥ	沖	30
	B	ㄅ			chou	ㄔㄡ	抽	30
ba	ㄅㄚ	八	5		chung	ㄔㄨㄢ	川	33
bai	ㄅㄞ	白	6		chuang	ㄔㄨㄤ	瘡	34
ban	ㄅㄢ	班	6		chui	ㄔㄨㄟ	吹	34
bang	ㄅㄤ	邦	8		chun	ㄔㄨㄣ	春	35
bao	ㄅㄠ	包	8		chuo	ㄔㄨㄛ	戳	35
bei	ㄅㄟ	杯	10		ci	ㄘ	疵	35
ben	ㄅㄣ	奔	11		cong	ㄘㄨㄥ	匆	37
beng	ㄅㄥ	崩	11		cu	ㄘㄨ	粗	37
bi	ㄅㄧ	逼	11		cui	ㄘㄨㄟ	崔	38
bian	ㄅㄧㄢ	邊	13		cun	ㄘㄨㄣ	村	39
biao	ㄅㄧㄠ	標	14		cuo	ㄘㄨㄛ	搓	39
bie	ㄅㄧㄝ	別	14			D	ㄉ	
bing	ㄅㄧㄥ	兵	15		da	ㄉㄚ	搭	41
bo	ㄅㄛ	撥	15		dai	ㄉㄞ	獃	41
bu	ㄅㄨ	捕	16		dan	ㄉㄤ	丹	42
	C	ㄘ			dang	ㄉㄠ	當	43
ca	ㄘㄚ	擦	17		dao	ㄉㄜ	刀	44
cai	ㄘㄞ	猜	17		de	ㄉㄥ	得	45
can	ㄘㄢ	參	18		deng	ㄉㄧ	燈	46
cang	ㄘㄤ	倉	18		di	ㄉㄧㄢ	低	46
cao	ㄘㄠ	操	19		dian	ㄉㄧㄠ	掂	48
ce	ㄘㄜ	冊	19		diao	ㄉㄧㄝ	刁	50
ceng	ㄘㄥ	層	20		die	ㄉㄧㄥ	跌	51
cha	ㄔㄚ	叉	20		ding	ㄉㄨㄥ	丁	51
chai	ㄔㄞ	拆	21		dong	ㄉㄡ	東	52
chan	ㄔㄢ	摻	21		dou	ㄉㄨ	都	53
chang	ㄔㄤ	昌	22		du	ㄉㄨ	督	54

kui	ㄎㄨㄟ	窺	159		ming	ㄇㄧㄥ	名	202
kun	ㄎㄨㄣ	坤	160		miu	ㄇㄧㄡ	謬	203
kuo	ㄎㄨㄛ	括	161		mo	ㄇㄛ	摸	204

L ㄌ					mou	ㄇㄡ	牟	205
la	ㄌㄚ	拉	162		mu	ㄇㄨ	畝	206
lai	ㄌㄞ	來	162		**N ㄋ**			
lan	ㄌㄢ	蘭	163		na	ㄋㄚ	拿	208
lang	ㄌㄤ	郎	164		nai	ㄋㄞ	乃	208
lao	ㄌㄠ	撈	165		nan	ㄋㄢ	男	209
le	ㄌㄜ	樂	166		nao	ㄋㄠ	撓	209
lei	ㄌㄟ	勒	166		nei	ㄋㄟ	餒	210
leng	ㄌㄥ	冷	168		nen	ㄋㄣ	嫩	210
li	ㄌㄧ	釐	168		neng	ㄋㄥ	能	210
lian	ㄌㄧㄢ	連	171		ni	ㄋㄧ	尼	210
liang	ㄌㄧㄤ	良	173		nian	ㄋㄧㄢ	年	211
liao	ㄌㄧㄠ	撩	174		niang	ㄋㄧㄤ	娘	212
lie	ㄌㄧㄝ	列	175		niao	ㄋㄧㄠ	鳥	212
lin	ㄌㄧㄣ	鄰	176		nie	ㄋㄧㄝ	捏	213
ling	ㄌㄧㄥ	玲	177		nin	ㄋㄧㄣ	您	213
liu	ㄌㄧㄡ	溜	178		ning	ㄋㄧㄥ	寧	213
long	ㄌㄨㄥ	龍	180		niu	ㄋㄧㄡ	妞	214
lou	ㄌㄡ	婁	181		nong	ㄋㄨㄥ	農	214
lu	ㄌㄨ	盧	182		nu	ㄋㄨ	奴	215
lu	ㄌㄩ	驢	184		nu	ㄋㄩ	女	215
luan	ㄌㄨㄢ	巒	186		nuan	ㄋㄨㄢ	暖	215
lue	ㄌㄩㄝ	掠	187		nue	ㄋㄩㄝ	虐	216
lun	ㄌㄨㄣ	淪	187		nuo	ㄋㄨㄛ	挪	216
luo	ㄌㄨㄛ	羅	187		**O ㄛ**			

M ㄇ					o	ㄛ	哦	217
ma	ㄇㄚ	媽	189		ou	ㄡ	謳	217
mai	ㄇㄞ	埋	190		**P ㄆ**			
man	ㄇㄢ	蠻	191		pa	ㄆㄚ	趴	218
mang	ㄇㄤ	忙	192		pai	ㄆㄞ	拍	219
mao	ㄇㄠ	貓	193		pan	ㄆㄢ	潘	219
me	ㄇㄜ	麼	194		pang	ㄆㄤ	乓	220
mei	ㄇㄟ	沒	194		pao	ㄆㄠ	拋	221
men	ㄇㄣ	門	196		pei	ㄆㄟ	呸	222
meng	ㄇㄥ	檬	196		peng	ㄆㄥ	抨	223
mi	ㄇㄧ	咪	197		pi	ㄆㄧ	批	224
mian	ㄇㄧㄢ	綿	199		pian	ㄆㄧㄢ	扁	226
miao	ㄇㄧㄠ	瞄	201		piao	ㄆㄧㄠ	漂	227
mie	ㄇㄧㄝ	滅	202		pie	ㄆㄧㄝ	撇	228
min	ㄇㄧㄣ	民	202		pin	ㄆㄧㄣ	拼	229

漢語拼音 注音音節索引(ㄅㄆㄇ排列)

	B	ㄅ	
ba	ㄅㄚ	八	5
bai	ㄅㄞ	白	6
ban	ㄅㄢ	班	6
bang	ㄅㄤ	邦	8
bao	ㄅㄠ	包	8
bei	ㄅㄟ	杯	10
ben	ㄅㄣ	奔	11
beng	ㄅㄥ	崩	11
bi	ㄅㄧ	逼	11
bian	ㄅㄧㄢ	邊	13
biao	ㄅㄧㄠ	標	14
bie	ㄅㄧㄝ	別	14
bing	ㄅㄧㄥ	兵	15
bo	ㄅㄛ	撥	15
bu	ㄅㄨ	捕	16

	P	ㄆ	
pa	ㄆㄚ	叭	218
pai	ㄆㄞ	拍	219
pan	ㄆㄢ	潘	219
pang	ㄆㄤ	乓	220
pao	ㄆㄠ	抛	221
pei	ㄆㄟ	呸	222
peng	ㄆㄥ	抨	223
pi	ㄆㄧ	批	224
pian	ㄆㄧㄢ	扁	226
piao	ㄆㄧㄝ	漂	227
pie	ㄆㄧㄝ	撇	228
pin	ㄆㄧㄣ	拚	229
ping	ㄆㄧㄥ	乒	219
po	ㄆㄛ	頗	231
pou	ㄆㄨ	剖	232
pu	ㄆㄨ	仆	232

	M	ㄇ	
ma	ㄇㄚ	媽	189
mai	ㄇㄞ	埋	190
man	ㄇㄢ	蠻	191
mang	ㄇㄤ	忙	192
mao	ㄇㄧㄠ	貓	193
me	ㄇㄜ	麼	194

mei	ㄇㄟ	沒	194
men	ㄇㄣ	門	196
meng	ㄇㄥ	檬	196
mi	ㄇㄧ	咪	197
mian	ㄇㄧㄢ	綿	199
miao	ㄇㄧㄠ	瞄	201
mie	ㄇㄧㄝ	滅	202
min	ㄇㄧㄣ	民	202
ming	ㄇㄧㄥ	名	202
miu	ㄇㄧㄡ	謬	203
mo	ㄇㄛ	摸	204
mou	ㄇㄡ	牟	205
mu	ㄇㄨ	畝	206

	F	ㄈ	
fa	ㄈㄚ	發	60
fan	ㄈㄢ	帆	60
fang	ㄈㄤ	方	62
fei	ㄈㄟ	飛	63
fen	ㄈㄣ	分	65
feng	ㄈㄥ	峰	66
fo	ㄈㄛ	佛	68
fu	ㄈㄨ	夫	68

	D	ㄉ	
da	ㄉㄚ	搭	41
dai	ㄉㄞ	獃	41
dan	ㄉㄤ	丹	42
dang	ㄉㄠ	當	43
dao	ㄉㄜ	刀	44
de	ㄉㄥ	得	45
deng	ㄉㄧ	燈	46
di	ㄉㄧㄢ	低	46
dian	ㄉㄧㄠ	掂	48
diao	ㄉㄧㄝ	刁	50
die	ㄉㄧㄥ	跌	51
ding	ㄉㄨㄥ	丁	51
dong	ㄉㄡ	東	52
dou	ㄉㄨ	都	53
du	ㄉㄨ	督	54
duan	ㄉㄨㄢ	端	55
dui	ㄉㄨㄟ	堆	55

dun	ㄉㄨㄣ	敦	56		nuo	ㄋㄨㄛ	挪	216
duo	ㄉㄨㄛ	多	56		**L**	**ㄌ**		
T	**ㄊ**				la	ㄌㄚ	拉	162
ta	ㄊㄚ	塌	296		lai	ㄌㄞ	來	162
tai	ㄊㄞ	胎	296		lan	ㄌㄢ	蘭	163
tan	ㄊㄢ	坍	298		lang	ㄌㄤ	郎	164
tang	ㄊㄤ	湯	300		lao	ㄌㄠ	撈	165
tao	ㄊㄠ	濤	301		le	ㄌㄜ	樂	166
te	ㄊㄜ	忑	302		lei	ㄌㄟ	勒	166
teng	ㄊㄥ	疼	302		leng	ㄌㄥ	冷	168
ti	ㄊㄧ	梯	303		li	ㄌㄧ	鰲	168
tian	ㄊㄧㄢ	天	304		lian	ㄌㄧㄢ	連	171
tiao	ㄊㄧㄠ	挑	305		liang	ㄌㄧㄤ	良	173
tie	ㄊㄧㄝ	貼	306		liao	ㄌㄧㄠ	撩	174
ting	ㄊㄧㄥ	聽	306		lie	ㄌㄧㄝ	列	175
tong	ㄊㄨㄥ	通	308		lin	ㄌㄧㄣ	鄰	176
tou	ㄊㄡ	偷	309		ling	ㄌㄧㄥ	玲	177
tu	ㄊㄨ	凸	309		liu	ㄌㄧㄡ	溜	178
tuan	ㄊㄨㄢ	湍	311		long	ㄌㄨㄥ	龍	180
tui	ㄊㄨㄟ	推	311		lou	ㄌㄡ	婁	181
tun	ㄊㄨㄣ	吞	312		lu	ㄌㄨ	盧	182
tuo	ㄊㄨㄛ	托	313		lu	ㄌㄩ	驢	184
N	**ㄋ**				luan	ㄌㄨㄢ	巒	186
na	ㄋㄚ	拿	208		lue	ㄌㄩㄝ	掠	187
nai	ㄋㄞ	乃	208		lun	ㄌㄨㄣ	淪	187
nan	ㄋㄢ	男	209		luo	ㄌㄨㄛ	羅	187
nao	ㄋㄠ	撓	209		**G**	**ㄍ**		
nei	ㄋㄟ	餒	210		gai	ㄍㄞ	該	73
nen	ㄋㄣ	嫩	210		gan	ㄍㄢ	肝	73
neng	ㄋㄥ	能	210		gang	ㄍㄤ	剛	75
ni	ㄋㄧ	尼	210		gao	ㄍㄠ	高	76
nian	ㄋㄧㄢ	年	211		ge	ㄍㄜ	鴿	77
niang	ㄋㄧㄤ	娘	212		gei	ㄍㄟ	給	78
niao	ㄋㄧㄠ	鳥	212		gen	ㄍㄣ	根	79
nie	ㄋㄧㄝ	捏	213		geng	ㄍㄥ	更	79
nin	ㄋㄧㄣ	您	213		gong	ㄍㄨㄥ	躬	79
ning	ㄋㄧㄥ	寧	213		gou	ㄍㄡ	勾	81
niu	ㄋㄧㄡ	妞	214		gu	ㄍㄨ	姑	82
nong	ㄋㄨㄥ	農	214		gua	ㄍㄨㄚ	颳	84
nu	ㄋㄨ	奴	215		guai	ㄍㄨㄞ	乖	85
nu	ㄋㄩ	女	215		guan	ㄍㄨㄢ	官	85
nuan	ㄋㄨㄢ	暖	215		guang	ㄍㄨㄤ	光	85
nue	ㄋㄩㄝ	虐	216		gui	ㄍㄨㄟ	歸	87

gun	ㄍㄨㄣ	滾	88
guo	ㄍㄨㄛ	鍋	89
K		**ㄎ**	
ka	ㄎㄚ	卡	150
kai	ㄎㄞ	開	150
kan	ㄎㄢ	刊	150
kang	ㄎㄤ	康	151
kao	ㄎㄠ	考	152
ke	ㄎㄜ	苛	153
ken	ㄎㄣ	肯	155
keng	ㄎㄥ	坑	155
kong	ㄎㄨㄥ	空	155
kou	ㄎㄡ	口	156
ku	ㄎㄨ	哭	156
kua	ㄎㄨㄚ	誇	157
kuai	ㄎㄨㄞ	快	157
kuan	ㄎㄨㄢ	寬	158
kuang	ㄎㄨㄤ	匡	158
kui	ㄎㄨㄟ	窺	159
kun	ㄎㄨㄣ	坤	160
kuo	ㄎㄨㄛ	括	161
H		**ㄏ**	
ha	ㄏㄚ	哈	90
gai	ㄏㄞ	孩	90
hang	ㄏㄤ	行	93
hao	ㄏㄠ	蠔	93
he	ㄏㄜ	呵	95
hei	ㄏㄟ	黑	97
hen	ㄏㄣ	痕	97
heng	ㄏㄥ	亨	98
hong	ㄏㄨㄥ	烘	98
hou	ㄏㄡ	瘊	100
hu	ㄏㄨ	乎	101
hua	ㄏㄚ	嘩	103
huai	ㄏㄨㄞ	懷	104
huan	ㄏㄨㄢ	歡	105
huang	ㄏㄨㄤ	肓	106
hui	ㄏㄨㄟ	輝	108
hun	ㄏㄨㄣ	昏	111
huo	ㄏㄨㄛ	豁	112
J		**ㄐ**	
ji	ㄐㄧ	几	114
jia	ㄐㄧㄚ	加	120
jian	ㄐㄧㄢ	尖	122
jiang	ㄐㄧㄤ	江	127
jiao	ㄐㄧㄠ	交	129
jie	ㄐㄧㄝ	階	133
jin	ㄐㄧㄣ	金	136
jing	ㄐㄧㄥ	京	138
jiong	ㄐㄩㄥ	窘	141
jiu	ㄐㄧㄡ	究	141
ju	ㄐㄩ	居	143
juan	ㄐㄩㄢ	捐	146
jue	ㄐㄩㄝ	抉	147
jun	ㄐㄩㄣ	軍	148
Q		**ㄑ**	
qi	ㄑㄧ	柒	234
qia	ㄑㄧㄚ	掐	238
qian	ㄑㄧㄢ	韆	239
qiang	ㄑㄧㄤ	槍	241
qiao	ㄑㄧㄠ	悄	242
qie	ㄑㄧㄝ	切	244
qin	ㄑㄧㄣ	欽	245
qing	ㄑㄧㄥ	青	246
qiong	ㄑㄩㄥ	窮	248
qiu	ㄑㄧㄡ	秋	248
qu	ㄑㄩ	區	249
quan	ㄑㄩㄢ	圈	251
que	ㄑㄩㄝ	缺	253
qun	ㄑㄩㄣ	群	253
X		**ㄒ**	
xi	ㄒㄧ	吸	328
xia	ㄒㄧㄚ	蝦	332
xian	ㄒㄧㄢ	纖	334
xiang	ㄒㄧㄤ	香	337
xiao	ㄒㄧㄠ	肖	339
xie	ㄒㄧㄝ	些	341
xin	ㄒㄧㄣ	新	344
xing	ㄒㄧㄥ	興	345
xiong	ㄒㄩㄥ	兄	347
xiu	ㄒㄧㄡ	休	347
xu	ㄒㄩ	須	349
xuan	ㄒㄩㄢ	宣	351
xue	ㄒㄩㄝ	削	353
xun	ㄒㄩㄣ	勛	353
Zh		**ㄓ**	

Pinyin	Zhuyin	Character	Page
zha	ㄓㄚ	閘	393
zhai	ㄓㄞ	齋	394
zhan	ㄓㄢ	粘	395
zhang	ㄓㄤ	張	397
zhao	ㄓㄠ	朝	398
zhe	ㄓㄜ	遮	400
zhen	ㄓㄣ	珍	401
zheng	ㄓㄥ	爭	403
zhi	ㄓ	汁	405
zhong	ㄓㄨㄥ	鐘	410
zhou	ㄓㄡ	州	412
zhu	ㄓㄨ	朱	414
zhua	ㄓㄨㄚ	抓	416
zhuan	ㄓㄨㄢ	專	416
zhuang	ㄓㄨㄤ	莊	417
zhui	ㄓㄨㄟ	椎	418
zhun	ㄓㄨㄣ	準	419
zhuo	ㄓㄨㄛ	捉	419
Ch	**ㄔ**		
cha	ㄔㄚ	叉	20
chai	ㄔㄞ	拆	21
chan	ㄔㄢ	摻	21
chang	ㄔㄤ	昌	22
chao	ㄔㄠ	抄	24
che	ㄔㄜ	車	25
chen	ㄔㄣ	嗔	25
cheng	ㄔㄥ	撐	27
chi	ㄔ	吃	28
chong	ㄔㄨㄥ	沖	30
chou	ㄔㄡ	抽	30
chung	ㄔㄨㄢ	川	33
chuang	ㄔㄨㄤ	瘡	34
chui	ㄔㄨㄟ	吹	34
chun	ㄔㄨㄣ	春	35
chuo	ㄔㄨㄛ	戳	35
Sh	**ㄕ**		
sha	ㄕㄚ	殺	263
shai	ㄕㄞ	篩	263
shan	ㄕㄢ	山	265
shang	ㄕㄤ	殤	267
shao	ㄕㄠ	稍	267
she	ㄕㄜ	賒	268
shei	ㄕㄟ	誰	270
shen	ㄕㄣ	伸	270
sheng	ㄕㄥ	生	272
shi	ㄕ	失	273
shou	ㄕㄡ	收	279
shu	ㄕㄨ	書	280
shua	ㄕㄨㄚ	刷	284
shuai	ㄕㄨㄞ	衰	284
shuan	ㄕㄨㄢ	栓	285
shuang	ㄕㄨㄤ	雙	285
shui	ㄕㄨㄟ	水	286
shun	ㄕㄨㄣ	順	286
shuo	ㄕㄨㄛ	說	287
R	**ㄖ**		
ran	ㄖㄢ	然	254
rang	ㄖㄤ	壤	254
rao	ㄖㄠ	饒	254
re	ㄖㄜ	惹	255
ren	ㄖㄣ	人	255
reng	ㄖㄥ	扔	256
ri	ㄖ	日	256
rong	ㄖㄨㄥ	榮	256
rou	ㄖㄡ	柔	257
ru	ㄖㄨ	如	258
ruan	ㄖㄨㄢ	軟	259
rui	ㄖㄨㄟ	蕊	259
run	ㄖㄨㄣ	閏	260
ruo	ㄖㄨㄛ	若	260
C	**ㄘ**		
ca	ㄘㄚ	擦	17
cai	ㄘㄞ	猜	17
can	ㄘㄢ	參	18
cang	ㄘㄤ	倉	18
cao	ㄘㄠ	操	19
ce	ㄘㄜ	冊	19
ceng	ㄘㄥ	層	20
ci	ㄘ	疵	35
cong	ㄘㄨㄥ	匆	37
cu	ㄘㄨ	粗	37
cui	ㄘㄨㄟ	崔	38
cun	ㄘㄨㄣ	村	39
cuo	ㄘㄨㄛ	搓	39
Z	**ㄗ**		
za	ㄗㄚ	札	389

拼音 拼音 Pinyin	正體 正体 Traditional Character	簡體 简体 Simplified Character	中英文註解 中英文注解 Chinese/English Definition	舉例 举例 Usage
A				
ā ㄚ	阿	阿	用于姓或名之前 use before name	阿李(ā lǐ) A Li 阿姨(ā yí) auntie
ā ㄚ	啊	啊	表贊嘆的感嘆詞 exclamation (showing agreement) 表赞叹的感叹词	啊！我忘記了！(ā! wǒ wàngjì le! 啊！我忘记了！) Oh! I forgot! 她真美麗啊！(tā zhēn měilì ā!) 她真美丽啊！She is really beautiful
āi ㄞ	哀	哀	悲痛 sorrow	哀悼(āi dào) to mourn 悲哀(bēi āi) grief
āi ㄞ	哎	哎	表不滿的感嘆詞 exclamation (showing dissatisfaction) 表不满的感叹词	哎！我有什麼辦法！(āi wǒ yǒu shénme bànfǎ) 哎！我有什么办法！ Ah! What can I do?
āi ㄞ	埃	埃	細的灰塵 dust 细的灰尘	塵埃 (chén āi)尘埃 dust 埃及(āi jí) Egypt
ái ㄞˊ	挨	挨	遭受，拖延 suffer, delay endure	挨餓 (ái è) 挨饿 be starved 挨罵 (ái mà) 挨骂 be scolded
ái ㄞˊ	癌	癌	發生於身體內外的惡性腫瘤 cancer 发生於身体内外的恶性肿瘤	癌症(ái zhèng) cancer 癌細胞(ái xì bāo) 癌细胞 cancer cell
ái ㄞˊ	皚	皑	雪白，潔白 white as snow 雪白，洁白	皚皚白雪 (ái ái bái xuě) white snow 皑皑白雪
ǎi ㄞˇ	藹	蔼	和氣 friendly 和气	和藹 (hé ǎi)和蔼 friendly 和藹可親(hé ǎi kě qīn) 和蔼可亲 cordial

ǎi ㄞˇ	矮	矮	短小 short	矮小(ǎi xiǎo) short 矮人(ǎi rén) dwarf
ài ㄞˋ	愛	爱	強烈喜歡 love 强烈喜欢	愛人(ài rén) 愛人 lover 可愛(kě ài)可爱 lovely
ài ㄞˋ	礙	碍	阻隔，妨害 obstruct	妨礙(fáng ài)妨碍obstruct 礙事(ài shì) 碍事 stand in the way of
ài ㄞˋ	嬡	嫒	稱對方的女兒 daughter 称对方的女儿	令嬡(lìng ài)令嫒 your daughter
ài ㄞˋ	艾	艾	1.開小黃花草本植物，可治病；2.停 moxa, mugwort, stop 1.开小黄花草本植物，可治病；2.停	艾草(ài cǎo) moxa 方興未艾(fāng xīng wèi ài) 方兴未艾 booming
ài ㄞˋ	唉	唉	表可惜的感嘆詞 to sigh 表可惜的感叹词	唉！我病了！(ài! wǒ bìng le)Ah! I am sick! 唉！我很累！(ài! wǒ hěn lèi) Ah! I am tired!
ān ㄢ	安	安	平靜 peace 平静	平安(píng ān) peaceful 安全(ān quán) safety 安排(ān pái) arrange
ān ㄢ	諳	谙	熟悉，知曉 well versed in 熟悉	不諳水性(bú ān shuǐ xìng) 不谙水性 not a swimmer
ān ㄢ	庵	庵	圓形的草屋 hut 圆形的草屋	尼姑庵(ní gū ān) Buddhist convent 庵堂(ān táng) nunnery
ǎn ㄢˇ	俺	俺	北方人稱"我"，"我們" I, we 北方人称"我"，"我们"	俺也不知道(ǎn yě bù zhī dào) I don't know either
àn ㄢˋ	案	案	長桌 long table 长桌	議案(yì àn) 议案 draft of law 破案(pò àn) crack a criminal case

2

àn ㄢˋ	暗	暗	不亮 not bright	黑暗(hēi àn) darkness 暗殺(àn shā) 暗杀 assassinate
àn ㄢˋ	岸	岸	江，河，湖，海邊 的地 the land by a river, lake or sea江， 河，湖，海边的地	河岸(hé àn) river bank 海岸(hǎi àn)seashore
àn ㄢˋ	按	按	用手壓 press with hand 用手压	按照(àn zhào) according to 按摩(àn mó) massage
àn ㄢˋ	黯	黯	昏暗 dim, gloomy	黯然(àn rán) depressed 黯淡無光(àn dàn wú guāng) 黯淡无光 gloomy
āng ㄤ	骯	肮	污穢，不清潔 dirty 污秽，不清洁	骯髒(āng zāng) 肮脏 dirty
áng ㄤˊ	昂	昂	高舉 hold high 高举	昂首(áng shǒu) hold high one's head 昂貴(áng guì) 昂贵 expensive
āo ㄠ	凹	凹	低陷下去或內縮進 去 dented	凹入(āo rù) dented 凹凸不平(āo tū bù píng) uneven
áo ㄠ	敖	敖	出去遊玩 stroll around 出去遊玩	敖遊(áo yóu) 敖遊 stroll around 孫叔敖(sūn shú áo) Sun Shuao, historical figure
áo ㄠˊ	熬	熬	久煮，忍受 stew, suffer	熬藥(áo yào) 熬药 decoct herb medicine 煎熬(jiān áo) 煎熬 torment
áo ㄠˊ	遨	遨	隨意出外玩，不受 拘束的樣子 stroll 随意出外玩，不受 拘束的样子	遨遊(áo yóu) 遨遊 roam 遨放(áo fàng) unrestrained
áo ㄠˊ	翱	翱	鳥飛的樣子；逍遙 自得的樣子 take wing 鸟飞的样子； 逍遥自得的样子	翱翔(áo xiáng)翱翔 hover
ào ㄠˋ	傲	傲	驕慢 arrogant 骄慢	驕傲(jiāo ào)骄傲 conceited 傲慢(ào màn) 傲慢arrogant

ào ㄠˋ	奧	奥	不容易懂 difficult to understand	奧妙(ào miào) 奥妙marvel 奧秘 (ào mì)奥秘 profound mystery 奧運會(ào yùn hùi)奥运会 Olympic Games
ào ㄠˋ	澳	澳	海邊彎曲可以停 靠船的地方 inlet, a bay 海边弯曲可以停 靠船的地方	澳洲(ào zhōu)澳洲 Australia
ào ㄠˋ	懊	懊	煩惱，悔恨 upset, regret 烦恼，悔恨	懊悔(ào huǐ) 懊悔regret 懊喪(ào sàng)懊丧 depressed
ào ㄠˋ	拗	拗	不順從 stubborn 不顺从	拗口(ào kǒu) hard to pronounce 拗令(ào lìng) tongue twister

B

bā ㄅㄚ	八	八	七加一得到的數 目字 eight 七加一得到的数 目字	八成(bā chéng) eighty percent 八面玲瓏(bā miàn líng lóng) 八面玲珑 very sociable
bā pá ㄅㄚ ㄆㄚˊ	扒	扒	抓住 hold on to	扒住不放(bā zhù bú fàng) cling tight to 扒手(pá shǒu) pickpocket
ba ㄅㄚ·	吧	吧	表商榷或祈使的 語尾助詞particle used after an imperative sentence 表商榷或祈使的 语尾助词	回家吧(huí jiā ba) Go home! 算了吧(suàn le ba) forget about it
bā ㄅㄚ	疤	疤	傷口愈後留下的 痕跡 scar 伤口愈后 留下的痕迹	疤痕(bā hén) scar 瘡疤(chuāng bā) 疮疤 scar
bá ㄅㄚˊ	拔	拔	抽起 pull up, pull out	選拔(xuǎn bá)选拔 choose 拔河(bá hé) tug-of-war
bá ㄅㄚˊ	跋	跋	在草裏走 walk on the grass 在草里走	跋涉(ba shè) trudge 跋扈(bá hù) domineering
bǎ ㄅㄚˇ	把	把	握 hold, grasp	把持(bǎ chí) control 把風(bǎ fēng) 把风 watch out for
bǎ ㄅㄚˇ	靶	靶	射擊的目標 target 射击的目标	靶場(bǎ chǎng) 靶场 shooting range 箭靶(jiàn bǎ) target for archery
bà ㄅㄚˋ	爸	爸	父親 father 父亲	爸爸(bà ba) father 乾爸(gān bà) godfather
bà ㄅㄚˋ	壩	坝	截住河流的建築物 dam 截住河流的建筑物	水壩(shuǐ bà) 水坝dam 河壩(hé bà) 河坝 river dam
bà ㄅㄚˋ	霸	霸	古時諸侯的首領 chief of feudal princes 古时诸侯的首领	惡霸(è bà)恶霸local tyrant 霸佔(bà zhàn) occupy forcibly

bà ㄅㄚˋ	罷	罢	停 stop	罷工(bà gōng) 罢工 strike 罷免(bà miǎn) 罢免 remove from office
bái ㄅㄞˊ	白	白	素色 white	白人(bái rén) white man, Caucasian 白天(bái tiān) day time
bǎi ㄅㄞˇ	百	百	十的十倍 hundred	一百(yì bǎi) one hundred 百分比(bǎi fēn bǐ) percentage
bǎi ㄅㄞˇ	佰	佰	"百"的大寫 the number 100 in word form "百"的大写	壹佰(yì bǎi) one hundred 壹佰萬(yì bǎi wàn) 一百萬 one million
bǎi ㄅㄞˇ	柏	柏	木質堅實的常綠喬 木 cypress 木质坚实的常绿乔 木	柏樹(bǎi shù) 柏树 cypress 柏油路(bǎi yóu lù) asphalt road
bǎi ㄅㄞˇ	擺	摆	安放 put, place	搖擺(yáo bǎi)摇摆 swaying 擺動(bǎi dòng) 摆动 swinging
bài ㄅㄞˋ	拜	拜	低頭拱手行禮或兩 手伏地行禮worship 低头拱手行礼或两 手伏地行礼	拜拜(bài bài) worship god 拜訪(bài fǎng) 拜访 pay a visit
bài ㄅㄞˋ	敗	败	戰不勝，輸 be defeated, lose 战不胜，输	失敗(shī bài)失败 failure 打敗(dǎ bài)打败 defeat
bān ㄅㄢ	班	班	一種小團體 a class, squad 一种小团体	值班(zhí bān) be on duty 班長(bān zhǎng) 班长 squad leader
bān ㄅㄢ	頒	颁	宣布，賜 proclaim, issue 宣布，赐	頒發(bān fā) 颁发 issue 頒獎(bān jiǎng) 颁奖 present award
bān ㄅㄢ	般	般	種類 sort 种类	百般(bǎi bān) in every possible way 一般(yì bān) in general

bān ㄅㄢ	搬	搬	移動位置 move, shift (furniture, etc) 移动位置	搬家(bān jiā) move one's residence 搬運工(bān yùn gōng) 搬运工 porter
bān ㄅㄢ	斑	斑	雜色 spot 杂色	斑點(bān diǎn) 斑点 stain 斑馬(bān mǎ) 斑马 zebra
bǎn ㄅㄢˇ	板	板	片木 board	黑板(hēi bǎn) blackboard 木板(mù bǎn) plank
bǎn ㄅㄢˇ	版	版	冊籍 printing plate	再版(zài bǎn) second edition 版權(bǎn quán) 版权 copyright
bǎn ㄅㄢˇ	闆	板	店主 boss	老闆(lǎo bǎn)老板 the boss 老闆娘(lǎo bǎn niáng) 老板娘female boss
bàn ㄅㄢˋ	辦	办	處理 handle, manage 处理	辦事(bàn shì) 办事 handle affairs 辦法(bàn fǎ) 办法 method, way
bàn ㄅㄢˋ	扮	扮	裝飾 to decorate 装饰	扮演(bàn yǎn) act 裝扮(zhuāng bàn)裝扮 to dress up
bàn ㄅㄢˋ	伴	伴	同伴 companion	伴侶(bàn lǚ) couple 陪伴(péi bàn) accompany
bàn ㄅㄢˋ	半	半	二分之一 half	一半(yí bàn) half 半價(bàn jià) 半价 half price
bàn ㄅㄢˋ	拌	拌	攪和 to mix 搅和	拌勻(bàn yún) mix well 攪拌(jiǎo bàn) 搅拌 to stir
bàn ㄅㄢˋ	絆	绊	繫馬腳的繩子，腳 受阻跌倒entangle, stumble 繫马脚的绳 子，脚受阻跌倒	絆了一跤(bàn le yī jiāo) 絆了一跤 trip and fall 絆腳石(bàn jiǎo shí) 絆脚石 stumbling block

bàn ㄅㄢˋ	瓣	瓣	花片 petal segment	花瓣(huā bàn) petal
bāng ㄅㄤ	邦	邦	國家 country 国家	邦交(bāng jiāo) diplomatic relations 聯邦(lián bāng) 联邦 federation
bāng ㄅㄤ	幫	帮	輔助，群，集團 help, gang, group 辅助，群，集团	幫手(bāng shǒu)帮手helper 幫派(bāng pài) 帮派gang
bǎng ㄅㄤˇ	綁	绑	捆起來 tie up	捆綁(kǔn bǎng)捆绑tie up 綁架(bǎng jià) 绑架kidnap
bǎng ㄅㄤˇ	榜	榜	牆上的通告 list of names posted on wall 揭在墙上的通告	榜樣(bǎng yàng) 榜样 example, model
bàng ㄅㄤˋ	蚌	蚌	淡水中的橢圓軟殼 動物 clam淡水中的 椭圆软壳动物	蚌殼(bàng ké)蚌壳 shell
bàng ㄅㄤˋ	棒	棒	木棍；好 stick; good	很棒(hěn bàng) very good 棒球(bàng qiú) baseball
bàng ㄅㄤˋ	謗	谤	斥他人過失 scold someone's mistake 斥他人过失	誹謗(fěi bàng)诽谤 slander
bàng ㄅㄤˋ	磅	磅	重量單位 pound (weight) 重量单位	磅秤(bàng chèng) scale (for weighing)
bàng ㄅㄤˋ	鎊	镑	貨幣單位 pound (currency) 货币单位	英鎊(yīng bàng) 英镑 pound sterling
bāo ㄅㄠ	包	包	裹起來 wrap up 裹起来	包裹(bāo guǒ) package 包圍(bāo wéi)包围 surround 錢包(qián bāo) purse 钱包
bāo ㄅㄠ	胞	胞	同父母的子女；裹 在胎兒外的薄膜 children of same parents, placenta 同父母的子女；裹 在胎儿外的薄膜	胞衣(bāo yī) placenta 同胞(tóng bāo) compatriot 細胞(xì bāo) cell
bāo ㄅㄠ	苞	苞	花沒開前包著的花 朵 bud 花没开前包著的花 朵	花苞(huā bāo) bud 含苞待放(hán bāo dài fàng) still in the bud

báo bo、 ㄅㄠˊ ㄅㄛˊ	薄	薄	不厚 not thick, thin	薄纸(báo zhǐ) 薄纸 thin paper 薄荷(bò hé)薄荷 mint
báo ㄅㄠˊ	雹	雹	空中水蒸汽遇冷结 成的冰粒 hail 空中水蒸汽遇 冷结成的冰粒	冰雹(bīng báo) hail
bǎo ㄅㄠˇ	保	保	守衛, 負責 guard, take responsibility 守卫, 负责	保護(bǎo hù) 保护 protect 保存(bǎo cún) preserve
bǎo ㄅㄠˇ	堡	堡	防御盗匪的土城 fortress 防御盗匪的土城	堡壘(bǎo lěi) 堡垒 fortress 城堡(chéng bǎo) castle
bǎo ㄅㄠˇ	寶	宝	珍貴的東西 treasure 珍贵的东西	寶貝(bǎo bèi)宝贝 precious object 寶物(bǎo wù)宝物treasure
bǎo ㄅㄠˇ	飽	饱	吃得足夠；豐滿； 充分 be full, plentiful, sufficient 吃得足够；丰满； 充分	飽和(bǎo hé) 饱和 saturated 吃飽(chī bǎo)吃饱 have eaten one's fill
bǎo ㄅㄠˇ	鴇	鸨	鳥名, 不善于飛, 性淫 bustard 鸟名, 不善于飞, 性淫	鴇母(bǎo mǔ) 鸨母 pimp
bào ㄅㄠˋ	刨	刨	削 to plane	刨冰(bào bīng) powdered ice 刨床(bào chuáng) planing machine
bào ㄅㄠˋ	報	报	告訴 report 告诉	電報(diàn bào)电报 telegram 報告(bào gào)报告report
bào ㄅㄠˋ	抱	抱	用手臂圍住 put one's arms around somebody 用手臂围住	抱怨(bào yuàn) complain 抱歉(bào qiàn) apologize
bào ㄅㄠˋ	暴	暴	突然又猛烈 sudden and violent	暴風雨(bào fēng yǔ) 暴风雨 storm 暴露(bào lù) expose
bào ㄅㄠˋ	豹	豹	比老虎小能爬樹的 動物 leopard 比老虎小能爬树的 动物	花豹(huā bào) leopard 黑豹(hēi bào) black leopard

bào pu、 ㄅㄠ、ㄆㄨ、	瀑	瀑	暴雨 rainstorm	瀑布(pù bù) waterfall
bào ㄅㄠ、	爆	爆	突然炸裂 explode	爆炸(bào zhà) explode 爆米花(bào mǐ huā) popcorn
bēi ㄅㄟ	盃	杯	通"杯"，比賽優勝 而頒發的杯狀獎品 trophy 通"杯"，比赛优胜 而颁发的杯状奖品	獎盃(jiǎng bēi) 奖杯 trophy
bēi ㄅㄟ	杯	杯	盛液體的器皿 cup 盛液体的器皿	一杯茶(yì bēi chá) a cup of tea 杯子(bēi zi) cup
bēi ㄅㄟ	碑	碑	刻上文字紀念事 業，功勛的石頭 monument 刻上文字纪念事 业，功勋的石头	紀念碑(jì niàn bēi)纪念碑 monument 石碑(shí bēi) stone tablet
bēi ㄅㄟ	悲	悲	哀傷 sad 哀伤	悲哀(bēi āi) sorrow 悲觀(bēi guān) 悲观 pessimistic
běi ㄅㄟˇ	北	北	方向 north	北極(běi jí) 北极 North Pole 北風(běi fēng) 北风 north wind
bèi ㄅㄟ、	背	背	胸部後邊的部分 back of body 胸部后边的部分	背痛(bèi tòng) back pain 背叛(bèi pàn) betray
bèi ㄅㄟ、	備	备	預備 prepare 预备	準備(zhǔn bèi)准备 prepare 備戰(bèi zhàn) 备战 be prepared against war
bèi ㄅㄟ、	倍	倍	照原數加上一個 或幾個全數 multiply by 照原数加上一个 或几个全数	加倍(jiā bèi) double 倍加小心(bèi jiā xiǎo xīn) exercise greater caution
bèi ㄅㄟ、	被	被	睡覺時蓋的東西， 覆蓋，遭受 blanket, cover, suffer 睡觉时盖的东西， 覆盖，遭受	棉被(mián bèi) blanket 被告(bèi gào) defendant

Pinyin	Traditional	Simplified	Meaning	Examples
bèi ㄅㄟˋ	貝	贝	水中有殼的動物 shell 水中有壳的动物	貝殼(bèi ké)贝壳 sea shell
bèi ㄅㄟˋ	臂	臂	人體從肩到腕的部份，動物的前肢 arm 人体从肩到腕的部分，动物的前肢	胳臂(gē bèi) arm 臂膀(bì bǎng) arm
bēn ㄅㄣ	奔	奔	急走 run quickly	奔跑(bēn pǎo) run In great hurry 奔波(bēn bō) be busy running about
běn ㄅㄣˇ	本	本	原始 origin	本來(běn lái) origin 資本(zī běn)资本 capital
bèn ㄅㄣˋ	笨	笨	不聰明 stupid 不聪明	笨人(bèn rén) stupid person
bēng ㄅㄥ	崩	崩	倒塌 collapse	山崩(shān bēng) avalanche 崩潰(bēng kuì)崩溃 collapse
bēng ㄅㄥ	繃	绷	拉緊 tighten 拉紧	繃帶(bēng dài)绷带 bandage
bèng ㄅㄥˋ	蹦	蹦	跳躍 pop out 跳跃	蹦蹦跳跳(bèng bèng tiào tiào) hop around
bī ㄅㄧ	逼	逼	強迫 force 强迫	逼迫(bī pò) force
bí ㄅㄧˊ	鼻	鼻	人及動物司嗅覺的器官 nose 人及动物司嗅覺的器官	鼻塞(bí sāi)鼻塞 stuffy nose 鼻孔(bí kǒng)鼻孔 nostril

11

bǐ ㄅ ㄧˇ	比	比	比較兩個同數量 間的關係 compare 比较两个 同数量间的关系	比較(bǐ jiào)比较 compare
bǐ ㄅ ㄧˇ	筆	笔	寫字，畫圖工具 pen 写字，画图工具	臘筆(là bǐ)腊笔 crayon 鉛筆(qiān bǐ)铅笔 pencil
bǐ ㄅ ㄧˇ	鄙	鄙	輕視 despise 轻视	卑鄙(bēi bǐ) mean, depraved 鄙人(bǐ rén) I
bì ㄅ ㄧˋ	庇	庇	保護, shelter protect, shelter 保护	庇護(bì hù)庇护 shield 庇佑(bì yòu) bless
bì ㄅ ㄧˋ	敝	敝	破爛的，我的 broken, my 破烂的，我的	敝姓王(bì xìng wáng) My lastname is Wang 敝屣(bì tǐ) worn-out shoes
bì ㄅ ㄧˋ	必	必	必定 surely	必定(bì dìng) certainly 必要(bì yào) required
bì ㄅ ㄧˋ	閉	闭	關閉，停止 close 关闭，停止	關閉(guān bì)关闭 close 閉嘴(bì zuǐ) shut up (the mouth) 闭嘴
bì ㄅ ㄧˋ	幣	币	錢幣，交換各種 商品的媒介 currency 钱币，交换各种 商品的媒介	貨幣(huò bì)货币currency 幣值(bì zhí) 币值 currency value
bì ㄅ ㄧˋ	畢	毕	做完 finish	畢生(bì shēng)毕生 whole life 完畢(wán bì)完毕 finish
bì ㄅ ㄧˋ	陛	陛	宮廷的台階 steps leading to a palace 宫廷的台阶	陛下(bì xià) Your Majesty
bì ㄅ ㄧˋ	臂	臂	肩到腕的部分 arm	手臂 (shǒu bì) arm 臂章 (bì zhāng) arm badge 左臂 (zuǒ bì) left arm
bì ㄅ ㄧˋ	痺	痹	麻木的病 numbness	麻痺(má bì) 麻痹 numb
bì ㄅ ㄧˋ	斃	毙	死 die	斃命(bì mìng) 毙命 die 槍斃(qiāng bì)枪毙 executed by firing squad

12

拼音	繁体	简体	释义	例词
bì ㄅㄧˋ	碧	碧	青綠色 green 青绿色	碧玉(bì yù) green jade 金碧輝煌(jīn bì huī huáng) 金碧辉煌 magnificent (building)
bì ㄅㄧˋ	避	避	躲 hide 躲	躲避(duǒ bì) 躲避avoid 逃避(táo bì) escape 避免(bì miǎn) prevent
bì ㄅㄧˋ	弊	弊	欺騙，害處 fraud, disadvantage 欺骗，害处	弊病(bì bìng) drawback 作弊(zuò bì) cheat
bì ㄅㄧˋ	壁	壁	牆壁 wall 墙壁	壁畫(bì huà) 壁画mural 壁報(bì bào) 壁报 wall newspaper
biān ㄅㄧㄢ	邊	边	物體周圍的部分 side 物体周围的部分	花邊(huā biān)花边 lace 邊界(biān jiè) 边界 border
biān ㄅㄧㄢ	編	编	交織，順序排列 weave, arrange in order 交织，顺序排列	編劇(biān jù) 编剧 write a play 編著(biān zhù) 编著 write a book
biān ㄅㄧㄢ	鞭	鞭	長形用具，用以 驅使牲畜whip 长形用具，用以 驱使牲畜	鞭炮(biān pào) fire cracker 鞭打(biān dǎ) to whip
biān biǎn ㄅㄧㄢ ㄅㄧㄢˇ	蝙	蝙	蝙蝠：會飛的鼠狀 哺乳動物 bat (mammal) 蝙蝠：會 飛的鼠狀哺乳動物	蝙蝠(biān fú) bat
biǎn ㄅㄧㄢˇ	貶	贬	給不好的評價 degrade 给不好的评价	褒貶(bāo biǎn)褒贬 pass judgment on 貶值(biǎn zhí) 贬值 devalue
biǎn piān ㄅㄧㄢˇ ㄆㄧㄢ	扁	扁	物體平而薄 flat 物体平而薄	扁平(biǎn píng) flat
biǎn ㄅㄧㄢˇ	匾	匾	掛在門或牆上有題 字的橫牌horizontal inscribed board 挂在门或墙上有题 字的横牌	匾額(biǎn é) 匾额 horizontal inscribed board

13

注音/拼音	繁體	簡體	釋義	詞例
biàn ㄅㄧㄢˋ	遍	遍	到處 everywhere 到处	一遍(yí biàn) one time 遍布(biàn bù) spread
biàn ㄅㄧㄢˋ	辮	辫	分股編成帶狀物 braid 分股编成带状物	辮子(biàn zi) 辫子 braid
biàn ㄅㄧㄢˋ	辨	辨	分別，分析 distinguish, analyze 分别，分析	分辨(fēn biàn) distinguish 辨認(biàn rèn) 辨认 identify
biàn ㄅㄧㄢˋ	辯	辩	爭論是非 debate 争论是非	辯論(biàn lùn) 辩论 debate
biàn pián ㄅㄧㄢˋ ㄆㄧㄢˊ	便	便	方便，順利 convenient 方便，顺利	方便(fāng biàn) convenient 便宜(pián yí) cheap
biàn ㄅㄧㄢˋ	變	变	更改事物 change	改變(gǎi biàn)改变 change 變化(biàn huà) 变化 change
biāo ㄅㄧㄠ	標	标	記號，表面 label, appearance 记号，表面	商標(shāng biāo)商标 trade mark 標本(biāo běn)标本 specimen
biāo ㄅㄧㄠ	飆	飙	暴風 whirlwind 暴风	飆車(biāo chē) 飙车 hot-rodding
biǎo ㄅㄧㄠˇ	表	表	在外面的 outside	發表(fā biǎo)发表 publish 外表(wài biǎo) appearance
biǎo ㄅㄧㄠˇ	裱	裱	用漿糊把紙糊上去 paste 用浆糊把纸糊上去	裱畫(biǎo huà) 裱画 mount a picture 裱糊(biǎo hú) paste paper on
bié ㄅㄧㄝˊ	別	别	分離 separate 分离	別針(bié zhēn) pin 別墅(bié shù) villa

bīn ㄅㄧㄣ	賓	宾	客人 guest	来賓(lái bīn) 来宾guest 賓主(bīn zhǔ) 宾主 host and guest
bīn ㄅㄧㄣ	鬢	鬓	面頰兩邊靠近耳朵 的頭髮 sideburns 面颊两边靠近耳朵 的头髮	鬢毛(bīn máo) 鬓毛 sideburns
bīng ㄅㄧㄥ	兵	兵	戰士，拿武器打 仗的人 soldier 战士，拿武器打 仗的人	兵器(bīng qì) weapon 當兵(dāng bīng)当兵 be a soldier
bīng ㄅㄧㄥ	冰	冰	水受冷後結成的固 體 ice 水受冷后所 結成的固体	冰塊(bīng kuài) 冰块 ice cube 冰河(bīng hé) glacier
bǐng ㄅㄧㄥˇ	餅	饼	麵製的扁圓形食品 cake 麵製的扁圓形食品	餅乾(bǐng gān) 饼乾cracker 月餅(yuè bǐng)月饼 moon cake
bǐng ㄅㄧㄥˇ	丙	丙	第三位 the third of the ten heavenly Stems	丙等(bǐng děng) the third place
bǐng ㄅㄧㄥˇ	炳	炳	光明 bright, brilliant	彪炳事業(biāo bǐng shì yè) 彪炳事业 glorious achievement
bǐng ㄅㄧㄥˇ	柄	柄	器物的手把 handle	把柄(bǎ bǐng) handle 笑柄(xiào bǐng) laughing stock
bìng ㄅㄧㄥˋ	併	併	把東西合起來 combine 把东西合起来	合併(hé bìng) combine 併吞(bìng tūn) to annex
bìng ㄅㄧㄥˋ	病	病	不健康的現象 sick 不健康的现象	生病(shēng bìng) become sick
bō ㄅㄛ	撥	拨	挑動 stir 挑动	撥款(bō kuǎn) 拨款 allocate fund 挑撥(tiǎo bō)挑拨 sow discord
bō ㄅㄛ	波	波	因震蕩而起伏的水 面 wave 因震蕩而 起伏的水面	波浪(bō làng) wave 波動(bō dòng) 波动 fluctuate
bō ㄅㄛ	播	播	撒種 sow seeds 撒种	傳播(chuán bō)传播 broadcast
bō bāo ㄅㄛ ㄅㄠ	剝	剥	把皮去掉 peel	剝皮(bāo pí) peel 剝奪(bō duó) 剥夺 deprive of

bō ㄅㄛ	玻	玻	一種硬而透明的物體 glass 一种硬而透明的物体	玻璃(bō lí) glass
bō ㄅㄛ	菠	菠	菠菜，菠蘿 spinach, pineapple 菠菜，菠萝	菠菜(bō cài) spinach 菠蘿(bō luó) 菠萝 pineapple
bō ㄅㄛ	缽	钵	陶製的碗 earthern bowl 陶製的碗	沿門托缽(yán mén tuō bō) 沿门托钵 begging alms from door to door
bó ㄅㄛˊ	伯	伯	父親的兄長 uncle (older than one's father) 父亲的兄长	伯父(bó fù) uncle
bó ㄅㄛˊ	脖	脖	頸，頭和身體相連的部分 neck 颈，头和身体相连的部分	脖子(bó zi) neck
bó ㄅㄛˊ	博	博	很多，很大 abundant, large	博士(bó shì) Ph.D. 博學(bó xué) 博学 knowledgeable
bó ㄅㄛˊ	搏	搏	用手抓住 to grab	搏鬥(bó dòu) 搏斗 to fight
bǔ ㄅㄨˇ	捕	捕	抓拿 catch	捕魚(bǔ yú) 捕鱼 catch fish 捕捉(bǔ zhuō) catch
bǔ ㄅㄨˇ	補	补	修理 mend	補習(bǔ xí) 补习 to tutor 補救(bǔ jiù) 补救 to remedy
bù ㄅㄨˋ	布	布	麻棉等織物 cloth 麻棉等织物	棉布(mián bù) cotton cloth 布告(bù gào) bulletin
bù ㄅㄨˋ	佈	布	用語言文字傳達事情，安排 publicize, arrange 用语言文字传达事情，安排	宣佈(xuān bù) 宣佈 declare 佈置(bù zhì) 佈置 arrange
bù ㄅㄨˋ	步	步	走路時兩隻腳前後的距離 step 走路时两隻脚前后的距离	一步(yí bù) a step 進步(jìn bù)进步 progress
bù ㄅㄨˋ	部	部	部分，行政機關 part, administrative organ 部分，行政机关	部落(bù luò) 部落 tribe 部長(bù zhǎng) 部长 department head
bù ㄅㄨˋ	不	不	否定詞，表示否定 no, not 否定词，表示否定	不可(bù kě) may not 不能(bù néng) cannot
bù ㄅㄨˋ	簿	簿	記事的本子 notebook 记事的本子	簿子(bù zi) notebook 簿記(bù jì) 簿记 bookkeeping

C

cā ㄘㄚ	擦	擦	抹掉，塗抹 wipe, put on 抹掉，涂抹	板擦(bǎn cā) eraser
cāi ㄘㄞ	猜	猜	推測 guess 推测	猜謎(cāi mí) 猜谜 solve riddles 猜疑(cāi yí) be suspicious
cái ㄘㄞˊ	材	材	木料 timber	木材(mù cái) timber 材料(cái liào) material
cái ㄘㄞˊ	才	才	學問，能力 knowledge, ability 学问，能力	才能(cái néng) talents 才幹(cái gàn) 才幹 ability
cái ㄘㄞˊ	財	财	金錢和物資 wealth 金钱和物资	發財(fā cái) 发财 make a fortune 財產(cái chǎn) 财产 property
cái ㄘㄞˊ	裁	裁	用刀把紙或布割裂 cut into parts 用刀把纸或布割裂	裁縫(cái féng) 裁缝 a tailor 裁員(cái yuán) 裁员 to lay off people
cǎi ㄘㄞˇ	采	采	同"彩"，顏色，風 度 colors, elegant manners 同"彩"， 颜色，风度	風采(fēng cǎi) 风采 elegant manners
cǎi ㄘㄞˇ	彩	彩	各種顏色 different colors 各种颜色	彩色(cǎi sè) colorful 彩虹(cǎi hóng) rainbow
cǎi ㄘㄞˇ	採	採	摘取 pick	採取(cǎi qǔ) 採取 adopt
cǎi ㄘㄞˇ	踩	踩	用腳踏在上面 step on 用脚踏在上面	踩油門(cǎi yóu mén) 踩油门 step on the gas

cài ㄘㄞˋ	菜	菜	蔬菜 vegetables	青菜(qīng cài)青菜 green vegetables
cài ㄘㄞˋ	蔡	蔡	姓氏 Chinese surname	
cān shēn ㄘㄢ ㄕㄣ	參	参	加入 participate	參加(cān jiā) 參加 participate 人參(rén shēn) 人参 ginseng
cān ㄘㄢ	餐	餐	食物，吃 food, eat	早餐(zǎo cān) breakfast 中餐(zhōng cān) lunch 晚餐(wǎn cān) dinner
cán ㄘㄢˊ	殘	残	傷害，不完整 injure, incomplete 伤害，不完整	殘殺(cán shā)残杀 massacre 殘酷(cán kù) 残酷 atrocious
cǎn ㄘㄢˇ	慚	惭	羞愧 feel ashamed	慚愧(cán kuì)惭愧 feel ashamed
cǎn ㄘㄢˇ	慘	惨	使人悲傷難受，狠 毒 tragic 使人悲伤 难受，狠毒	悲慘(bēi cǎn)悲惨 tragic 慘無人道(cǎn wú rén dào) 惨无人道 atrocious
càn ㄘㄢˋ	燦	灿	光亮奪目 brilliant 光亮夺目	燦爛(càn làn)灿烂 brilliant
cāng ㄘㄤ	倉	仓	藏物品的房子 storage house	倉庫(cāng kù)仓库 warehouse 倉促(cāng cù)仓促 in a hurry
cāng ㄘㄤ	蒼	苍	百姓，深綠，藍色 common people, deep green, blue 百姓，深绿，蓝色	蒼生(cāng shēng)苍生 the common people 蒼天(chāng tiān)苍天 blue sky
cāng ㄘㄤ	艙	舱	船隻內部 cabin 船隻内部	船艙(chuán cāng)船舱 cabin
cáng zàng ㄘㄤˊ ㄗㄤˋ	藏	藏	收貯，躲避 store, hide	躲藏(duǒ cáng) hide 收藏(shōu cáng) collect

cāo ㄘㄠ	操	操	抓在手裏，演習軍事 grasp, drill troops 抓在手里，演习军事	操守(cāo shǒu) moral integrity 體操(tǐ cāo) 体操 gymnastics
cāo ㄘㄠ	糙	糙	不精細 rough 不精细	糙米(cāo mǐ) brown rice 粗糙(cū cāo) coarse
cáo ㄘㄠˊ	曹	曹	姓氏 a Chinese surname	
cǎo ㄘㄠˇ	草	草	草木植物 grass 草木植物	草藥(cǎo yào) 草药 herbal medicine 青草(qīng cǎo) green grass 草坪(cǎo píng) lawn
cè ㄘㄜˋ	冊	册	本子 volume	紀念冊(jì niàn cè) 纪念册 yearbook
cè ㄘㄜˋ	側	侧	旁邊 side 旁边	側面(cè miàn) 侧面 on the side 側門(cè mén) 侧门 side door
cè ㄘㄜˋ	策	策	計劃 plan 计划	策劃(cè huà) 策划 plot 策略(ce lüè) tactics
cè ㄘㄜˋ	廁	厕	大小便的地方， 擠在中間 lavatory 大小便的地方， 挤在中间	廁所(cè suǒ) 厕所 washroom 廁身(cè shēn) 厕身 occupy a humble place
cè ㄘㄜˋ	測	测	用器具量大小， 高低，深淺，遠近 to measure 用器具量大小， 高低，深浅，远近	測量(cè liáng) 测量 survey 測驗(cè yàn) 测验 test

Pinyin	Traditional	Simplified	Meaning	Examples
cè ㄘ ㄜ	惻	恻	悲傷 sorrowful 悲伤	惻隱之心(cè yǐn zhī xīn) 恻隐之心 compassion 悲惻(bēi cè) 悲恻 sad
céng ㄘ ㄥ	層	层	用于重疊物 layer 用于重叠物	一層(yì céng) 一层 one layer 十層大樓(shí céng dà lóu) 十层大楼 ten-story building
céng zēng ㄘ ㄗ ㄥ ㄥ	曾	曾	表示發生過的行爲 indicate past action 表示发生过的行为	曾經(céng jīng) 曾经 have taken part in
chā ㄔ ㄚ	叉	叉	分開，扎取物品的 器皿 split, fork 分开，扎取物品的 器皿	叉路(chā lù) a forked road 叉子(chā zi) fork
chā ㄔ ㄚ	插	插	插入，刺進去 insert 插入，刺进去	插花(chā huā) arrange flowers 安插(ān chā) to place (a person) on a job
chā chà ㄔ ㄔ ㄚ ㄚ	差	差	不同，區別，錯誤 difference, mistake 不同，区别，错误	差別(chā bié) difference 差不多(chà bù duō) approximately
chá ㄔ ㄚ	茶	茶	常綠灌木，葉焙 乾後可做飲料 tea 常绿灌木，叶焙 乾后可做饮料	茶匙(chá chí) teaspoon 喝茶(hē chá) drink tea
chá ㄔ ㄚ	查	查	考察 check, examine	檢查(jiǎn chá) 检查 examine 調查(diao cha) 调查 investigate
chá ㄔ ㄚ	察	察	細看 look closely 细看	察看(chá kàn) to view 察言觀色(chá yán guān sè) 察言观色 to observe somebody's words and facial expressions

chà ㄔ ㄚˋ	岔	岔	分歧的道路，轉移 主題 forked road, interrupt 分歧的道路，转移 主题	岔路(chà lù) forked road 打岔(dǎ chà) interrupt
chà chā ㄔ ㄔ ㄚˋ ㄚ	差	差	低劣 of poor quality	差勁(chà jìng) 差劲 no good
chāi ㄔ ㄞ	拆	拆	打開合著的東西 tear open 打开合著的东西	拆開(chāi kāi) 拆开 to open 拆毀(chāi huǐ)拆毁 to demolish
chāi chā ㄔ ㄔ ㄞ ㄚ	差	差	派遣，使喚 dispatch, order about	當差(dāng chāi) 当差 be a messenger 差事(chāi shì) assignment
chāi ㄔ ㄞ	釵	钗	婦人插在頭上的 一種飾物 hairpin 妇人插在头上的 一种饰物	玉釵(yù chāi) 玉钗 jade pin 金釵(jīn chāi)金钗 gold pin
chái ㄔ ㄞˊ	柴	柴	燒火用的草木 firewood 烧火用的草木	柴火(chái huǒ) firewood, faggot 火柴(huǒ chái) match
chái ㄔ ㄞˊ	豺	豺	肉食動物，與狼 同類 jackal 肉食动物，与狼 同类	豺狼(chái láng) beasts, evil people
chān ㄔ ㄢ	摻	掺	混合 mix	摻和(chān huò) 掺和 blend
chán ㄔ ㄢˊ	纏	缠	困擾他人 to pester 困扰他人	糾纏(jiū chán) 纠缠 be entangled 纏繞(chán rào) 缠绕 twine
chán ㄔ ㄢˊ	饞	馋	貪吃 gluttons 贪吃	嘴饞(zuǐ chán) 嘴馋 fond of good food 饞嘴(chán zuǐ)馋嘴 gluttonous

chán ㄔㄢˊ	讒	谗	用語言毀謗 slander, backbite 用语言毁谤	讒言(chán yán) 谗言 slanderous remarks
chán ㄔㄢˊ	蟬	蝉	昆蟲名，頭短，翼 透明，夏日有鳴聲 cicada 昆虫名，头短，翼 透明，夏日有鸣声	蟬聯(chán lián) 蝉联 continue to hold title
chán ㄔㄢˊ	蟾	蟾	屬蛙類，皮膚多疣 toad 属蛙类，皮肤多疣	蟾蜍(chán chú) toad
chǎn ㄔㄢˇ	產	产	出生，財物 give birth to, property 出生，财物	產生(chǎn shēng) 产生 produce 財產(cái chǎn) 财产 property
chǎn ㄔㄢˇ	諂	谄	用語言求人喜悅 flatter 用语言求人喜悦	諂媚(chǎn mèi) 谄媚 curry favor with 諂諛(chǎn yú) 谄谀 fawn on
chǎn ㄔㄢˇ	闡	阐	講明白 explain 讲明白	闡述(chǎn shù) 阐述 expound
chàn ㄔㄢˋ	懺	忏	承認罪過並力求改 正 repent 承认罪过并力求改 正	懺悔(chàn huǐ) 忏悔 repent
chàn ㄔㄢˋ	顫	颤	身體抖動 quiver 身体抖动	顫抖(chàn dǒu) 颤抖 trembling
chāng ㄔㄤ	昌	昌	興盛 prosperous 兴盛	昌明(chāng míng) thriving
chāng ㄔㄤ	娼	娼	靠賣淫為生的人 prostitute 靠卖淫为生的人	娼妓(chāng jì) prostitute
chāng ㄔㄤ	猖	猖	狂妄 unruly	猖狂(chāng kuáng) savage, furious 猖獗(chāng jué) run wild

cháng zhǎng ㄔ ㄤˊ ㄓ ㄤˇ	長	长	兩端中間的距離，優點 long, advantage 两端中间的距离，优点	長度(cháng dù) 长度 length 長處(cháng chù) 长处 advantage
cháng ㄔ ㄤˊ	腸	肠	消化器官之一 intestine	大腸(dà cháng) 大肠 big intestine 腸胃(cháng wèi) 肠胃 stomach
cháng ㄔ ㄤˊ	償	偿	歸還 to return 归还	償還(cháng huán) 偿还 compensate for 償債(cháng zhài) 偿债 repay debt
cháng ㄔ ㄤˊ	嘗	尝	試，辨別滋味 taste 试，辨别滋味	嘗試 (cháng shì) 尝试 try
cháng ㄔ ㄤˊ	常	常	一般的 usual	平常 (píng cháng) as usual 經常(jīng cháng) 经常 always, frequently
cháng sháng ㄔ ㄤˊ ㄕ ㄤˊ	裳	裳	衣裙 skirt	衣裳(yī sháng) clothes
chǎng ㄔ ㄤˇ	廠	厂	製造產品的場所 factory 製造产品的场所	工廠 (gōng chǎng) 工厂 factory
chǎng ㄔ ㄤˇ	敞	敞	張開 open 张开	敞開(chǎng kāi) 敞开 open wide
chǎng ㄔ ㄤˇ	場	场	處所，聚集的地方 site 处所，聚集的地方	場合 (chǎng hé) 场合 situation 場所 (chǎng suǒ) 场所 place
chàng ㄔ ㄤˋ	悵	怅	失意，不痛快 disappointed	悵然(chàng rán) 怅然 feel upset

chàng ㄔㄤˋ	暢	畅	沒有阻礙，痛快 unimpeded, to one's heart's content 没有阻碍，痛快	暢銷(chàng xiāo)畅销 good-selling 暢談(chàng tán)畅谈 have a good talk
chàng ㄔㄤˋ	唱	唱	發出歌聲 sing 发出歌声	唱歌(chàng gē) sing 合唱團(hé chàng tuán) 合唱团 chorus
chàng ㄔㄤˋ	倡	倡	發動，首先提出 start, initiate 发动，首先提出	提倡(tí chàng) advocate 倡議(chàng yì)倡议 propose
chāo ㄔㄠ	抄	抄	照原文寫 copy 照原文写	抄襲(chāo xí)抄袭 plagiarize 抄寫(chāo xiě)抄写 copy, transcribe
chāo ㄔㄠ	超	超	越過 exceed 越过	超過(chāo guò)超过 surpass 超齡(chāo líng)超龄 overaged
chāo ㄔㄠ	勦	剿	抄取 plagiarize	勦襲(chāo xí)剿袭 plagiarize
chāo ㄔㄠ	鈔	钞	鈔票 paper money 钞票	鈔票(chāo piào)钞票 bank note 外鈔(wài chāo)外钞 foreign currency
cháo zhāo ㄔㄠˊ ㄓㄠ	朝	朝	對著，當政 face toward, be in power 对著，当政	朝廷(cháo tíng) imperial court 朝代(cháo dài) dynasty 綽綽記記(zhāo zhāo mù mù) day and night
cháo ㄔㄠˊ	巢	巢	鳥搭的窩 nest 鸟搭的窝	鳥巢 (niǎo cháo) 乌巢 nest 築巢(zhú cháo) 筑巢 make a nest
cháo ㄔㄠˊ	潮	潮	海水漲落的現象 tide 海水涨落的现象	思潮(sī cháo) ideological trend 海潮(hǎi cháo) tide

cháo ㄔㄠˊ	嘲	嘲	譏笑，取笑 jeer 讥笑，取笑	嘲笑 (cháo xiào) jeer 嘲弄 (cháo nòng) tease
chǎo ㄔㄠˇ	吵	吵	聲音擾亂人 noisy 声音扰乱人	吵鬧 (chǎo nào) 吵闹 noisy 吵架 (chǎo jià) quarrel
chǎo ㄔㄠˇ	炒	炒	把東西放在鍋裏加 熱攪拌 stir fry 把东西放在锅里加 热搅拌	炒菜 (chǎo cài) 炒菜 stir fry vegetables
chē ㄔㄜ	車	车	陸地上有輪子的運 輸工具 vehicle 陆地上有轮子的运 输工具	火車(huǒ chē) 火车 train 汽車(qì chē) 汽车 automobile
chě ㄔㄜˇ	扯	扯	拉，撕，閒談 pull, tear, chat 拉，撕，闲谈	扯謊 (chě huǎng) 扯谎 tell a lie
chè ㄔㄜˋ	徹	彻	透徹 thorough 透彻	徹底(chè dǐ) 彻底 thorough 徹夜(chè yè) 彻夜 all night long
chè ㄔㄜˋ	澈	澈	清澄 clear (water)	清澈 (qīng chè) clear
chè ㄔㄜˋ	撤	撤	除去 remove	撤除 (chè chú) remove 撤回 (chè huí) withdraw
chēn ㄔㄣ	嗔	嗔	生氣 be angry 生气	嗔怒 (chēn nù)嗔怒 get angry
chén ㄔㄣˊ	臣	臣	幫皇帝統治的官吏 official under a feudal ruler 帮皇帝统治的官吏	大臣 (dà chén) minister
chén ㄔㄣˊ	辰	辰	日子，時間，時運 date, time, luck 日子，时间，时运	時辰(shí chén) time 誕辰(dàn chén) 诞辰 birthday

chén ㄔㄣˊ	晨	晨	清早 morning	早晨 (zǎo chén) morning 清晨 (qīng chén) early morning
chén ㄔㄣˊ	塵	尘	飛揚的灰土 dust 飞扬的灰土	飛塵 (fēi chén) 飞尘 flying dust 塵土 (chén tǔ) 尘土 dust
chén ㄔㄣˊ	忱	忱	真實的心情 sincere feeling 真实的心情	熱忱 (rè chén) 热忱 zeal
chén ㄔㄣˊ	陳	陈	排列 layout	陳列 (chén liè) 陈列 exhibit 陳腐 (chén fǔ) 陈腐 decayed
chén ㄔㄣˊ	沉	沉	沒入水中，落下 sink, lower	沉沒 (chén mò) sink 沉悶 (chén mèn) 沉闷 depressing
chèn ㄔㄣˋ	襯	衬	搭配上別的東西 lining 搭配上别的东西	襯托 (chèn tuō) 衬托 provide a contrast
chèn chēng ㄔㄣˋ ㄔㄥ	稱	称	量輕重，叫做 weigh, address somebody 量轻重，叫做	稱呼 (chēng hū) 称呼 address somebody 相稱 (xiāng chèn) 相称 fit, match
chèn ㄔㄣˋ	趁	趁	利用機會 take advantage of 利用机会	趁早 (chèn zǎo) as soon as possible 趁熱 (chèn rè) 趁热 while it is hot

chēng ㄔㄥ	撐	撑	支持 prop up, support, maintain	撐竿跳 (chēng gān tiào) 撑竿跳 pole vault
chēng ㄔㄥ	瞠	瞠	瞪著眼，直看 stare 瞪著眼，直看	瞠目結舌 (chēng mù jié shé) 瞠目结舌 stare tongue-tied
chéng ㄔㄥˊ	成	成	做好 accomplish	成功(chéng gōng) succeed 完成(wán chéng) finish
chéng ㄔㄥˊ	乘	乘	坐，算術中用一個 數使另一數變成幾 倍 ride, multiply 坐，算术中用一个 数使另一数变成几 倍	乘法(chéng fǎ) multiplication 乘客(chéng kè) passenger
chéng ㄔㄥˊ	承	承	繼續，托著 carry on, undertake 继续，托著	承認(chéng rèn) 承认 recognize 繼承(jì chéng) 继承 inherit
chéng ㄔㄥˊ	丞	丞	幫助，輔佐，古時 最高一級官吏 assist 帮助，辅佐，古时 最高一级官吏	丞相(chéng xiàng) prime minister
chéng ㄔㄥˊ	城	城	圍繞一個可防守的 牆垣 city wall, wall 围绕一个可防守的 墙垣	城堡(chéng bǎo) castle 城市(chéng shì) city
chéng ㄔㄥˊ	懲	惩	處罰，警戒 punish 处罚，警戒	懲罰(chéng fá) 惩罚 punish
chéng ㄔㄥˊ	橙	橙	橘類水果，紅和黃 合成的顏色 orange, orange color 橘类水果，红和黄 合成的颜色	橙黃色(chéng huáng sè) orange color
chéng shèng ㄔㄥˊ ㄕ ㄥˋ	盛	盛	把東西放進去 fill 把东西放进去	盛飯(chéng fàn) 盛饭 fill a bowl with rice

chéng ㄔㄥˊ	誠	诚	眞實，確實 sincere, honest 真实，确实	誠意(chéng yì) 诚意 sincerity 誠實(chéng shí) 诚实 honesty
chéng ㄔㄥˊ	程	程	規章，路途 rule, journey 规章，路途	程度(chéng dù) degree 程序(chéng xù) procedure
chěng ㄔㄥˇ	逞	逞	賣弄 show off, flaunt 卖弄	逞強(chěng qiáng) 逞强 flaunt one's power
chěng ㄔㄥˇ	騁	骋	直馳 gallop 直驰	馳騁(chí chěng) 驰骋 gallop about
chèng ㄔㄥˋ	秤	秤	衡量輕重的器具 weighing instrument 衡量轻重的器具	秤米(chèng mǐ) weigh rice
chī jí ㄔ ㄐ	吃	吃	食 eat	吃飯(chī fàn) 吃饭 eat, have a meal 吃不下(chī bú xià) cannot eat anymore 口吃(kǒu jí) stuttering
chī ㄔ	嗤	嗤	譏笑，笑的樣子 laugh at 讥笑，笑的样子	嗤笑(chī xiào) sneer at
chī ㄔ	癡	痴	呆傻，愛戀沉迷 silly, be infatuated with 呆傻，爱恋沉迷	白癡(bái chī) 白痴 idiot 癡情(chī qíng) 痴情 infatuation
chí ㄔˊ	持	持	保守不變 maintain 保守不变	支持(zhī chí) support 保持(bǎo chí) maintain
chí ㄔˊ	池	池	積水的凹地 pond 积水的凹地	水池(shuǐ chí) pond 游泳池(yóu yǒng chí) swimming pool
chí ㄔˊ	遲	迟	慢，晚 slow, tardy	遲到(chí dào) 迟到 late

chí ㄔˊ	踟	踟	心裏猶豫 hesitate 心里犹豫	踟躕(chí chú) 踟躕 hesitate, waver
chí ㄔˊ	弛	弛	放鬆 relax, slacken 放松	鬆弛(sōng chí) 松弛 relax
chí ㄔˊ	馳	驰	車馬快跑 speed, gallop 车马快跑	奔馳(bēn chí) 奔驰 run quickly 馳騁(chí chěng) 驰骋 gallop
chǐ ㄔˇ	尺	尺	長度單位，十寸 10 inches 长度单位，十寸	一尺(yì chǐ) 1 foot 尺寸(chǐ cùn) measurement
chǐ ㄔˇ	呎	呎	一呎是12吋，英美 制長度單位 1 foot 一呎是12吋，英美 制长度单位	英呎(yīng chǐ) 1 foot
chǐ ㄔˇ	齒	齿	咬嚼的器官 tooth	不齒(bù chǐ) 不齿 despise 牙齒(yá chǐ) 牙齿 tooth
chǐ ㄔˇ	恥	耻	羞辱 shame, disgrace	恥辱(chǐ rǔ) 耻辱 humiliation 羞恥(xiū chǐ) 羞耻 shame
chǐ ㄔˇ	侈	侈	不節儉 wasteful 不节俭	奢侈(shē chǐ) extravagant
chì ㄔˋ	赤	赤	紅色 red 红色	赤誠(chì chéng) 赤诚 absolute sincerity 赤道(chì dào) equator
chì ㄔˋ	叱	叱	大聲斥罵 shout at 大声斥骂	叱罵(chì mà) 叱骂 scold
chì ㄔˋ	斥	斥	責罵，拒絕 scold, reject 责骂，拒绝	斥責(chì zé) 斥责 rebuke
chì ㄔˋ	翅	翅	鳥和昆蟲等用來飛 行的器官 wing 鸟和昆虫等用来飞 行的器官	翅膀(chì bǎng) wing

chì 彳ˋ	熾	炽	火旺盛 flaming	熾熱(chì rè)炽热 red-hot
chōng 彳ㄨㄥ	沖	冲	用水澆下去 pour water on 用水浇下去	沖洗(chōng xǐ)冲洗 rinse 沖淡(chōng dàn)冲淡 dilute
chōng 彳ㄨㄥ	充	充	滿，實，假冒 full, sufficient, feign 满，实，假冒	充實(chōng shí)充实 fulfill 冒充(mào chōng) pretend
chōng 彳ㄨㄥ	憧	憧	心志不定的樣子 flickering, moving 心志不定的样子	憧憧(chōng chōng) moving
chōng chòng 彳 彳 ㄨ ㄨˋ ㄥ ㄥ	衝	冲	用力向前推進 dash forward 用力向前推进	衝動(chōng dòng)冲动 impulse 衝鋒槍(chōng fēng qiāng) 冲锋枪 submachine gun 說話很衝(shuō huà hěn chòng) 说话很冲 speak bluntly
chóng zhòng 彳 ㄓ ㄨ ㄨ ㄥ ㄥˋ	重	重	再次，物體分量 必需要的 repeat, weight, important 再次，物体分量 必需要的	重新(chóng xīn) again 重視(zhòng shì)重视 attach importance to
chóng 彳ㄨㄥˊ	蟲	虫	昆蟲 insect 昆虫	昆蟲(kūn chóng)昆虫 insect 蟲子(chóng zi)虫子 insects
chóng 彳ㄨㄥˊ	崇	崇	尊敬 respect	尊崇(zūn chóng) respect 崇拜(chóng bài) adore, worship
chōu 彳ㄡ	抽	抽	從多數中提出一部 分，拔出 take out 从多数中提出一部 分，拔出	抽樣(chōu yàng)抽样 sampling 抽屜(chōu tì)抽屉 drawer
chóu 彳ㄡˊ	稠	稠	多，濃，密 thick 多，浓，密	稠密(chóu mì) dense

chóu ㄔ ㄡˊ	籌	筹	計算數目的器具， 打算 chip, counter 计算数目的器具， 打算	籌款(chóu kuǎn) 筹款 to raise funds 籌備(chóu bèi) 筹备 prepare, arrange
chóu ㄔ ㄡˊ	躊	踌	猶豫不決的樣子， 自滿的樣子， hesitate, conceited 犹豫不决的样子， 自满的样子	躊躇(chóu chú) 踌躇 hesitate 躊躇滿志(chóu chú mǎn zhì) 踌躇满志smug
chóu ㄔ ㄡˊ	仇	仇	和自己有仇恨的樣 子，當做敵人看待 enemy, foe 和自己有仇恨的样 子，当做敌人看待	仇人(chóu rén) enemy 仇恨(chóu hèn) hatred
chóu ㄔ ㄡˊ	愁	愁	憂慮不樂 worried 忧虑不乐	憂愁(yōu chóu) 忧愁 worried 愁悶(chóu mèn) 愁闷 boredom
chóu ㄔ ㄡˊ	酬	酬	報答，親友來往交 際 reward, social intercourse 报答，亲友来往交 际	酬勞(chóu láo) 酬劳 reward 應酬(yìng chóu) 应酬 attend social functions
chǒu ㄔ ㄡˇ	醜	醜	相貌不美 ugly	醜陋(chǒu lòu) 醜陋 ugly 醜化(chǒu huà) 醜化 to tarnish image
chǒu ㄔ ㄡˇ	丑	丑	戲中表演滑稽的角 色 clown 戏中表演滑稽的角 色	小丑(xiǎo chǒu) clown
chòu ㄔ ㄡˋ	臭	臭	氣味惡劣 smelly, stinky 气味恶劣	臭罵(chòu mà) 臭骂 scold abusively 惡臭(è chòu) 恶臭
chū ㄔ ㄨ	出	出	從裏面到外面，發 生 come out 从里面到外面，发 生	日出(rì chū) sunrise 出口(chū kǒu) export

31

chū ㄔ ㄨ	初	初	起頭 beginning 起头	起初(qǐ chū) at the beginning 初級(chū jí) 初级 beginner's level
chú ㄔ ㄨˊ	除	除	算法的一種，符號 爲÷；去掉 division, remove 算法的一种，符号 为÷；去掉	除法(chú fǎ) division 除去(chú qù) remove
chú ㄔ ㄨˊ	廚	厨	烹調食物的地方 kitchen 烹调食物的地方	廚房(chú fáng) 厨房 kitchen 廚師(chú shī) 厨师 chef
chú ㄔ ㄨˊ	雛	雏	剛孵出不久的幼禽 ，幼小的 young bird, nestling 刚孵出不久的幼禽 ，幼小的	孤雛(gū chú) 孤雏 orphan 雛形(chú xíng) 雏形 embryo
chú ㄔ ㄨˊ	鋤	锄	一種用來翻鬆土地 和除草的農具 hoe 一种用来翻松土地 和除草的农具	鋤頭(chú tóu) 锄头 hoe 鋤奸(chú jiān) 锄奸 eliminate evils
chú ㄔ ㄨˊ	櫥	橱	櫃子 cabinet 柜子	衣櫥(yī chú) 衣橱 closet 書櫥(shū chú) 书橱 book case
chú ㄔ ㄨˊ	躇	躇	猶豫不決的樣子 hesitate 犹豫不决的样子	躊躇(chóu chú) 踌躇 hesitant
chú chǔ ㄔ ㄔ ㄨˊ ㄨˇ	儲	储	將繼承王位的人， 積藏起來 crown price, store up 将继承王位的人， 积藏起来	皇儲(huáng chú) 皇储 crown prince 儲蓄(chú xù) 储蓄 savings
chǔ ㄔ ㄨˇ	楚	楚	痛苦，清晰 painful, clear	痛楚(tòng chǔ) painful 清楚(qīng chǔ) clear
chǔ ㄔ ㄨˇ	褚	褚	姓氏 Chinese surname	

32

chǔ chù ㄔㄨˇ ㄔㄨˋ	處	处	辦理，地方 handle affairs, site 办理，地方	處理(chǔ lǐ) 处理 handle affairs 處方(chǔ fāng) 处方 prescription
chǔ ㄔㄨˇ	礎	础	柱子下面的石塊 foundation 柱子下面的石块	基礎(jī chǔ) 基础 basis 礎石(chǔ shí) 础石 foundation stone
chǔ ㄔㄨˇ	杵	杵	舂米的木棍 pound, pestle	杵錘(chǔ chuí) 杵锤 tail hammer 杵臼(chǔ jiù) mortar and pestle
chù xù ㄔㄨˋ ㄒㄩˋ	畜	畜	禽獸 beast 禽兽	家畜(jiā chù) domesticated animal 牲畜(shēng chù) beast
chuān ㄔㄨㄢ	川	川	江河的總稱 river 江河的总称	大川(dà chuān) rivers 川流不息(chuān liú bù xí) flow endlessly
chuān ㄔㄨㄢ	穿	穿	從窟窿裏通過去 pierce through, penetrate 从窟窿里通过去	穿針(chuān zhēn) 穿针 thread needle 穿衣(chuān yī) put on clothes
chuán ㄔㄨㄢˊ	船	船	水上載人，運貨的 交通工具 boat, ship 水上载人，运货的 交通工具	帆船(fān chuān) sail boat 船長(chuán zhǎng) 船长 captain
chuán zhuàn ㄔㄨㄢˊ ㄓㄨㄢˋ	傳	传	轉給別人 pass, pass on 转给别人	傳染(chuán rǎn) 传染 contagious 自傳(zì zhuàn) 自传 autobiography
chuǎn ㄔㄨㄢˇ	喘	喘	呼吸急促 panting	氣喘(qì chuǎn) 气喘 asthma 喘氣(chuǎn qì) 喘气 gasp for air
chuàn ㄔㄨㄢˋ	串	串	連貫東西的量詞 string together 连贯东西的量词	串通(chuàn tōng) collaborate 客串(kè chuàn) be a guest performer

chuàn ㄔㄨㄢˋ	釧	钏	臂環，手環 bracelet 臂环，手环	金釧(jīn chuàn) 金钏 gold bracelet
chuāng ㄔㄨㄤ	瘡	疮	腫起或潰爛的皮膚 病 skin ulcer 肿起或溃烂的皮肤 病	瘡疤(chuāng bā) 疮疤 scar
chuāng ㄔㄨㄤ	窗	窗	房屋中，車子裏透 光通氣的開口 window 房屋中，车子里透 光通气的开口	窗戶(chuāng hù) window 窗簾(chuāng lián) 窗帘 drape
chuáng ㄔㄨㄤˊ	床	床	睡覺的家具 bed 睡觉的家具	床鋪(chuáng pù) 床铺 bed 床單(chuáng dān) 床单 bedsheet
chuǎng ㄔㄨㄤˇ	闖	闯	擾動 rush 扰动	闖禍(chuǎng huò) 闯祸 get into trouble
chuàng chuāng ㄔㄨㄤˋ ㄔㄨㄤ	創	创	傷，開始做某件事 to injure, start doing something 伤，开始做某件事	創傷(chuāng shāng) 创伤 injure 創造(chuàng zào) 创造 create
chuī ㄔㄨㄟ	吹	吹	從嘴裏呼出氣 blow 从嘴里呼出气	吹牛(chuī niú) boast 吹奏(chuī zòu) play wind instrument
chuī ㄔㄨㄟ	炊	炊	燒煮 cook a meal 烧煮	炊煙(chuī yān) 炊烟 chimney smoke
chuí ㄔㄨㄟˊ	垂	垂	掛下來 hang down	垂危(chuí wéi) critically ill 垂直(chuí zhí) vertical
chuí ㄔㄨㄟˊ	鎚	锤	可擊物的工具，敲 擊 hammer 可击物 的工具，敲击	鐵鎚(tiě chuí) 铁锤 hammer

chuí ㄔㄨㄟˊ	槌	槌	敲打的工具 mallet	鼓槌(gǔ chuí) drumstick
chuí ㄔㄨㄟˊ	捶	捶	敲打 pound, beat	捶打(chuí dǎ) beat
chūn ㄔㄨㄣ	春	春	四季的第一季 spring	春季(chūn jì) spring season 春風(chūn fēng) 春风 spring breeze
chún ㄔㄨㄣˊ	純	纯	專一，不雜 pure, unmired 专一，不杂	純潔(chún jié) 纯洁 pure 單純(dān chún) 单纯 simplistic
chún ㄔㄨㄣˊ	唇	唇	嘴的邊緣 lip 嘴的边缘	嘴唇(zuǐ chún) 嘴唇 lip 唇膏(chún gāo) lipstick
chǔn ㄔㄨㄣˇ	蠢	蠢	愚笨 stupid, foolish	愚蠢(yú chǔn) foolish 蠢動(chǔn dòng) 蠢动 wriggle
chuō ㄔㄨㄛ	戳	戳	圖章，用尖銳的器 具刺東西 stamp, poke, stab 图章，用尖锐的器 具刺东西	郵戳(yóu chuō) 邮戳 postmark 戳穿(chuō chuān) puncture
chuò ㄔㄨㄛˋ	齪	龊	污穢 filthy 污秽	齷齪(wò chuò) 龌龊 dirty
cī ㄘ	疵	疵	毛病，缺點 defect 毛病，缺点	瑕疵(xiá cī) defect

cí ㄘˊ	詞	词	表示一個觀念的語言或文字 word, term 表示一个观念的语言或文字	名詞(míng cí) 名词 noun 詞典(cí diǎn) 词典 dictionary
cí ㄘˊ	雌	雌	陰性的生物 female 阴性的生物	英雌(yīng cí) heroine 雌性(cí xìng) female
cí ㄘˊ	辭	辞	短語或文字，告別 diction, phrase, to leave 短语或文字，告别	告辭(gào cí) 告辞 say goodbye 辭呈(cí chéng) 辞呈 resignation letter
cí ㄘˊ	祠	祠	供奉祖先，鬼神或先賢烈士的廟 ancestral temple 供奉祖先，鬼神或先贤烈士的庙	祠堂(cí táng) memorial temple
cí ㄘˊ	慈	慈	疼愛 kind, loving 疼爱	慈祥(cí xiáng) kindly 慈善(cí shàn) charity
cí ㄘˊ	瓷	瓷	質地緊密細致的陶器 china 质地紧密细致的陶器	瓷碗(cí wǎn) china bowl 瓷器(cí qì) ceramics
cí ㄘˊ	磁	磁	能吸引金屬的性質 magnetism 能吸引金属的性质	磁場(cí chǎng) 磁场 magnetic field 磁鐵(cí tiě) 磁铁 magnet
cǐ ㄘˇ	此	此	這個 this 这个	彼此(bǐ cǐ) each other 此後(cǐ hòu) 此后 from now on
cì ㄘˋ	刺	刺	植物莖上尖銳的芒，用尖的東西戳入 thorn, pierce 植物茎上尖锐的芒，用尖的东西戳入	魚刺(yú cì) 鱼刺 fish bone 刺客(cì kè) assassin
cì sì ㄘˋ、ㄙ	伺	伺	服侍 to serve	伺侯(cì hòu) to serve 窺伺(kuī sì) 窥伺 to keep an eye on

cì ㄘˋ	次	次	照著大小，高低， 好壞順序排列 order, sequence 照着大小，高低， 好坏顺序排列	次序(cì xù) order 次要(cì yào) secondary
cì ㄘˋ	賜	赐	恩惠，上級賞給下 級 favor, grant 恩惠，上级赏给下 级	恩賜(ēn cì) 恩赐 favor 賜與(cì yǔ) 赐与 bestow, grant
cōng ㄘㄨㄥ	匆	匆	忙 hastily, hurriedly	匆匆(cōng cōng) hurriedly 匆促(cōng cù) in a hurry
cōng ㄘㄨㄥ	囪	囱	爐上通氣的管道 pipe 炉上通气的管道	煙囪(yān cōng) 烟囱 chimney
cōng ㄘㄨㄥ	聰	聪	聽力好，智力好 acute hearing, intelligent 听力好，智力好	聰明(cōng míng) 聪明 smart, clever 失聰(shī cōng) 失聪 hearing loss
cōng ㄘㄨㄥ	蔥	葱	蔬菜的一種 green onion 蔬菜的一种	蔥花(cōng huā) 葱花 chopped green onion 蔥白(cōng baí) 葱白 very light green
cóng ㄘㄨㄥˊ	從	从	跟隨，自，由 follow, from 跟随，自，由	跟從(gēn cóng) 跟从 follow 從前(cóng qián) 从前 before 你從那裏來？(nǐ cóng nǎ lǐ lái) 你从那里来？ Where did you come from?
cóng ㄘㄨㄥˊ	叢	丛	聚集 crowd together	樹叢(shù cóng) 树丛 bush 叢書(cóng shū) 丛书 book series
cū ㄘㄨ	粗	粗	不精細 rough 不精细	粗心(cū xīn) careless 粗俗(cū sú) vulgar

cù ㄘ ㄨˋ	促	促	催迫 urge, push	倉促(cāng cù)仓促 in a hurry 督促(dū cù) supervise
cù ㄘ ㄨˋ	醋	醋	用米，麥，高粱等 釀製成的酸味液體 ，可以調味 vinegar 用米，麦，高粱等 酿製成的酸味液体 ，可以调味	白醋(bái cù) white vinegar 醋意(cù yì) jealousy
cù ㄘ ㄨˋ	簇	簇	聚集 form a cluster, pile up	花團錦簇(huā tuán jǐn cù) 花团锦簇 colorful decorations
cù ㄘ ㄨˋ	蹙	蹙	急迫 pressed	蹙眉(cù méi) frown 蹙額(cù é) 蹙额
cuī ㄘ ㄨㄟ	崔	崔	姓 a Chinese surname	
cuī ㄘ ㄨㄟ	催	催	促迫 urge, hurry, press	催促(cuī cù) urge 催眠(cuī mián) hypnotize
cuī ㄘ ㄨㄟ	摧	摧	破壞，折斷 break, destroy 破坏，折断	摧毀(cuī huǐ) 摧毁 destroy 摧殘(cuī cán) 摧残 devastate, ruin
cuì ㄘ ㄨㄟˋ	翠	翠	青色 emerald green	蒼翠(cāng cuì) 苍翠 green 翡翠(fěi cuì) emerald

cuì ㄘㄨㄟˋ	瘁	瘁	勞苦 overworked, tired 劳苦	心力交瘁(xīn lì jiāo cuì) be physically and mentally exhausted
cuì ㄘㄨㄟˋ	脆	脆	容易破碎的 fragile	脆弱(cuì ruò) fragile
cuì ㄘㄨㄟˋ	粹	粹	純一不雜 pure 纯一不杂	純粹(chún cuì) 纯粹 pure; 國粹(guó cuì) 国粹 quintessence of Chinese culture
cuì ㄘㄨㄟˋ	悴	悴	臉色不好，很疲倦 look pallid, tired 脸色不好，很疲倦	憔悴(qiáo cuì) look pallid
cūn ㄘㄨㄣ	村	村	鄉人聚居的地方 village 乡人聚居的地方	鄉村(xiāng cūn) 乡村 village 村長(cūn zhǎng) 村长 village head
cún ㄘㄨㄣˊ	存	存	寄放，活著 store, keep; exist, survive 寄放，活著	保存(bǎo cún) preserve 生存(shēng cún) live
cùn ㄘㄨㄣˋ	寸	寸	長度單位，極少 inch, very little 长度单位，极少	寸步(cùn bù) a tiny step 寸土(cùn tǔ) an inch of land
cuō ㄘㄨㄛ	搓	搓	兩手相摩擦 rub hands 两手相摩擦	搓手(cuō shǒu) rub hands
cuō ㄘㄨㄛ	磋	磋	失誤，差誤 idle away one's time 失误，差误	磋跎歲月(cuō tuó suì yuè) 磋跎岁月 let time slip by

cuò ㄘㄨㄛˋ	錯	错	謬誤，交叉雜亂 error, interlocked and jagged 谬误，交叉杂乱	錯誤(cuò wù) 错误 mistake 錯亂(cuò luàn) 错乱 disorder
cuò ㄘㄨㄛˋ	措	措	安排 arrange	措施(cuò shī) arrangement, measure
cuò ㄘㄨㄛˋ	挫	挫	阻礙 defect, frustrate 阻碍	挫折(cuò zhé) setback 下挫(xià cuò) going down

D

dā ㄉㄚ	搭	搭	架設起來，乘坐 erect a structure, ride a vehicle 架设起来，乘坐	搭棚(dā péng) erect a shed 搭車 (dā chē) 搭车 ride a car
dá dā ㄉㄚˊ ㄉㄚ	答	答	應對，回報 respond, repay 应对，回报	回答 (huí dá) answer 答應 (dá yìng) 答应 promise 羞答答(xiū dā dā) shy
dá ㄉㄚˊ	達	达	通，到，實現，明 白 reach, achieve, understand 通，到，实现，明 白	到達 (dào dá) 到达 arrive 傳達(chuán dá) 传达 transmit
dǎ ㄉㄚˇ	打	打	敲擊 hit 敲击	打仗(dǎ zhàng) at war 打字(dǎ zì) typing
dà ㄉㄚˋ	大	大	不小，生長 big, grow 不小，生长	大人(dà rén) adult 長大(zhǎng dà) 长大 grow up
dāi ㄉㄞ	獃	呆	癡傻的，不靈敏 dull-witted, not keen 痴傻的，不灵敏	獃子(dāi zi) 呆子 simpleton 癡獃(chī dāi) 痴呆 silly
dǎi ㄉㄞˇ	歹	歹	壞事，不好的 evil, sinister 坏事，不好的	歹徒(dǎi tú) rascal 為非作歹(wéi fēi zuò dǎi) 为非作歹 do evil
dǎi ㄉㄞˇ	逮	逮	追捕，捉 arrest, catch	逮捕(dǎi bǔ) arrest
dài dāi ㄉㄞˋ ㄉㄞ	待	待	停留，等候 remain, wait	招待(zhāo dài) entertain a guest 對待(duì dài) 对待 treat 待一會兒(dāi yì huǐ ér) wait a minute 待一会儿

41

dài ㄉ ㄞ丶	黛	黛	畫眉用青黑色顏料 dark green dye for blackening eyebrows 画眉用青黑色颜料	黛筆(dài bǐ)黛笔 eyebrow pencil 粉黛(fěn dài) palace girls
dài ㄉ ㄞ丶	帶	带	布或皮革做成的 長條物，引導belt, guide布或皮革做 成的长条物，引导	皮帶(pí dài) 皮带 belt 帶領(dài lǐng) 带领 lead
dài ㄉ ㄞ丶	代	代	時世，指時間； 輪流更換 era, times; to supersede 时世，指时间； 轮流更换	古代(gǔ dài) ancient times 後代(hòu dài) 后代 future generations
dài ㄉ ㄞ丶	戴	戴	把東西套在頭上， 手指、手臂上 wear, support 把东西套在 头上，手指、手臂上	戴帽子(dài mào zi) wear hat 愛戴(ài dài) 爱戴 love and support
dài ㄉ ㄞ丶	怠	怠	做事懶散，不勤勞 slack in work, lazy 做事懒散，不勤劳	怠慢(dài màn) to treat with neglect 怠工(dài gōng) slowdown in work
dài ㄉ ㄞ丶	殆	殆	幾乎，差不多，危險 virtually, danger 几乎 ，差不多，危险	殆盡(dài jìn) 殆尽 virtually, almost 危殆(wéi dài) in great danger
dài ㄉ ㄞ丶	貸	贷	借出或借入 loan	借貸(jiè dài) 借贷 borrow money 貸款(dài kuǎn) 贷款 loan
dài ㄉ ㄞ丶	袋	袋	可以裝東西的；袋 裝物品一包 叫一袋 a sack 可以装东西 的；袋装物品一包 叫一袋	口袋(kǒu dài) pocket 袋鼠(dài shǔ) kangaroo
dān ㄉ ㄢ	丹	丹	精煉配制的藥劑； 紅色 pill, red 精炼配制的药剂； 红色	仙丹(xiān dān) magic pill 丹心(dān xīn) utter devotion
dān ㄉ ㄢ	單	单	記事紙張，用一層 布製成的衣物 sheet 记事纸张，用一层 布制成的衣物	名單(míng dān) 名单 name list 床單(chuáng dān) 床单 bedsheet
dān dàn ㄉ ㄉ ㄢ ㄢ丶	擔	担	用肩膀挑；負責 shoulder, undertake 用肩膀挑；负责	擔心(dān xīn) 担心 worry 重擔(zhòng dàn) 重担 heavy burden

42

dān ㄉㄢ	耽	耽	延遲，沉迷 delay, indulge in 延迟，沉迷	耽擱(dān gē) 耽搁 delay 耽溺(dān nì) be indulged in
dān ㄉㄢ	眈	眈	眼向下看 look downward	虎視眈眈(hǔ shì dān dān) cast a covetous eye at
dǎn ㄉㄢˇ	膽	胆	位于肝臟下面圓形 的消化器官 gall bladder 位于肝脏下面圆形 的消化器官	膽子(dǎn zi) 胆子 courage, nerves 膽小(dǎn xiǎo) 胆小 coward
dǎn ㄉㄢˇ	疸	疸	黃疸：皮膚眼白呈 黃色的病症 jaundice 黄疸：皮肤眼白呈 黄色的病症	黃疸病(huáng dǎn bìng) jaundice
dàn ㄉㄢˋ	旦	旦	早晨，天，日 morning, day	元旦(yuán dàn) New Year's Day 一旦(yí dàn) once
dàn ㄉㄢˋ	但	但	只是 only	但是(dàn shì) but 不但(bú dàn) not only
dàn ㄉㄢˋ	誕	诞	出生 birth	誕生(dàn shēng) 诞生 be born
dàn tan ˊ ㄉ ㄊ ㄢˋ ㄢˊ	彈	弹	可以發射出的小丸 子 ball, pellet, bullet 可以发射出的小丸 子	子彈(zǐ dàn) 子弹 bullet 彈弓(dàn gōng) 弹弓 slingshot
dàn ㄉㄢˋ	淡	淡	含鹽分少，稀薄 insipid, diluted 含盐分少，稀薄	淡水(dàn shuǐ) fresh water 淡季(dàn jì) slack season
dàn ㄉㄢˋ	蛋	蛋	硬殼的卵，受精後 可孵出小動物 egg 硬壳的卵，受精后 可孵出小动物	蛋糕(dàn gāo) cake 蛋白(dàn bái) egg white
dāng dàng ㄉ ㄉ ㄤ ㄤˋ	當	当	恰當，適宜 appropriate, suitable 恰当，适宜	當時(dāng shí) 当时 at that time 相當(xiāng dāng) 相当 equal to

43

dàng ㄉㄤˋ	當	当	抵押，抵得 mortgage	當鋪(dàng pù) 当铺 pawn shop 上當(shàng dàng) 上当 be deceived
dǎng ㄉㄤˇ	黨	党	志同道合的人組成 的團體 party, political party 志同道合的人组成 的团体	黨員(dǎng yuán) 党员 party members 政黨(zhèng dǎng) 政党 political party
dǎng dang、 ㄉㄤˇ ㄉㄤˋ	擋	挡	攔住 to block something 拦住	阻擋(zǔ dǎng) 阻挡 obstruct
dàng ㄉㄤˋ	蕩	荡	搖晃，清除 sway, clean up	掃蕩(sǎo dàng) 扫荡 mopping-up operation 傾家蕩產(qīng jiā dàng chǎn) 倾家荡产 go bankrupt
dàng ㄉㄤˋ	盪	荡	擺動 swaying 摆动	動盪(dòng dàng) 动荡 turmoil 盪鞦韆(dàng qiū qiān) 荡秋韆 play the swing
dāo ㄉㄠ	刀	刀	用來切割的工具 knife 用来切割的工具	刀口(dāo kǒu) knife edge 剪刀(jiǎn dāo) scissors
dāo ㄉㄠ	叨	叨	話多，翻來復去地 說 annoyingly talkative 话多，翻来复去地 说	嘮叨(láo dāo) 唠叨 talk on and on
dǎo ㄉㄠˇ	導	导	引導 guide 引导	指導(zhǐ dǎo) 指导guide 導播(dǎo bō) 导播 TV program director
dǎo ㄉㄠˇ	島	岛	海洋或湖泊裏四周 被水圍著的陸地 island 海洋或湖泊里四周 被水围著的陆地	半島(bàn dǎo) 半岛 peninsula 島嶼(dǎo yǔ) 岛屿 island
dǎo ㄉㄠˇ	禱	祷	教徒向天，神求助 pray	禱告(dǎo gào) 祷告 pray 禱詞(dǎo cí) 祷词 prayer

dǎo ㄉ ㄠˇ	倒	倒	豎立的東西平躺下來 fall down 竖立的东西平躺下来	倒閉(dǎo bì) 倒闭 go bankrupt 倒霉(dǎo méi) tough luck
dǎo ㄉ ㄠˇ	搗	搗	舂，攪擾 pound at, stir up 舂，搅扰	搗亂(dǎo luàn) 搗乱 stir up trouble 搗碎(dǎo suì) 搗碎 crush to pieces
dǎo ㄉ ㄠˇ	蹈	蹈	踐踏，遵循 trample on, follow 践踏，遵循	手舞足蹈(shǒu wǔ zú dǎo) jump about in joy 重蹈覆轍(chóng dǎo fù zhé) 重蹈覆辙 commit same mistake
dào ㄉ ㄠˋ	到	到	往 go to	到達(dào dá) 到达 arrive 遲到(chí dào) 迟到 tardy
dào ㄉ ㄠˋ	悼	悼	表達哀念 show grievance 表达哀念	哀悼(āi dào) mourn
dào ㄉ ㄠˋ	稻	稻	一種穀類植物 rice 一种谷类植物	水稻(shuǐ dào) paddy 稻田(dào tián) rice field
dào ㄉ ㄠˋ	道	道	路，方向 way, direction	道路(dào lù) road 道德(dào dé) morality
dào ㄉ ㄠˋ	盜	盜	偷 steal	盜賊(dào zéi) 盜贼 thief 盜用(dào yòng) 盜用 use without authorization
dé děi ㄉ ㄉ ㄜˊ ㄟˇ	得	得	得到，必須 gain, should	得意(dé yì) feel elated 得當(dé dàng) 得当 proper 說得好(shuō dé hǎo) 说得好 well said!

45

拼音	繁體	简体	解释	例词
dé ㄉㄜˊ	德	德	好的品行 good conduct	德國(dé guó) 德国 Germany 德育(dé yù) moral education
de ㄉㄜ·	的	的	表示所屬 expressing possession 表示所属	我的書(wǒ de shū) 我的书 my book 誠實的人(chéng shí de rén) 诚实的人 an honest person
dēng ㄉㄥ	燈	灯	照明的器具 lamp	燈泡(dēng pāo) 灯泡 light bulb 燈塔(dēng tǎ) 灯塔 lighthouse
dēng ㄉㄥ	登	登	升上去,記錄 go up, to record 升上去,记录	登山(dēng shān) climb mountain 登記(dēng jì) 登记 register
děng ㄉㄥˇ	等	等	級別,待 category, wait 级别,待	等級(děng jí) 等级 level 等待(děng dài) wait
dèng ㄉㄥˋ	鄧	邓	姓氏 Chinese surname	
dèng ㄉㄥˋ	凳	凳	沒有靠背的椅子 bench	凳子(dèng zi) bench
dèng ㄉㄥˋ	瞪	瞪	張大眼睛直看 stare 张大眼睛直看	目瞪口呆(mù dèng kǒu dāi) rendered speechless
dī ㄉㄧ	低	低	不高,垂下來 low, hang down	低等(dī děng) low grade 低頭(dī tóu) 低头 hang one's head
dī ㄉㄧ	滴	滴	液體顆粒狀 a drop of liquid 液体颗粒状	滴管(dī guǎn) medicine dropper 水滴(shuǐ dī) water drop
dí dì ㄉㄧˊ ㄉㄧˋ	的	的	確實,心裏想要達到的境地 certainly, goal 确实,心里想要达到的境地	的確(dí què) 的确 definitely 目的(mù dì) objective

dí ㄉ 一ˊ	敵	敌	懷有仇恨的對手 enemy 怀有仇恨的对手	敵對(dí duì) 敌对 antagonistic 敵人(dí rén) 敌人 enemy
dí ㄉ 一ˊ	笛	笛	管樂器的一種 flute 管乐器的一种	吹笛(chuī dí) play flute 汽笛(qì dí) siren
dí ㄉ 一ˊ	滌	涤	清洗 cleanse	洗滌(xǐ dí) 洗涤 wash 滌除(dí chú) 涤除 get rid of
dí ㄉ 一ˊ	迪	迪	開導 enlighten 开导	啓迪(qǐ dí) 启迪 enlighten
dí ㄉ 一ˊ	嫡	嫡	家族中血統最近的 the closest of blood relation 家族中血统最近的	嫡親兄弟(dí qīn xiōng dì) 嫡亲兄弟 whole brothers
dǐ ㄉ 一ˇ	底	底	物體的最下側 bottom 物体的最下侧	根底(gēn dǐ) foundation 底漆(dǐ qī) undercoat
dǐ ㄉ 一ˇ	邸	邸	重要官員住的地方 residence of an important official 重要官员住的地方	官邸(guān dǐ) official residence
dǐ ㄉ 一ˇ	砥	砥	磨刀石 whetstone	中流砥柱(zhōng liú dǐ zhù) main support
dǐ ㄉ 一ˇ	抵	抵	支持，抗拒 support, resist	抵押(dǐ yā) mortgage 抵抗 (dǐ kàng) resist
dǐ ㄉ 一ˇ	詆	诋	說別人壞話 to badmouth 说别人坏话	詆毀(dǐ huǐ) 诋毁 to slander, defame

47

dì ㄉ 一、	地	地	土地，位置 land, position 土地，位置	地方(dì fāng) place 地位(dì wèi) status
dì ㄉ 一、	第	第	加在數詞前表示次序的字 used before a sequential number 加在数词前表示次序的字	第一(dì yī) number one, first
dì ㄉ 一、	帝	帝	古代君主 emperor	皇帝(huáng dì) emperor
dì ㄉ 一、	弟	弟	同父母比自己年幼的男子 younger brother	弟子(dì zi) disciple 內弟(nèi dì) brother-in-law
dì ㄉ 一、	遞	递	傳送 transmit 传送	遞增(dì zēng) 递增 increase progressively 遞交(dì jiāo) 递交 deliver
dì ㄉ 一、	締	缔	結合 form relationship 结合	締造(dì zào) 缔造 establish 締約(dì yuē) 缔约 sign a treaty
diān ㄉ 一 ㄢ	掂	掂	用手托著物件估量輕重 weigh in the hand 用手托著物件估量轻重	掂斤估兩(diān jīn gū liǎng) 度斤估兩 haggle over details
diān ㄉ 一 ㄢ	顛	颠	搖晃震動 shaky, bumpy 摇晃震动	顛覆(diān fù) 颠覆 overturn 顛倒(diān dǎo) 颠倒 turn upside down
diān ㄉ 一 ㄢ	癲	癫	精神失常 deranged	瘋癲(fēng diān) 疯癫 deranged
diǎn ㄉ 一ˇ ㄢ	點	点	細小的痕跡，小時，指示 dot, hour, guide 细小的痕迹，小时，指示	一點(yì diǎn) 一点 one o'clock, a little 指點(zhǐ diǎn) 指点 provide guidance

diǎn ㄉ一ˇㄢ	典	典	法則，抵押 standardized rules, mortgage 法则，抵押	典型(diǎn xíng) model 典押(diǎn yā) mortgage
diàn ㄉ一ˋㄢ	電	电	實物具有的感應力 electricity 实物具有的感应力	電話(diàn huà) 电话 telephone 電腦(diàn nǎo) 电脑 computer 電冰箱(diàn bīng xiāng) 电冰箱 refrigerator
diàn ㄉ一ˋㄢ	佃	佃	租用土地以耕種 rent a piece of land for farming 租用土地以耕种	佃農(diàn nóng) 佃农 tenant farmer
diàn ㄉ一ˋㄢ	店	店	陳列出賣商品的鋪子 shop 陈列出卖商品的铺子	店鋪(diàn pù) 店铺 shop 店東(diàn dōng) 店东 shop owner
diàn ㄉ一ˋㄢ	惦	惦	掛念 be concerned about a person or something	惦記(diàn jì) 惦记 keep in mind
diàn ㄉ一ˋㄢ	墊	垫	襯托物，代爲付款 cushion, advance money to others 衬托物，代为付款	椅墊(yǐ diàn) 椅垫 chair cushion 墊錢(diàn qián) 垫钱 advance money
diàn ㄉ一ˋㄢ	奠	奠	創立，獻給死者的祭品 establish, offering to the dead 创立，献给死者的祭品	奠都(diàn dū) establish the capital 奠定(diàn dìng) lay down (foundation)
diàn ㄉ一ˋㄢ	殿	殿	皇宮或寺廟裏的大廳 main hall of palace or temple 皇宫或寺庙里的大厅	殿下(diàn xià) Your Highness 殿軍(diàn jūn) 殿军 fourth-place winner
diàn ㄉ一ˋㄢ	澱	淀	沉渣 sediment	沉澱(chén diàn) 沉淀 sediment 澱粉(diàn fěn) 淀粉 starch

diāo ㄉ ㄧ ㄠ	刁	刁	狡詐的 crafty 狡诈的	刁蠻(diāo mán) 刁蛮 stubborn 刁難(diāo nán) 刁难 give people a hard time
diāo ㄉ ㄧ ㄠ	叼	叼	銜在嘴裏 hold something in the mouth 衔在嘴里	叼著香煙(diāo zhe xiāng yān) with cigarette dangling from the lip
diāo ㄉ ㄧ ㄠ	碉	碉	石頭房子 blockhouse 石头房子	碉堡(diāo bǎo) fortress
diāo ㄉ ㄧ ㄠ	貂	貂	鼠類小動物 marten 鼠类小动物	貂皮大衣(diāo pí dà yī) mink coat
diāo ㄉ ㄧ ㄠ	凋	凋	花草樹葉枯萎 wither 花草树叶枯萎	凋謝(diāo xiè) 凋谢 wither and fall
diāo ㄉ ㄧ ㄠ	雕	雕	一種凶猛的鳥；刻畫在金屬、石頭、木料上 vulture, engrave一种凶猛的鸟；刻画在金属、石头、木料上	雕刻(diāo kè) sculpture 雕像(diāo xiàng) monument
diào ㄉ ㄧ ㄠ	吊	吊	懸掛著 hang 悬挂著	吊床(diào chuáng) hammock 吊帶(diào dài) 吊带 suspenders
diào ㄉ ㄧ ㄠ	掉	掉	跌落，遺失，替換 drop, miss from possession, substitute 跌落，遗失，替换	掉色(diào sè) discolor 掉換(diào huàn) 掉换 exchange
diào ㄉ ㄧ ㄠ	釣	钓	用鉤子捕魚 angling 用钩子捕鱼	釣竿(diào gān) 钓竿 fishing pole 釣餌(diào ěr) 钓饵 bait
diào tiáo ㄉ ㄧ ㄠ ㄊ ㄧ ㄠ	調	调	音的高低，移動 tune, transfer 音的高低，移动	曲調(qǔ diào) 曲调 melody 調查(diào chá) 调查 investigate

diē dié ㄉ一 ㄝ ㄉ一ˊㄝ	跌	跌	失足倒下 fall	跌倒(diē dǎo) tumble 跌價(diē jià) 跌价 price decline
diē ㄉ一ㄝ	爹	爹	父親 father 父亲	爹娘(diē niáng) mom and dad 爹爹(diē diē) father
dié ㄉ一ˊㄝ	碟	碟	盛放食物的盤子 plate, saucer 盛放食物的盘子	碟子(dié zi) dish 飛碟(fēi dié) 飞碟 flying saucer
dié ㄉ一ˊㄝ	蝶	蝶	蝴蝶簡稱 butterfly 蝴蝶简称	蝴蝶(hú dié) butterfly 蝶泳(dié yǒng) butterfly stroke
dié ㄉ一ˊㄝ	諜	谍	探聽敵情 to spy on 探听敌情	間諜(jiàn dié) 间谍 a spy 諜報(dié bào) 谍报 intelligence report
dié ㄉ一ˊㄝ	疊	叠	一層層搭架起來 pile up 一层层搭架起来	折疊(zhé dié) 折叠 fold up
dīng ㄉ一ㄥ	丁	丁	第四，成年男子 fourth, man	丁等(dīng děng) the fourth place 壯丁(zhuàng dīng) able-bodied man
dīng ㄉ一ㄥ	叮	叮	囑咐，被蟲子咬 remind, stung by insect 嘱咐，被虫子咬	叮嚀(dīng níng) 叮咛 repeatedly remind 叮咬(dīng yǎo) bitten by insect
dīng ㄉ一ㄥ	釘	钉	一端尖利的金屬或 木制細粳，跟蹤 nail, to tail a person 一端尖利的金属或 木制细粳，跟踪	釘子 (dīng zi) 钉子 nail 釘人(dīng rén) 钉人 watch over a person

dīng ㄉ ㄧ ㄥ	盯	盯	專心地看人 stare at a person 专心地看人	盯著他看(dīng zhe tā kàn) 盯著他看 stare straight at him
dǐng ㄉ ㄧ ㄥ	鼎	鼎	古代烹飪器，盛大 ancient cooking pot, magnificent 古代烹饪器，盛大	鼎力相助(dǐng lì xiāng zhù) render full support 鼎鼎大名(dǐng dǐng dà míng) a name well known
dǐng ㄉ ㄧ ㄥ	頂	顶	最高的部位，反駁 top part, support, retort 最高的部位 ，支撐，反駁	屋頂(wū dǐng) 屋顶 roof 頂嘴(dǐng zuǐ) 顶嘴 talk back
dìng ㄉ ㄧ ㄥ	定	定	平穩，必然，不變 的 stable, definitely, fixed 平稳，必然， 不变的	平定(píng dìng) calm down, quell 一定(yí dìng) definitely
dìng ㄉ ㄧ ㄥ	訂	订	商量後確定，修改 reach agreement, make amendment 商量后确定，修改	訂婚(dìng hūn) 订婚 engaged to be married 訂正(dìng zhèng) 订正 make correction
dìng ㄉ ㄧ ㄥ	錠	锭	金屬或藥品呈塊狀 的 a block of metal or medicine 金属或 药品呈块状的	錠劑(dìng jì) 锭剂 lozenge 鋼錠(gāng dìng) 钢锭 steel slab
diū ㄉ ㄧ ㄡ	丟	丟	遺失，遺棄 lost, discard 遗失，遗弃	丟掉(diū diào) lost, discard 丟臉(diū liǎn) 丢脸 lose face
dōng ㄉ ㄨ ㄥ	東	东	太陽升起的一邊 east 太阳升起的一边	東西(dōng xī) 东西 thing, article 東道(dōng dào) 东道 the host
dōng ㄉ ㄨ ㄥ	冬	冬	一年四季中的最後 一季 winter 一年 四季中的最后一季	冬天(dōng tiān) winter 冬眠(dōng mián) hibernation
dǒng ㄉ ㄨ ㄥ	董	董	監督管理；姓氏 direct, manage; a Chinese surname 监督管理；姓氏	董事(dǒng shì) board directors 董事會(dǒng shì huì) 董事会 board directors
dǒng ㄉ ㄨ ㄥ	懂	懂	明瞭 understand 明了	懂事(dǒng shì) intellectually mature 懂行(dǒng háng) know the trade
dòng ㄉ ㄨ ㄥ	恫	恫	恐嚇別人 to threaten other 恐吓别人	恫嚇(dòng hè) 恫吓 to threaten

dòng ㄉ ㄨˋ ㄥ	動	动	非靜止狀態 moving 非静止状态	動物(dòng wù) 动物 animal 擺動(bǎi dòng) 摆动 swaying
dòng ㄉ ㄨˋ ㄥ	凍	冻	液體遇冷而凝固 freeze 液体遇冷而凝固	凍結(dòng jié) 冻结 to freeze 冷凍(lěng dòng) 冷冻 frozen
dòng ㄉ ㄨˋ ㄥ	棟	栋	房屋的脊檁 ridgepole 房屋的脊檩	棟樑(dòng liáng) 栋樑 ridge beam
dòng ㄉ ㄨˋ ㄥ	洞	洞	表面上凹進去較深 的部分，徹底 hole, thoroughly 表面上凹进去较深 的部分，彻底	洞穴(dong xuè) cave 洞察(dòng chá) thorougly observe
dōu dū ㄉ ㄉ ㄡ ㄨ	都	都	全部，程度深 all, to a greater extent	都去(dōu qù) all will go 天都亮了(tiān dōu liàng le) the day has dawned
dōu ㄉ ㄡ	兜	兜	繞著走，招攬生意 going around, solicit business 绕着走，招揽生意	兜風(dōu fēng) 兜风 go for a ride 兜售(dōu shòu) peddle goods
dǒu ㄉ ㄡˇ	蚪	蚪	蝌蚪 tadpole	蝌蚪(kē dǒu) tadpole
dǒu ㄉ ㄡˇ	抖	抖	顫動，甩動 tremble, shake 颤动，甩动	發抖(fā dǒu) 发抖 shivering 抖掉(dǒu diào) shake off
dǒu ㄉ ㄡˇ	斗	斗	糧食容量單位 unit of measure for grain 粮食容量单位	斗室(dǒu shì) little room 漏斗(lòu dǒu) funnel
dòu ㄉ ㄡˋ	豆	豆	豆類作物 bean, pea 豆类作物	豆腐(dòu fǔ) bean curd 黃豆(huáng dòu) soybean
dòu ㄉ ㄡˋ	逗	逗	停留，引人發笑 stop over, to amuse	逗留(dòu liú) stay over 逗趣(dòu qù) interesting

dòu ㄉ ㄡˋ	鬥	斗	相對抗 fight 相对抗	鬥爭(dòu zhēng) 斗争 struggle 奮鬥(fèn dòu) 奋斗 to strive for
dòu ㄉ ㄡˋ	竇	窦	洞孔 hole	啓人疑竇(qǐ rén yí dòu) 启人疑窦 arouse people's suspicion
dū ㄉ ㄨ	督	督	看管 supervise	監督(jiān dū) 监督 watch over 總督(zǒng dū) 总督 governor
dū dōu ㄉ ㄉ ㄨ ㄡ	都	都	城市，中央政府所 地 city, capital	都市計劃(dū shì jì huà) 都市计划 urban planning 首都(shǒu dū) capital city 大都會(dà dū huì)大都会 metropolis
dú ㄉ ㄨ	讀	读	用眼睛看文字以瞭 解其意思 read 用眼睛看文字以了 解其意思	閱讀(yuè dú) 阅读 reading 讀者(dú zhě) 读者 readers
dú ㄉ ㄨ	毒	毒	有害物質 poison 有害物质	毒品(dú pǐn) narcotics 中毒(zhòng dú) poisoned
dú ㄉ ㄨ	獨	独	單個的 single 单个的	獨立(dú lì) 独立 independence 獨特(dú tè) 独特 unique
dǔ ㄉ ㄨˇ	賭	赌	爲贏取錢財而玩的 遊戲 gamble 为赢取钱财而玩的 遊戏	打賭(dǎ dǔ) 打赌 to bet 賭博(dǔ bó) 赌博 gambling
dù ㄉ ㄨˋ	妒	妒	心懷嫉恨 jealous 心怀嫉恨	妒忌(dù jì) jealous
dù ㄉ ㄨˋ	度	度	衡量標準，渡過 standard of measurement, spend time 衡量标准，渡过	程度(chéng dù) degree 度假(dù jià) to vacation

dù ㄉ ㄨˋ	肚	肚	腹部 abdomen	肚子(dù zi) belly 有肚量(yǒu dù liàng) tolerant, forgiving
dù ㄉ ㄨˋ	渡	渡	越過水面 cross a stretch of water 越过水面	過渡期(guò dù qí) 过渡期 transition period 渡輪(dù lún) 渡轮 ferry boat
dù ㄉ ㄨˋ	杜	杜	停止 stop	杜絕(dù jué) 杜绝 eradicate 杜鵑花(dù juān huā) azalea
duān ㄉ ㄨ ㄢ	端	端	事物的起源或末尾 ，正直 beginning or end; upright	開端(kāi duān) 开端 beginning 端正(duān zhèng) upright
duǎn ㄉ ㄨˇ ㄢ	短	短	不長，缺乏 short, lack 不长，缺乏	短波(duǎn bō) short wave 短期(duǎn qí) short term
duàn ㄉ ㄨˋ ㄢ	段	段	事情或時間的某一 部分 section, period 事情或时间的某一 部分	段落(duàn luò) paragraph 一段(yí duàn) one section
duàn ㄉ ㄨˋ ㄢ	緞	缎	絲織品的一種 satin 丝织品的一种	綢緞(chóu duàn) 绸缎 silk fabrics 緞帶(duàn dài) 缎带 silk ribbon
duàn ㄉ ㄨˋ ㄢ	斷	断	失去連接 break	斷絕(duàn jué) 断绝 break off 中斷(zhōng duàn) 中断 terminate
duī ㄉ ㄨ ㄟ	堆	堆	積在一起 stack 积在一起	堆積(duī jī) 堆积 pile up 一大堆(yí dà duī) a whole bunch
duì ㄉ ㄨˋ ㄟ	對	对	朝向，正確 face toward, correct 朝向，正确	對手(duì shǒu) 对手 opponent 不對(bú duì) 不对 wrong

duì ㄉㄨㄟˋ	隊	队	有組織的團體 organized group 有组织的团体	部隊(bù duì) 部队 troop, army 隊員(duì yuán) 队员 team member
duì ㄉㄨㄟˋ	兌	兑	換取 exchange 换取	兌換(duì huàn) 兑换 exchange 承兌(chéng duì) accept
dūn ㄉㄨㄣ	敦	敦	懇切，忠厚 sincere, honest 恳切，忠厚	敦請(dūn qǐng) 敦请 sincerely invite 敦厚(dūn hòu) honest
dǔn ㄉㄨㄣˇ	盹	盹	閉目小睡 doze off 闭目小睡	打盹(dǎ dǔn) take a nap
dùn ㄉㄨㄣˋ	盾	盾	手提防護裝備 shield 手提防护装备	矛盾(máo dùn) contradiction 盾牌(dùn pái) shield
dùn ㄉㄨㄣˋ	頓	顿	暫停，突然 pause, suddenly 暂停，突然	停頓(tíng dùn) 停顿 pause 頓時(dùn shí) 顿时 suddenly
dùn ㄉㄨㄣˋ	噸	吨	重量單位，一噸是 1,000公斤 one ton 重量单位，一吨是 1,000公斤	一噸(yí dùn) 一吨 one ton 噸位(dùn wèi) 吨位 tonnage
duō ㄉㄨㄛ	多	多	不少，過分 many, excessive 不少，过分	多少(duō shǎo) how many? 多心(duō xīn) too sensitive
duō ㄉㄨㄛ	咄	咄	表示斥責，不信 expressing disapproval or disbelief 表示斥责，不信	咄咄逼人(duō duō bī rén) arrogant 咄咄怪事(duō duō guài shì) unbelievable
duó ㄉㄨㄛˊ	奪	夺	強取，爭取 snatch, win 强取，争取	爭奪(zhēng duó) 争夺 contend for 奪回(duó huí) 夺回 recapture

duǒ ㄉㄨㄛˇ	朵	朵	花和雲的量詞 used to count flowers, clouds 花和云的量词	花朵(huā duǒ) flower 一朵雲(yì duǒ yún)一朵云 a cloud 一朵花(yì duǒ huā) a flower
duǒ ㄉㄨㄛˇ	躲	躲	藏起來，避開 hide, avoid 藏起来，避开	躲藏(duǒ cáng)躲藏 hide 躲開(duǒ kāi) 躲开 avoid
duò ㄉㄨㄛˋ	舵	舵	控制航行工具方向 的裝置 helm 控制航行工具方向 的装置	舵手(duò shǒu) helmsman 掌舵(zhǎng duò) take the helm
duò tuó ㄉㄨㄛˋ ㄊㄨㄛˊ	馱	馱	牲畜背負的貨物 load carried by draft animals 牲畜背负的货物	馱運(tuó yùn) 驮运 transport by draft animals
duò ㄉㄨㄛˋ	惰	惰	懶 lazy 懒	懶惰(lǎn duò) 懒惰 lazy 惰性(duò xìng) listlessness
duò ㄉㄨㄛˋ	墮	堕	掉下來，思想或行 爲向壞的方面發展 fall, degenerate 掉下来，思想或行 爲向壞的方面發展	墮落(duò luò) 堕落 degenerate 墮胎(duò tāi) 堕胎 abortion

E				
é さ′	額	额	眉上髪下部分 forehead 眉上髪下部分	額頭(é tóu) 额头 forehead 額外(é wài) 额外 extra
é さ′	娥	娥	美女 pretty woman	娥眉(é méi) delicate eyebrows
é さ′	鵝	鹅	一種家禽，比鴨大 ，頸長 goose 一种家禽，比鸭大 ，颈长	鵝毛(é máo) 鹅毛 goose feather
é さ′	蛾	蛾	節枝動物，蝶類昆 蟲，翅面灰白moth 节枝动物，蝶类昆 虫，翅面灰白	飛蛾(fēi é) 飞蛾 moth
é さ′	俄	俄	很短的時間 very short time 很短的时间	俄國(é guó) 俄国 Russia 俄羅斯(é luó sī) 俄罗斯 Russia
ě è wù さˇ さˋ ㄨˋ	惡 噁	恶	要嘔吐，厭惡，不 善 nauseating, disgusting, evil 要呕吐，厌恶，不 善	罪惡(zuì è) evil 噁心(ě xīn) feel like vomiting
è さˋ	貳	贰	"二"字的大寫 word form of 2 "二"字的大写	貳拾(è shí) 贰拾 twenty
è さˋ	扼	扼	掐住 to clutch	扼要(è yào) summary
è さˋ	噩	噩	驚人的 shocking 惊人的	噩耗(è hào) shocking news 渾渾噩噩(hún hún è è) 浑浑噩噩 live aimlessly
è さˋ	餓	饿	飢，不飽 hungry 饥，不饱	饑餓(jī è) 饥饿 hunger
è さˋ	愕	愕	驚訝 stunned, astounded 惊讶	愕然(è rán) be stunned

è さ、	鱷	鳄	一種凶猛的爬行動物，皮和鱗很硬 alligator 一种凶猛的爬行动物，皮和鳞很硬	鱷魚(è yú) 鳄鱼 alligator
è さ、	遏	遏	阻止，制止 to stop	遏止(è zhǐ) to stop
ēn ㄣ	恩	恩	好處 kindness 好处	恩惠(ēn huì) kindness 恩人(ēn rén) benefactor 報恩(bào ēn) 报恩 return one's kindness 恩賜(ēn cì) 恩赐 blessing
ér ㄦˊ	而	而	連接同類的詞或句子 connecting word 连接同类的词或句子	而且(ér qiě) also 而已(ér yǐ) that is all
ér ㄦˊ	兒	儿	小孩子，父母稱子 child 小孩子，父母称子	兒童(ér tóng) child 女兒(nǚ ér) 女儿 daughter
ěr ㄦˇ	爾	尔	你，此，這兒 you, that 你，此，这儿	爾虞我詐(ěr yú wǒ zhà) 尔虞我诈 deceive each other
ěr ㄦˇ	耳	耳	聽覺器官 ear 听觉器官	耳朵(ěr duo) ear 中耳(zhōng ěr) middle ear
ěr ㄦˇ	餌	饵	釣魚用的魚食 bait 钓鱼用的鱼食	魚餌(yú ěr) 鱼饵 bait
èr ㄦ、	二	二	一加一的總和 two 一加一的总和	三心二意(sān xīn èr yì) constant change of mind

F				
fā ㄈㄚ	發	发	送出，動身 send, set out on a trip 送出，动身	發送(fā sòng) 发送 transmit 出發(chū fā) 出发 set out
fá ㄈㄚˊ	乏	乏	缺少，疲倦 lack, tiresome	貧乏(pín fá) 贫乏 poverty 缺乏(quē fá) shortage
fá ㄈㄚˊ	伐	伐	砍 chop down	伐木(fá mù) timber logging
fá ㄈㄚˊ	罰	罚	處分犯錯的人 punish 处分犯错的人	懲罰(chéng fá) 惩罚 punish
fǎ ㄈㄚˇ	法	法	國家制定，頒布的 規則 law, decree 国家制定，颁布的 规则	法律(fǎ lǜ) law
fǎ ㄈㄚˇ	髮	发	頭髮 hair 头发	理髮(lǐ fǎ) 理发 hair-dressing 脫髮(tuō fǎ) 脱发 lose hair
fà ㄈㄚˋ	琺	珐	一種玻璃質的塗料 ，不透明白色 enamel 一种玻璃质的涂料 ，不透明白色	琺瑯(fà láng) 珐琅 enamel
fān ㄈㄢ	帆	帆	利用風力使船前進 的布篷 sail 利用风力使船前进 的布篷	帆船(fān chuán) sail boat 揚帆(yáng fān) 扬帆 set sail
fān ㄈㄢ	番	番	遍數，來自外國的 one time, foreign country 遍数，来自外国的	番茄(fān qié) tomato 番薯(fān shǔ) sweet potato

fān ㄈㄢ	翻	翻	歪倒了，改變 overturn, change 歪倒了，改变	翻修(fān xiū) overhaul 翻譯(fān yì) 翻译 translate
fán ㄈㄢˊ	煩	烦	苦悶，急躁 depressed, vexed, 苦闷，急躁	麻煩(má fán) 麻烦 troublesome 煩躁(fán zào) 烦躁 irritating
fán ㄈㄢˊ	凡	凡	平常的，所有的 ordinary, all	平凡(píng fán) ordinary 凡是(fán shì) whatever
fán ㄈㄢˊ	繁	繁	許多，興盛 many, prosperous 许多，兴盛	繁殖(fán zhí) 繁殖 to breed 繁榮(fán róng) 繁荣 prosperity
fǎn ㄈㄢˇ	反	反	翻轉，顛倒 turn about, turn upside down 翻转，颠倒	反面(fǎn miàn) opposite 相反(xiāng fǎn) on the contrary
fǎn ㄈㄢˇ	返	返	回去 return	往返(wǎng fǎn) back and forth 返鄉(fǎn xiāng) 返乡 return home
fàn ㄈㄢˋ	范	范	姓氏 Chinese surname	
fàn ㄈㄢˋ	範	范	榜樣，模子 example, mould 榜样，模子	模範(mó fàn) 模范 model 範圍(fàn wéi) 范围 scope
fàn ㄈㄢˋ	飯	饭	煮熟的穀類食品 cooked rice 煮熟的谷类食品	午飯(wǔ fàn) 午饭 lunch 飯店(fàn diàn) 饭店 restaurant
fàn ㄈㄢˋ	泛	泛	水向外漫流，漂浮 flood, float	泛濫(fàn làn) 泛滥 flooding 泛舟(fàn zhōu) row a boat

fàn ㄈㄢˋ	犯	犯	違反 violate 违反	犯罪(fàn zuì) commit crime 罪犯(zuì fàn) criminal
fàn ㄈㄢˋ	販	販	商人，兜售 peddler, peddle	小販(xiǎo fàn) 小贩 hawker 販毒(fàn dú) 贩毒 drug trafficking
fàn ㄈㄢˋ	梵	梵	有關佛教的事物 relating to Buddhism 有关佛教的事物	梵文(fàn wén) Sanskrit script 梵蒂岡(fàn dì gāng)梵蒂冈 Vatican
fāng ㄈㄤ	方	方	四個角全是九十度 的四邊形 square 四个角全是九十度 的四边形	方便(fāng biàn) convenience 方向(fāng xiàng) direction
fāng ㄈㄤ-	芳	芳	花草的香味；美好 的德行 fragrance, virtue	芬芳(fēn fāng) fragrance 流芳百世(liú fāng bǎi shì) good name lasts forever
fáng ㄈㄤˊ	防	防	戒備，避免 guard against, prevent 戒备，避免	國防(guó fáng) 国防 national defense 防水(fáng shuǐ) waterproof
fáng ㄈㄤˊ	房	房	住人的建築物 shelter 住人的建筑物	房屋(fáng wū) house 房東(fáng dōng) 房东 landlord
fáng ㄈㄤˊ	坊	坊	工作場所 work place 工作场所	街坊(jiē fáng) neighborhood 茶坊(chá fáng) tea house
fáng ㄈㄤˊ	肪	肪	厚的脂膏 fat	脂肪(zhī fáng) fat

fǎng ㄈㄤˇ	妨	妨	阻礙 hamper 阻碍	妨害(fáng hài) jeopardize 不妨(bù fáng) it doesn't hurt to ...
fǎng ㄈㄤˇ	訪	访	看望 visit	訪問(fǎng wèn) 访问 pay a visit to 訪客(fǎng kè) 访客 visitor
fǎng ㄈㄤˇ	紡	纺	把絲，棉等做成紗 spin 把丝，棉等做成纱	紡織品 (fǎng zhī pǐn) 纺织品 textiles 紡織業(fǎng zhī yè) 纺织业 textile industry
fǎng ㄈㄤˇ	仿	仿	效法，類似 imitate, resemble 效法，类似	仿照(fǎng zhào) model after 相仿(xiāng fǎng) be alike
fàng ㄈㄤˋ	放	放	解除約束 release 解除约束	釋放(shì fàng) 释放 to release 放款(fàng kuǎn) lend money to
fei ㄈㄟ	飛	飞	鳥類或蟲類用翅膀 在空中往來活動 fly 鸟类或虫类用翅膀 在空中往来活动	飛機(fēi jī) 飞机 airplane 試飛(shì fēi) 试飞 test fly
fei ㄈㄟ	妃	妃	皇帝的妾 imperial concubine	妃子(fēi zi) imperial concubine 王妃(wáng fēi) princess consort
fei ㄈㄟ	非	非	不是，十分 no, not, very	講是非(jiǎng shì fēi) 讲是非 to gossip 非常(fēi cháng) unusually
fei ㄈㄟ	菲	菲	花草茂盛 abundant growth	芳菲(fāng fēi) flowers and grasses 菲律賓(fēi lǜ bīn) 菲律宾 the Philippines

fēi ㄈㄟ	緋	绯	紅色 red	面頰緋紅(miàn jiá fēi hóng) 面颊绯红 blush 緋聞(fēi wén) 绯闻 sex scandal
féi ㄈㄟˊ	肥	肥	胖，含脂肪多 fat	肥胖(féi pàng) fat 肥沃(féi wò) fertile
fěi ㄈㄟˇ	匪	匪	強盜，非 bandit, not 强盗，非	土匪(tǔ fěi) bandit 匪夷所思(fěi yí suǒ sī) unbelievable
fěi ㄈㄟˇ	誹	诽	說別人的壞話 slander 说别人的坏话	誹謗(fěi bàng) 诽谤 make slander
fěi ㄈㄟˇ	翡	翡	綠色的硬玉 emerald 绿色的硬玉	翡翠(fěi cuì) emerald
fèi ㄈㄟˋ	廢	废	停止，沒有用的 stop, useless	廢除(fèi chú) 废除 abolish 廢紙(fèi zhǐ) 废纸 scratch paper
fèi ㄈㄟˋ	肺	肺	呼吸器官 lung	肺癌(fèi ái) lung cancer 肺癆(fèi láo) 肺痨 tuberculosis
fèi ㄈㄟˋ	費	费	消耗，所需要的款項 consume, fee 消耗，所需要的款项	費用(fèi yòng) expense 學費(xué fèi) 学费 tuition
fèi ㄈㄟˋ	吠	吠	狗叫 bark	狂吠(kuáng fèi) bark furiously

64

fèi ㄈㄟˋ	沸	沸	滾燙 boiling 滚烫	沸騰(fèi téng) 沸腾 filled with excitement 沸點(fèi diǎn) 沸点 boiling point
fēn ㄈㄣ	分	分	由整體中取出一部 分 divide, separate 由整体中取出一部 分	分裂(fēn liè) split 分別(fēn bié) separately
fēn ㄈㄣ	芬	芬	花草的香氣 fragrance 花草的香气	芬蘭(fēn lán) 芬兰 Finland 芬芳(fēn fāng) fragrance
fēn ㄈㄣ	氛	氛	氣象，情勢 atmosphere (the surrounding influence) 气象，情势	氣氛(qì fēn) 气氛 atmosphere
fēn ㄈㄣ	紛	纷	眾多、雜亂 numerous, disorderly 众多，杂乱	紛擾(fēn rǎo) 纷扰 confusion 議論紛紛(yì lùn fēn fēn) 议论纷纷 controversial
fēn ㄈㄣ	吩	吩	口頭指派或命令 oral instruction or order 口头指派或命令	吩咐(fēn fù) orally instruct
fén ㄈㄣˊ	墳	坟	埋葬死者的土堆 grave	墳墓(fén mù) 坟墓 graveyard 祖墳(zǔ fén) 祖坟 ancestral grave
fén ㄈㄣˊ	焚	焚	燒 burn 烧	焚毀(fén huǐ) 焚毁 destroy by burning 自焚(zì fén) set oneself on fire
fěn ㄈㄣˇ	粉	粉	細末 powder 细末	粉筆(fěn bǐ) 粉笔 chalk 粉碎(fěn suì) to crush

fèn ㄈㄣˋ	份	份	整體中的一個單位 a share 整体中的一个单位	成份(chéng fèn) ingredient, component 股份(gǔ fèn) stock share
fèn ㄈㄣˋ	糞	粪	由腸內排出的廢物 excrement 由肠内排出的废物	糞便(fèn biàn) 粪便 excrement 牛糞(niú fèn) 牛粪 cow dung
fèn ㄈㄣˋ	奮	奋	振作，有力地 exert oneself, forcefully	興奮(xīng fèn) 兴奋 excited 奮戰(fèn zhàn) 奋战 fight bravely
fèn ㄈㄣˋ	憤	愤	不滿意，生氣而感 情激動 indignant 不满意，生气而感 情激动	憤怒(fèn nù) 愤怒 anger 憤恨(fèn hèn) 愤恨 resentment
fèn ㄈㄣˋ	忿	忿	生氣，不服氣 angry, unconvinced 生气，不服气	忿忿不平(fèn fèn bù píng) harbor resentment
fēng ㄈㄥ	峰	峰	高而尖的山頭 summit 高而尖的山头	巔峰(diān fēng) 巅峰 peak 群峰(qún fēng) a group of mountains
fēng ㄈㄥ	風	风	流動的空氣，表現 在外的豐采 wind, style 流动的空气，表现 在外的丰采	北風(běi fēng) 北风 northwind 風度(fēng dù) 风度 graceful behavior
fēng ㄈㄥ	封	封	密封 sealed	信封(xìn fēng) envelope 封面(fēng miàn) cover page
fēng ㄈㄥ	豐	丰	多 abundant, plentiful	豐盛(fēng shèng) 丰盛 bountiful 豐收(fēng shōu) 丰收 bumper harvest

fēng ㄈㄥ	楓	枫	落葉喬木，邊緣有細鋸齒，秋天葉轉紅 maple 落叶乔木，边缘有细锯齿，秋天叶转红	楓樹(fēng shù) 枫树 maple tree
fēng ㄈㄥ	鋒	锋	刀劍等器械尖端部分 sharp point of cutlery 刀剑等器械尖端部分	先鋒(xiān fēng) 先锋 vanguard 鋒利(fēng lì) 锋利 sharp
fēng ㄈㄥ	蜂	蜂	昆蟲名，會螫人 bee 昆虫名，会螫人	蜜蜂(mì fēng) bee 蜂蜜(fēng mì) honey
fēng ㄈㄥ	瘋	疯	神經錯亂 mentally deranged 神经错乱	瘋狂(fēng kuáng) 疯狂 wild, mad 麻瘋(má fēng) 麻风 leprosy
fēng ㄈㄥ	烽	烽	古時邊防報警的煙火 beacon fire 古时边防报警的烟火	烽火(fēng huǒ) beacon fire
féng ㄈㄥˊ	逢	逢	遇到，迎合 meet with, cater to	相逢(xiāng féng) meeting 逢迎(féng yíng) curry favor with
féng fèng ㄈㄥˊ ㄈㄥ	縫	缝	用針線做衣服，補合 sew, stitch 用针线做衣服，补合	縫紉(féng rèn) 缝纫 sewing 縫隙(fèng xì) 缝隙 slit
fěng ㄈㄥˇ	諷	讽	含蓄地責罵 satirize 含蓄地责骂	諷刺(fěng cì) 讽刺 satirize 嘲諷(cháo fěng) 嘲讽 sneer at
fèng ㄈㄥ丶	奉	奉	給 give	奉送(fèng sòng) present as gift 奉陪(fèng péi) accompany

fèng ㄈㄥˋ	鳳	凤	古代傳說的詳瑞鳥 phoenix 古代传说的详瑞鸟	鳳梨(fèng lí) 凤梨 pineapple 鳳凰(fèng huáng) 凤凰 phoenix
fèng ㄈㄥˋ	俸	俸	官員的薪酬 government official's salary 官员的薪酬	俸祿(fèng lù) 俸禄 official's salary
fó ㄈㄛˊ	佛	佛	佛教徒稱得道的人 Buddha 佛教徒称得道的人	佛教(fó jiào) Buddhism 佛事(fó shì) Buddhist ceremony
fǒu ㄈㄡˇ	否	否	不，用在字尾表示 詢問 denial, no 不，用在字尾表示 询问	否決(fǒu jué) veto 是否(shì fǒu) whether or not
fū ㄈㄨ	夫	夫	成年男子的通稱， 男性配偶 man, husband 成年男子的通称， 男性配偶	丈夫(zhàng fū) husband 夫婦(fū fù) 夫妇 husband and wife
fū ㄈㄨ	膚	肤	肉體表面的皮 skin 肉体表面的皮	皮膚(pí fū) 皮肤 skin 膚色(fū sè) 肤色 complexion
fū ㄈㄨ	敷	敷	塗上，搽上 apply powder, ointment	敷藥(fū yào) 敷药 apply medicine 敷衍(fū yǎn) go through the motions
fú ㄈㄨˊ	氟	氟	化學元素，符號F， 淡黃色有臭味的毒 氣 fluorine 化学元 素，符号F, 淡黄色 有臭味的毒气	
fú ㄈㄨˊ	扶	扶	攙，用手支持人或 物以免倒下 support 搀，用手支持人或 物以免倒下	扶持(fú chí) support 扶養(fú yǎng) 扶养 to provide for
fú ㄈㄨˊ	伏	伏	隱藏，承認，屈服 hide, admit, subjugate 隐藏，承认，屈服	埋伏(mái fú) ambush 伏罪(fú zuì) plead guilty

fú ㄈㄨˊ	浮	浮	漂 float	漂浮(piāo fú) float 浮標(fú biāo) 浮标 buoy
fú ㄈㄨˊ	芙	芙	落葉灌木，花有紅白黃色 hibiscus 落叶灌木，花有紅白黃色	芙蓉(fú róng) lotus
fú ㄈㄨˊ	福	福	吉祥之事 good fortune	幸福(xìng fú) happiness 福利(fú lì) welfare
fú ㄈㄨˊ	幅	幅	量詞，布匹的寬度 classifier for painting, width of cloth 量词，布匹的宽度	一幅畫(yì fú huà) 一幅画 a painting 幅度(fú dù) range, scope, extent
fú ㄈㄨˊ	符	符	代表事物的標記 symbol 代表事物的标记	符號(fú hào) 符号 symbol 符合(fú hé) conform to
fú ㄈㄨˊ	服	服	衣裳 dress	衣服(yī fú) dress 服裝(fú zhuāng) garment
fú ㄈㄨˊ	孚	孚	信用，使人信服 trust, convincing	深孚眾望(shēn fú zhòng wàng) 深孚众望 enjoy high prestige
fú ㄈㄨˊ	輻	辐	車輪中連接軸和輪的直木 spoke 车轮中连接轴和轮的直木	輻射(fú shè) 辐射 radiation
fú ㄈㄨˊ	蝠	蝠	一種會飛，狀似老鼠的哺乳動物 bat 一种会飞，状似老鼠的哺乳动物	蝙蝠(biān fú) bat (mammal)
fǔ ㄈㄨˇ	撫	抚	養育，輕輕按摩 nurture, caress 养育，轻轻按摩	撫育(fǔ yù) 抚育 nurture 撫摸(fǔ mō) 抚摸 caress

69

fǔ ㄈㄨˇ	府	府	國家統治機關，尊稱別人的居處 government, your home (honorific) 国家统治机关，尊称别人的居处	政府(zhèng fǔ) government 府上(fǔ shàng) your home
fǔ ㄈㄨˇ	輔	辅	幫助 assist 帮助	輔助(fǔ zhù) 辅助 assist 輔導(fǔ dǎo) 辅导 counseling
fǔ ㄈㄨˇ	甫	甫	古代男子的美稱 used in addressing a man in ancient times 古代男子的美称	台甫(tái fǔ) your personal name 甫畢(fǔ bì) 甫毕 just finish
fǔ ㄈㄨˇ	腐	腐	變質，行為墮落，思想陳舊 decomposed, decadent 变质，行为堕落，思想陈旧	腐敗(fǔ bài) 腐败 corrupt 豆腐(dòu fǔ) bean curd
fǔ ㄈㄨˇ	脯	脯	肉乾 dried cooked meat 肉干	肉脯(ròu fǔ) dried cooked meat
fǔ ㄈㄨˇ	釜	釜	古代的一種鍋 an ancient cookery 古代的一种锅	破釜沉舟(pò fǔ chén zhōu) be determined to forge ahead without turning back
fǔ ㄈㄨˇ	腑	腑	胸腹內器官的總稱 internal organs inside chest and abdomen 胸腹内器官的总称	肺腑之言(fèi fǔ zhī yán) talk from the bottom of the heart
fǔ ㄈㄨˇ	斧	斧	砍東西的工具 axe 砍东西的工具	斧頭(fǔ tóu) 斧头 hatchet 鬼斧神工(guǐ fǔ shén gōng) exquisite craftsmanship
fù ㄈㄨˋ	付	付	交，給 give, offer, pay 交，给	付款(fù kuǎn) make payment 交付(jiāo fù) turn over to

fù ㄈㄨˋ	負	负	背，擔任，欠 carry on the back, shoulder, owe 背，担任，欠	負責(fù zé) 负责 be responsible for 負債(fù zhài) 负债 be in debt
fù ㄈㄨˋ	赴	赴	往，去 go to	赴會(fù huì) 赴会 attend a meeting 赴任(fù rèn) go to one's new post
fù ㄈㄨˋ	婦	妇	已婚的女子 married woman	婦女(fù nǚ) 妇女 women 婦科(fù kē) 妇科 gynecology
fù ㄈㄨˋ	富	富	財產，充滿 wealth, abundance 财产，充满	財富(cái fù) 财富 wealth 富足(fù zú) abundance 富豪(fù háo) rich and powerful people
fù ㄈㄨˋ	賦	赋	田地稅，給予 land tax, bestow on 田地税，给予	田賦(tián fù) 田赋 land tax 天賦(tiān fù) 天赋 gifted talents
fù ㄈㄨˋ	父	父	爸爸，對男性長輩 的稱呼 father, uncle 爸爸，对男性长辈 的称呼	父親(fù qīn) 父亲 father 伯父(bó fù) uncle
fù ㄈㄨˋ	復	复	返回，還報 return, retaliate 返回，还报	復原(fù yuán) 复原 recover from illness 復仇(fù chóu) 复仇 to avenge
fù ㄈㄨˋ	副	副	居第二位的，輔助 的 righthand man, assistant 居第二位的，辅助 的	副總統(fù zǒng tǒng) 副总统 vice president 副本(fù běn) copy
fù ㄈㄨˋ	傅	傅	輔助，教導 help, instruct 辅助，教导	師傅(shī fù) 师傅 master

fù ㄈㄨˋ	覆	覆	遮蓋，翻倒 cover, overturn 遮盖，翻倒	覆沒(fù mò) capsize 顛覆(diān fù) 颠覆 overthrow
fù ㄈㄨˋ	訃	讣	報喪 obituary 报丧	訃聞(fù wén) 讣闻 obituary
fù ㄈㄨˋ	阜	阜	土山，昌盛 mound, abundance	丘阜(qiū fù) mound
fù ㄈㄨˋ	腹	腹	肚子 abdomen	果腹(guǒ fù) eat 腹部(fù bù) abdomen
fù ㄈㄨˋ	咐	咐	口頭指派或命令 oral instruction 口头指派或命令	吩咐(fēn fù) oral instruction 囑咐(zhǔ fù) 嘱咐 enjoin
fù ㄈㄨˋ	附	附	連帶，依靠 attached, depend 连带，依靠	附件(fù jiàn) appendix 附屬(fù shǔ) 附属 attached
fù ㄈㄨˋ	駙	驸	八匹馬共同拉車， 在旁邊的叫"駙" a kind of horse 八匹马共同拉车， 在旁边的叫"驸"	駙馬(fù mǎ) 驸马 an emporor's son-in-law
fù ㄈㄨˋ	複	复	再 again	重複(chóng fù) 重复 repeat 複習(fù xí) 复习 review (lesson)

G

gāi 《 ㄞ	該	该	應當，那個 should, that 应当，那个	應該(yīng gāi) 应该 should 該校(gāi xiào) 该校 that school
gǎi 《 ㄞˇ	改	改	變更，訂正 change, correct 变更，订正	修改(xiū gǎi) amend, revise 改正(gǎi zhèng) correct
gài 《 ㄞˋ	鈣	钙	化學金屬元素名 calcium 化学金属元素名	鈣片(gài piàn) 钙片 calcium tablet
gài 《 ㄞˋ	丐	丐	乞討者 beggar 乞讨者	乞丐(qǐ gài) beggar
gài 《 ㄞˋ	概	概	大略，總括 roughly, generally 大略，总括	大概(dà gài) more or less 概論(gài lùn) 概论 introduction
gài 《 ㄞˋ	溉	溉	澆灌 irrigate 浇灌	灌溉(guàn gài) irrigation
gài 《 ㄞˋ	蓋	盖	遮蔽在器物上面的 東西 a cover 遮蔽在器物上面的 东西	遮蓋(zhē gài) 遮盖 cover up 蓋子(gài zi) 盖子 lid
gān 《 ㄢ	肝	肝	消化器官之一，分 泌膽汁存于膽囊 liver 消化器官之一，分 泌胆汁存于胆囊	肝炎(gān yán) hepatitis 心肝(xīn gān) conscience, darling
gān 《 ㄢ	甘	甘	味道好，願意 tasty, willing to 味道好，愿意	甘蔗(gān zhè) sugarcane 甘心(gān xīn) willingly
gān 《 ㄢ	乾	干	不濕 dry 不湿	乾燥(gān zào) 干燥 dry 乾淨(gān jìng) 干净 clear

gān 《ㄢ	尷	尬	處境窘困，不易處理 embarrassing 處境窘困，不易处理	尷尬(gān gà) 尷尬 embarrassing
gān 《ㄢ	桿	杆	較小的木條 pole 较小的木条	旗桿(qí gān) 旗杆 flag pole 球桿(qiú gān) 球杆 club (for golf, etc)
gān 《ㄢ	柑	柑	橘類水果，味甘美 tangerine 橘类水果，味甘美	柑橘(gān jú) tangerines and oranges
gān 《ㄢ	竿	竿	竹的莖幹 rod 竹的茎幹	竹竿(zhú gān) bamboo pole 撐竿跳(chēng gān tiào) 撐竿跳 pole jump
gǎn 《ㄢˇ	趕	赶	追，盡早或及時到達 chase, hurry 追，尽早或及时到达	趕走(gǎn zǒu) 赶走 expel 趕快(gǎn kuài) 赶快 hurriedly
gǎn 《ㄢˇ	敢	敢	有勇氣，有膽量 bold, courageous 有勇气，有胆量	勇敢(yǒng gǎn) courageous 敢死隊(gǎn sǐ duì) 敢死队 suicide squad
gǎn 《ㄢˇ	感	感	覺得，因受刺激引起的心理變化 sense, feel 觉得，因受刺激引起的心理变化	感覺(gǎn jué) 感觉 perception 感謝(gǎn xiè) 感谢 thank
gǎn 《ㄢˇ	橄	橄	常綠喬木，葉子羽狀，果實尖長，種子可榨油 olive 常绿乔木，叶子羽状，果实尖长，种子可榨油	橄欖(gǎn lǎn) 橄榄 olive
gàn 《ㄢˋ	幹	幹	樹木的主莖，才能 tree trunk, talent 树木的主茎，才能	樹幹(shù gàn) 树幹 tree trunk 能幹(néng gàn) 能幹 capable

74

gàn 《ㄢˋ	贛	赣	地名，江西省的簡稱 Jiangxi Province 地名，江西省的简称	
gāng 《ㄤ	剛	刚	堅強，正好 strong, just right 坚强，正好	剛強(gāng qiáng) 刚强 staunch 剛好(gāng hǎo) 刚好 just right
gāng 《ㄤ	肛	肛	肛門：在直腸末端，排泄糞便的器官 anus 肛门：在直肠末端，排泄粪便的器官	肛門(gāng mén) 肛门 anus
gāng 《ㄤ	缸	缸	用陶土或瓷土制成的容器 crock 用陶土或瓷土制成的容器	浴缸(yù gāng) bath tub 汽缸(qì gāng) cylinder (of car)
gāng 《ㄤ	岡	冈	山脊 ridge	山岡(shān gāng) small hill
gāng 《ㄤ	鋼	钢	生鐵制成，不含磷，硫，矽等雜質的鐵 steel 生铁制成，不含磷，硫，矽等杂质的铁	不銹鋼(bú xiù gāng) 不锈钢 stainless steel 鋼琴(gāng qín) 钢琴 piano
gāng 《ㄤ	綱	纲	文章，言論或事物的主要部分 gist 文章，言论或事物的主要部分	綱要(gāng yào) 纲要 outline 綱領(gāng lǐng) 纲领 guiding principle
gǎng 《ㄤˇ	崗	岗	巡邏兵或警察擔任守望時站立的地方 sentry 巡逻兵或警察担任守望时站立的地方	崗位(gǎng wèi) post 站崗(zhàn gǎng) stand guard
gǎng 《ㄤˇ	港	港	可以停泊大船的江海口岸 port 可以停泊大船的江海口岸	港口(gǎng kǒu) port 香港(xiāng gǎng) Hong Kong
gàng 《ㄤˋ	槓	杠	較粗的棍子 rod 较粗的棍子	杠桿(gàng gǎn) 杠杆 lever 單杠(dān gàng) 单杠 horizontal bar

gāo 《 ㄠ	高	高	"低"的反面，等级在上的 high "低"的反面，等级在上的	高樓(gāo lóu) 高楼 high-rise 跳高(tiào gāo) high jump
gāo 《 ㄠ	膏	膏	油脂，稠厚的糊狀物 fat, paste 油脂，稠厚的糊狀物	牙膏(yá gāo) tooth paste 膏藥(gāo yào) 膏药 plaster
gāo 《 ㄠ	糕	糕	用米粉或麵粉攪和其他材料做成的食品 cake 用米粉或麵粉攪和其他材料做成的食品	蛋糕(dàn gāo) cake 糕點(gāo diǎn) 糕点 pastry
gāo 《 ㄠ	睪	睾	雄性動物性器官的一部分，能產生精子 testicle 雄性动物性器官的一部分，能产生精子	睪丸(gāo wán) 睾丸 testicle
gāo 《 ㄠ	羔	羔	小羊 lamb	羔羊(gāo yáng) lamb
gǎo 《 ㄠˇ	搞	搞	做，弄 do	搞懂(gǎo dǒng) to understand 搞鬼(gǎo guǐ) play tricks
gǎo 《 ㄠˇ	稿	稿	文字，圖畫的草底，事先考慮的計劃 manuscript, draft 文字，图画的草底，事先考虑的计划	草稿(cǎo gǎo) manuscript 定稿(dìng gǎo) finalize the script
gǎo 《 ㄠˇ	鎬	镐	刨土的工具 hoe-type farm implement	十字鎬(shí zì gǎo) 十字镐 hoe
gào 《 ㄠˋ	告	告	通知 inform	報告(bào gào) 报告 report 告訴(gào sù) 告诉 tell

gào ㄍㄠˋ	誥	诰	告誡的文體 a written admonition 告诫的文体	誥誡(gào jiè) 诰诫 admonition
gē ㄍㄜ	鴿	鸽	鳥名，常成群飛翔 。有些能傳遞書信 pigeon 鸟名，常成群飞翔 。有些能传递书信	鴿子(gē zi) 鸽子 pigeon 信鴿(xìn gē) 信鸽 carrier pigeon
gē ㄍㄜ	割	割	用刀剝開 cut 用刀剥开	割傷(gē shāng) 割伤 a cut wound 割讓(gē ràng) 割让 to cede
gē ㄍㄜ	哥	哥	同父母比自己年長 的男子 elder brother 同父母比自己年长 的男子	大哥(dà gē) big brother 哥倫布(gē lún bù) 哥伦布 Columbus
gē ㄍㄜ	疙	疙	皮膚腫起的小塊 lump on the body 皮肤肿起的小块	疙瘩(gē dā) goose bumps
gē ㄍㄜ	胳	胳	腋下，從肩膀到手 的部分 armpit, arm 腋下，从肩膀到手 的部分	胳臂(gē bèi) arm
gē ㄍㄜ	擱	搁	放置，事情停頓 put aside, delay 放置，事情停顿	擱置(gē zhì) 搁置 to shelve a matter 擱淺(gē qiǎn) 搁浅 stranded
gē ㄍㄜ	戈	戈	古代一種兵器 an ancient armament 古代一种兵器	干戈(gān gē) a warfare
gē kǎ ㄍㄜ ㄎㄚˇ	咯	咯	象聲詞，吐，用力 使東西從食道或氣 管裏出來 giggle, vomit 象声词，吐，用力 使东西从食道或气 管里出来	咯咯笑(gē gē xiào) giggle 咯血(kǎ xiě) vomit blood

77

gē ㄍ ㄜ	歌	歌	合樂的曲子，有節奏的發聲 song 合乐的曲子，有节奏的发声	歌曲(gē qǔ) song 歌頌(gē sòng) 歌颂 sing praise to
gé ㄍ ㄜ	革	革	去了毛加工過的皮，改變 leather, change 去了毛加工过的皮，改变	皮革(pí gé) leather 改革(gǎi gé) reform
gé ㄍ ㄜˊ	格	格	劃分成的空欄和框框，標準 grid, standards 划分成的空栏和框框，标准	格式(gé shì) format 品格(pǐn gé) character
gé ㄍ ㄜˊ	隔	隔	阻絕，分開 obstruct, separate 阻绝，分开	隔絕(gé jué) 隔绝 separated 隔壁(gé bì) next door
gé ㄍ ㄜˊ	閣	阁	樓房的一種，四周有欄干；官署之稱 pavilion, government 楼房的一种，四周有栏干；官署之称	出閣(chū gé) 出阁 get married(for a girl) 組閣(zǔ gé) 组阁 form a cabinet
gě ㄍ ㄜˇ	葛	葛	多年生蔓草，莖細長，纖維可織布 a kind of creeping plant 多年生蔓草，茎细长，纤维可织布	
gè ㄍ ㄜˋ	各	各	每個，彼此，不同的 every, each, different 每个，彼此，不同的	各種(gè zhǒng) 各种 all kinds of 各處(gè chù) 各处 everywhere
gè ㄍ ㄜˋ	個	个	數量詞 numerical coefficient 数量词	一個(yí gè) 一个 one 個性(gè xìng) 个性 personality
gěi jǐ ㄍ ㄐ ㄟ 一	給	给	交付，為 give, do something for 交付，为	送給(sòng gěi) 送给 give to 供給(gōng jǐ) 供给 supply

78

gēn ㄍㄣ	根	根	植物體向土裏伸長的部分，事物的本源 root, basis 植物体向土里伸长的部分，事物的本源	根本(gēn běn) fundamentals 根據(gēn jù) 根据 basis 一根香蕉(yì gēn xiāng jiāo) a banana
gēn ㄍㄣ	跟	跟	腳底的後部，在後面隨行 heel, follow 脚底的后部，在后面随行	鞋跟(xié gēn) heel (of shoe) 跟隨(gēn suí) 跟随 follow
gēng gèng jīng ㄍㄥ ㄍㄥˋ ㄐㄧㄥ	更	更	改變，再 change, even more 改变，再	更改(gēng gǎi) make changes 更加(gèng jiā) even more 三更半夜(sān jīng bàn yè) midnight
gēng ㄍㄥ	庚	庚	年齡 age 年龄	貴庚(guì gēng) 貴庚 your age
gēng ㄍㄥ	耕	耕	用犁把土翻鬆 plough 用犁把土翻松	耕田(gēng tián) till the land 耕耘(gēng yún) farming
gěng ㄍㄥˇ	耿	耿	光明，正直 honest, upright	耿直(gěng zhí) 耿直 straightforward 忠心耿耿(zhōng xīn gěng gěng) utmost loyalty
gěng ㄍㄥˇ	梗	梗	植物的枝莖，挺立 stem, straighten up 植物的枝茎，挺立	花梗(huā gěng) flower stem 梗著脖子(gěng zhe bó zi) 梗著脖子 straighten up the neck
gōng ㄍㄨㄥ	躬	躬	身體 body 身体	鞠躬(jú gōng) to bow 事必躬親(shì bì gōng qīn) 事必躬亲 do things personally
gōng ㄍㄨㄥ	功	功	貢獻 contribution 贡献	功勞(gōng láo) 功劳 meritorious service 成功(chéng gōng) success

79

gōng 《ㄨㄥ	攻	攻	打擊 attack 打击	攻擊(gōng jí) 攻击 attack 攻勢(gōng shì) 攻势 offensive
gōng 《ㄨㄥ	龔	龚	姓 a Chinese surname	
gōng 《ㄨㄥ	宮	宫	房屋，帝王的住所 palace 房屋，帝王的住所	皇宮(huáng gōng) palace 迷宮(mí gōng) maze
gōng 《ㄨㄥ	恭	恭	肅敬，謙遜，有禮貌 respectful, humble, courteous 肃敬，谦逊，有礼貌	恭敬(gōng jìng) respect 恭維(gōng wéi) 恭维 to compliment
gōng 《ㄨㄥ	工	工	從事勞動生產的人，勞動 worker, work 从事劳动生产的人，劳动	工人(gōng rén) worker 工廠(gōng chǎng) 工厂 factory
gōng 《ㄨㄥ	公	公	祖父或丈夫的父親，共同的 grandfather, common 祖父或丈夫的父亲，共同的	公平(gōng píng) equality 公用(gōng yòng) for public use 充公(chōng gōng) confiscate 公園(gōng yuán) park
gōng 《ㄨㄥ	弓	弓	射箭或發射彈丸的工具 a bow 射箭或发射弹丸的工具	弓箭(gōng jiàn) bow and arrow 彈弓(dàn gōng) 弹弓 slingshot
gǒng 《ㄨㄥˇ	鞏	巩	堅固 firm and solid 坚固	鞏固(gǒng gù) 巩固 consolidated
gǒng 《ㄨㄥˇ	汞	汞	一種金屬元素，符號Hg,另稱水銀 mercury 一种金属元素，符号Hg,另称水银	

gǒng ㄍ ㄨˇ ㄥ	拱	拱	兩手在胸前合抱 cup both hands in front of the chest 两手在胸前合抱	拱手(gǒng shǒu) cup both hands 拱橋(gǒng qiáo) 拱桥 arch bridge
gòng ㄍ ㄨˇ ㄥ	共	共	同，合計 common, total 同，合计	共同(gòng tóng) common 總共(zǒng gòng) 总共 total
gòng ㄍ ㄨˋ ㄥ	供	供	向神佛或死者奉獻 祭 offerings 向神佛或死者奉献 祭	供奉(gòng fèng) worship 供詞(gòng cí) 供词 confession
gòng ㄍ ㄨˇ ㄥˋ	貢	贡	臣民向君主獻東西 pay tribute to 臣民向君主献东西	貢獻(gòng xiàn) 贡献 contribution 進貢(jìn gòng) 进贡 pay tribute to
gōu ㄍ ㄡ	勾	勾	書寫的一種符號 「ㄠ」，引起，挑 動 checkmark, incite, provoke 书写的一种符号 「ㄠ」，引起，挑 动	打勾(dǎ gōu) put a checkmark on 勾引(gōu yǐn) to seduce
gōu ㄍ ㄡ	溝	沟	流水道，疏通 gutter, communicate	水溝(shuǐ gōu) 水沟 gutter 溝通(gōu tōng) 沟通 communicate
gōu ㄍ ㄡ	鉤	钩	形狀彎曲的器物， 一端尖銳 hook 形狀弯曲的器物， 一端尖锐	釣魚鉤(diào yú gōu) 钓鱼钩 fishing hook 鉤子(gōu zi) 钩子 hook
gǒu ㄍ ㄡˇ	狗	狗	一種家畜，看守門 戶；幫助惡人者 dog 一种家畜，看守门 户；帮助恶人者	獵狗(liè gǒu) 猎狗 hound 走狗(zǒu gǒu) running dog, lackey
gǒu ㄍ ㄡˇ	苟	苟	姑且，暫且，馬虎 temporarily, careless 姑且，暂且，马虎	苟且(gǒu qiě) just for now 一絲不苟(yì sī bù gǒu) 一丝不苟 detail oriented

gòu ㄍ ㄡ、	購	购	買 buy 买	購物(gòu wù) 购物 shopping 采購(cǎi gòu) 采购 make purchase
gòu ㄍ ㄡ、	夠	够	達到某種程度，滿 足 enough, satisfy 达到某种程度，满 足	夠高(gòu gāo) 够高 tall enough 足夠(zú gòu) 足够 sufficient
gòu ㄍ ㄡ、	垢	垢	髒東西，邪惡 dirt, evil 脏东西，邪恶	污垢(wū gòu) dirt 藏污納垢(cáng wū nà gòu) 藏污纳垢 shelter for evil things
gòu ㄍ ㄡ、	構	构	組織，連結 organize, associate 组织，连结	結構(jié gòu) 结构 structure 構成(gòu chéng) 构成 composition
gòu ㄍ ㄡ、	詬	诟	辱罵 denounce 辱骂	爲人詬病(wéi rén gòu bìng) 为人诟病 denounced by people
gū ㄍ ㄨ	姑	姑	父親的姊妹，暫且 father's sister, for the time being 父亲的姊妹，暂且	姑媽(gū mā) 姑妈 auntie 姑且(gū qiě) for the time being
gū ㄍ ㄨ	辜	辜	罪惡 guilt 罪恶	無辜(wú gū) 无辜 innocent 辜負(gū fù) 辜负 fail to live up to
gū ㄍ ㄨ	孤	孤	幼年失去父母，單 獨 orphan, lonely 幼年失去父母，单 独	孤兒(gū ér) 孤儿 orphan 孤立(gū lì) isolate
gū ㄍ ㄨ	估	估	推測，概算 estimate 推测，概算	估計(gū jì) 估计 estimate 評估(píng gū) 评估 evaluate

gū ㄍ ㄨ	菇	菇	菌類植物 mushroom 菌类植物	蘑菇(mó gū) 蘑菇 mushroom
gū ㄍ ㄨ	鴣	鸪	鳥名 a king of pigeon 鸟名	鷓鴣(zhè gū) 鹧鸪 partridge
gǔ ㄍ ㄨˇ	古	古	過去久遠的時代， 舊的 ancient, old 过去久远的时代， 旧的	古代(gǔ dài) ancient times 古怪(gǔ guài) weird
gǔ ㄍ ㄨˇ	谷	谷	兩山之間 valley 两山之间	山谷(shān gǔ) valley
gǔ ㄍ ㄨˇ	股	股	從胯到膝蓋的部分 ，計算公司資本的 單位 hip, share 從 胯到膝蓋的部分 ，計算公司資本的 单位	股東(gǔ dōng) 股东 shareholder 屁股(pì gǔ) buttocks
gǔ ㄍ ㄨˇ	骨	骨	脊椎動物體內支持 身體的堅硬組織 bone 脊椎动物体内支持 身体的坚硬组织	骨骼(gǔ gé) skeleton 骨灰(gǔ huī) ashes
gǔ ㄍ ㄨˇ	蠱	蛊	毒蟲，迷惑心意 poisonous insect, to befuddle 毒虫，迷惑心意	蠱惑人心(gǔ huò rén xīn) 蛊惑人心 to confuse the people's minds
gǔ ㄍ ㄨˇ	鼓	鼓	打擊樂器，脹起 drum, swelling 打击乐器，胀起	鼓手(gǔ shǒu) drummer 鼓起(gǔ qǐ) swelling
gù ㄍ ㄨˋ	故	故	過去的，原因 of the past, reason 过去的，原因	故事(gù shì) story 無故(wú gù) 无故 without any reason 故意(gù yì) purposely
gù ㄍ ㄨˋ	僱	雇	出錢請人給自己做 事 hire 出钱请人给自己做 事	解僱(jiě gù) 解雇 lay off 僱用(gù yòng) 雇用 hire

gù ㄍ ㄨ ˋ	固	固	堅硬 hard 坚硬	堅固(jiān gù) 坚固 solid 固定(gù dìng) fixed 固執(gù zhí) 固执 stubborn 固有(gù yǒu) inherent
gù ㄍ ㄨ ˋ	顧	顾	回頭看，看管 look back, watch over 回头看，看管	回顧(huí gù) 回顾 review 照顧(zhào gù) 照顾 take care of
gù ㄍ ㄨ ˋ	痼	痼	長久不易治療的 chronic 长久不易治疗的	痼疾(gù jí) chronic disease 痼癖(gù pǐ) steeped in bad habit
gù ㄍ ㄨ ˋ	雇	雇	出錢請人幫忙做事 hire 出钱请人都忙做事	雇員(gù yuán) 雇员 employee 雇用(gù yòng) to hire
guā ㄍ ㄨ ㄚ	颳	刮	風吹動 the wind blows 风吹动	颳風(guā fēng) 刮风 the wind blows
guā ㄍ ㄨ ㄚ	刮	刮	用刀子去掉物體表面的東西 scrape, shave 用刀子去掉物体表面的东西	刮鬍子(guā hú zi) 刮胡子 shave 搜刮(sōu guā) plunder
guā ㄍ ㄨ ㄚ	瓜	瓜	蔓生植物，果實可吃 melon 蔓生植物，果实可吃	西瓜(xī guā) water melon 南瓜(nán guā) pumpkin
guǎ ㄍ ㄨ ㄚ ˇ	寡	寡	很少，丈夫已經去世的婦女 small in number, widow 很少，丈夫已经去世的妇女	寡言(guǎ yán) not inclined to talk 寡婦(guǎ fù) 寡妇 widow
guà ㄍ ㄨ ㄚ ˋ	掛	挂	牽繫，懸起 hang 牵系，悬起	掛念(guà niàn) 挂念 to worry about 掛號(guà hào) 挂号 to register

guà 《 ㄨ ㄚ	卦	卦	古代占卜用的符號 symbol used for divining 古代占卜用的符号	八卦(bā guà) the eight symbols used in the "Book of Changes"
guà 《 ㄨ ㄚ	褂	褂	上身衣服 upper garment	馬褂(mǎ guà) 马褂 a mandarin's jacket
guāi 《 ㄨ ㄞ	乖	乖	溫順機靈，反常 meek and clever, perverted 温顺机灵，反常	乖巧(guāi qiǎo) meek and clever 乖張(guāi zhāng) 乖张 unreasonable
guāi guo 《 《 ㄨ ㄨ ㄞ ㄛ	摑	掴	用巴掌打 slap	摑耳光(guāi ěr guāng) 掴耳光 smack somebody on the face
guǎi 《 ㄨ ㄞ	拐	拐	走路時用來支撐身 體的棍子，哄騙 crutch, abduct 走路时用来支撑身 体的棍子，哄骗	拐杖(guǎi zhàng) walking stick 拐騙(guǎi piàn) 拐骗 kidnap
guài 《 ㄨ ㄞ	怪	怪	不平常 strange	奇怪(qí guài) strange 怪物(guài wù) monster
guān 《 ㄨ ㄢ	官	官	政府機關的高級人 員，身體上有特殊 功能的部分 official, organ 政府机关的高级人 员，身体上有特殊 功能的部分	官員(guān yuán) 官员 government official 感官(gǎn guān) sense organ
guān 《 ㄨ ㄢ	關	关	合起來，牽連 close, connect 合起来，牵连	關閉(guān bì) 关闭 close 關係(guān xì) 关系 relationship
guān 《 ㄨ ㄢ	觀	观	看 look	觀察(guān chá) 观察 observe 參觀(cān guān) 参观 to visit

85

guān ㄍㄨㄢ	棺	棺	裝殮死者的器具 coffin 装殓死者的器具	棺材(guān cái) coffin
guǎn ㄍㄨㄢˇ	管	管	中空的圓柱，吹奏 的樂器，料理 pipe, flute, manage 中空的圆柱，吹奏 的乐器，料理	管家(guǎn jiā) housekeeper 管理(guǎn lǐ) manage
guǎn ㄍㄨㄢˇ	館	馆	招待旅客的房舍 ，一些文化場所 hotel, public building 招待旅客的房舍 ，一些文化场所	旅館(lǚ guǎn) 旅馆 hotel 博物館(bó wù guǎn) 博物馆 museum
guàn ㄍㄨㄢˋ	貫	贯	一直連串下去，向 來如此 pass through, always 一直连串下去，向 来如此	連貫(lián guàn) 连贯 continuous 一貫(yí guàn) 一贯 always
guàn ㄍㄨㄢˋ	慣	惯	習以爲常的行爲 habit 习以为常的行为	習慣(xí guàn) 习惯 habit 慣例(guàn lì) 惯例 convention
guàn ㄍㄨㄢˋ	灌	灌	澆 pour water on 浇	灌水(guàn shuǐ) to water 灌木(guàn mù) shrub
guàn ㄍㄨㄢˋ	冠	冠	最優秀的，帽子 champion, hat 最优秀的，帽子	冠軍(guàn jūn) 冠军 champion 冠冕(guàn miǎn) crown
guàn ㄍㄨㄢˋ	罐	罐	盛東西或水的器皿 a can 盛东西或水的器皿	罐頭(guàn tóu) 罐头 a can 罐子(guàn zi) a jar
guāng ㄍㄨㄤ	光	光	物體發射或反射的 電磁波，亮 light, bright 物体发射或反射的 电磁波，亮	日光(rì guāng) sunlight 光明(guāng míng) light

guāng 《 ㄨ ㄤ	胱	胱	儲藏尿液的器官 bladder 储藏尿液的器官	膀胱(páng guāng) urinary bladder
guǎng 《 ㄨˇ ㄤ	廣	广	寬大 wide 宽大	寬廣(kuān guǎng) 宽广 spacious 廣播(guǎng bō) 广播 broadcast
guàng 《 ㄨˋ ㄤ	逛	逛	閑遊 stroll about 闲遊	逛街(guàng jiē) stroll the street 閑逛(xián guàng) 闲逛 stroll about aimlessly
guī 《 ㄨ ㄟ	歸	归	回到原處，還給 return 回到原处，还给	歸還(guī huán) 归还 return something 歸化(guī huà) 归化 naturalization
guī 《 ㄨ ㄟ	瑰	瑰	奇特，珍奇 peculiar, rare	玫瑰(méi guī) rose (flower) 瑰寶(guī bǎo) 瑰宝 treasure
guī 《 ㄨ ㄟ	閨	闺	女子居住的内室 maiden's private room	閨房(guī fáng) 闺房 maiden's private room 閨女(guī nǚ) 闺女 maiden
guī 《 ㄨ ㄟ	規	规	標準，法則 standards, rules 标准，法则	規矩(guī jǔ) 规矩 rules 規定(guī dìng) 规定 regulations
guī 《 ㄨ ㄟ	皈	皈	佛教入教儀式； 信奉宗教 inducted into a church 佛教入教仪式； 信奉宗教	皈依(guī yī) convert into a believer
guī 《 ㄨ ㄟ	龜	龟	爬行動物，腹背有 硬甲，頭尾和腳能 縮入甲中 tortoise 爬行动物，腹背有 硬甲，头尾和脚能 缩入甲中	烏龜(wū guī) 乌龟 tortoise 龜甲(guī jiǎ) 龟甲 tortoise shell
guǐ 《 ㄨˇ ㄟ	軌	轨	一定的路線 route 一定的路线	軌道(guǐ dào) 轨道 track, orbit 鐵軌(tiě guǐ) 铁轨 railway track

guǐ ㄍㄨㄟˇ	鬼	鬼	人死後的精靈 ghost 人死后的精灵	鬼魂(guǐ hún) specter 鬼話(guǐ huà) 鬼话 talk nonsense
guǐ ㄍㄨㄟˇ	詭	诡	欺詐，奸猾 crafty 欺诈，奸猾	詭計(guǐ jì) 诡计 crafty plot 詭辯(guǐ biàn) 诡辩 sophistry
guì ㄍㄨㄟˋ	桂	桂	植物品，常綠喬木 cinnamon 植物品，常绿乔木	桂花(guì huā) sweet osmanthus
guì ㄍㄨㄟˋ	劊	刽	砍斷 chop off 砍断	劊子手(guì zi shǒu) 刽子手 executioner
guì ㄍㄨㄟˋ	貴	贵	價錢高，價值高， 地位高 expensive, high value, high status 价钱高，价值高， 地位高	貴重(guì zhòng) 贵重 valuables 貴賓(guì bīn) 贵宾 distinguished guests
guì ㄍㄨㄟˋ	櫃	柜	收藏存放東西的家 具，通常是長方形 ，有屜或門 cabinet 收藏存放东西的家 具，通常是长方形 ，有屉或门	櫃子(guì zi) 柜子 cabinet 貨櫃(huò guì) 货柜 shipping container
guì ㄍㄨㄟˋ	跪	跪	屈膝使膝蓋著地 kneel 屈膝使膝盖著地	下跪(xià guì) kneel down 跪拜(guì bài) kneel and worship
gǔn ㄍㄨㄣˇ	滾	滚	水流翻騰，旋轉移 動 rolling water 水流翻腾，旋转移 动	滾水(gǔn shuǐ) 滚水 boiling water 滾筒(gǔn tǒng) 滚筒 roller
gùn ㄍㄨㄣˋ	棍	棍	棒，壞人俗稱 rod, ruffian 棒，坏人俗称	木棍(mù gùn) stick 惡棍(è gùn) 恶棍 ruffian

guō ㄍㄨㄛ	鍋	锅	煮食的器皿 cooking pot 煮食的器皿	鍋子(guō zi) 锅子 cooking pot 飯鍋(fàn guò) 饭锅 rice cooker
guō ㄍㄨㄛ	聒	聒	聲音嘈雜，使人厭煩 irritating noise 声音嘈杂，使人厌烦	聒耳(guō ěr) irritating noise
guō ㄍㄨㄛ	郭	郭	城外圍著城的牆；姓 outer wall of a city, surname 城外围著城的墙；姓	城郭(chéng guō) outer wall of a city
guō ㄍㄨㄛ	蟈	蝈	一種昆蟲，身體綠色或褐色，翅短，腹大，害蟲 grasshopper 一种昆虫，身体绿色或褐色，翅短，腹大，害虫	蟈蟈(guō guo) 蝈蝈 a king of grasshopper
guó ㄍㄨㄛˊ	國	国	有土地，人民，主權，政府或軍權的團體 nation有土地，人民，主权，政府或军权的团体	國家(guó jiā) 国家 nation, country 國籍(guó jí) 国籍 nationality
guó ㄍㄨㄛˊ	幗	帼	古代婦女包頭的巾 kerchief worn by ancient women 古代妇女包头的巾	巾幗英雄(jīn guó yīng xióng) 巾帼英雄 a heroine
guǒ ㄍㄨㄛˇ	果	果	植物開花後所結的含有種子的部分 fruit 植物开花后所结的含有种子的部分	水果(shuǐ guǒ) fruits 結果(jié guǒ) 结果 bear fruit, result
guǒ ㄍㄨㄛˇ	裹	裹	包東西，纏繞 wrap up, twine around 包东西，缠绕	包裹(bāo guǒ) parcel 裹脅(guǒ xié) 裹胁 to coerce
guò ㄍㄨㄛˋ	過	过	錯誤，在動詞後表示曾經的意思 error, completed action 错误，在动词后表示已经或曾经的意思	過失(guò shī) 过失 mistake 經過(jīng guò) 经过 pass by 超過(chāo guò) 超过 exceed

hā ㄏㄚ	哈	哈	張口呼氣，笑 exhale with open mouth, laugh 张口呼气，笑	打哈欠 (dǎ hā qiàn) to yawn 哈哈笑 (hā hā xiào) laugh
há ㄏㄚˊ	蛤	蛤	似青蛙的兩棲動物 toad 似青蛙的两栖动物	蛤蟆 (há ma) toad
hái ㄏㄞˊ	孩	孩	幼童，子女 small kid, one's children	孩童 (hái tóng) children 男孩 (nán hái) a boy
hái huán ㄏㄞˊ ㄏㄨㄢˊ	還	还	仍然 still	還是 (hái shì) 还是 is still 還會 (hái huì) 还会 can also
hái ㄏㄞˊ	骸	骸	骨的總稱，身體和 形體的總稱skeleton, body structure 骨的总称，身体和 形体的总称	殘骸 (cán hái) 残骸 the wreckage 骸骨 (hái gǔ) 骸骨 bones
hǎi ㄏㄞˇ	海	海	靠近大陸比洋小的 水域，巨大的 sea, huge 靠近大陆比洋小的 水域，巨大的	海岸 (hǎi àn) seashore 海量 (hǎi liàng) broadmindedness
hài ㄏㄞˋ	害	害	有損的，謀殺 harm, murder 有损的，谋杀	禍害 (huò hài) calamity 遇害 (yù hài) be murdered
hài ㄏㄞˋ	駭	骇	驚恐，驚嚇 fear 惊恐，惊吓	駭人聽聞 (hài rén tīng wén) 骇人听闻 horrifying news
hài ㄏㄞˋ	亥	亥	晚上九點到十一點 the hour between 9 pm and 11 pm 晚上九点到十一点	亥時時分 (hài shí shí fēn) 亥时时分 during the hour between 9 and 11 pm

hài ㄏㄞˋ	氦	氦	很輕的氣體，可充注氣球使其升空，符號為He helium 很轻的气体，可充注气球使其升空，符号为He	氦氣(hài qì) 氦气 helium
hān ㄏㄢ	酣	酣	酒喝得很暢快，盡量 drink as much as one wishes 酒喝得很畅快，尽量	酣飲(hān yǐn) 酣饮 drink freely 酣睡(hān shuì) sound asleep
hān ㄏㄢ	蚶	蚶	軟體動物，有貝殼，生活在淺海泥沙中 clam 软体动物，有贝壳，生活在浅海泥沙中	血蚶(xuè hān) clam
hān ㄏㄢ	憨	憨	傻，癡，厚道 foolish, naive, sincere 傻，痴，厚道	憨厚(hān hòu) simple and sincere
hān ㄏㄢ	鼾	鼾	熟睡時的鼻息聲 snore 熟睡时的鼻息声	打鼾(dǎ hān) to snore 鼾聲(hān shēng) 鼾声 the snore
hán ㄏㄢˊ	含	含	東西銜在嘴裏；感情不完全表露 keep in mouth; implied 东西衔在嘴里；感情不完全表露	包含(bāo hán) include 含蓄(hán xù)含蓄 implied
hán ㄏㄢˊ	函	函	信件，古時寄信用的木匣子 letter 信件，古时寄信用的木匣子	信函(xìn hán) letters 函授(hán shòu) teach by correspondence
hán ㄏㄢˊ	涵	涵	包容 accommodate	包涵(bāo hán) tolerant 涵養(hán yǎng) 涵养 self-discipline
hán ㄏㄢˊ	韓	韩	姓，戰國時代國名 Chinese surname, name of an ancient state 姓，战国时代国名	韓國(hán guó) 韩国 Korea 南韓(nán hán) 南韩 South Korea

hán ㄏㄢˊ	寒	寒	冷，痛心，灰心 cold, distressed disappointed	寒冷(hán lěng) cold 心寒(xīn hán) feel pain in heart
hǎn ㄏㄢˇ	罕	罕	稀少 rare	罕見(hǎn jiàn) 罕见 rarely seen 罕用(hǎn yòng) seldom used
hǎn ㄏㄢˇ	喊	喊	大聲叫 shout 大声叫	呼喊(hū hǎn) shout 喊口號(hǎn kǒu hào) 喊口号 shout slogan
hàn ㄏㄢˋ	汗	汗	皮膚毛孔排出的液 體 sweat 皮肤毛孔排出的液 体	流汗(liú hàn) to sweat 出汗(chū hàn) to sweat
hàn ㄏㄢˋ	漢	汉	朝代名，中國五大 民族之一，男子 dynasty name, Han people, man 朝代名，中国五大 民族之一，男子	漢朝(hàn cháo) 汉朝 the Han Dynasty 老漢(lǎo hàn) 老汉 an old man 漢學(hàn xué) 汉学 Sinology
hàn ㄏㄢˋ	翰	翰	毛筆 writing brush 毛笔	揮翰(huī hàn) 挥翰 write with a brush 翰林(hàn lín) member of Imperial Academy
hàn ㄏㄢˋ	瀚	瀚	廣大 vast 广大	浩瀚(hào hàn) vast 瀚海(hàn hǎi) vast desert (the Gobi Desert)
hàn ㄏㄢˋ	旱	旱	長時間不下雨而缺 水 drought 長时间不下雨而缺 水	乾旱(gān hàn) 干旱 drought 旱季(hàn jì) dry season
hàn ㄏㄢˋ	捍	捍	保衛，抵禦 defend, resist 保卫，抵御	捍衛(hàn wèi) 捍卫 defend
hàn ㄏㄢˋ	悍	悍	勇敢，凶暴 bold, violent	強悍(qiáng hàn) 强悍 intrepid 悍然(hàn rán) flagrantly

hàn ㄏㄢˋ	撼	撼	搖動 shake 摇动	震撼(zhèn hàn) a jolt
hàn ㄏㄢˋ	憾	憾	悔恨 regret	遺憾(yí hàn) 遗憾 regret 憾事(hàn shì) a regretful thing
hàn ㄏㄢˋ	焊	焊	將金屬或玻璃等活 部加熱，熔化使相 互連接 weld, solder 将金属或玻璃等活 部加热，熔化使相 互连接	焊接(hàn jiē) weld, solder 焊槍(hàn qiāng) 焊枪 solder gun
hàn hé ㄏㄢˋㄏㄜˊ	和	和	跟，與，日本 and, Japan 跟，与，日本	你和我(nǐ hàn wǒ) you and me
háng xíng ㄏㄤˊㄒㄧㄥˊ	行	行	排列，職業 row, occupation 排列，职业	行列(háng liè) ranks 行家(háng jiā) expert
háng kēng ㄏㄤˊㄎㄥ	吭	吭	嗓子，高歌，出聲 voice, sing loudly, utter a sound 嗓子，高歌，出声	高吭(gāo háng) sing loudly
háng ㄏㄤˊ	杭	杭	杭州簡稱 abbreviation for Hangzhou 杭州简称	杭州(háng zhōu) Hangzhou 蘇杭(sū háng) 苏杭 Suzhou and Hangzhou
háng ㄏㄤˊ	航	航	在海上或空中運行 navigate 在海上或空中运行	航程(háng chéng) voyage 航空(háng kōng) aviation
háo ㄏㄠˊ	蠔	蚝	牡蠣的別名，屬軟 體動物，肉鮮美 oyster 牡蛎的别名，属软 体动物，肉鲜美	蠔油(háo yóu) 蚝油 oyster sauce

háo ㄏㄠˊ	毫	毫	長而尖銳的毛，一點，數量少 sharp, long hair; a little 长而尖锐的毛，一点，数量少	毫米(háo mǐ) millimeter 毫不(háo bù) not the least
háo luò ㄏㄠˊ ㄌㄨㄛ	貉	貉	動物名，小耳尖嘴，皮很珍貴 fox-like animal 动物名，小耳尖嘴，皮很珍贵	一丘之貉(yì qiū zhī háo) a group of bad people
háo ㄏㄠˊ	豪	豪	才能出眾的人，奔放 talented person, unrestrained 才能出众的人，奔放	文豪(wén háo) man of letter 豪放(háo fàng) unrestrained
háo hào ㄏㄠˊ ㄏㄠˋ	號	号	呼喊，大聲哭 cry, wail 呼喊，大声哭	呼號(hū háo) 呼号 wail 怒號(nù háo) 怒号 angry cry
háo ㄏㄠˊ	壕	壕	溝 ditch 沟	壕溝(háo gōu) 壕沟 trench 防空壕(fáng kōng háo) air-raid shelter
háo ㄏㄠˊ	嚎	嚎	大聲哭喊 loud cry 大声哭喊	嚎啕大哭(háo táo dà kū) give out a loud cry
hǎo hào ㄏㄠˇ ㄏㄠˋ	好	好	優點多，不壞，喜歡 good, like to 优点多，不坏，喜欢	好人(hǎo rén) good man 好吃(hào chī) gluttonous
hǎo ㄏㄠˇ	郝	郝	姓 a Chinese surname	
hào ㄏㄠˋ	浩	浩	廣大 vast 广大	聲勢浩大(shēng shì hào dà) 声势浩大 of great momentum, on a grand scale

Pinyin	Traditional	Simplified	Meaning	Examples
hào ㄏㄠˋ	皓	皓	白，明亮 white, bright	皓齒(hào chǐ)皓齿 white teeth 皓月(hào yuè) bright moon
hào háo ㄏㄠˋ ㄏㄠˊ	號	号	名稱，表示大小，命令 name, expressing size, order 名称，表示大小，命令	別號(bié hào)别号 nickname 號碼(hào mǎ)号码 number
hào ㄏㄠˋ	耗	耗	減損，拖延 wear and tear, consume 减损，拖延	消耗(xiāo hào) consume 損耗(sǔn hào)损耗 attrition
hē ㄏㄜ	呵	呵	怒責，形容笑 angrily scold, describing a smile 怒责，形容笑	呵責(hē zé)呵责 angrily scold 笑呵呵(xiào hē hē) smilingly
hē hè ㄏㄜ ㄏㄜˋ	喝	喝	吸食飲料或流質食物 drink 吸食饮料或流质食物	喝水(hē shuǐ) drink water 喝酒(hē jiǔ) drink wine 喝彩(hè cǎi) acclaim
hé hàn huò ㄏㄜˊ ㄏㄨㄛˋ ㄏㄢˋ	和	和	平靜，不猛烈，日本，總數 calm, not violent, Japan, sum 平静，不猛烈，日本，总数	和平(hé píng) peace 溫和(wēn hé) 温和gentle 和解(hé jiě) reconciliation 和服(hé fú) kimono 和數(hé shù) 和数 sum
hé ㄏㄜˊ	禾	禾	穀類的通稱 standing grain 谷类的通称	禾穗(hé suì) ear of grain 禾苗(hé miáo) rice seedling
hé ㄏㄜˊ	合	合	聚集 gather	合同(hé tóng) contract 合作(hé zuò) cooperate
hé ㄏㄜˊ	何	何	姓，那裏，什麼 Chinese surname, where, what 姓，那里，什么	何處(hé chù)何处 where 為何(wèi hé) 为何 why

hé hè ㄏㄜˊ ㄏㄜˋ	荷	荷	水生植物，葉大， 開紅色或白色花； 負擔 lotus, burden 水生植物，叶大， 开红色或白色花； 负担	荷花(hé huā) lotus 負荷(fù hè) 负荷 burden
hé ㄏㄜˊ	河	河	流水的通稱 river 流水的通称	河流(hé liú) rivers 河岸(hé àn) riverbank
hé ㄏㄜˊ	核	核	果子內硬質保護果 仁部分；事物重點 pit of fruit, core 果子内硬质保护果 仁部分；事物重点	核能(hé néng) nuclear power 核心(hé xīn) core
hé ㄏㄜˊ	閡	阂	阻隔 severed	隔閡(gé hé)隔阂 lack communication
hé ㄏㄜˊ	闔	阖	全部，關閉 entire, close 全部，关闭	闔府(hé fǔ)阖府 the whole family 闔眼(hé yǎn)阖眼 close the eyes
hé ㄏㄜˊ	涸	涸	水乾掉了 dry up 水干掉了	乾涸(gān hé)干涸 dry up
hé ㄏㄜˊ	盒	盒	底蓋相合可裝東西 的器物 box 底盖相合可装东西 的器物	紙盒(zhǐ hé) 纸盒 carton 盒子(hé zi) a box
hé ㄏㄜˊ	劾	劾	揭發罪狀 expose crime 揭发罪状	彈劾(tán hé)弹劾 impeach
hé ㄏㄜˊ	褐	褐	淺咖啡色，粗布 brown, coarse cloth 浅咖啡色，粗布	褐色(hé sè) brown color 褐夫(hé fū) poor, lowly person

hè ㄏㄜˋ	賀	贺	慶祝，恭喜，送禮物給人 celebrate, congratulate 庆祝，恭喜，送礼物给人	祝賀(zhù hè) 祝贺 greet 賀禮(hè lǐ) 贺礼 gift
hè ㄏㄜˋ	赫	赫	盛大，非常顯明 grandiose, impressive 盛大，非常显明	顯赫(xiǎn hè) 显赫 distinguished 赫然(hè rán) appear suddenly
hè ㄏㄜˋ	鶴	鹤	全身白色，頸腿細長，翅膀大善飛的鳥 crane 全身白色，颈腿细长，翅膀大善飞的鸟	白鶴(bái hè) 白鹤 white crane 鶴立雞群(hè lì jī qún) 鹤立鸡群 very tall, very capable
hè ㄏㄜˋ	壑	壑	山溝 gully 山沟	千山萬壑(qiān shān wàn hè) 千山万壑 numerous hills and valleys
hēi ㄏㄟ	黑	黑	墨或煤炭的顏色，白色的相反，惡毒 black, evil 墨或煤炭的颜色，白色的相反，恶毒	黑暗(hēi àn) darkness 黑心(hēi xīn) evil-minded
hén ㄏㄣˊ	痕	痕	事物留下的印跡 mark 事物留下的印迹	痕跡(hén jī) 痕迹 mark, trace 傷痕(shāng hén) 伤痕 scar
hěn ㄏㄣˇ	很	很	非常 very	很好(hěn hǎo) very good 很快樂(hěn kuài lè) 很快乐 very happy
hěn ㄏㄣˇ	狠	狠	凶惡，殘忍，用盡全力 vicious, cruel, try desperately 凶恶，残忍，用尽全力	狠毒(hěn dú) vicious 狠命(hěn mìng) try desperately
hèn ㄏㄣˋ	恨	恨	仇視，怨，懊悔 hate, hold grievance against, regret 仇视，怨，懊悔	怨恨(yuàn hèn) hate 悔恨(huǐ hèn) deeply regret

hēng ㄏ ㄥ	亨	亨	通達，順利 proceed smoothly 通达，顺利	萬事亨通(wàn shì hēng tōng) 万事亨通 prosperous in everything
hēng ㄏ ㄥ	哼	哼	輕聲隨唱,表示痛苦的聲音 hum, groan 轻声随唱,表示痛苦的声音	哼著歌(hēng zhe gē) 哼著歌 humming a song
héng ㄏ ㄥ	橫	横	從左到右和地面平行 horizontal 从左到右和地面平行	橫跨(héng kuà) to span 橫渡(héng dù) sail across
héng ㄏ ㄥˊ	恆	恒	持久 to persevere	恆心(héng xīn) 恒心 perseverance 永恆(yǒng héng) 永恒 eternity
héng ㄏ ㄥˊ	珩	珩	古人佩掛在身上的玉石 jade worn by ancient people 古人佩挂在身上的玉石	
héng ㄏ ㄥˊ	衡	衡	稱東西輕重的器具，稱量instrument for weighing, measure 称东西轻重的器具，称量	平衡(píng héng) equilibrium 衡量(héng liáng) to measure
hōng hǒng ㄏ ㄏ ㄨ ㄨˇ ㄥ ㄥ	哄	哄	很多人同時發聲，騙 uproar, deceive 很多人同时发声，骗	哄抬(hōng tái) drive up (prices) 哄骗(hòng piàn) 哄骗 cajole
hōng ㄏ ㄨ ㄥ	烘	烘	用火烤乾，襯托 to dry by heat, ontrast 用火烤干，衬托	烘烤(hōng kǎo) to dry by heat 烘托(hōng tuō) create a contrast
hōng ㄏ ㄨ ㄥ	轟	轰	象聲詞，巨大的聲音 a loud boom 象声词，巨大的声音	轟動(hōng dòng) 轰动 sensational 轟炸(hōng zhà) 轰炸 to bomb

hóng ㄏㄨㄥˊ	紅	红	像鮮血的顏色，營業的利潤 red, business profit 像鲜血的颜色，营业的利润	紅色(hóng sè) 红色 red 紅利(hóng lì) 红利 bonus
hóng ㄏㄨㄥˊ	洪	洪	大水 flood	洪水(hóng shuǐ) flood water 防洪(fáng hóng) flood prevention
hóng ㄏㄨㄥˊ	虹	虹	雨後天空出現的七彩圓弧 rainbow 雨后天空出现的七彩圆弧	彩虹(cǎi hóng) rainbow 虹管(hóng guǎn) tube
hóng ㄏㄨㄥˊ	宏	宏	廣大 broad 广大	寬宏(kuān hóng) 宽宏 broadminded 宏觀(hóng guān) 宏观 macroscopic
hóng ㄏㄨㄥˊ	弘	弘	大 big, grand	弘揚(hóng yáng) 弘扬 promote and expand 弘願(hóng yuàn) 弘愿 grand wishes
hóng ㄏㄨㄥˊ	鴻	鸿	雁的一種，大 swan goose, grand 雁的一种，大	鴻運(hóng yùn) 鸿运 good fortune 鴻儒(hóng rú) 鸿儒 great scholar
hóng ㄏㄨㄥˊ	泓	泓	水深而廣 a stretch of broad and 水深而广 deep water	一泓清水(yì hóng qīng shuǐ) a stretch of clear water
hóng ㄏㄨㄥˊ	閎	闳	巷門，宏大 lane door, vast 巷门，宏大	閎論(hóng lùn) 闳论 grand opinion
hòng ㄏㄨㄥˋ	訌	讧	衝突，亂 conflict, chaos 冲突，乱	內訌(nèi hòng) 内讧 internal strife
hòng ㄏㄨㄥˋ	鬨 哄	哄	吵鬧 commotion 吵闹	起哄(qǐ hòng) kick up a fuss 內鬨(nèi hòng) 内哄 internal strife

hóu ㄏ ㄡˊ	瘊	瘊	皮膚上長的小疙瘩 wart 皮肤上长的小疙瘩	瘊子(hóu zi) wart
hóu ㄏ ㄡˊ	侯	侯	古代第二等爵位， 達官貴人: marquess, nobleman 古代第二等爵位， 达官贵人	諸侯(zhū hóu) 诸侯 feudal princes 侯門(hóu mén) 侯门 a noble family
hóu ㄏ ㄡˊ	喉	喉	頸的前部和氣管相 通的部分，嗓子 throat, voice 颈的前部和气管相 通的部分，嗓子	喉嚨(hóu lóng) 喉咙 throat 歌喉(gē hóu) a singer's voice
hóu ㄏ ㄡˊ	猴	猴	似猩猩的哺乳動物 monkey 似猩猩的哺乳动物	猴子(hóu zi) monkey 猴急(hóu jí) impatient
hǒu ㄏ ㄡˇ	吼	吼	大聲叫；因憤怒而 呼喊 roar 大声叫；因愤怒而 呼喊	怒吼(nù hǒu) an angry roar 吼叫(hǒu jiào) howl
hòu ㄏ ㄡˋ	後	后	"前"的相反，指 時間很晚 back, late "前"的相反，指 时间很晚	後門(hòu mén) 后门 back door 後退(hòu tuì) 后退 retreat
hòu ㄏ ㄡˋ	逅	逅	沒有約好而相會 meet somebody unexpectedly 没有约好而相会	邂逅(xiè hòu) run into somebody
hòu ㄏ ㄡˋ	厚	厚	不薄，重視 thick, attach great importance to 不薄，重视	厚禮(hòu lǐ) 厚礼 expensive gift 厚待(hòu dài) treat with kindness
hòu ㄏ ㄡˋ	后	后	皇帝的妻子 empress 皇帝的妻子	皇后(huáng hòu) empress

			等待，問好 wait, send one's regards to 等待，问好	等候(děng hòu) wait 問候(wèn hòu) 问候 give one's regards to
hòu ㄏ ㄡ ˋ	候	候		
hū ㄏ ㄨ	乎	乎	表示疑問，驚嘆 expressing doubt, exclamation 表示疑问，惊叹	出乎意料(chū hū yì liào) unexpectedly
hū ㄏ ㄨ	呼	呼	吐氣，高聲叫喊 exhale, shout 吐气，高声叫喊	呼吸(hū xī) exhale, inhale (breathe) 呼喚(hū huàn) 呼唤 a loud call
hū ㄏ ㄨ	忽	忽	粗心，不在意，突然 careless, suddenly	疏忽(shū hū) negligence 忽然(hū rán) suddenly
hū ㄏ ㄨ	惚	惚	神志不清，精神不集中 absentminded	恍惚(huǎng hū) absentminded
hú ㄏ ㄨ ˊ	胡	胡	亂，沒道理 unreasonable 乱，没道理	胡説(hú shuō) 胡说 talk nonsense 胡同(hú tòng) alley
hú ㄏ ㄨ ˊ	湖	湖	陸地上聚集大片水域的地方 lake 陆地上聚集大片水域的地方	湖泊(hú pó) lakes 湖畔(hú pàn) by the lake
hú ㄏ ㄨ ˊ	葫	葫	一年生草本植物，爬蔓，果實像大小兩球連一起 gourd 一年生草本植物，爬蔓，果实像大小两球连一起	葫蘆(hú lú) 葫芦 gourd
hú ㄏ ㄨ ˊ	猢	猢	猴子的一種，全身長滿毛，耐寒，擅長攀緣 a type of monkey 猴子的一种，全身长满毛，耐寒，擅长攀缘	猢猻(hú sūn) a type of monkey

hú ㄏㄨˊ	糊	糊	黏合粥 paste 粘合粥	漿糊(jiāng hú) glue, paste 糊口(hú kǒu) eke out a living
hú ㄏㄨˊ	瑚	瑚	一種海底動物所分泌的石灰質東西，形狀像樹枝 coral 一种海底动物所分泌的石灰质东西，形状像树枝	珊瑚(shān hú) coral
hú ㄏㄨˊ	蝴	蝴	昆蟲，喜在花間草地飛行，翅膀漂亮 butterfly 昆虫，喜在花间草地飞行，翅膀漂亮	蝴蝶(hú dié) butterfly
hú ㄏㄨˊ	鬍	胡	長在嘴唇上下的毛 moustache, beard 长在嘴唇上下的毛	鬍鬚(hú xū) 胡须 moustache, beard 鬍子(hú zi) 胡子 moustache
hú ㄏㄨˊ	狐	狐	哺乳肉食動物，形狀像狗，嘴尖，性狡猾 fox 哺乳肉食动物，形状像狗，嘴尖，性狡猾	狐狸(hú lí) fox 狐疑(hú yí) full of suspicion
hú ㄏㄨˊ	弧	弧	木弓，圓周的任何一段稱作弧 wooden bow, arc 木弓，圆周的任何一段称作弧	弧形(hú xíng) arc-shaped 括弧(kuò hú) parenthesis
hú ㄏㄨˊ	囫	囫	整個的 entirely 整个的	囫圇吞棗(hú lún tūn zǎo) 囫囵吞枣 accept something indiscriminately
hú ㄏㄨˊ	壺	壶	一種有把柄有嘴的器皿，可用以泡茶 kettle 一种有把柄有嘴的器皿，可用以泡茶	茶壺(chá hú) 茶壶 tea pot 水壺(shuǐ hú) 水壶 water jug
hǔ ㄏㄨˇ	虎	虎	凶猛野獸，毛黃褐色，有條紋 tiger 凶猛野兽，毛黄褐色，有条纹	老虎(lǎo hǔ) tiger 虎膽(hǔ dǎn) 虎胆 brave as a tiger

hǔ ㄏㄨˇ	唬	唬	威嚇 bluff somebody off 威吓	唬人(hǔ rén) bluff people off
hǔ ㄏㄨˇ	滸	浒	水邊的陸地 water margin 水边的陆地	水滸傳(shuǐ hǔ zhuàn) 水浒传 The Water Margin (popular Chinese novel)
hù ㄏㄨˋ	戶	户	門，人家 door, family 门，人家	戶外(hù wài) outdoor 開戶頭(hù tóu) 开户头 open account
hù ㄏㄨˋ	護	护	包庇，保衛，掩蔽 protect, defend, shelter 包庇，保卫，掩蔽	保護(bǎo hù) 保护 protect 護照(hù zhào) 护照 passport
hù ㄏㄨˋ	滬	沪	上海別稱 abbreviation of Shanghai 上海别称	京滬鐵路(jīng hù tiě lù) 京沪铁路 Beijing-Shanghai Railway
hù ㄏㄨˋ	互	互	彼此 mutual	互助(hù zhù) help each other 互利(hù lì) benefit each other
huā ㄏㄨㄚ	嘩	哗	亂吵 boisterous 乱吵	喧嘩(xuān huá) 喧哗 noisy
huā ㄏㄨㄚ	花	花	植物的一部分，生 于莖枝之上；耗費 flower, spend 植物的一部分，生 于茎枝之上；耗费	火花(huǒ huā) spark 花費(huā fèi) 花费 expenditure
huá ㄏㄨㄚˊ	華	华	中國簡稱，事物的 精粹部分 China, essence 中国简称，事物的 精粹部分	中華(zhōng huá) 中华 Chinese 精華(jīng huá) 精华 quintessence
huá ㄏㄨㄚˊ	划	划	撥水前進，合算 to paddle, reasonable 拨水前进，合算	划算(huá suàn) reasonable 划船(huá chuán) row a boat

huá ㄏㄨㄚˊ	猾	猾	奸詐 crafty 奸诈	狡猾(jiǎo huá) cunning
huá ㄏㄨㄚˊ	滑	滑	不粗糙，在平坦的 表面上溜動 smooth, slide 不粗糙，在平坦的 表面上溜动	光滑(guāng huá) smooth 滑雪(huá xuě) to ski
huà ㄏㄨㄚˋ	劃	划	分開，設計 divide, plan 分开，设计	劃分(huà fēn) 划分 divide into parts 計劃(jì huà) 计划 plan
huà ㄏㄨㄚˋ	化	化	改變性質 qualitative change 改变性质	變化(biàn huà) 变化 change 化學(huà xué) 化学 chemistry
huà ㄏㄨㄚˋ	畫	画	繪圖，中國字一筆 稱一畫 draw, a stroke of Chinese character 绘图，中国字一笔 称一画	圖畫(tú huà) 图画 drawing 畫像(huà xiàng) 画像 portrait
huà ㄏㄨㄚˋ	話	话	語言，談談 language, talk 语言，谈谈	説話(shuō huà) 说话 talk 話題(huà tí) 话题 topic of discussion
huái ㄏㄨㄞˊ	懷	怀	思念，存於內心 cherish the memory of, harbor a feeling 思念，存于内心	懷念(huái niàn) 怀念 miss a person 懷疑(huái yí) 怀疑 feel suspicious
huái ㄏㄨㄞˊ	淮	淮	河名，發源於河南 省 Huai River 河名，发源於河南 省	淮河(huái hé) Huai River
huái ㄏㄨㄞˊ	徊	徊	來回走動，猶豫不 決 walk back and forth, feel hesitant 来回走动，犹豫不 决	徘徊(pái huái) walk back and forth

huái ㄏ ㄨˊ ㄞ	槐	槐	落葉喬木，果實長莢形，木料可做家具 locust tree 落叶乔木，果实长荚形，木料可做家具	槐樹(huái shù) 槐树 locust tree
huài ㄏ ㄨˋ ㄞ	壞	坏	不好，東西有破損 bad, defective 不好，东西有破损	壞人(huài rén) 坏人 bad people 破壞(pò huài) 破坏 sabotage
huān ㄏ ㄨ ㄢ	歡	欢	快樂，高興 happy, joyful 快乐，高兴	喜歡(xǐ huān) 喜欢 like 歡迎(huān yíng) 欢迎 welcome
huán hái ㄏ ㄏ ㄨˊ ㄞˊ ㄢ	還	还	返回，給回，恢復原狀 return, give back, restore 返回，给回，恢复原状	還鄉(huán xiāng) 还乡 return home 還債(huán zhài) 还债 repay debt
huán ㄏ ㄨˊ ㄢ	環	环	圓形的東西，圍繞 a circle, encircle 圆形的东西，围绕	環境(huán jìng) 环境 cnvironment 環球(huán qiú) 环球 global
huán ㄏ ㄨˊ ㄢ	寰	寰	廣大的地域，全世界 a vast space, the whole world 广大的地域，全世界	人寰(rén huán) world of mankind
huán ㄏ ㄨˊ ㄢ	桓	桓	木名，葉似柳，皮黃白色；姓 plant name, surname 木名，叶似柳，皮黄白色；姓	
huàn ㄏ ㄨˋ ㄢ	換	换	以物易物；更改 exchange; change	交換(jiāo huàn) 交换 exchange 替換(tì huàn) 替换 to replace
huàn ㄏ ㄨˋ ㄢ	喚	唤	呼叫，叫喊 shout, call	呼喚(hū huàn) 呼唤 a loud call 喚醒(huàn xǐng) 唤醒 to awaken

huàn ㄏㄨㄢˋ	煥	焕	光明，光彩的樣子 bright, shining 光明，光彩的样子	煥發(huàn fā) 焕发 freshen up 煥然一新(huàn rán yì xīn) look anew
huàn ㄏㄨㄢˋ	奐	奂	文采鮮明燦爛 bright-colored 文采鲜明灿烂	美侖美奐(měi lún méi huàn) 美仑美奂 magnificent (building)
huàn ㄏㄨㄢˋ	豢	豢	餵養牲畜 breed livestock 喂养牲畜	豢養(huàn yǎng) 豢养 breed livestock
huàn ㄏㄨㄢˋ	浣	浣	洗 wash	浣衣(huàn yī) wash clothes
huàn ㄏㄨㄢˋ	患	患	生病，禍害，憂慮 fall ill, disaster, apprehensions 生病，祸害，忧虑	患病(huàn bìng) fall ill 禍患(huò huàn) disaster
huàn ㄏㄨㄢˋ	幻	幻	不真實的，空虛的 unreal, empty 不真实的，空虚的	夢幻(mèng huàn) 梦幻 dream 幻想(huàn xiǎng) fantasy
huàn ㄏㄨㄢˋ	宦	宦	古時經過閹割後伺 候皇帝的男人，也 稱"太監" eunuch 古时经过阉割后伺 候皇帝的男人，也 称"太监"	宦官(huàn guān) eunuch as high official
huāng ㄏㄨㄤ	肓	肓	心臟以下橫隔膜以 上的部位 between heart and diaphragm 心脏以下横隔膜以 上的部位	病入膏肓(bìng rù gāo huāng) terminally ill
huāng ㄏㄨㄤ	荒	荒	五穀歉收，嚴重 缺乏 lean harvest, severe shortage 五谷歉收，严重 缺乏	荒年(huāng nián) a lean year 荒蕪(huāng wú) 荒芜 barren

huāng ㄏㄨㄤ	慌	慌	不安，難忍受，驚恐 uneasy, unbearable, panic 不安，难忍受，惊恐	恐慌(kǒng huāng) panicking 餓慌了(è huāng le) 饿慌了 be terribly hungry
huáng ㄏㄨㄤˊ	黃	黄	香蕉皮的顏色，墮落低級的 yellow, degrading 香蕉皮的颜色，堕落低级的	黃色(huáng sè) yellow 黃金(huáng jīn) gold
huáng ㄏㄨㄤˊ	潢	潢	積水池，裱褙字畫 pond, mount a picture 积水池，裱褙字画	裝潢(zhuāng huáng) 装潢 decoration
huáng ㄏㄨㄤˊ	璜	璜	半環形的玉飾 semi-circular jade ornament 半环形的玉饰	
huáng ㄏㄨㄤˊ	簧	簧	器物里有彈性的小零件 spring in a mechanical device 器物里有弹性的小零件	彈簧(tán huáng) 弹簧 spring
huáng ㄏㄨㄤˊ	磺	磺	非金屬元素 sulphur 非金属元素	硫磺(liú huáng) sulphur
huáng ㄏㄨㄤˊ	蟥	蟥	水蛭的一種 a kind of leech 水蛭的一种	螞蟥(mǎ huáng)蚂蟥 leech
huáng ㄏㄨㄤˊ	凰	凰	傳說中的鳥王，雄的叫鳳，雌的叫凰 female phoenix 传说中的鸟王，雄的叫凤，雌的叫凰	鳳凰(fèng huáng) 凤凰 phoenix
huáng ㄏㄨㄤˊ	惶	惶	恐懼 fear 恐惧	惶恐(huáng kǒng) fear 人心惶惶(rén xīn huáng huáng) public feeling of uneasiness
huáng ㄏㄨㄤˊ	蝗	蝗	一種吃農作物會飛的害蟲 locust 一种吃农作物会飞的害虫	蝗蟲(huáng chóng) 蝗虫 locust

huáng ㄏㄨㄤˊ	皇	皇	君主 emporer	皇帝(huáng dì) emperor 皇宮(huáng gōng) palace
huáng ㄏㄨㄤˊ	煌	煌	光明 brilliant	輝煌成果(huī huáng chéng guǒ) 辉煌成果 magnificent results
huáng ㄏㄨㄤˊ	徨	徨	不定，不知去哪 undecided, not knowing where to go	彷徨(páng huáng) not knowing where to go
huǎng ㄏㄨㄤˇ	恍	恍	忽然，彷彿，不清晰 suddenly, as if, absentminded	恍然(huǎng rán) suddenly 恍惚(huǎng hū) be in a trance
huǎng ㄏㄨㄤˇ	謊	谎	不真實的話 a lie 不真实的话	謊話(huǎng huà) 谎话 a lie 撒謊(sā huǎng) 撒谎 tell a lie
huǎng ㄏㄨㄤˇ	幌	幌	爲了進行某種活動而假借名義 smoke screen 为了进行某种活动而假借名义	幌子(huǎng zi) smoke screen
huǎng ㄏㄨㄤˇ	晃	晃	很快地閃過，搖擺 flash past, dazzle 很快地闪过，摇摆	一晃(yì huǎng) suddenly 晃動(huǎng dòng) 晃动 dazzle
huī ㄏㄨㄟ	輝	辉	閃射的光彩，光彩耀眼 brilliance 闪射的光彩，光彩耀眼	光輝(guāng huī) 光辉 brilliance 輝煌(huī huáng) 辉煌 magnificent
huī ㄏㄨㄟ	揮	挥	散開，發散，發號司令 scatter, command 散开，发散，发号司令	指揮(zhǐ huī) 指挥 to command, direct 揮手(huī shǒu) 挥手 wave hand
huī ㄏㄨㄟ	暉	晖	日光 sunlight	餘暉(yú huī) 余晖 sunset

huī ㄏㄨㄟ	灰	灰	物體燃燒後剩下的東西，黑白之間的顏色 ash, grey 物体燃烧后剩下的东西，黑白之间的颜色	灰色(huī sè) grey color 灰塵(huī chén) 灰尘 dust
huī ㄏㄨㄟ	恢	恢	寬廣，失而復得 vast, recover 宽广，失而复得	恢復(huī fù)恢复 recover, restore 恢恢(huī huī) vast, extensive
huī ㄏㄨㄟ	詼	诙	說話有趣 humorous 说话有趣	詼諧(huī xié)诙谐 humorous
huī ㄏㄨㄟ	徽	徽	標誌 mark, sign 标志	國徽(guó huī)国徽 national emblem 徽章(huī zhāng) badge
huī ㄏㄨㄟ	麾	麾	指揮用的旗，指揮 commander's banner, command 指揮用的旗，指揮	麾軍南下(huī jūn nán xià) 麾军南下 lead the army south
huí ㄏㄨㄟˊ	回	回	走到原來的地方，答復 return, reply 走到原来的地方，答复	回家(huí jiā) return home 回信(huí xìn) reply to a letter
huǐ ㄏㄨㄟˇ	悔	悔	懊惱過去做的事 regret 懊恼过去做的事	後悔(hòu huǐ)后悔 regret 悔過(huǐ guò)悔过 show remorse
huǐ ㄏㄨㄟˇ	毀	毁	破壞，損害 destroy, damage 破坏，损害	毀壞(huǐ huài)毁坏 destroy 毀容(huǐ róng) 毁容 disfigure
huǐ ㄏㄨㄟˇ	燬	毁	用火燒壞，烈火 burn down, fiery fire 用火烧坏，烈火	燒燬(shāo huǐ)烧毁 burn down
huì huǐ kuài ㄏㄨㄟˋ ㄎㄨㄞˇ ㄏㄨㄟˇ ㄎㄨㄞ	會	会	集合，能夠，善于 meet, able to, good at 集合，能够，善于	會面(huì miàn)会面meet 不會(bú huì)不会unable to 一會兒(yì huǐ er)一会儿 pretty soon

huì ㄏㄨㄟˋ	繪	绘	畫，描畫 draw 画，描画	繪畫(huì huà) 绘画 drawing
huì ㄏㄨㄟˋ	薈	荟	草木茂盛的樣子 ；聚集 abundant growth, gather 草木茂盛的样子 ；聚集	蘆薈(lú huì) 芦荟 aloe 薈萃(huì cuì) 荟萃 gathering of talents
huì ㄏㄨㄟˋ	燴	烩	將多種菜煮熟並加 上濃汁的烹調 a method of cooking 将多种菜煮熟並加 上浓汁的烹调	燴飯(huì fàn) 烩饭 cooked rice topped with meat, gravy
huì ㄏㄨㄟˋ	諱	讳	有顧忌不敢說 avoid as taboo 有顾忌不敢说	諱言(huì yán) 讳言 dare not say 忌諱(jì huì) 忌讳 a taboo
huì ㄏㄨㄟˋ	誨	诲	教導，勸說 teach, persuade 教导，劝说	教誨(jiào huì) 教诲 teaching
huì ㄏㄨㄟˋ	晦	晦	昏暗不明，倒霉 gloomy, unlucky 昏暗不明，倒霉	晦氣(huì qì) 晦气 bad luck 晦澀(huì sè) 晦涩 difficult to understand
huì ㄏㄨㄟˋ	卉	卉	草的總稱 grass 草的总称	花卉(huā huì) flowers and grasses
huì ㄏㄨㄟˋ	彗	彗	掃把 broomstick 扫把	彗星(huì xīng) comet
huì ㄏㄨㄟˋ	慧	慧	聰明，有才智 clever, talented 聪明，有才智	智慧(zhì huì) wisdom 慧眼(huì yǎn) discerning eyes

huì ㄏㄨㄟˋ	賄	贿	用財物買通別人 bribe 用财物买通别人	賄賂(huì lù) 贿赂 to bribe 受賄(shòu huì) 受贿 accept bribe
huì ㄏㄨㄟˋ	惠	惠	好處，給人好處 favor, give favor to 好处，给人好处	恩惠(ēn huì) kindness 互惠(hù huì) mutually beneficial
huì ㄏㄨㄟˋ	匯	汇	水流會合，把錢從 一處劃撥到別處 confluence, remit 水流会合，把钱从 一处划拨到别处	匯合(huì hé) 汇合 confluence 匯款(huì kuǎn) 汇款 remit money
huì ㄏㄨㄟˋ	穢	秽	骯髒 filthy 肮脏	污穢(wū huì) 污秽 filthy 穢行(huì xíng) 秽行 indecent act
hūn ㄏㄨㄣ	昏	昏	天將黑的時候，神 志不清 dusk, lose consciousness 天将黑的时候，神 志不清	黃昏(huáng hūn) dusk 頭昏(tóu hūn) 头昏 feel giddy
hūn ㄏㄨㄣ	婚	婚	男女結爲夫婦 marry 男女结为夫妇	結婚(jié hūn) 结婚 get married 婚禮(hūn lǐ) 婚礼 wedding ceremony
hūn ㄏㄨㄣ	葷	荤	食肉 non-vegetarian	葷菜(hūn cài) 荤菜 non-vegetarian dishes 吃葷(chī hūn) 吃荤 not a vegetarian
hún ㄏㄨㄣˊ	渾	浑	水不清，全部，不 明事理 muddy, entirely unreasonable	渾水(hún shuǐ) 浑水 muddy water 渾身(hún shēn) 浑身 all over the body
hún ㄏㄨㄣˊ	餛	馄	在薄麵皮上包上餡 做成的食品 wonton 在薄麵皮上包上馅 做成的食品	餛飩(hún tún) 馄饨 wonton

hún ㄏㄨㄣˊ	魂	魂	離肉體而存在的精神 soul 离肉体而存在的精神	靈魂(líng hún) 灵魂 soul 鬼魂(guǐ hún) ghost
hùn ㄏㄨㄣˋ	混	混	攙在一起，苟且渡過 mix, drift along 搀在一起，苟且渡过	混合物(hùn hé wù) mixture 混日子(hùn rì zi) idle away the time
huō huò ㄏㄨㄛ ㄏㄨㄛˋ	豁	豁	拼命，免除 at all costs, exempt	豁出去(huò chū qù) go ahead at all cost 豁免(huò miǎn) exemption
huó ㄏㄨㄛˊ	活	活	生存，"死"的反面，不固定，可移動的 living, movable 生存，"死"的反面，不固定，可移动的	生活(shēng huó) livelihood 活動(huó dòng) 活动 activity
huǒ ㄏㄨㄛˇ	火	火	物體燃燒時產生的光和熱 fire 物体燃烧时产生的光和热	火車(huǒ chē) 火车 train 點火(diǎn huǒ) 点火 start the fire, ignite
huǒ ㄏㄨㄛˇ	伙	伙	一同做事的人 colleague 一同做事的人	伙伴(huǒ bàn) companion 伙計(huǒ jì) 伙计 partner
huǒ ㄏㄨㄛˇ	夥	伙	合作，多人結伴，親近的朋友 cooperate, companion 合作，多人结伴，亲近的朋友	合夥(hé huǒ) 合伙 go into partnership 一夥人(yì huǒ rén) 一伙人 a group of people
huò ㄏㄨㄛˋ	或	或	也許 probably 也许	或者(huò zhě) or 或許(huò xǔ) 或许 maybe
huò ㄏㄨㄛˋ	貨	货	商品，錢幣 commodity, currency 商品，钱币	貨物(huò wù) 货物 commodity 貨幣(huò bì) 货币 money

huò				
huò ㄏㄨㄛˋ	獲	获	得到 gain 得到	獲得(huò dé) 获得 obtain 獲獎(huò jiǎng) 获奖 win prize
huò ㄏㄨㄛˋ	穫	获	收割農作物，農作 物收成 harvest 收割农作物，农作 物收成	收穫(shōu huò) 收获 harvest 一年四穫(yì nián sì huò) 一年四穫4 crops a year
huò ㄏㄨㄛˋ	惑	惑	不知道是對是錯， 使迷亂 confused, befuddle 不知道是对是错， 使迷乱	疑惑(yí huò) doubt 惑眾(huò zhòng) 惑众 confuse the public
huò ㄏㄨㄛˋ	禍	祸	災殃，損害，苦難 disaster, harm, suffering 灾殃，损 害，苦难	車禍(chē huò) 车祸 traffic accident 禍首(huò shǒu) chief culprit
huò ㄏㄨㄛˋ	霍	霍	迅速 rapidly	霍然大怒(huò rán dà nù) fly into a rage 霍亂(huò luàn) 霍乱 cholera
huò hè ㄏㄨㄛˋ ㄏㄜˋ	壑	壑	溝，坑谷 gully 沟，坑谷	溝壑(gōu huò) 沟壑 gully
huò hàn hé ㄏㄨㄛˋ ㄏㄢˋ ㄏㄜˊ	和	和	混合，加水攪拌調 勻 blend 混合，加水搅拌调 匀	和麵(huò miàn) 和面 mix flour with water
huò ㄏㄨㄛˋ	豁	豁	開通，免除 open up, exempt 开通，免除	豁然開朗(huò rán kāi lǎng) 豁然开朗the mind suddenly opens up 豁免(huò miǎn) exempt 豁達(huò dá) 豁达 broadminded

J				
jī ㄐㄧ	几	几	矮小的桌子 small table	茶几(chá jī) tea table
jī ㄐㄧ	譏	讥	譏笑，諷刺 jeer 讥笑，讽刺	譏笑(jī xiào) 讥笑 jeer at 譏諷(jī fěng) 讥讽 to satirize
jī ㄐㄧ	饑	饥	餓，收成不好 hungry, poor harvest 饿，收成不好	饑餓(jī è) 饥饿 hunger 饑荒(jī huāng) 饥荒 famine
jī ㄐㄧ	肌	肌	肌肉 muscle	肌肉(jī ròu) muscle
jī ㄐㄧ	機	机	合適的時候，機器 opportunity, machine 合适的时候，机器	機會(jī huì) 机会 opportunity 飛機(fēi jī) 飞机 airplane
jī ㄐㄧ	圾	圾	垃圾 garbage	垃圾(lā jī) garbage
jī jí ㄐㄧ ㄐㄧˊ	擊	击	打，敲打，攻打 strike, attack	攻擊(gōng jī) 攻击 attack 擊敗(jī bài) 击败 to defeat
jī ㄐㄧ	雞	鸡	一種家禽 chicken 一种家禽	公雞(gōng jī) 公鸡 cock 母雞(mǔ jī) 母鸡 hen
jī ㄐㄧ	積	积	聚集 accumulate	積極(jī jí) 积极 positive 堆積(duī jī) 堆积 pile up

jī ㄐ丨ー	基	基	建築物的根底 foundation 建筑物的根底	基礎(jī chǔ) 基础 foundation 基督教(jī dū jiào) Christianity
jī ㄐ丨ー	跡	迹	腳印 trace 脚印	跡象(jī xiàng) 迹象 indication 古跡(gǔ jī) 古迹 historical relics
jī ㄐ丨ー	績	绩	成果 achievement	學業成績(xué yè chéng jī) 学业成绩 academic result
jī ㄐ丨ー	蹟	迹	事物留下來的痕跡 ，同"跡" the trace 事物留下来的痕迹 ，同"迹"	奇蹟(qí jī) 奇迹 miracle 事蹟(shì jī) 事迹 exploit of a person
jī ㄐ丨ー	畸	畸	不整齊，不正常 deformed, abnormal 不整齐，不正常	畸形(jī xíng) deformed
jī ㄐ丨ー	激	激	水受阻而濺出，引 發 surge, arouse 水受阻而溅出，引 发	刺激(cì jī) stimulus, stimulate 激動(jī dòng) 激动 excited, emotional
jī ㄐ丨ー	箕	箕	揚米去糠或清除垃 圾的用具 winnow, dustpan 扬米去糠或清除垃 圾的用具	簸箕(bǒ jī) winnow
jī ㄐ丨ー	屐	屐	木底鞋 a clog	木屐(mù jī) a clog
jī ㄐ丨ー	姬	姬	美女，姓 pretty woman, Chinese surname	姬妾(jī qiè) charming concubine
jī ㄐ丨ー	稽	稽	查究 inspect	稽查(jī chá) inspector

jī 丩ㄧ	缉	缉	抓拿 arrest	缉捕(jī bǔ) 缉捕 arrest, seize 缉私(jī sī) 缉私 anti-smuggling
jí 丩ㄧˊ	及	及	和，趕上 and, be up to 和，赶上	以及(yǐ jí) as well as 及時(jí shí) 及时 just in time
jí 丩ㄧˊ	極	极	盡頭，非常 the extreme, very 尽头，非常	北極(běi jí) 北极 North Pole 極端(jí duān) 极端 the extreme
jí 丩ㄧˊ	級	级	等次，台階 rank, step 等次，台阶	等級(děng jí) 等级 the grade 階級(jiē jí) 阶级 a social class
jí 丩ㄧˊ	吉	吉	美好順利 auspicious 美好顺利	吉祥(jí xiáng) auspicious 吉人(jí rén) good person
jí 丩ㄧˊ	汲	汲	從井裏取水 draw water from the well 从井里取水	汲水(jí shuǐ) draw water from well
jí 丩ㄧˊ	瘠	瘠	瘦弱，土地不肥沃 thin and weak, infertile	貧瘠(pín jí) infertile
jí 丩ㄧˊ	即	即	就是，當時，當地 that is, immediately 就是，当时，当地	即將(jí jiāng) 即将 will soon 即使(jí shǐ) even though
jí 丩ㄧˊ	急	急	匆忙 hastily	急忙(jí máng) hastily 緊急(jǐn jí) 紧急 emergency

Pinyin	Traditional	Simplified	Meaning	Examples
jí ㄐㄧˊ	集	集	會合，許多人合起來 gather , a group of people 会合，许多人合起来	聚集(jù jí) gather together 集體(jí tǐ) 集体 collective
jí ㄐㄧˊ	疾	疾	病 illness	疾病(jí bìng) disease 疾苦(jí kǔ) sufferings
jí ㄐㄧˊ	嫉	嫉	妒忌，痛恨 jealous, hate	嫉惡如仇(jí è rú chóu) 嫉恶如仇 extreme hatred for evil 嫉妒(jí dù) jealous
jí ㄐㄧˊ	棘	棘	多刺的灌木 bramble	荆棘(jīng jí) bramble 棘手(jí shǒu) tough (problem)
jí ㄐㄧˊ	輯	辑	搜集材料編書 compile 搜集材料编书	編輯(biān jí) 编辑 compile, editor
jí ㄐㄧˊ	籍	籍	書本，戶口冊子 books, household registry 书本，户口册子	書籍(shū jí) 书籍 books 國籍(guó jí) 国籍 nationality
jí jiè ㄐㄧˊ ㄐㄧㄝˋ	藉	藉	亂七八槽 messy 乱七八糟	杯盤狼藉(bēi pán láng jí) 杯盘狼藉 a mess of cups and dishes 聲名狼藉(shēng míng láng jí) 声名狼藉 notorious
jí jī ㄐㄧˊ ㄐㄧ	幾	几	多少，問有多少的疑問詞 how many 多少，问有多少的疑问词	幾個(jǐ gè) 几个 how many 幾何(jǐ hé) 几何 geometry
jǐ ㄐㄧˇ	己	己	自身 oneself	自己(zì jǐ) oneself 律己(lǜ jǐ) practice self-discipline

jǐ ㄐ ㄧ ˇ	擠	挤	許多人，物緊緊靠 在一起，不易動彈 ；用力壓出 crowded, squeeze 许多人，物紧紧靠 在一起，不易动弹 ；用力压出	擁擠(yōng jǐ) 拥挤 crowded 擠牛奶(jǐ niú nǎi) 挤牛奶 to milk a cow
jǐ ㄐ ㄧ ˇ	濟	济	眾多 multitude 众多	人才濟濟(rén cái jǐ jǐ) 人才济济a lot of talented people
jǐ ㄐ ㄧ ˇ	戟	戟	一種古代兵器，長 桿頭上附有月牙狀 的利刃 an ancient weapon 一种古代兵器，长 杆头上附有月牙状 的利刃	
jǐ jí ㄐ ㄐ ㄧ ㄧˇ ´	脊	脊	背中間的骨頭，中 間高起的部分 spine, ridge 背中间的骨头，中 间高起的部分	脊椎(jí zhuī) spine 屋脊(wū jǐ) ridge of roof
jì ㄐ ㄧ ˋ	計	计	核算，主意 calculate, idea 核算，主意	計算(jì suàn) 计算 calculate 計劃(jì huà) 计划 plan
jì ㄐ ㄧ ˋ	記	记	暗號，標誌，登錄 sign, symbol, register 暗号，标志，登录	標記(biāo jì) 标记 a mark 登記(dēng jì) 登记 to register
jì ㄐ ㄧ ˋ	紀	纪	歲，一百年，不忘 age, one century, remember 岁，一百年，不忘	年紀(nián jì) 年纪 age 世紀(shì jì) 世纪 century
jì ㄐ ㄧ ˋ	忌	忌	禁戒，避免做會產 生不良後果的事 taboo 禁戒，避免做会产 生不良后果的事	禁忌(jìn jì) taboo 忌日(jì rì) death anniversary
jì ㄐ ㄧ ˋ	寄	寄	傳送，托付 send, entrust 传送，托付	郵寄(yóu jì) 邮寄 send by mail 寄托(jì tuō) something to rely on

jì ㄐㄧˋ	際	际	交界，靠邊的地方 ，中間 border, between 交界，靠边的地方 ，中间	國際(guó jì) 国际 international 交際(jiāo jì) 交际 socialization
jì ㄐㄧˋ	技	技	才能，本領 talent, skill	技能(jì néng) skills 技術(jì shù) 技术 technology
jì ㄐㄧˋ	伎	伎	手段，花招 means, tricks	伎倆(jì liǎng) 伎俩 sleight of hand
jì ㄐㄧˋ	妓	妓	靠賣淫爲生的人 prostitute 靠卖淫为生的人	妓女(jì nǚ) prostitute 娼妓(chāng jì) prostitute
jì ㄐㄧˋ	季	季	三個月爲一季，兄 弟排行中最小的 season, quarter, youngest sibling 三个月为一季，兄 弟排行中最小的	四季(sì jì) four seasons 一季度(yí jì dù) first quarter
jì ㄐㄧˋ	悸	悸	心跳，害怕 palpitate with fear	心有餘悸(xīn yǒu yú jì) 心有余悸 still palpitating with fear
jì ㄐㄧˋ	繼	继	連續，接著 continue, next 连续，接著	繼續(jì xù) 继续 continue 繼母(jì mǔ) 继母 stepmother
jì ㄐㄧˋ	濟	济	幫助苦難的人，渡 過 help the needy, tide over hardship 帮助苦难的人，渡 过	救濟(jiù jì) 救济 relief for the needy 經濟(jīng jì) 经济 economy
jì ㄐㄧˋ	劑	剂	藥量，配制的藥物 ，適當的調整 dosage, readjust 药量，配制的药物 ，适当的调整	藥劑(yào jì) 药剂 pharmaceutical 調劑(tiáo jì) 调剂 make adjustments

jì ㄐㄧˋ	祭	祭	追悼死者的儀式 memorial service 追悼死者的仪式	祭祖(jì zǔ) offer sacrifices to ancestor
jì ㄐㄧˋ	既	既	已經 already 已经	既然(jì rán) this being the case 既得利益(jì dé lì yì) vested interest
jì ㄐㄧˋ	冀	冀	希望，河北省的別稱 hope, Hebei Province 希望，河北省的别称	冀望(jì wàng) expect, wish
jì ㄐㄧˋ	暨	暨	至，以及 until, and	暨今(jì jīn) up til now
jì ㄐㄧˋ	鯽	鲫	淡水魚的一種 crucian carp 淡水鱼的一种	鯽魚(jì yú) 鲫鱼 crucian carp
jì ㄐㄧˋ	稷	稷	一年生草本，白色種子可食，葉細長 a kind of grain 一年生草本，白色种子可食，叶细长	社稷(shè jì) society
jì jí ㄐㄧˋ ㄐㄧˊ	寂	寂	靜，沒有聲音，孤獨 quiet, silent, lonely 静，没有声音，孤独	寂靜(jì jìng) 寂静 tranquil 寂寞(jì mò) lonesome
jiā ㄐㄧㄚ	加	加	把數目合起來的算法，增多 add, increase 把数目合起来的算法，增多	加法(jiā fǎ) addition 增加(zēng jiā) increase
jiā ㄐㄧㄚ	袈	袈	和尚披的外衣 robe worn by Buddhist monk	袈裟(jiā shā) robe worn by Buddhist monk

jiā ㄐ 丨 ㄚ	枷	枷	古時套在罪犯脖子上的刑具 shackle 古时套在罪犯脖子上的刑具	枷鎖(jiā suǒ) 枷锁 shackle
jiā ㄐ 丨 ㄚ	痂	痂	傷口，瘡口上的血乾後凝結成的東西 scab 伤口，疮口上的血乾后凝结成的东西	結痂(jié jiā) 结痂 to form scab
jiā ㄐ 丨 ㄚ	嘉	嘉	贊美，美好 praise, good 赞美，美好	嘉獎(jiā jiǎng) 嘉奖 to commend 嘉賓(jiā bīn) 嘉宾 honorable guest
jiā ㄐ 丨 ㄚ	佳	佳	美好的 fine	佳人(jiā rén) pretty woman 佳作(jiā zuò) masterpieces
jiā ㄐ 丨 ㄚ	家	家	住所，對人稱自己的雙親和兄長 home, my 住所，对人称自己的双亲和兄长	家庭(jiā tíng) family 家慈(jiā cí) my mother
jiā ㄐ 丨 ㄚ	傢	家	家用器具 furniture	傢俱(jiā jù) 家具 furniture
jiá ㄐ 丨 ㄚˊ	莢	荚	豆類植物，長形果實 pod 豆类植物，长形果实	豆莢(dòu jiá) 豆荚 pea pod
jiá ㄐ 丨 ㄚˊ	頰	颊	臉的兩側 cheek 脸的两侧	面頰(miàn jiá) 面颊 cheek 頰骨(jiá gǔ) 颊骨 cheekbone
jiǎ ㄐ 丨 ㄚˇ	甲	甲	打仗護身的金屬衣，硬殼 armor, shell 打仗护身的金属衣，硬壳	盔甲(kuī jiǎ) armor 指甲(zhǐ jiǎ) finger nail

jiǎ gǔ ㄐ一ˇ ㄍㄨˇ	賈	贾	姓，做買賣 Chinese surname, do business 姓，做买卖	商賈(shāng gǔ) 商贾 merchants
jià ㄐ一ˋ	駕	驾	操縱 operate 操纵	駕駛(jià shǐ) 驾驶 operate a vehicle 駕臨(jià lín) 驾临 your arrival
jià ㄐ一ˋ	價	价	商品所值的錢數 price 商品所值的钱数	價格(jià gé) 价格 price 減價(jiǎn jià) 减价 reduce price
jià ㄐ一ˋ	架	架	用來支持或擱置物品的器具，爭吵毆打 shelf, fight 用来支持或搁置物品的器具，爭吵殴打	書架(shū jià) 书架 bookshelf 打架(dǎ jià) fight
jià ㄐ一ˋ	嫁	嫁	女子結婚；把禍害怨恨推到別人身上 marry, shift blame to others 女子结婚；把祸害怨恨推到别人身上	嫁妝(jià zhuāng) 嫁妆 dowry 嫁禍(jià huò) shift blame
jià ㄐ一ˋ	稼	稼	種田 till the land 种田	莊稼(zhuāng jià) 庄稼 crops
jià jiǎ ㄐ一ˋ ㄐ一ˇ	假	假	暫時不工作，不真 vacation, false 暂时不工作，不真	假日(jià rì) holiday 假如(jiǎ rú) if
jiān ㄐ一ㄢ	尖	尖	物體末端細小部分，銳利 pointed end of object, sharp 物體末端細小部分，銳利	尖銳(jiān ruì) 尖锐 sharp 尖峰(jiān fēng) peak
jiān ㄐ一ㄢ	姦	奸	不正常的性行為 illicit sexual intercourse 不正常的性行为	強姦(qiáng jiān) 强奸 rape 通姦(tōng jiān) 通奸 adultery

jiān jiàn ㄐㄧㄢ ㄐㄧㄢˋ	間	间	當中，使人不合 middle, sow discord 当中，使人不合	中間(zhōng jiān) 中间 middle 離間(lí jiàn) 离间 sow discord 空間(kōng jiān) 空间 space
jiān ㄐㄧㄢ	堅	坚	結實，硬 sturdy, hard 结实，硬	堅強(jiān qiáng) 坚强 strong 堅定(jiān dìng) 坚定 resolute
jiān ㄐㄧㄢ	奸	奸	狡詐，虛偽 cunning, hypocritic 狡诈，虚伪	奸細(jiān xì) 奸细 enemy's spy 奸笑(jiān xiào) evil smile
jiān ㄐㄧㄢ	殲	歼	殺盡，滅絕 exterminate 杀尽，灭绝	殲滅(jiān miè) 歼灭 exterminate, annihilate 殲敵(jiān dí) 歼敌 kill the enemy
jiān ㄐㄧㄢ	肩	肩	膀子旁胳臂上邊部 分，擔負 shoulder 膀子旁胳臂上边部 分，担负	肩膀(jiān bǎng) shoulder 肩負(jiān fù) 肩负 take up (responsbility)
jiān ㄐㄧㄢ	兼	兼	從事額外的工作 do something part-time 从事额外的工作	兼職(jiān zhí) 兼职 take a part-time job 兼併(jiān bìng) merge
jiān ㄐㄧㄢ	艱	艰	困難 hardship 困难	艱難(jiān nán) 艰难 hardship 艱巨(jiān jù) 艰巨 arduous
jiān ㄐㄧㄢ	監	监	牢獄，看守 prison, watch over 牢狱，看守	監牢(jiān láo) 监牢 prison 監督(jiān dū) 监督 supervise
jiān ㄐㄧㄢ	煎	煎	把食物放在少量的 熱油裏煮熟或煮熱 fry 把食物放在少量的 热油里煮熟或煮热	煎熬(jiān áo) torment 煎魚(jiān yú) 煎鱼 fried fish

jiān ㄐㄧㄢ	菅	菅	多年生草本植物， 葉細長；輕視 a kind of plant, disregard 多年生草本植物， 叶细长；轻视	草菅人命(cǎo jiān rén mìng) 草菅人命 without regard to human lives
jiān ㄐㄧㄢ	緘	缄	封閉 closed 封闭	緘默(jiān mò) 缄默 silence
jiān ㄐㄧㄢ	箋	笺	書信，小便條 letter, memo 书信，小便条	便箋(biàn jiān) 便笺 memo pad 信箋(xìn jiān) 信笺 letter pad
jiǎn ㄐㄧㄢˇ	柬	柬	信件，請客的帖子 letter, invitation card 信件，请客的帖子	請柬(qǐng jiǎn) 请柬 invitation card
jiǎn ㄐㄧㄢˇ	揀	拣	選擇，僥倖獲得 choose, obtain effortlessly 选择，侥幸获得	揀選(jiǎn xuǎn) 拣选 pick and choose 揀便宜(jiǎn pián yí) 拣便宜 go after petty gains
jiǎn ㄐㄧㄢˇ	撿	捡	拾取，選取 pick up, select 拾取，选取	撿破爛(jiǎn pò làn) 捡破烂 collect scrap
jiǎn ㄐㄧㄢˇ	檢	检	告發壞人的事 report misdeed 告发坏人的事	檢查(jiǎn chá) 检查 inspect 檢舉(jiǎn jǔ) 检举 report a crime
jiǎn ㄐㄧㄢˇ	儉	俭	不浪費 frugal 不浪费	節儉(jié jiǎn) 节俭 frugal
jiǎn ㄐㄧㄢˇ	繭	茧	蠶吐絲所結的巢， 手腳上長的厚皮 cocoon, callus 蚕吐丝所结的巢， 手脚上长的厚皮	蠶繭(cán jiǎn) 蚕茧 cocoon

jiǎn ㄐ 一ˇ ㄢ	剪	剪	刀刃交叉可把物品 分開的用具，割斷 scissors, cut 刀刃交叉可把物品 分开的用具，割断	剪刀(jiǎn dāo) scissors 剪斷(jiǎn duàn) 剪断 cut off
jiǎn ㄐ 一ˇ ㄢ	簡	简	書信，不難 letter, simple 书信，不难	書簡(shū jiǎn) 书简 letters 簡單(jiǎn dān) 简单 simple
jiǎn ㄐ 一ˇ ㄢ	減	减	從整體中去掉一部 份 deduct, subtract 从整体中去掉一部 份	減法(jiǎn fǎ) 减法 subtraction 減價(jiǎn jià) 减价 price reduction
jiàn ㄐ 一ˋ ㄢ	見	见	看到，會面，對事 物的看法 see, meet, opinion 看到，会面，对事 物的看法	會見(huì jiàn) 会见 meet 見解(jiàn jiě) 见解 opinion
jiàn ㄐ 一ˋ ㄢ	件	件	量詞 numerical coefficient 量词	一件衣服(yí jiàn yī fú) a dress 一件事(yí jiàn shì) a matter
jiàn ㄐ 一ˋ ㄢ	艦	舰	戰船 battleship 战船	軍艦(jūn jiàn) 军舰 battleship 艦隊(jiàn duì) 舰队 fleet
jiàn ㄐ 一ˋ ㄢ	薦	荐	推舉，介紹 recommend, introduce 推举，介绍	推薦(tuī jiàn) 推荐 recommend
jiàn ㄐ 一ˋ ㄢ	澗	涧	兩山之間的深溝 ravine 两山之间的深沟	溪澗(xī jiàn) 溪涧 mountain stream

jiàn ㄐㄧㄢˋ	漸	渐	慢慢地 slowly	逐漸(zhú jiàn) 逐渐 gradually 漸進(jiàn jìn) 渐进 gradual progress
jiàn ㄐㄧㄢˋ	餞	饯	請客送朋友遠行， 用蜜糖浸漬的果品 give farewell party, preserves 请客送朋友远行， 用蜜糖浸渍的果品	餞行(jiàn xíng) 饯行 give farewell party 蜜餞(mì jiàn) 蜜饯 preserves
jiàn ㄐㄧㄢˋ	踐	践	踩，履行 trample on, put into practice	踐踏(jiàn tà) 践踏 trample on 實踐(shí jiàn) 实践 put into practice
jiàn ㄐㄧㄢˋ	賤	贱	地位低下，價錢低 lowly, low price 地位低下，价钱低	卑賤(bēi jiàn) 卑贱 lowly 貧賤(pín jiàn) 贫贱 poor and lowly
jiàn ㄐㄧㄢˋ	濺	溅	液體受沖激向四方 飛射 splash 液体受冲激向四方 飞射	飛濺(fēi jiàn) 飞溅 splash
jiàn ㄐㄧㄢˋ	毽	毽	一種用腳踢的玩具 shuttlecock 一种用脚踢的玩具	毽子(jiàn zi) shuttlecock
jiàn ㄐㄧㄢˋ	劍	剑	兵器，兩邊有刃 sword 兵器，两边有刃	劍術(jiàn shù) 剑术 swordsmanship 刀劍(dāo jiàn) 刀剑 knife and sword
jiàn ㄐㄧㄢˋ	建	建	設立，創立，提出 意見 establish, suggest 设立，创立，提出 意见	建立(jiàn lì) establish 建議(jiàn yì) 建议 suggest

jiàn ㄐㄧㄢˋ	健	健	身體好 healthy 身体好	強健(qiáng jiàn)强健 strong and healthy 健康(jiàn kāng) healthy
jiàn ㄐㄧㄢˋ	鍵	键	彈琴或打字機上被 按動的部分 key of piano or typewriter 弹琴或打字机上被 按动的部分	琴鍵(qín jiàn)琴键 key of piano 鍵盤(jiàn pán)键盘 keyboard
jiàn ㄐㄧㄢˋ	鑒	鉴	做爲教訓，觀察 draw lesson from, observe 做为教训，观察	借鑒(jiè jiàn)借鉴 draw lesson from 鑒定(jiàn dìng)鉴定 authenticate
jiàn ㄐㄧㄢˋ	箭	箭	用來射到遠處的兵 器 arrow 用来射到远处的兵 器	射箭(shè jiàn) archery 火箭(huǒ jiàn) rocket
jiàn ㄐㄧㄢˋ	諫	谏	歡君主、長輩改正 錯誤 plead with emperor to correct mistake 欢君主、长辈改正 错误	力諫(lì jiàn)力谏 strongly advise against
jiāng ㄐㄧㄤ	江	江	大河 big river	江山(jiāng shān) territory 長江(cháng jiāng)长江 Yangtze River
jiāng ㄐㄧㄤ	薑	姜	多年生草木植物， 味辣，調味作料， 去腥 ginger 多年生草木植物， 味辣，调味作料， 去腥	生薑(shēng jiāng)生姜 ginger 薑湯(jiāng tāng)姜汤 ginger soup
jiāng jiàng ㄐㄧㄤ ㄐㄧㄤˋ	將	将	未來，快要，湊合 future, will do, accommodate 未来，快要，凑合	將來(jiāng lái)将来 the future 將要(jiāng yào)将要 is going to do 五星上將(wǔ xīng shàng jiàng)五星上将 five-star general

jiāng ㄐ ㄧ ㄤ	漿	浆	糊狀物，流質 paste, fluid 糊状物，流质	漿糊(jiāng hú) 浆糊 glue 豆漿(dòu jiāng) 豆浆 soybean milk
jiāng ㄐ ㄧ ㄤ	疆	疆	邊界，戰場 border, battlefield 边界，战场	疆土(jiāng tǔ) territory 疆場(jiāng chǎng) 疆场 battleground
jiāng ㄐ ㄧ ㄤ	僵	僵	不靈活，不易彎曲 ；意見不合 stiff, rigid, stalemate 不灵活，不易弯曲 ；意见不合	凍僵(dòng jiāng)冻僵 frozen stiff 僵局(jiāng jú) a stalemate
jiāng ㄐ ㄧ ㄤ	韁	缰	繫在馬脖子上的繩 子 halter 繫在马脖子上的绳 子	韁繩(jiāng shéng) 缰绳 halter
jiǎng ㄐ ㄧ ㄤˇ	講	讲	说，解釋 speak, explain 说，解释	講解(jiǎng jiě) 讲解 explain 演講(yǎn jiǎng) 演讲 public speaking
jiǎng ㄐ ㄧ ㄤˇ	蔣	蒋	姓 Chinese surname	
jiǎng ㄐ ㄧ ㄤˇ	獎	奖	勉勵，稱贊 award, praise 勉励，称赞	獎品(jiǎng pǐn) 奖品 prize 獎勵(jiǎng lì) 奖励 reward
jiàng ㄐ ㄧ ㄤˋ	匠	匠	有手藝的人，靈巧 craftsman, dexterous 有手艺的人，灵巧	木匠(mù jiàng) carpenter 匠心(jiàng xīn) ingenuity
jiàng ㄐ ㄧ ㄤˋ	強	强	固執 obstinate, stubborn 固执	倔強(jué jiàng)倔强 obstinate, stubborn

jiàng xiáng ㄐ丨ㄤ ˋ ㄒ丨ㄤ ˊ	降	降	下落 descend	下降(xià jiàng) decrease 降落傘(jiàng luò shǎn) 降落傘 parachute 投降(tóu xiáng) surrender
jiàng ㄐ丨ㄤ ˋ	醬	酱	調味品，搗爛的東西 sauce, jam 调味品，捣烂的东西	醬油(jiàng yóu)酱油 soybean sauce 果醬(guǒ jiàng)果酱 jam
jiāo ㄐ丨ㄠ	交	交	付給，互相往來，交叉 hand over to, exchange, cross 付给，互相往来，交叉	交通(jiāo tōng) communication 交稅(jiāo shuì) pay tax
jiāo ㄐ丨ㄠ	膠	胶	黏性物質，樹皮分泌的黏液 glue, gum 黏性物质，树皮分泌的黏液	橡膠(xiàng jiāo)橡胶 rubber 膠卷(jiāo juǎn)胶卷 film
jiāo ㄐ丨ㄠ	蛟	蛟	古時傳說能發大水的龍 a kind of dragon 古时传说能发大水的龙	蛟龍(jiāo lóng)蛟龙 legendary dragon capable of causing flood
jiāo ㄐ丨ㄠ	姣	姣	美貌 pretty	姣好(jiāo hǎo) pretty
jiāo ㄐ丨ㄠ	澆	浇	灌溉，淋 irrigate, to water	澆花(jiāo huā)浇花 water the plant 澆地(jiāo dì)浇地 irrigate the land
jiāo ㄐ丨ㄠ	跤	交	筋斗，一種角力運動 fall, wrestling 筋斗，一种角力运动	跌跤(dié jiāo)跌交 fall on the ground 摔跤(shuāi jiāo)摔交 wrestling

jiāo ㄐ一ㄠ	郊	郊	城外 outside the city	郊區(jiāo qū) 郊区 suburban area 郊遊(jiāo yóu) 郊遊 field trip
jiāo jiào ㄐ一ㄠ ㄐ一ㄠ	教	教	傳授 teach 传授	教學(jiāo xué) 教学 teaching 教授(jiào shòu) professor
jiāo ㄐ一ㄠ	嬌	娇	美麗可愛，寵愛 pretty and lovely, pampered 美丽可爱，宠爱	嬌艷(jiāo yàn) 娇艳 charming 嬌縱(jiāo zòng) 娇纵 pampered
jiāo ㄐ一ㄠ	驕	骄	自大，看不起他人 arrogant, conceited	驕傲(jiāo ào) 骄傲 conceited 驕陽(jiāo yáng) 骄阳 scorching sun
jiāo ㄐ一ㄠ	焦	焦	火力過猛燒乾；著 急 charred, worried 火力过猛烧干；著 急	燒焦(shāo jiāo) 烧焦 charred 焦點(jiāo diǎn) 焦点 focus
jiāo ㄐ一ㄠ	蕉	蕉	多年生草本植物， 葉寬大，果實和香 蕉相似 a broadleaf plant 多年生草本植物， 叶宽大，果实和香 蕉相似	香蕉(xiāng jiāo) 香蕉 banana
jiāo ㄐ一ㄠ	礁	礁	海裏或江裏的岩石 reef 海里或江里的岩石	暗礁(àn jiāo) hidden reef 觸礁(chù jiāo) 触礁 hit upon a reef
jiāo ㄐ一ㄠ	椒	椒	植物名 a kind of spicy plant 植物名	辣椒(là jiāo) chili 胡椒(hú jiāo) black pepper

jiáo jué ㄐㄧㄠˊ ㄐㄩㄝˊ	嚼	嚼	用牙齒咬碎食物； 搬弄是非 chew, gossip 用牙齿咬碎食物； 搬弄是非	咀嚼(jǔ jué) chew, munch 嚼舌(jiáo shé) gossip
jiǎo ㄐㄧㄠˇ	角	角	動物頭上長出的堅 硬東西；兩直線相 交而成的形狀 horn, angle 动物头上长出的坚 硬东西；两直线相 交而成的形状	牛角(niú jiǎo) ox horn 角落(jiǎo luò) corner
jiǎo ㄐㄧㄠˇ	腳	脚	用來走路的肢體 leg 用来走路的肢体	腳步(jiǎo bù) 脚步 step 右腳(yòu jiǎo) 右脚 right leg
jiǎo ㄐㄧㄠˇ	攪	搅	擾亂，拌 disturb, stir 扰乱，拌	攪亂(jiǎo luàn) 搅乱 make trouble 攪勻(jiǎo yún) 搅匀 stir well
jiǎo ㄐㄧㄠˇ	僥	侥	僥倖：運氣好 good luck 侥幸：运气好	僥倖(jiǎo xìng) 侥幸 lucky
jiǎo ㄐㄧㄠˇ	餃	饺	將和好的麵扞成圓 形，裏面放菜肉等 餡再包起來的食品 dumpling 将和好的面扞成圆 形，里面放菜肉等 馅再包起来的食品	水餃(shuǐ jiǎo) 水饺 boiled dumpling
jiǎo ㄐㄧㄠˇ	佼	佼	美好 good and pretty	佼好(jiǎo hǎo) beautiful, handsome 佼佼者(jiǎo jiǎo zhě) eminent people
jiǎo ㄐㄧㄠˇ	狡	狡	詭詐 crafty 诡诈	狡猾(jiǎo huá) cunning, crafty

jiǎo ㄐ ㄧˇ ㄠ	絞	绞	扭緊，用繩子把人 勒死 wring, hang a person 扭紧，用绳 子把人勒死	絞衣服(jiǎo yī fú) 绞衣服 wring a clothe dry 絞刑(jiǎo xíng) 绞刑 execution by hanging
jiǎo ㄐ ㄧˇ ㄠ	皎	皎	明亮，潔白 bright, pure white 明亮，洁白	皎月(jiǎo yuè) bright moon
jiǎo ㄐ ㄧˇ ㄠ	繳	缴	交付 make payment	繳稅(jiǎo shuì) 缴税 pay tax 繳械(jiǎo xiè) 缴械 surrender weapons
jiǎo ㄐ ㄧˇ ㄠ	矯	矫	糾正，違反常情， 與眾不同 to correct, affected manners 纠正，违反常情， 与众不同	矯正(jiǎo zhèng) 矫正 to correct 矯情(jiǎo qíng) 矫情 affected manners
jiǎo ㄐ ㄧˇ ㄠ	剿	剿	消滅，討伐 annihilate, conquer 消灭，讨伐	圍剿(wéi jiǎo) 围剿 encircle and annihilate 剿匪(jiǎo fěi) eliminate the bandits
jiào ㄐ ㄧˋ ㄠ	叫	叫	呼喊，稱呼，招喚 shout, address, beckon 呼喊，称呼，招唤	大叫(dà jiào) cry out loud 叫座(jiào zuò) draw a large audience
jiào jue ㄐ ㄐ ㄧˋ ㄩˊ ㄠ ㄝ	覺	觉	睡眠 sleep	睡覺(shuì jiào) 睡觉 sleep 感覺(gǎn jué) 感觉 feeling
jiào ㄐ ㄧˋ ㄠ	窖	窖	地洞，儲藏東西的 地下室 cellar or pit 地洞，储藏东西的 地下室	地窖(dì jiào) storage pit 冰窖(bīng jiào) cold storage
jiào ㄐ ㄧˋ ㄠ	轎	轿	交通工具，四人或 二人抬著走 palanguin 交通工具，四人或 二人抬著走	轎子(jiào zi) 轿子 palanquin 花轎(huā jiào) 花轿 palanquin

Pinyin	Traditional	Simplified	Definition	Examples
jiào xiào ㄐㄧㄠˋ ㄒㄧㄠˋ	校	校	比較，訂正 compare, correct 比较，订正	校對(jiào duì)校对 proofread 校正(jiào zhèng) adjust
jiào ㄐㄧㄠˋ	較	较	比，對比 compare 比，对比	比較(bǐ jiào)比较 compare 較量(jiào liàng)较量 test of strength
jiào jiāo ㄐㄧㄠˋ ㄐㄧㄠ	教	教	指導，傳授知識技能 guide, teach 指导，传授知识技能	教師(jiào shī)教师 teacher 教育(jiào yù) education 教書(jiāo shū) teach at school
jiē ㄐㄧㄝ	階	阶	等級高低，次序，用磚頭砌成的梯形建築 grade, stairs 等级高低，次序，用砖头砌成的梯形建筑	階級(jiē jí)阶级 social class 階梯(jiē tī)阶梯 a flight of stairs
jiē ㄐㄧㄝ	接	接	繼續，迎接 continue, welcome 继续，迎接	接受(jiē shòu) accept 接觸(jiē chù)接触 contact, connection
jiē ㄐㄧㄝ	揭	揭	把蓋在上面的東西拿掉，使隱藏的東西顯露 uncover, expose 把盖在上面的东西拿掉，使隐藏的东西显露	揭開(jiē kāi)揭开 uncover 揭露(jiē lòu) expose
jiē ㄐㄧㄝ	皆	皆	全，都 all	比比皆是(bǐ bǐ jiē shì) it is everywhere 人人皆知(rén rén jiē zhī) everybody knows
jiē ㄐㄧㄝ	街	街	城裏兩旁有房屋的道路 street 城里两旁有房屋的道路	街道(jiē dào) road, street 逛街(guàng jiē) go shopping

jié ㄐㄧㄝˊ	節	节	段落，紀念或慶祝的日子，音調高低 section, festival, tone 段落，纪念或庆祝的日子，音调高低	節目(jié mù) 节目 program 節日(jié rì) 节日 festival
jié ㄐㄧㄝˊ	傑	傑	才能出眾的人 man of great talents 才能出众的人	傑出(jié chū) 傑出 eminent 傑作(jié zuò) 傑作 masterpiece
jié ㄐㄧㄝˊ	孑	孑	單獨，孤單 lonely 单独，孤单	孑然一身(jié rán yì shēn) all alone
jié ㄐㄧㄝˊ	潔	洁	乾淨，不貪污 clean, not corrupt 干净，不贪污	清潔(qīng jié) 清洁 clean 廉潔(lián jié) 廉洁 not corrupt
jié ㄐㄧㄝˊ	捷	捷	快 rapid	敏捷(mǐn jié) agile 捷徑(jié jìng) 捷径 shortcut
jié ㄐㄧㄝˊ	睫	睫	上下眼邊的毛 eyelash 上下眼边的毛	睫毛(jié máo) eyelash
jié ㄐㄧㄝˊ	竭	竭	用盡 use up 用尽	竭誠(jié chéng) 竭诚 with utmost sincerity 竭力(jié lì) do one's best
jié ㄐㄧㄝˊ	截	截	割斷，弄斷，限期停止 cut, break off, set a deadline 割斷，弄斷，限期停止	截斷(jié duàn) 截断 cut off 截止日期 (jié zhǐ rì qí) deadline
jié ㄐㄧㄝˊ	劫	劫	災難，以武力相逼迫 disaster, plunder 灾难，以武力相逼迫	搶劫(qiǎng jié) 抢劫 robbery 劫持(jié chí) hijack
jié ㄐㄧㄝˊ	結	结	繩帶結成的紐；植物開花而成的果實 knot, bear fruit 绳带结成的纽；植物开花而成的果实	結束(jié shù) 结束 conclude 結果(jié guǒ) 结果 result, bear fruits

jié ㄐㄧㄝ	姐	姐	未結婚的女子 maiden 未结婚的女子	小姐(xiǎo jiě) miss
jiě zǐ ㄐㄧㄝ ㄗ	姊	姊	同父母比自己年長 的女子，親戚中比 自己年長的女性 elder sister 同父母比自己年长 的女子，亲戚中比 自己年长的女性	姊姊(jiě jie) elder sister 表姊(biǎo jiě) female cousin 姊妹(zǐ mèi) sister 學姊(xué jiě) 学姊 elder female schoolmate
jiě ㄐㄧㄝ	解	解	分開，除去 separate, remove 分开，除去	解剖(jiě pōu) anatomy 解除(jiě chú) remove 解釋(jiě shì) 解释 explain 解決(jiě jué) settle, solve 解開(jiě kāi) 解开 untie
jiè ji ㄐㄧㄝ ㄐㄧ	藉	借	假借 pretext 假借	藉口(jiè kǒu) 借口 pretext 憑藉(píng jiè) 凭借 rely on
jiè ㄐㄧㄝ	戒	戒	防備，停止不良習 慣或嗜好 guard against, quit a bad habit 防备，停止不良习 惯或嗜好	戒備(jiè bèi) 戒备 be on guard 戒酒(jiè jiǔ) quit drinking
jiè ㄐㄧㄝ	誡	诫	教條，命令，警告 dogma, order, warning 教条，命令，警告	十誡(shí jiè) 十诫 the Ten Commandments 告誡(gào jiè) 告诫 admonition
jiè ㄐㄧㄝ	介	介	在兩者之中，正直 不屈 mediate, upright and unyielding 在两者之中，正直 不屈	介紹(jiè shào) 介绍 introduce 耿介(gěng jiè) upright and unyielding
jiè ㄐㄧㄝ	芥	芥	二年生草本，開黃 花，味辛辣，研成 細末付用於調味 mustard 二年生草本，开黄 花，味辛辣，研成 细末付用於调味	芥末(jiè mò) mustard

135

jiè ㄐ 一 ㄝˋ	屆	屆	到期，次 at that time, session	屆時(jiè shí) 届时 at that time 上屆(shàng jiè) 上届 the last session
jiè ㄐ 一 ㄝˋ	界	界	相交的地方，範圍 border, scope 相交的地方，范围	世界(shì jiè) the world 教育界(jiào yù jiè)教育界 educational circles
jiè ㄐ 一 ㄝˋ	借	借	暫時使用別人的物 品 borrow 暂时使用别人的物 品	借錢(jiè qián) 借钱 borrow money 借口(jiè kǒu) pretext, excuse
jīn ㄐ 一 ㄣ	金	金	金屬，錢 metal, money 金属，钱	黄金(huáng jīn) gold 現金(xiàn jīn) 现金 cash
jīn ㄐ 一 ㄣ	斤	斤	重量單位；注意小 利害 unit of weight, haggle over petty gains 重量单位；注意小 利害	斤斤計較(jīn jīn jì jiào) 斤斤计较 haggle over petty gains 缺斤少兩(quē jīn shǎo liǎng) 缺斤少两 to be shortchanged
jīn ㄐ 一 ㄣ	巾	巾	擦、包或蓋東西的 紡織品 towel, handkerchief , scarf, and the like 擦、包或盖东西的 纺织品	毛巾(máo jīn) towel 手巾(shǒu jīn) handkerchief
jīn ㄐ 一 ㄣ	今	今	現在 now 现在	今天(jīn tiān) today 現今(xiàn jīn) 现今 nowadays
jīn ㄐ 一 ㄣ	衿	衿	同"襟"，衣服前 面有鈕扣開合的部 分 front of garment 同"襟"，衣服前 面有钮扣开合的部 分	衣衿(yī jīn) lapel of coat

jīn ㄐ丨ㄣ	矜	矜	拘謹 discreet 拘谨	矜持(jīn chí) in a reserved manner
jīn ㄐ丨ㄣ	津	津	唾液，形容有滋味 的，用財物助人 sali va, tasty, subsidize 唾液，形容有滋味 的，用财物助人	津津有味(jīn jīn yǒu wèi) interesting 津貼(jīn tiē) 津贴 subsidize
jīn ㄐ丨ㄣ	筋	筋	骨頭上的勒帶，身 體上下翻轉的動作 tendon, somersault 骨头上的勒带，身 体上下翻转的动作	筋疲力盡(jīn pí lì jìn) 筋疲力尽 thoroughly exhausted 翻筋斗(fān jīn dǒu) do a somersault
jīn ㄐ丨ㄣ	襟	襟	衣服胸前的部分 front of garment	胸襟(xiōng jīn) tolerance
jǐn ㄐ丨ㄣ	僅	仅	只 only	不僅(bù jǐn) 不仅 not only 僅有(jǐn yǒu) 仅有 only have
jǐn ㄐ丨ㄣ	儘	尽	極盡，無限制 as much as possible, without restraint 极尽，无限制	儘快(jǐn kuài) 尽快 as soon as possible 儘量(jǐn liàng) 尽量 as much as possible
jǐn ㄐ丨ㄣ	謹	谨	慎重，小心 discreet, cautious 慎重，小心	謹慎(jǐn shèn) 谨慎 cautious 嚴謹(yán jǐn) 严谨 stringent
jǐn ㄐ丨ㄣ	錦	锦	五彩繽紛，鮮明美 麗 bright and colorful 五彩缤纷，鲜明美 丽	錦標(jǐn biāo) 锦标trophy 錦繡河山(jǐn xiù hé shān) 錦绣河山 beautiful country
jǐn ㄐ丨ㄣ	緊	紧	"鬆" 的反面，靠得 太近，受壓力而呈 現的狀態 tight, very close, tension "松" 的反面，靠得 太近，受压力而呈 现的状态	緊張(jǐn zhāng) 紧张 nervous 緊跟(jǐn gēn) follow close behind

jìn ㄐ ㄧ ㄣ、	進	进	向前 forward	進步(jìn bù) 进步 progress 進攻(jìn gōng) 进攻 attack
jìn ㄐ ㄧ ㄣ、	勁	劲	力氣，力量，有精神 energy, strength 力气，力量，有精神	使勁(shǐ jìn) 使劲 make great effort 帶勁(dài jìn) 带劲 enthusiastic
jìn ㄐ ㄧ ㄣ、	盡	尽	終結，完 end, finish 终结，完	盡頭(jìn tóu) 尽头 the end 盡職(jìn zhí) 尽职 work dutifully
jìn ㄐ ㄧ ㄣ、	近	近	不遠，距離短 near, short distance 不远，距离短	靠近(kào jìn) approach 近年(jìn nián) recent years
jìn ㄐ ㄧ ㄣ、	浸	浸	泡在液體裏，滲透 immerse 泡在液体里，渗透	沈浸在(chén jìn) be immersed in 浸透(jìn tòu) be soaked in
jìn ㄐ ㄧ ㄣ、	禁	禁	不許可 prohibited 不许可	禁止(jìn zhǐ) be prohibited to 監禁(jiān jìn) 监禁 imprison
jìn ㄐ ㄧ ㄣ、	晉	晋	向前，朝代名 advance, name of Chinese dynasty	晉見(jìn jiàn) 晋见 have a audience with 晉級(jìn jí) 晋级 promoted to higher rank
jīng ㄐ ㄧ ㄥ	京	京	首都，國都 capital 首都，国都	京城(jīng chéng) capital city 京戲(jīng xì) 京戏 Beijing opera
jīng ㄐ ㄧ ㄥ	鯨	鲸	海裏哺乳動物，體大，鼻孔位於頭頂，常露出水面噴水 whale 海里哺乳动物，体大，鼻孔位於头顶，常露出水面喷水	鯨魚(jīng yú) 鲸鱼 whale 鯨吞(jīng tūn) 鲸吞 annex territory

jīng ㄐㄧㄥ	驚	惊	害怕，出人意料的感覺 frightened, surprised 害怕，出人意料的感觉	受驚(shòu jīng) 受惊 frightened 驚奇(jīng qí) 惊奇 surprised
jīng ㄐㄧㄥ	兢	兢	小心，謹慎 careful, discreet 小心，谨慎	兢兢業業(jīng jīng yè yè) 兢兢业业 conscientious 戰戰兢兢(zhàn zhàn jīng jīng) 战战兢兢 tremble with fear
jīng ㄐㄧㄥ	莖	茎	植物的主幹，可支撐 stem of plant 植物的主干，可支撑	根莖(gēn jīng) 根茎 tuber
jīng ㄐㄧㄥ	經	经	通過，管理 pass through, manage 通过，管理	經度(jīng dù) 经度 longitude 經理(jīng lǐ) 经理 manager 經費(jīng fèi) 经费 funds 經紀(jīng jì) 经纪 broker
jīng ㄐㄧㄥ	菁	菁	草木茂盛，精華 luxuriant, quintessence 草木茂盛，精华	去蕪存菁(qù wú cún jīng) 去芜存菁 remove the scum and retain the pith
jīng ㄐㄧㄥ	睛	睛	眼珠 eyeball	眼睛(yǎn jīng) eye 目不轉睛(mù bù zhuǎn jīng) 目不转睛 stare at
jīng ㄐㄧㄥ	精	精	細密，聰明能幹，活力 refined, clever, energetic 细密，聪明能干，活力	精細(jīng xì) 精细 refined 精神(jīng shén) spirit
jīng ㄐㄧㄥ	荊	荆	有刺的灌木，困難和障礙 bramble, hardship, obstruction 有刺的灌木，困难和障碍	荊棘(jīng jí) bramble
jīng ㄐㄧㄥ	旌	旌	旗子，表揚 banner, commend 旗子，表扬	旌旗(jīng qí) banners and flags

jīng ㄐ一ㄥ	晶	晶	成果，礦物品，堅硬透明光亮 crystal 成果，矿物品，坚硬透明光亮	結晶(jié jīng) 结晶 crystalize 亮晶晶(liàng jīng jīng) glittering
jǐng ㄐ一ㄥˇ	井	井	挖鑿地面可取水的深洞，整齊 well, orderly 挖凿地面可取水的深洞，整齐	油井(yóu jǐng) oil well 井井有條(jǐng jǐng yǒu tiáo) 井井有条orderly
jǐng ㄐ一ㄥˇ	頸	颈	脖子，頭和身體 相連的部分 neck 脖子，头和身体 相连的部分	頸項(jǐng xiàng) 颈项 neck 長頸鹿(cháng jǐng lù) 长颈鹿 giraffe
jǐng ㄐ一ㄥˇ	景	景	可供觀賞的地方，佩服 scenic place, admire 可供观赏的地方，佩服	風景(fēng jǐng) 风景 scenery 景仰(jǐng yǎng) admire and respect
jǐng ㄐ一ㄥˇ	警	警	維護治安的人員，告誡 police, admonish 维护治安的人员，告诫	警察(jǐng chá) police 警告(jǐng gào) warning
jǐng ㄐ一ㄥˇ	憬	憬	覺悟 awaken 觉悟	憬悟(jǐng wù) realize one's error 憧憬(chōng jǐng) yearning
jìng ㄐ一ㄥ	徑	径	小路，方法 path, method	路徑圖(lù jìng tú) 路径图 roadmap 直徑(zhí jìng) 直径 diameter
jìng ㄐ一ㄥˋ	痙	痉	抽筋 cramp	痙攣(jìng luán) 痉挛 cramp
jìng ㄐ一ㄥˋ	竟	竟	整個，居然 all, go so far as to 整个，居然	竟日(jìng rì) all day long 竟敢(jìng gǎn) have the audacity to

140

jìng ㄐ ㄧˋ ㄥ	境	境	疆界，情況 border area, situation 疆界，情况	邊境(biān jìng) 边境 border area 境況(jìng kuàng) 境況 circumstances
jìng ㄐ ㄧˋ ㄥ	鏡	镜	可看自己形象的器 具 mirror	鏡子(jìng zi) 镜子 mirror 鏡片(jìng pian) 镜片 lens 眼鏡(yǎn jìng) 眼镜 eyeglasses
jìng ㄐ ㄧˋ ㄥ	淨	净	清潔 clean 清洁	乾淨(gān jìng) 干净 clean 淨化(jìng huà) 净化 purify
jìng ㄐ ㄧˋ ㄥ	靜	静	不動，沒有聲音， 停止 still, quiet 不动，没有声音， 停止	安靜(ān jìng) 安静 quiet 靜脈(jìng mài) 静脉 vein
jìng ㄐ ㄧˋ ㄥ	敬	敬	尊重，有禮貌地對 待 respect, courteously 尊重，有礼貌地对 待	恭敬(gōng jìng) respect 敬贈(jìng zèng) 敬赠 give courteously
jìng ㄐ ㄧˋ ㄥ	靖	靖	平定 suppress	靖亂(jìng luàn) 靖乱 put down rebellion
jìng ㄐ ㄧˋ ㄥ	競	竞	比賽爭勝 compete 比赛争胜	競爭(jìng zhēng) 竞争 to compete 競選(jìng xuǎn) 竞选 to run in an election
jìng ㄐ ㄧˋ ㄥ	靚	靓	妝飾，打扮 put on makeup, dress up 妆饰，打扮	靚妝(jìng zhuāng) 靓妆 put on makeup
jiǒng ㄐ ㄩˇ ㄥ	窘	窘	窮困，為難，不好 意思 distressed, embarrassing 穷困，为难，不好 意思	窘境(jiǒng jìng) predicament 窘迫(jiǒng pò) financially distressed
jiū jiù ㄐ ㄐ ㄧ ㄧ ㄡ ㄡˋ	究	究	追查，到底 investigate, what in the world...	追究(zhuī jiū) investigate 究竟(jiū jìng) what in the world ...

			威武健壯的樣子 a commanding appearance 威武健壮的样子	雄赳赳(xióng jiū jiū) in a commanding manner
jiū ㄐ ㄧ ㄡ	赳	赳		
jiū ㄐ ㄧ ㄡ	糾	纠	纏繞，改正，集合 pester, rectify, gather a crowd 缠绕，改正，集合	糾紛(jiū fēn) 纠纷 dispute 糾正(jiū zhèng) 纠正 to rectify
jiū ㄐ ㄧ ㄡ	鳩	鸠	鴿子類的鳥 a kind of pigeon 鸽子类的鸟	斑鳩(bān jiū) 斑鸠 turtledove
jiǔ ㄐ ㄧ ㄡ	九	九	八加一之和，形容 很多 nine, many	九死一生(jiǔ sǐ yì shēng) a narrow brush with death 九泉(jiǔ quán) the grave
jiǔ ㄐ ㄧ ㄡ	久	久	時間長，時間的長 短 long time, length of time 时间长，时 间的长短	久別(jiǔ bié) separated for a long time 多久以前(duō jiǔ yǐ qián) how long ago
jiǔ ㄐ ㄧ ㄡ	灸	灸	燒，指用藥薰烤身 體某部分治病的方 法 cauterize 烧，指 用药薰烤身体某部 分治病的方法	針灸(zhēn jiǔ) 针灸 acupuncture
jiǔ ㄐ ㄧ ㄡ	韭	韭	多年生草本植物， 葉細長，可生小白 花 chives 多年生草 本植物，叶细长， 可生小白花	韭菜(jiǔ cài) chives
jiǔ ㄐ ㄧ ㄡ	酒	酒	用米，麥發酵製成 的含有刺激性的飲 料 wine 用米，麦 发酵制成的含有刺 激性的饮料	喝酒(hē jiǔ) drink wine 酒精(jiǔ jīng) alcohol
jiù ㄐ ㄧ ㄡ	舊	旧	不新，過時，有交 情的人old, outdated, old acquaintance 不新，过时，有交 情的人	守舊(shǒu jiù) 守旧 antiquated 故舊(gù jiù) 故旧 old acquiantance

jiù ㄐ 一 ㄡˋ	臼	臼	舂米的器具，形狀 像盆子 mortar 舂米的器具，形狀 像盆子	脱臼(tuō jiù) dislocation of joints 臼齒(jiù chǐ) 臼齿 molar tooth
jiù ㄐ 一 ㄡˋ	咎	咎	過失，處分 fault, punishment 过失，处分	歸咎他人(guī jiù tā rén) 归咎他人 lay blame on others 咎由自取(jiù yóu zì qǔ) ask for trouble
jiù ㄐ 一 ㄡˋ	疚	疚	心裏的痛苦 agony 心里的痛苦	内疚(nèi jiù) feel guilty
jiù ㄐ 一 ㄡˋ	舅	舅	母親的弟兄 uncle (mother's brother) 母亲的弟兄	舅舅(jiù jiù) mother's brother 小舅子(xiǎo jiù zi) wife's brother
jiù ㄐ 一 ㄡˋ	救	救	幫助脱離困難 rescue 帮助脱离困难	拯救(zhěng jiù) rescue 求救(qiú jiù) ask for help
jiù ㄐ 一 ㄡˋ	廄	厩	牲口棚 stable	馬廄(mǎ jiù) 马厩 horse stable
jiù ㄐ 一 ㄡˋ	就	就	靠近，立刻 close by, at once,	就地(jiù dì) on the spot 就來(jiù lái) 就来 come immediately
jū ㄐ ㄩ	居	居	住，住所 live, residence	居住(jū zhù) live 居民(jū mín) resident
jū ㄐ ㄩ	拘	拘	逮捕，限制 arrest, restrict	拘留(jū liú) detain 拘束(jū shù) restriction

jú ㄐㄩˊ	鞠	鞠	彎身行禮，表示恭敬 to bow in respect 弯身行礼，表示恭敬	鞠躬(jú gōng) to bow in respect
jú ㄐㄩˊ	菊	菊	多年生草本植物，秋天開花 chrysanthemum 多年生草本植物，秋天开花	菊花(jú huā) chrysanthemum
jú ㄐㄩˊ	局	局	情況，部分，機關團體 situation, part, a department 情况，部分，机关团体	局勢(jú shì)局势 situation 郵局(yóu jú)邮局 post office
jú ㄐㄩˊ	桔	桔	橘子的俗稱 tangerine 橘子的俗称	柑桔(gān jú) tangerine
jú ㄐㄩˊ	橘	橘	常綠喬木，初夏開花，果實可吃，果皮可做藥 tangerine 常绿乔木，初夏开花，果实可吃，果皮可做药	橘黃色(jú huáng sè) orange color 橘子汁(jú zi zhī) orange juice
jǔ ㄐㄩˇ	莒	莒	周代諸候國名 name of state during the Chou Dynasty 周代诸候国名	
jǔ ㄐㄩˇ	咀	咀	細嚼品味，含在嘴裏細細品嘗 chew 细嚼品味，含在嘴里细细品尝	咀嚼(jǔ jué) chew
jǔ ㄐㄩˇ	沮	沮	阻止，懊喪 stop, dejected 阻止，懊丧	沮喪(jǔ sàng) feel dejected
jǔ ㄐㄩˇ	齟	齟	意見不合，牙齒上下不合 dissension, irregular teeth 意见不合，牙齿上下不合	齟齬(jǔ yǔ)齟齬 dissension
jǔ ㄐㄩˇ	矩	矩	畫方形的工具，規則 carpenter's square, rules 画方形的工具，规则	規矩(guī jǔ)规矩 rules 矩形(jǔ xíng) rectangle

jǔ ㄐㄩˇ	舉	举	向上抬，提出 hold up, present,	舉重(jǔ zhòng) 举重 weightlifting 舉例(jǔ lì) 举例 show an example
jù ㄐㄩˋ	巨	巨	大 big	巨款(jù kuǎn) large sum of money 巨人(jù rén) giant
jù ㄐㄩˋ	拒	拒	不接受，抵抗 reject, resist	拒絕(jù jué) 拒绝 reject 抗拒(kàng jù) resist
jù ㄐㄩˋ	距	距	相隔 distance	距離(jù lí) 距离 distance
jù ㄐㄩˋ	炬	炬	火把 torch	火炬(huǒ jù) torch 付之一炬(fù zhī yí jù) burn something down
jù ㄐㄩˋ	具	具	器物，明顯，不抽 象 tool, concrete 器物，明显，不抽 象	玩具(wán jù) toy 具體(jù tǐ) 具体 concrete
jù ㄐㄩˋ	俱	俱	全，都，皆，同 all	萬事俱備(wàn shì jù bèi) 万事俱备 everything is ready 俱樂部(jù lè bù) 俱乐部 club
jù ㄐㄩˋ	懼	惧	害怕 frightened	恐懼(kǒng jù) 恐惧 fear 毫無所懼(háo wú suǒ jù) 毫无所惧 dauntless
jù ㄐㄩˋ	颶	飓	在熱帶海岸上的風 暴，同時有暴雨 hurricane 在热带海岸上的风 暴，同时有暴雨	颶風(jù fēng) 飓风 hurricane

jù ㄐㄩˋ	句	句	由字或詞組成能表達完整意思的話 sentence 由字或词组成能表达完整意思的话	造句(zào jù) make sentence 句型(jù xíng) sentence pattern
jù ㄐㄩˋ	劇	剧	戲，猛烈 drama, intense 戏，猛烈	戲劇(xì jù) 戏剧 drama 劇烈(jù liè) 剧烈 intense
jù ㄐㄩˋ	據	据	占領，按照 occupy, according to 占领，按照	占據(zhàn jù) 占据 occupy (a position) 根據(gēn jù) 根据 according to
jù ㄐㄩˋ	鋸	锯	邊緣有尖齒的鋼製薄片，可截斷物品 a saw 边缘有尖齿的钢製薄片，可截斷物品	鋸子(jù zi) 锯子 a saw 鋸斷(jù duàn) 锯断 to saw off
jù ㄐㄩˋ	聚	聚	會合，集合 meet, gather together 会合，集合	聚會(jù huì) 聚会 meeting 聚集(jù jí) gather together
juān ㄐㄩㄢ	捐	捐	獻出 to offer 献出	捐贈(juān zèng) 捐赠 donate 捐軀(juān qū) 捐躯 sacrifice one's life
juān ㄐㄩㄢ	涓	涓	細小的流水 brook 细小的流水	涓涓流水(juān juān liú shuǐ) trickling water
juān ㄐㄩㄢ	鵑	鹃	鳥名，口大尾長；植物名，常綠灌木 cuckoo, azalea 鸟名，口大尾长；植物名，常绿灌木	杜鵑(dù juān) cuckoo 杜鵑花(dù juān huā) azalea
juān ㄐㄩㄢ	娟	娟	美好的樣子 pretty 美好的样子	娟秀(juān xiù) pretty
juǎn ㄐㄩㄢˇ	捲	卷	把東西向裏面彎轉成圓筒形，裹住 roll up, wrap up 把东西向里面弯转	捲起袖子(juǎn qǐ xiù zi) 卷起袖子 roll up sleeves 捲入(juǎn rù) 卷入 get involved in

146

juàn juǎn ㄐㄩㄢ ㄐㄩˇㄢ	卷	卷	書本，裹成圓筒形，一梱 book, roll up, a roll 书本，裹成圆筒形，一梱	手不釋卷(shǒu bú shì juàn) 手不释卷 voracious reader 卷髮(juǎn fǎ) 卷发 curly hair
juàn ㄐㄩㄢˋ	倦	倦	身心疲憊，厭煩 exhausted, be tired of 身心疲惫，厌烦	疲倦(pí juàn) exhausted 厭倦(yàn juàn) 厌倦 be tired of
juàn ㄐㄩㄢˋ	雋	隽	指言論、文章意味深長 profound meaning of speeches, writings 指言论、文章意味深长	雋永(juàn yǒng) 隽永 profound meaning
juàn ㄐㄩㄢˋ	狷	狷	心胸狹窄，急躁 narrowminded, impetuous 心胸狭窄，急躁	狷急(juàn jí) impatient
juàn ㄐㄩㄢˋ	絹	绢	一種薄的絲織品，手帕 thin silk, handkerchief 一种薄的丝织品，手帕	手絹(shǒu juàn) 手绢 handkerchief
juàn ㄐㄩㄢˋ	眷	眷	愛戀，親屬 cling on to, dependent 爱恋，亲属	眷戀(juàn liàn) 眷恋 cling on to 家眷(jiā juàn) dependents
jué ㄐㄩㄝ	抉	抉	挑選 choose 挑选	抉擇(jué zé) 抉择 make a choice
jué ㄐㄩㄝ	決	决	拿定主意，感情或會談破裂 decide, break up 拿定主意，感情或会谈破裂	決定(jué dìng) 决定 decide 決裂(jué liè) 决裂 breakup
jué ㄐㄩㄝˊ	訣	诀	分別不再相見，高明的方法 bid farewell, clever trick 分别不再相见，高明的方法	訣別(jué bié) 诀别 bid farewell 祕訣(mì jué) 秘诀 secret trick

jué ㄐㄩㄝˊ	覺	觉	對事物的看法和感受，醒悟 perceive, awaken, feel 对事物的看法和感受，醒悟	感覺(gǎn jué) 感觉 perception 覺醒(jué xǐng) 觉醒 be awakened 覺得(jué dé) 觉得 feel
jué ㄐㄩㄝˊ	絕	绝	斷裂，極爲 cut off, extremely 断裂，极为	絕路(jué lù) 绝路 road to destruction 絕對(jué duì) 绝对 absolutely
jué ㄐㄩㄝˊ	倔	倔	態度頑強不屈的 stubborn 态度顽强不屈的	倔強(jué jiàng) 倔强 stubborn
jué ㄐㄩㄝˊ	掘	掘	挖，鑿 dig 挖，凿	挖掘(wā jué) dig 掘土機(jué tǔ jī) 掘土机 excavator
jué ㄐㄩㄝˊ	厥	厥	氣悶而昏倒 fainted 气闷而昏倒	昏厥(hūn jué) fainted
jué ㄐㄩㄝˊ	蹶	蹶	跌倒，挫敗 fall, defeat 跌倒，挫败	一蹶不振(yì jué bú zhèn) never recover from a defeat
jué ㄐㄩㄝˊ	爵	爵	古代封給貴族和功臣的名位 peerage 古代封给贵族和功臣的名位	爵位(jué wèi) peerage
jué ㄐㄩㄝˊ	嚼	嚼	用牙齒咬碎食物 chew 用牙齿咬碎食物	咀嚼(jǔ jué) chew
jūn ㄐㄩㄣ	軍	军	武裝部隊 armed forces 武装部队	海軍(hǎi jūn) 海军 navy 空軍(kōng jūn) 空军 air force 軍人(jūn rén) 军人 soldier

jūn jùn ㄐㄩ ㄐㄩ ㄣ ㄣ	菌	菌	使人生病的病原； 生於朽木 bacterium, mushroom 使人生病的病原； 生於朽木	细菌(xì jùn) 细菌 bacterium 食用菌(shí yòng jūn) mushroom
jūn ㄐㄩ ㄣ	君	君	古時的帝王，有地 位品行的人 king, virtuous person 古时的帝王，有地 位品行的人	君王(jūn wáng) king 君子(jūn zi) virtuous person
jūn ㄐㄩ ㄣ	均	均	平等，勻 equal, even	平均(píng jūn) average 均匀(jūn yún) even
jūn ㄐㄩ ㄣ	鈞	钧	古代重量單位，合 三十斤；敬辭 unit of weight, an honorific "you" 古代重量单位，合 三十斤；敬辞	千鈞(qiān jūn) 千钧 heavy weight 鈞安(jūn ān) 钧安 wishing you well
jùn ㄐㄩ ㄣ	郡	郡	古代行政區域，比 現在的縣大 prefecture 古代行政区域，比 现在的县大	郡主(jùn zhǔ) prefecture head
jùn ㄐㄩ ㄣ	俊	俊	才智傑出的人，相 貌好看 talened person, handsome 才智傑出的人，相 貌好看	俊傑(jùn jié) 俊傑 talented person 英俊(yīng jùn) handsome
jùn ㄐㄩ ㄣ	峻	峻	高而險要 tall and steep 高而险要	峻嶺(jùn lǐng) 峻岭 tall and steep mountain 嚴峻(yán jùn) 严峻 harsh, severe
jùn ㄐㄩ ㄣ	駿	骏	好馬 fine horse 好马	駿馬(jùn mǎ) 骏马 fine horse
jùn ㄐㄩ ㄣ	雋	隽	同"俊"，才智傑 出 man of great talents 同"俊"，才智傑 出	英雋(yīng jùn) 英隽 man of great talents

K

kǎ ㄎㄚˇ	卡	卡	堵住，付費或检查 的關口 get stuck, checkpoint 堵住，付费或检查 的关口	被卡住(bèi kǎ zhù) get stuck 關卡(guān kǎ) 关卡 checkpoint
kǎ ㄎㄚˇ	咯	咯	從氣管咳出東西 cough up 从气管咳出东西	咯血(kǎ xiě) cough up blood
kāi ㄎㄞ	開	开	"關"或"閉"的 相反，啓動，沸 open, start, boil "关"或"闭"的 相反，启动，沸	開車(kāi chē) 开车 drive a car 開水(kāi shuǐ) 开水 boiled water
kǎi ㄎㄞˇ	凱	凯	打勝仗 triumphant 打胜仗	凱旋(kǎi xuán) 凯旋 victory
kǎi ㄎㄞˇ	楷	楷	一種書法字體，模 範 a calligraphic style, a model 一种书法字体，模 范	楷書(kǎi shū) 楷书 standard writing script 楷模(kǎi mó) model
kǎi kài ㄎㄞˇ ㄎㄞˋ	慨	慨	激憤，嘆息，不吝 嗇 indignant, sigh, generous 激愤，叹息，不吝 啬	憤慨(fèn kǎi) 愤慨 indignance 慷慨(kāng kǎi) generous
kān ㄎㄢ	刊	刊	報紙等出版物 publication 报纸等出版物	刊物(kān wù) publication 年刊(nián kān) yearbook
kān ㄎㄢ	看	看	守護，照顧 watch over, take care of 守护，照顾	看守(kān shǒu) guard 看護(kān hù) 看护 nurse

kān ㄎ ㄢ	堪	堪	可以，能忍受 capable of, tolerable	難堪(nán kān) 难堪 embarrassing 不堪入目(bù kān rù mù) unsightly
kǎn ㄎ ㄢˇ	坎	坎	坑穴，道路不平 pit, bumpy (road)	坎坷(kǎn kě) bumpy (road)
kǎn ㄎ ㄢˇ	砍	砍	用力劈 to chop, cut	砍柴(kǎn chái) chop firewood 砍伐(kǎn fá) to log (trees)
kǎn ㄎ ㄢˇ	檻	檻	門下面的橫木 threshold 门下面的横木	門檻(mén kǎn) 门槛 threshold
kǎn ㄎ ㄢˇ	侃	侃	理直氣壯，從容的 assertively, fluently 理直气壮，从容的	侃侃而談(kǎn kǎn ér tán) 侃侃而谈 speak freely
kàn ㄎ ㄢˋ	看	看	瞧，訪問，診治 look, visit, seek medical treatment 瞧，访问，诊治	看電影(kàn diàn yǐng) 看电影 go to the movies 看病(kàn bìng) seek medical treatment
kāng ㄎ ㄤ	康	康	身體好 healthy 身体好	康樂(kāng lè) 康乐 recreation 康復(kāng fù) 康复 recuperate
kāng ㄎ ㄤ	慷	慷	大方，情緒激動 generous, emotional 大方，情绪激动	慷慨激昂(kāng kǎi jī áng) very emotional 慷慨解囊(kāng kǎi jiě náng) donate generously

kāng ㄎㄤ	糠	糠	稻米，穀類等的皮或殼 chaff, bran 稻米，谷类等的皮或壳	米糠(mǐ kāng) rice bran
káng ㄎㄤˊ	扛	扛	用肩膀承擔，抬一東西，負責 carry on shoulder, take responsibility 用肩膀承担，抬一东西，负责	扛行李(káng xíng lǐ) carry baggage on shoulder 扛下這結果(káng xià zhè jié guǒ) 扛下这结果 take responsibility for the consequence
kàng ㄎㄤˋ	抗	抗	抵禦，拒絕，不接受 resist, reject 抵禦，拒絕，不接受	抵抗(dǐ kàng) resist 對抗(duì kàng) 对抗 confrontation
kàng ㄎㄤˋ	伉	伉	夫婦 married couple 夫妇	伉儷(kàng lì) 伉俪 husband and wife
kǎo ㄎㄠˇ	考	考	測驗，斟酌 test, assess 测验，斟酌	考試(kǎo shì) 考试 examination 考慮(kǎo lǜ) 考虑 consider
kǎo ㄎㄠˇ	拷	拷	折磨 torture	拷打(kǎo dǎ) torture by beating 拷問(kǎo wèn) 拷问 torture and interrogate
kǎo ㄎㄠˇ	烤	烤	用火烘乾或燒熟食物，借火取暖 roast, keep warm by the fire 用火烘乾或燒熟食物，借火取暖	烤肉(kǎo ròu) barbecue 烤火(kǎo huǒ) keep warm by the fire
kào ㄎㄠˋ	銬	铐	把犯人鎖起來的刑具 handcuffs 把犯人锁起来的刑具	手銬(shǒu kào) 手铐 handcuffs
kào ㄎㄠˋ	犒	犒	以食物金錢等慰勞 reward with food or money 以食物金钱等慰劳	犒賞(kào shǎng) 犒赏 reward the troops

kào ㄎㄠˋ	靠	靠	依賴，可信，挨近 depend, reliable, to approach 依赖，可信，挨近	依靠(yī kào) depend on 可靠(kě kào) reliable
kē ㄎㄜ	苛	苛	過分，難以忍受 excessive, intolerable 过分，难以忍受	苛責(kē zé) 苛责 scold harshly 苛政(kē zhèng) tyrannical rule
kē ㄎㄜ	柯	柯	姓氏，斧頭的柄 Chinese surname, ax handle 姓氏，斧头的柄	
kē ㄎㄜ	科	科	類別 category 类别	科目(kē mù) subject 科學(kē xué) 科学 science
kē ㄎㄜ	顆	颗	量詞，指圓形或粒狀的東西 classifier for round objects 量词，指圆形或粒状的东西	一顆心 (yì kē xīn) 一颗心 a heart 一顆珍珠(yì kē zhēn zhū) 一颗珍珠a pearl
kē ㄎㄜ	棵	棵	指樹或植物的數詞 classifier for trees or plants 指树或植物的数词	一棵樹(yì kē shù) 一棵树 a tree
kē ㄎㄜ	磕	磕	把頭碰在地上跪拜 kowtow 把头碰在地上跪拜	磕頭(kē tóu) 磕头 kowtow
kē ㄎㄜ	瞌	瞌	困倦打盹兒，半睡眠 doze off 困倦打盹儿，半睡眠	打瞌睡(dǎ kē shuì) doze off
ké ㄎㄜˊ	殼	壳	物體外的硬表殼 shell 物体外的硬表壳	蛋殼(dàn ké) 蛋壳 egg shell 花生殼(huā shēng ké) 花生壳 peanut shell

ké ㄎㄜˊ	咳	咳	氣管用力排出刺激物 cough 气管用力排出刺激物	咳嗽(ké sòu) cough
kě ㄎㄜˇ	可	可	表示允許，值得 can, worthy of 表示允许，值得	可以(kě yǐ) can, may 可愛(kě ài) 可爱 lovable
kě ㄎㄜˇ	坷	坷	低陷不平的地方，坑穴，不得志 bumpy, pit 低陷不平的地方，坑穴，不得志	坎坷(kǎn kě) bumpy (road)
kě ㄎㄜˇ	渴	渴	口乾想喝水，急切 thirsty, yearn for 口干想喝水，急切	口渴(kǒu kě) thirsty 渴望(kě wàng) yearn for
kè ㄎㄜˋ	克	克	能，控制 able to, restrain	不克(bú kè) unable to 克制(kè zhì) exercise restraint
kè ㄎㄜˋ	刻	刻	雕，十五分鐘，待人不厚道 sculpting, 15 minutes, mean 雕，十五分钟，待人不厚道	雕刻(diāo kè) sculpting 一刻鐘(yí kè zhōng) 一刻钟15 minutes
kè ㄎㄜˋ	客	客	"主"的相反，到外地或別人家去拜訪 guest "主"的相反，到外地或别人家去拜访	客人(kè rén) guest 客觀(kè guān) 客观 objective
kè kē ㄎㄜˋ ㄎㄜ	課	课	教學過程的一段落，繳納 lesson, make payment 教学过程的一段落，缴纳	功課(gōng kè) 功课 homework 課稅(kè shuì) 课税 pay taxes 課長(kē zhǎng) 课长 Section Chief

kěn 万 ㄣˇ	肯	肯	願意 willing to 愿意	不肯(bù kěn) refuse to 肯定(kěn dìng) definitely
kěn 万 ㄣˇ	墾	垦	翻土耕種 till the land 翻土耕种	墾荒(kěn huāng) 垦荒 reclaim wasteland 墾殖(kěn zhí) 垦殖 reclaim land for farming
kěn 万 ㄣˇ	懇	恳	真誠 sincere 真诚	誠懇(chéng kěn) 诚恳 sincere 懇求(kěn qiú) 恳求 implore
kēng 万 ㄥ	坑	坑	注下去的地方 pit 注下去的地方	坑道(kēng dào) mine pit 水坑(shuǐ kēng) water pit
kēng háng 万 ㄏ ㄥ ㄤˊ	吭	吭	發出聲音 make a sound 发出声音	不吭氣(bù kēng qì) 不吭气 do not utter a word 不吭聲(bù kēng shēng) 不吭声 say not a word
kōng kòng 万 万 ㄨ ㄨˋ ㄥ ㄥ	空	空	沒有內容，天 empty, sky	空洞(kōng dòng) empty 天空(tiān kōng) sky 空位(kòng wèi) empty seat 空閑(kòng xián) 空闲 free time 空白(kòng bái) blank 有空(yǒu kòng) have leisure
kǒng 万 ㄨˇ ㄥ	孔	孔	小洞 hole	針孔(zhēn kǒng) 针孔 needle hole 鼻孔(bí kǒng) nostril
kǒng 万 ㄨˇ ㄥ	恐	恐	害怕，心慌不安 fearful, uneasy	恐懼(kǒng jù) 恐惧 fear 恐慌(kǒng huāng) panic

kòng ㄎㄨㄥˋ	控	控	告狀，支配，掌握 sue, control, grasp 告状，支配，掌握	控告(kòng gào) file lawsuit against 控制(kòng zhì) control
kǒu ㄎㄡˇ	口	口	嘴，進出必經之處 mouth, entrance or exit 嘴，进出必经之处	口才(kǒu cái) eloquence 進出口(jìn chū kǒu) 进出口 import and export
kòu ㄎㄡˋ	寇	寇	盜匪，侵略者 bandit, aggressor 盗匪，侵略者	寇仇(kòu chóu) enemy 匪寇(fěi kòu) bandit
kòu ㄎㄡˋ	扣	扣	衣鈕，留置 button, detain 衣钮，留置	鈕扣(niǔ kòu) 钮扣 button 扣留(kòu liú) detain
kòu ㄎㄡˋ	叩	叩	敲打，磕頭 knock, kowtow 敲打，磕头	叩門(kòu mén) 叩门 knock on the door 叩首(kòu shǒu) kowtow
kū ㄎㄨ	哭	哭	因哀傷而流淚發聲 crying 因哀伤而流泪发声	痛哭(tòng kū) wailing 哭訴(kū sù) 哭诉 tearful complaint
kū ㄎㄨ	枯	枯	乾，沒趣味 wither, dull 干，没趣味	枯樹(kū shù) 枯树 withered tree 枯燥(kū zào) dull
kū ㄎㄨ	窟	窟	洞穴，人、獸、蟲 等聚集的地方 cave, hole 洞穴，人、兽、虫 等聚集的地方	窟窿(kū lóng) hole 賊窟(zéi kū) 贼窟 bandits' hideout

kū ㄎㄨ	骷	骷	沒有皮肉的屍骨 human skeleton	骷髏(kū lóu) 骷髏 human skeleton
kǔ ㄎㄨˇ	苦	苦	似黄蓮的滋味，"甜"的相反，耐心 bitter, patiently 似黄莲的滋味，"甜"的相反，耐心	痛苦(tòng kǔ) pain, suffering 苦等(kǔ děng) wait patiently
kù ㄎㄨˋ	庫	库	貯存東西的地方 storage 贮存东西的地方	倉庫(cāng kù) 仓库 warehouse 水庫(shuǐ kù) 水库 reservoir
kù ㄎㄨˋ	酷	酷	殘忍的，極爲 cruel, extremely 残忍的，极为	殘酷(cán kù) 残酷 atrocious 酷熱(kù rè) 酷热 extremely hot
kù ㄎㄨˋ	褲	裤	穿在下身和腿部的服裝 trousers 穿在下身和腿部的服裝	褲子(kù zi) 裤子 trousers, pants 短褲(duǎn kù) 短裤 shorts
kuā ㄎㄨㄚ	誇	夸	説大話，向別人炫耀 overstate, boast 说大话，向别人炫耀	誇張(kuā zhāng) 夸张 exaggerate 誇獎(kuā jiǎng) 夸奖 commend, praise
kuǎ ㄎㄨㄚˇ	垮	垮	倒塌，敗壞，崩潰 collapse, corrupt, crumble 倒塌，败坏，崩溃	垮台(kuǎ tái) downfall 搞垮(gǎo kuǎ) to topple something
kuà ㄎㄨㄚˋ	跨	跨	叉腿 straddle	橫跨(héng kuà) stretch across 跨國(kuà guó) 跨国 multinational
kuà ㄎㄨㄚˋ	胯	胯	腰和大腿間的部分 groin 腰和大腿间的部分	胯下之辱(kuà xià zhī rǔ) made to crawl between the legs of a person as an insult

kuài ㄎ ㄨ ㄞ丶	快	快	不慢，速度，銳利 quick, speed, sharp 不慢，速度，锐利	快樂(kuài lè) 快乐 happy 快刀(kuài dāo) sharp knife
kuài ㄎ ㄨ ㄞ丶	塊	块	成圍的東西，量詞 a mass, classifier 成团的东西，量词	木塊(mù kuài) 木块 a block of wood 一塊錢(yí kuài qián) 一块钱 one dollar
kuài ㄎ ㄨ ㄞ丶	筷	筷	夾菜的細棍子 chopstick 夹菜的细棍子	筷子(kuài zi) chopstick
kuài ㄎ ㄨ丶 ㄞㄟ	會	会	總計 sum total 总计	會計(kuài jì) 会计 accounting, accountant
kuài ㄎ ㄨ ㄞ丶	儈	侩	介紹買賣從中年利 的人，自私庸俗的 人 broker, mundane person 介绍买卖从中年利 的人，自私庸俗的 人	市儈(shì kuài) 市侩 selfish, mundane person
kuān ㄎ ㄨ ㄢ	寬	宽	不窄，廣闊 broad 不窄，广阔	寬大(kuān dà) 宽大 generous 放寬(fàng kuān) 放宽 liberalize
kuǎn ㄎ ㄨ ㄢˇ	款	款	法令規章的項目， 錢財，誠懇 provisions of law, money 法令规章的项目， 钱财，诚恳	條款(tiáo kuǎn) 条款 provisions of law 存款(cún kuǎn) savings
kuāng ㄎ ㄨ ㄤ	匡	匡	糾正 correct 纠正	匡正(kuāng zhèng) make correction
kuāng ㄎ ㄨ ㄤ	筐	筐	盛物的竹器 basket	籮筐(luó kuāng) 箩筐 basket

kuāng ㄎㄨㄤ	框	框	安裝在門窗上的架子 door or window frame 安装在门窗上的架子	門框(mén kuāng) 门框 door frame 鏡框(jìng kuāng) 镜框 mirror frame 相框(xiàng kuāng) picture frame
kuáng ㄎㄨㄤˊ	狂	狂	瘋癲，精神失常，任意的 deranged, wild 疯癫，精神失常，任意的	狂妄(kuáng wàng) arrogant 狂熱(kuáng rè) 狂热 feverish
kuáng ㄎㄨㄤˊ	誑	诳	欺騙 deceive 欺骗	誑語(kuáng yǔ) 诳语 a lie
kuàng ㄎㄨㄤˋ	曠	旷	空闊，心境寬大，荒廢 spacious, desert 空阔，心境宽大，荒废	空曠(kōng kuàng) 空旷 empty and spacious 曠課(kuàng kè) 旷课 ditch class
kuàng ㄎㄨㄤˋ	況	况	情形；連接詞意思是"再說" condition, moreover 情形；连接词意思是"再说"	情況(qíng kuàng) 情况 circumstances 況且(kuàng qiě) 况且 moreover
kuàng ㄎㄨㄤˋ	眶	眶	眼睛的周圍 eye socket 眼睛的周围	眼眶(yǎn kuàng) eye socket
kuàng ㄎㄨㄤˋ	礦	矿	地下埋藏的金、銀、銅、鐵等 mineral deposit 地下埋藏的金、银、铜、铁等	礦物(kuàng wù) 矿物 minerals 煤礦(méi kuàng) 煤矿 coal mine
kuī ㄎㄨㄟ	窺	窺	偷看 peek	窺見(kuī jiàn) sneak a peek 偷窺(tōu kuī) 偷窥 to peep
kuī ㄎㄨㄟ	盔	盔	打仗時用來保護頭的帽子 helmet 打仗时用来保护头的帽子	頭盔(tóu kuī) 头盔 helmet 盔甲(kuī jiǎ) helmet and armor

Pinyin	Traditional	Simplified	Definition	Examples
kuī ㄎㄨㄟ	虧	亏	缺損，缺少，損失 loss, shortage 缺损，缺少，损失	虧損(kuī sǔn) 亏损 loss 虧待(kuī dài) 亏待 unfair treatment
kuí ㄎㄨㄟˊ	魁	魁	比賽得第一名，高大強壯 champion, sturdy 比赛得第一名，高大强壮	奪魁(duó kuí) 夺魁 win first place 魁偉(kuí wěi) 魁伟 sturdy
kuí ㄎㄨㄟˊ	葵	葵	一年生草本植物，黃色花芯常向日，種子可食 sunflower 一年生草本植物，黄色花芯常向日，种子可食	向日葵(xiàng rì kuí) sunflower
kuí ㄎㄨㄟˊ	睽	睽	張大眼睛注視 stare at 张大眼睛注视	眾目睽睽(zhòng mù kuí kuí) 众目睽睽 in full view of the public
kuǐ ㄎㄨㄟˇ	傀	傀	木偶戲裏的木頭人，受人操縱的人或組織 puppet 木偶戏里的木头人，受人操纵的人或组织	傀儡(kuí lěi) puppet
kuì ㄎㄨㄟˋ	愧	愧	羞慚 shameful 羞惭	慚愧(cán kuì) 惭愧 feel ashamed 問心無愧(wèn xīn wú kuì) 问心无愧 have a clear conscience
kūn ㄎㄨㄣ	坤	坤	八卦之一，"地"的意思；婦女 earth, woman 八卦之一，"地"的意思；妇女	乾坤(qián kūn) heaven and earth 坤伶(kūn líng) actress
kūn ㄎㄨㄣ	昆	昆	哥哥 elder brother	昆仲(kūn zhòng) brothers 昆蟲(kūn chóng) 昆虫 insect
kǔn ㄎㄨㄣˇ	捆	捆	用繩子等綁緊，量詞 bundle up, classifier 用绳子等绑紧，量词	捆綁(kǔn bǎng) 捆绑 一捆(yì kǔn) a bundle of

kùn ㄎㄨㄣˋ	睏	睏	疲倦想睡覺 feel drowsy 疲倦想睡觉	我睏了 (wǒ kùn le) I feel drowsy 睏倦(kùn juàn) tired and sleepy
kùn ㄎㄨㄣˋ	困	困	陷在艱難痛苦裏， 包圍住，窮苦 beset with hardship, surrounded, poverty 陷在艰难痛苦里， 包围住，穷苦	困境(kùn jìng) predicament 窮困(qióng kùn) 穷困 poverty
kuò ㄎㄨㄛˋ	括	括	包容 include	包括(bāo kuò) include 總括(zǒng kuò) 总括 summarize
kuò ㄎㄨㄛˋ	闊	阔	面積寬廣，富裕 spacious, abundance 面积宽广，富裕	寬闊(kuān kuò) 宽阔 spacious 闊氣(kuò qì) 阔气 extravagance
kuò ㄎㄨㄛˋ	擴	扩	放大，張大 enlarge, expand 放大，张大	擴張(kuò zhāng) 扩张 expand 擴散(kuò sàn) 扩散 proliferate
kuò ㄎㄨㄛˋ	廓	廓	開闊 wide 开阔	空廓(kōng kuò) empty and spacious 輪廓(lún kuò) 轮廓 contour

L				
Lā ㄌㄚ	拉	拉	牽引，聯絡，排泄 pull, contact, excrete 牵引，联络，排泄	拉門(lā mén) 拉门 pull the door 拉屎(lā shǐ) defecate
Lā ㄌㄚ	啦	啦	表示聲響的字，感 嘆助詞 mimetic word, exclamatory expression 表示聲響 的字，感嘆助詞	啦啦隊(lā lā duì) 啦啦队 cheering team 啦啦隊員(lā lā duì yuan) 啦啦队员 cheerleaders 當然啦(dāng rán la) 当然啦 of course
Lā ㄌㄚ	垃	垃	扔掉的東西 garbage 扔掉的东西	垃圾(lā jī) garbage
Lā ㄌㄚ	邋	邋	不利落 sloppy	邋遢(lā tā) sloppy
Lǎ ㄌㄚˇ	喇	喇	銅管樂器，西藏語 指出家男子 trumpet, lama 铜管乐器，西藏语 指出家男子	喇叭(lǎ ba) trumpet 喇嘛(lǎ ma) lama
Là ㄌㄚˋ	辣	辣	濃烈的辛味 hot (like chilli) 浓烈的辛味	辣椒(là jiāo) chilli 辣手(là shǒu) ruthless
Là ㄌㄚˋ	臘	腊	十二月 12th month of lunar calendar	臘月(là yuè) 腊月 the 12th month 臘肉(là ròu) 腊肉 salted dried meat
Lái ㄌㄞˊ	來	来	"去" 的相反 come	來信(lái xìn) 来信 incoming letter 未來(wèi lái) 未来 the future
Lài ㄌㄞˋ	賴	赖	依靠，仗持，推諉 過錯 rely, shift the blame 依靠，仗持，推诿 过错	依賴(yī lài) 依赖 rely on 抵賴(dǐ lài) 抵赖 deny wrongdoing

Lài ㄌㄞˋ	癩	癩	痲瘋 leprosy 麻风	癩病(lài bìng) 癞病 leprosy 癩蛤蟆(lài há ma) 癞蛤蟆 toad
Lán ㄌㄢˊ	蘭	兰	常綠多年生草本植物，花味清香 orchid 常绿多年生草本植物，花味清香	蘭花(lán huā) 兰花 orchid 蘭州(lán zhōu) 兰州 Lanzhou Province
Lán ㄌㄢˊ	欄	栏	圍牆，書報雜誌上用線條隔開的部分 fence, column 围墙，书报杂誌上用线条隔开的部分	佈告欄(bù gào lán) 佈告栏 bulletin board 豬欄(zhū lán) 猪栏 pig sty
Lán ㄌㄢˊ	攔	拦	阻擋 to block 阻挡	攔截(lán jié) 拦截 intercept 阻攔(zǔ lán) 阻拦 obstruct
Lán ㄌㄢˊ	嵐	岚	山中霧氣 hillside haze 山中雾气	山嵐(shān lán) 山岚 hillside haze
Lán ㄌㄢˊ	婪	婪	貪愛財物 greedy 贪爱财物	貪婪(tān lán) 贪婪 greedy
Lán ㄌㄢˊ	瀾	澜	大波浪 huge wave 大波浪	波瀾(bō lán) 波澜 huge wave
Lán ㄌㄢˊ	藍	蓝	晴天天空的顏色 blue	藍色(lán sè) 蓝色 blue color 藍圖(lán tú) 蓝图 blueprint
Lán ㄌㄢˊ	籃	篮	藤或竹制的容器 basket	菜籃(cài lán) 菜篮 vegetable basket 籃球(lán qiú) 篮球 basketball
Lán ㄌㄢˊ	襤	褴	衣服破爛 tattered clothes 衣服破烂	襤褸(lán lǚ) 褴褛 dressed in tatters

Lǎn ㄌㄢˇ	覽	览	觀看 view, browse 观看	瀏覽(liú lǎn) 浏览 browse 遊覽(yóu lǎn) 遊览 to tour a place
Lǎn ㄌㄢˇ	懶	懒	怠惰，不勤快 lazy, slack	懶惰(lǎn duò) 懒惰 lazy 懶散 (lǎn sàn) 懒散 slack
Lǎn ㄌㄢˇ	攬	揽	抱住，把持 hold somebody in the arms, grasp	一攬子(yì lǎn zi) 一揽子 a bundle 攬權(lǎn quán) 揽权 assume all powers
Lǎn ㄌㄢˇ	纜	缆	繫船的繩索，繫， 綁 mooring rope, to tighten with rope 系船的绳索，繫， 绑	纜車(lǎn chē) 缆车 cable car 電纜(diàn lǎn) 电缆 electric cable
Lǎn ㄌㄢˇ	欖	榄	常綠喬木，果實尖 長，種子可榨油 olive 常绿乔木，果实尖 长，种子可榨油	橄欖(gǎn lǎn) 橄榄 olive
Làn ㄌㄢˋ	爛	烂	軟，東西腐壞，破 碎 soft, rotten, broken 软，东西腐坏，破 碎	煮爛(zhǔ làn) 煮烂 thoroughly cooked 腐爛(fǔ làn) 腐烂 rotten
Làn ㄌㄢˋ	濫	滥	水滿而四溢，過度 flooded, excessive 水满而四溢，过度	泛濫(fàn làn) 泛滥 flooding 濫用(làn yòng) 滥用 abuse
Láng ㄌㄤˊ	郎	郎	青年男女 young person	新郎(xīn láng) bridegroom 女郎(nǚ láng) a girl
Láng ㄌㄤˊ	廊	廊	有頂的過道，可避 風雨，遮太陽 corridor, veranda 有顶的过道，可避 风雨，遮太阳	走廊(zǒu láng) corridor 畫廊(huà láng) art gallery

Láng ㄌ ㄤˊ	狼	狼	哺乳動物，性殘忍 ，以食小動物爲生 ；處境窘困 wolf, awkwardness 哺乳动物，性残忍 ，以食小动物为生 ；处境窘困	色狼(sè láng) lady-killer 狼狽(láng bèi) 狼狈 in an awkward state
Lǎng ㄌ ㄤˇ	朗	朗	明亮，坦白 bright, candid	明朗(míng lǎng) clear and bright 開朗(kāi lǎng) 开朗 openminded
Làng ㄌ ㄤˋ	浪	浪	因振動而起伏，濫 用，放縱 bobbing, abuse, uninhibited 因振动而起伏，滥 用，放纵	波浪(bō làng) wave 浪費(làng fèi) 浪费 wasteful
Lāo ㄌ ㄠ	撈	捞	從水或其他流質液 體裏拿東西，取得 salvage from water, obtain 从水或其他流质液 体里拿东西，取得	打撈(dǎ lāo) 打捞 salvage from water 撈取(lāo qǔ) 捞取 obtain (profit)
Láo Lào ㄌ ㄌ ㄠˊ ㄠˋ	勞	劳	辛苦 labor	勞動(láo dòng) 劳动labor 疲勞(pí láo) 疲劳tired
Láo ㄌ ㄠˊ	癆	痨	肺結核病 tuberculosis 肺结核病	肺癆(fèi láo) 肺痨 tuberculosis
Láo ㄌ ㄠˊ	牢	牢	囚禁犯人的地方， 堅固 prison, firm 囚禁犯人的地方， 坚固	監牢(jiān láo) 监牢 prison 牢固(láo gù) hard and fast
Lǎo ㄌ ㄠˇ	老	老	年紀大，舊的 old-aged, used 年纪大，旧的	老人(lǎo rén) old person 古老(gǔ lǎo) ancient

Lǎo ㄌㄠˇ	姥	姥	外祖母 grandmother (on mother's side)	姥姥(lǎo lao) grandmother
Lǎo ㄌㄠˇ	佬	佬	成年男子 a man	闊佬(kuò lǎo) 阔佬 a rich guy
Lào Láo ㄌㄠˋ ㄌㄠˊ	勞	劳	慰問別人的辛苦 to comfort other people for their hardwork 慰问别人的辛苦	慰勞(wèi lào) 慰劳 to entertain and cheer 勞軍(lào jūn)劳军 cheer and entertain troops
Lào ㄌㄠˋ	烙	烙	用燒紅的鐵燙東西 to brand 用烧红的铁烫东西	烙印(lào yìn) brand
Lào ㄌㄠˋ	酪	酪	用動物的乳汁做成的半凝固食品 cheese 用动物的乳汁做成的半凝固食品	乳酪(rǔ lào) cheese
Lè yuè ㄌㄜˋ ㄩㄝˋ	樂	乐	歡喜，有規律的聲音 happy, music 欢喜，有规律的声音	快樂(kuài lè) 快乐 happy 音樂(yīn yuè) 音乐 music
Le Liǎo ㄌㄜˋ ㄌㄠˇ	了	了	動作完畢，結束 end 动作完毕，结束	看了(kàn le) has seen 了結(liǎo jié) 了结 an end
Lēi ㄌㄟ	勒	勒	用繩子拉緊 tighten the rope 用绳子拉紧	勒緊褲帶(lēi jǐn kù dài) 勒紧裤带 practice austerity
Léi ㄌㄟˊ	雷	雷	閃電後發出的強大聲音，爆炸武器 thunder, land mine 闪电后发出的强大声音，爆炸武器	打雷(dǎ léi) thundering 地雷(dì léi) land mine

Léi ㄌㄟˊ	擂	擂	打，吹嘘 strike, boast	擂鼓(léi gǔ) beat the drum 自吹自擂(zì chuī zì léi) boasting
Lěi Lei、 ㄌㄟˇ ㄌㄟˋ	累	累	堆積，疲勞 accumulate, tired 堆积，疲劳	累積(lěi jī)累积 accumulate 勞累(láo lèi)劳累 tired from work
Lěi ㄌㄟˇ	壘	垒	防守用的墙壁 rampart 防守用的墙壁	壘球(lěi qiú)垒球 softball 堡壘(bǎo lěi)堡垒 fortification
Lěi ㄌㄟˇ	儡	儡	傀儡：木偶，虛有 其名，甘心受人操 縱者puppet 傀儡： 木偶，虛有其名， 甘心受人操纵者	傀儡(kuí lěi) puppet
Lěi ㄌㄟˇ	磊	磊	石頭多，光明正大 stony, open and aboveboard 石头多，光明正大	磊落(lěi luò) open and aboveboard
Lěi ㄌㄟˇ	蕾	蕾	花苞 bud	花蕾(huā lěi) flower bud
Lèi ㄌㄟˋ	淚	泪	哀傷時從眼睛流出 的液體 tear 哀伤时从眼睛流出 的液体	眼淚(yǎn lèi)眼泪 tear 流淚(liú lèi)流泪 shed tears
Lèi ㄌㄟˋ	類	类	種，相似的集合體 ，相像 category, similar to 种，相似的集合体 ，相像	分類(fēn lèi)分类 categorize 類似(lèi sì)类似 similar to
Lèi Lěi ㄌㄟˋ ㄌㄟˇ	累	累	疲勞 tired 疲劳	勞累(láo lèi)劳累 tired from work 累犯(lěi fàn)累犯 repeated offender

Lèi Lē ㄌㄟˋ ㄌㄜ	肋	肋	胸的兩旁 rib 胸的两旁	肋骨(lèi gǔ) rib
Lěng ㄌㄥˇ	冷	冷	溫度低，寒 cold 温度低，寒	寒冷(hán lěng) cold 冷氣(lěng qì) 冷气 air-conditioning
Lí ㄌㄧˊ	釐	厘	度量單位，訂正 unit of measure, to correct 度量单位，订正	釐正(lí zhèng) 厘正 to correct 釐定(lí dìng) 厘定 collate, stipulate rules
Lí ㄌㄧˊ	離	离	分開 separate 分开	距離(jù lí) 距离 distance 離婚(lí hūn) 离婚 divorce
Lí ㄌㄧˊ	梨	梨	落葉喬木，果實可 食 pear 落叶乔木，果实可 食	梨子(lí zi) pear 鳳梨(fèng lí) 凤梨 pineapple
Lí ㄌㄧˊ	罹	罹	遭受困境 meet with misfortune	罹難(lí nàn) 罹难 killed in a disaster
Lí ㄌㄧˊ	驪	骊	純黑色的馬 black horse 纯黑色的马	驪歌(lí gē) 骊歌 song of farewell
Lí ㄌㄧˊ	鸝	鹂	鳥類，羽毛黃色， 叫聲悅耳 oriole 鸟类，羽毛黄色， 叫声悦耳	黃鸝(huáng lí) 黄鹂 oriole
Lí ㄌㄧˊ	璃	璃	玻璃：透明物體， 可做鏡子，窗戶等 用具 glass 玻璃： 透明物体，可做镜 子，窗户等用具	玻璃(bō lí) glass
Lí ㄌㄧˊ	黎	黎	姓氏 Chinese surname	巴黎(bā lí) Paris

Lǐ ㄌ 一ˇ	裏	里	内部，一定範圍之内 inside, in a certain area 内部，一定范围之内	裏面(lǐ miàn) 里面 inside 這裏(zhè lǐ) 这里 here
Lǐ ㄌ 一ˇ	李	李	李樹，春天開白花，果實呈黃色或暗紅色，可食 plum 李树，春天开白花，果实呈黄色或暗红色，可食	李樹(lǐ shù) 李树 plum tree 桃李滿天下(táo lǐ mǎn tiān xià) 桃李满天下 said of a teacher who has students all over the world
Lǐ ㄌ 一ˇ	禮	礼	表示尊敬的行爲，送他人的東西 rite, gift 表示尊敬的行为，送他人的东西	行禮(xíng lǐ) 行礼 salute 送禮(sòng lǐ) 送礼 present a gift to 禮物(lǐ wù) 礼物 a gift
Lǐ ㄌ 一ˇ	理	理	原則，辦事 principle, handle a matter 原则，办事	合理(hé lǐ) reasonable 料理(liào lǐ) manage 理由(lǐ yóu) reason 理想(lǐ xiǎng) ideal
Lǐ ㄌ 一ˇ	鯉	鲤	身體扁肥，肉味鮮美的魚 carp 身体扁肥，肉味鲜美的鱼	鯉魚(lǐ yú) 鲤鱼 carp
Lì ㄌ 一ˋ	力	力	施於人體或物體的作用 power, energy 施於人体或物体的作用	力量(lì liàng) strength 能力(néng lì) ability
Lì ㄌ 一ˋ	麗	丽	漂亮 beautiful	美麗(měi lì) 美丽 beautiful 風和日麗(fēng hé rì lì) 风和日丽 gentle breeze and warm sunshine
Lì ㄌ 一ˋ	立	立	站著，設置 stand, establish 站著，设置	起立(qǐ lì) stand up 設立(shè lì) 设立 establish
Lì ㄌ 一ˋ	粒	粒	一顆細小的東西 a pellet 一颗细小的东西	一粒米(yí lì mǐ) a grain of rice 粒子(lì zi) particle

Lì ㄌ 一ˋ	笠	笠	用竹篾等編成的帽子 bamboo hat 用竹篾等编成的帽子	斗笠(dǒu lì) bamboo hat
Lì ㄌ 一ˋ	隸	隶	社會地位低聽差的，附屬 slave, subordinate to 社会地位低听差的，附属	奴隸(nú lì) 奴隶 slave 隸屬(lì shǔ) 隶属 subordinate to
Lì ㄌ 一ˋ	例	例	可作依據的事物，規則 example, rule 可作依据的事物，规则	舉例(jǔ lì) 举例 show by example 條例(tiáo lì) 条例 regulations
Lì ㄌ 一ˋ	吏	吏	古時候的官員 old-time government official 古时候的官员	官吏(guān lì) government official
Lì ㄌ 一ˋ	歷	历	人類漫長的過去，所做過的事 history, experience 人类漫长的过去，所做过的事	歷史(lì shǐ) 历史 history 經歷(jīng lì) 经历 experience
Lì ㄌ 一ˋ	厲	厉	嚴格，兇惡 stringent, grim 严格，兇恶	嚴厲(yán lì) 严厉 rigorous 厲害(lì hài) 厉害 formidable
Lì ㄌ 一ˋ	栗	栗	落葉喬木，果實可食；因害怕而發抖 chestnut, shiver 落叶乔木，果实可食；因害怕而发抖	栗子(lì zi) chestnut 不寒而栗(bù hán ér lì) shiver from fear
Lì ㄌ 一ˋ	戾	戾	罪惡，暴虐，兇狠 evil, violent, ruthless 罪恶，暴虐，兇狠	暴戾(bào lì) violent 乖戾(guāi lì) perverted
Lì ㄌ 一ˋ	礪	砺	粗磨刀石 coarse whetstone	磨礪(mó lì) 磨砺 to steel oneself 砥礪(dǐ lì) 砥砺 to discipline, polish oneself
Lì ㄌ 一ˋ	莉	莉	初夏開的小白花，味清香 jasmine 初夏开的小白花，	茉莉花(mò lì huā) jasmine

			味清香	
Lì ㄌ 一、	礫	砾	小石頭 gravel 小石头	瓦礫(wǎ lì) 瓦砾 rubbles 砂礫(shā lì) 砂砾 gravel
Lì ㄌ 一、	利	利	好處，和"害" "弊"相反 benefit, advantage 好处，和"害"" 弊"相反	利益(lì yì) benefit, profit 利用(lì yòng) utilize
Lì ㄌ 一、	俐	俐	聰明的樣子，敏捷 smart, agile 聪明的样子，敏捷	伶俐(líng lì) smart 俐落(lì luò) not sloppy
Lì ㄌ 一、	痢	痢	傳染病，腹痛，發 燒，糞便帶血或黏 液 dysentery 传染病，腹痛，发 烧，粪便带血或黏 液	痢疾(lì jí) dysentery
Lì ㄌ 一、	勵	励	勸勉 encourage 劝勉	鼓勵(gǔ lì) 鼓励 encourage 再接再勵(zài jiē zài lì) 再接再励 redouble the efforts
Lì ㄌ 一、	靂	雳	雷擊聲 thunder 雷击声	霹靂(pī lì) 霹雳 thunderbolt
Lì ㄌ 一、	荔	荔	常綠喬木，果皮暗 紅色，果肉白色， 汁多味甜 litchi 常绿乔木，果皮暗 红色，果肉白色， 汁多味甜	荔枝(lì zhī) litchi
Lián ㄌ 一 ㄢ	連	连	相接不斷，接，合 continuous, join 相接不断，接，合	連續(lián xù) 连续 continuous 連鎖(lián suǒ) 连锁 chain

Lián ㄌㄧㄢˊ	聯	联	結合，彼此接洽 connect, contact 结合，彼此接洽	聯合國(lián hé guó) 联合国 United Nations 聯絡(lián luò) 联络 contact
Lián ㄌㄧㄢˊ	憐	怜	愛惜 sympathize with 爱惜	憐愛(lián ài) 怜爱 show tender care for 可憐(kě lián) 可怜 pitiful
Lián ㄌㄧㄢˊ	廉	廉	不貪污，樸素的作 風，便宜 not corrupt, plain workstyle, cheap 不贪污，朴素的作 风，便宜	廉潔(lián jié) 廉洁 not corrupt, honest 廉價(lián jià) 廉价 low price
Lián ㄌㄧㄢˊ	簾	帘	用布，竹，塑膠等 做成遮蓋門窗的東 西 curtain 用布，竹，塑胶等 做成遮盖门窗的东 西	窗簾(chuāng lián) 窗帘 window curtain 竹簾(zhú lián) 竹帘 bamboo curtain
Liǎn ㄌㄧㄢˇ	臉	脸	面孔，從額頭到下 巴部分 face 面孔，从额头到下 巴部分	丟臉(diū liǎn) 丢脸 shameless 臉孔(liǎn kǒng) 脸孔 face
Liàn ㄌㄧㄢˋ	斂	敛	聚集 collect	收斂(shōu liàn) 收敛 collect (taxes)
Liàn ㄌㄧㄢˋ	戀	恋	男女相愛 courtship 男女相爱	戀愛(liàn ài) 恋爱 courtship 留戀(liú liàn) 留恋 reluctant to part with
Liàn ㄌㄧㄢˋ	練	练	有經驗，反覆學習 experienced, practice 有经验，反复学习	練習(liàn xí) 练习 exercise 老練(lǎo liàn) 老练 experienced

Liàn ㄌ 一ˋ ㄢ	殮	殓	把死人裝進棺材裏 lay a dead body into a coffin 把死人装进棺材里	入殮(rù liàn) 入殓 lay a body in coffin
Liàn ㄌ 一ˋ ㄢ	煉	炼	用火燒製 refine by heating 用火烧製	鍛煉(duàn liàn) 锻炼 do exercise 提煉(tí liàn) 提炼 refine, extract
Liáng ㄌ 一ˊ ㄤ	良	良	好 good	優良(yōu liáng) 优良 good 良藥(liáng yào) 良药 good medicine
Liáng ㄌ 一ˊ ㄤ	涼	凉	溫度低，灰心 cool, disappointed 温度低，灰心	涼快(liáng kuài) 凉快 cool 心涼(xīn liáng) 心凉 chilled to the heart
Liáng ㄌ 一ˊ ㄤ	樑	樑	房架，支持屋頂的柱子 beam of a building 房架，支持屋顶的柱子	屋樑(wū liáng) 屋樑 beam of a building 橋樑(qiáo liáng) 桥樑 bridge
Liáng ㄌ 一ˊ ㄤ	梁	梁	姓 Chinese surname	高梁(gāo liáng) sorghum
Liáng Liàng ㄌ ㄌ 一ˊ 一ˋ ㄤ ㄤ	量	量	計算東西的大小，多少 measure 计算东西的大小，多少	商量(shāng liáng) consult 量杯(liáng bēi) measuring cup 測量(cè liáng) 测量 measure
Liáng ㄌ 一ˊ ㄤ	糧	粮	食物 grain, food	糧食(liáng shí) 粮食 grain, food 糧票(liáng piào) 粮票 food coupon
Liǎng ㄌ 一ˇ ㄤ	兩	两	"二"的意思，表示不定的數目 two, a rough number "二"的意思，表示不定的数目	兩個人(liǎng gè rén) 两个人 two persons 過兩天(guò liǎng tiān) 过两天 a few days later
Liǎng Liǎ ㄌ ㄌ 一ˇ 一ˇ ㄤ	倆	俩	手段，花招，兩人 means, tricks, both persons 手段，花招，两人	伎倆(jì liǎng) 伎俩 tricks 他倆兒(tā liǎ ér) 他俩儿 both of them

Liàng ㄌ ㄧ ㄤ丶	亮	亮	有光線 bright 有光线	明亮(míng liàng) bright 月亮 (yuè liàng) moon 天亮了(tiān liàng le) the day is breaking 亮晶晶(liàng jīng jīng) sparkling, glittering
Liàng ㄌ ㄧ ㄤ丶	諒	谅	寬恕 forgive 宽恕	原諒(yuán liàng) 原谅 forgive 諒解(liàng jiě) 谅解 understanding
Liàng Liáng ㄌ ㄌ ㄧ ㄧ ㄤ丶 ㄤˊ	量	量	可容納的限度， 數量 capacity, quantity 可容纳的限度， 数量	重量(zhòng liàng) weight 分量(fèn liàng) importance 量子(liàng zǐ) quantum 力量(lì liàng) 力量strength
Liàng ㄌ ㄧ ㄤ丶	輛	辆	計算車數目的單位 classifier for motor vehicles 计算车数目的单位	一輛車(yí liàng chē) 一辆车 a car 車輛(chē liàng) 车辆 motor vehicles
Liāo ㄌ ㄧ ㄠ	撩	撩	掀起來 lift up	撩窗簾(liāo chuāng lián) 撩窗帘 lift up the curtain
Liáo ㄌ ㄧ ㄠˊ	遼	辽	遠而闊 far and spacious 远而阔	遼闊(liáo kuò) 辽阔 vast
Liáo ㄌ ㄧ ㄠˊ	聊	聊	閒談，興趣 chat, interest 闲谈，兴趣	聊天(liáo tiān) chat 無聊(wú liáo) 无聊 bored
Liáo Liào ㄌ ㄌ ㄧ ㄧ ㄠˊ ㄠˋ	廖	廖	稀疏，姓氏 very few, Chinese surname	廖廖無幾(liáo liáo wú jǐ) 廖廖无几 very few

Liáo ㄌㄧㄠˊ	療	疗	醫治，治病 give medical treatment 医治，治病	治療(zhì liáo)治疗 medical treatment 療養(liáo yǎng)疗养 recuperate
Liáo ㄌㄧㄠˊ	僚	僚	官員的助理或下屬 assistant to government official 官员的助理或下属	同僚(tóng liáo) colleague 官僚(guān liáo) bureaucrat
Liáo ㄌㄧㄠˊ	燎	燎	延燒 spreading fire 延烧	燎原(liáo yuán) set a prairie on fire
Liǎo Liào ㄌㄧㄠˇ ㄌㄧㄠˋ	瞭	了	遠遠地望 look at from a distance 远远地望	瞭解(liǎo jiě) 了解 understand 瞭望(liào wàng) 了望 look from afar
Liào ㄌㄧㄠˋ	料	料	估計，可供製造其他東西的物質 estimate, material 估计，可供制造其他东西的物质	不料(bú liào) unexpectedly 原料(yuán liào) raw material
Liào ㄌㄧㄠˋ	廖	廖	姓 Chinese surname	
Liè ㄌㄧㄝˋ	列	列	行列，擺出來 row, exhibit 行列，摆出来	排列(pái liè) put into order 陳列(chén liè)陈列 exhibit
Liè ㄌㄧㄝˋ	烈	烈	氣勢大，為國家主義而犧牲者 strong, martyr 气势大，为国家主义而牺牲者	猛烈(měng liè) violent 烈士(liè shì) martyr
Liè ㄌㄧㄝˋ	裂	裂	破開 ripped open 破开	分裂(fēn liè) split 裂痕(liè hén) crack

Liè ㄌ 一 ㄝ ˋ	劣	劣	不好，品質差 bad, of poor quality 不好，品质差	劣勢(liè shì) 劣势 disadvantage 惡劣(è liè) 恶劣 bad
Liè ㄌ 一 ㄝ ˋ	獵	猎	捕捉動物 hunting 捕捉动物	打獵(dǎ liè) 打猎 hunting 獵人(liè rén) 猎人 hunter
Lín ㄌ 一 ㄣ ˊ	鄰	邻	住在靠近的人家 neighbor	鄰居(lín jū) 邻居 neighbor 睦鄰(mù lín) 睦邻 good-neighborliness
Lín ㄌ 一 ㄣ ˊ	林	林	許多樹木 woods 许多树木	森林(sēn lín) forest
Lín ㄌ 一 ㄣ ˊ	臨	临	來到，遭遇，靠近 arrive, encounter, approach 来到，遭遇，靠近	臨近(lín jìn) 临近 draw near 面臨(miàn lín) 面临 be faced with
Lín ㄌ 一 ㄣ ˊ	麟	麟	麒麟 unicorn	麟兒(lín ér) 麟儿 baby boy
Lín ㄌ 一 ㄣ ˊ	霖	霖	連下兩三天不停的 雨，恩澤 continuous rain, kindness 连下两三天不停的 雨，恩泽	甘霖(gān lín) timely rain for the crop
Lín ㄌ 一 ㄣ ˊ	鱗	鳞	魚類或動物表面的 硬小薄片，瑣碎的 事fish scale, titbit 鱼类或动物表面的 硬小薄片，琐碎的 事	魚鱗(yú lín) 鱼鳞 fish scale 鱗爪(lín zhuǎ) 鳞爪 tidbits

Lín ㄌ ㄧ ㄣ	淋	淋	一種性病，水從上澆下 gonorrhoea, take a shower 一种性病，水从上浇下	淋病(lín bìng) gonorrhoea 淋浴(lín yù) take a shower
Lǐn ㄌ ㄧˇ ㄣ	凜	凛	寒冷 cold	凜冽(lìn liè) 凛冽 bone-chilling (wind) 威風凜凜(wēi fēng lǐn lǐn) 威风凛凛 look majestic
Lìn ㄌ ㄧˋ ㄣ	吝	吝	該用的捨不得用，過分愛惜 stingy, be overly attached to 该用的捨不得用，过份爱惜	吝嗇(lìn sè) stingy 吝惜(lìn xí) be overly attached to
Lìn ㄌ ㄧˋ ㄣ	賃	赁	租用 rent	租賃(zū lìn) 租赁 rental
Líng ㄌ ㄧˊ ㄥ	玲	玲	靈巧的樣子 clever 灵巧的样子	玲瓏(líng lóng) 玲珑 good and clever
Líng ㄌ ㄧˊ ㄥ	零	零	"0"，代表"無"；小部分 zero, piecemeal "0"，代表"无"；小部分	歸零(guī líng) 归零 reset to zero 零售(líng shòu) retail
Líng ㄌ ㄧˊ ㄥ	齡	龄	年紀 age 年纪	年齡(nián líng) 年龄 age 高齡(gāo líng) 高龄 old-aged
Líng ㄌ ㄧˊ ㄥ	鈴	铃	鐘狀金屬，中間有個小鐵丸，搖動時會發聲 bell 钟狀金属，中间有个小铁丸，摇动时会发声	電鈴(diàn líng) 电铃 doorbell 打鈴了(dǎ líng le) 打铃了 the bell rings

Líng 为 一 ㄥ	聆	聆	聽 listen 听	聆聽(líng tīng) 聆听 listen respectfully 聆教(líng jiào) 聆教 listen to your advice
Líng 为 一 ㄥ	陵	陵	大土山，帝王的墳墓 mound, mausoleum 大土山，帝王的坟墓	丘陵(qiū líng) mountains 陵墓(líng mù) mausoleum
Líng 为 一 ㄥ	凌	凌	欺負，高出 bully, high over 欺负，高出	凌辱(líng rǔ) insult 凌空(líng kōng) soar into the sky
Líng 为 一 ㄥ	靈	灵	敏捷，乖巧，有效的 agile, clever, efficacious	靈敏(líng mǐn) 灵敏 clever 靈魂(líng hún) 灵魂 soul
Lǐng 为 一 ㄥ	領	领	衣服頸項部分，統率，本事 collar, command, ability 衣服颈项部分，统率，本事	領子(lǐng zi) 领子 collar 領袖(lǐng xiù) 领袖 leader
Lǐng 为 一 ㄥ	嶺	岭	山脈 mountain ridge 山脉	山嶺(shān lǐng) 山岭 mountain ridge 分水嶺(fēn shuǐ lǐng) 分水岭watershed
Lìng 为 一 ㄥ	另	另	額外，別的，分開 extra, another, separate 额外，别的，分开	另外(lìng wài) in addition 另函(lìng hán) a separate letter
Lìng 为 一 ㄥ	令	令	上級對下級的指示，規定 an order, regulations 上级对下级的指示，规定	命令(mìng lìng) an order 法令(fǎ lìng) decree
Liū 为 一 又	溜	溜	滑行，趁人不注意時走開 slide, sneak out 滑行，趁人不注意时走开	溜冰(liū bīng) ice skating 溜走(liū zǒu) sneak out

Liú ㄌ ㄧ ˊ ㄡ	留	留	停在某處，接受，注意 stop over, receive, heed 停在某处，接受，注意	停留(tíng liú) stop over 留心(liú xīn) pay attention to
Liú ㄌ ㄧ ˊ ㄡ	瘤	瘤	皮膚或身體內部長出不正常的肉塊 tumor 皮肤或身体内部长出不正常的肉块	腫瘤(zhǒng liú)腫瘤 tumor 肉瘤(ròu liú) sarcoma
Liú ㄌ ㄧ ˊ ㄡ	流	流	液體流動，漂泊不定 flow, drift 液体流动，漂泊不定	河流(hé liú) rivers 流浪(liú làng) roam about
Liú ㄌ ㄧ ˊ ㄡ	劉	刘	姓 Chinese surname	
Liú ㄌ ㄧ ˊ ㄡ	榴	榴	落葉灌木，開紅花，果實球狀，內有很多種子 pomegranate 落叶灌木，开红花，果实球状，内有很多种子	石榴(shí liú) pomegranate 手榴彈(shǒu liú dàn) 手榴弹 hand grenade
Liú ㄌ ㄧ ˊ ㄡ	琉	琉	一種用鈉和鋁的硅酸化合物燒成的釉料品 glaze 一种用钠和铝的硅酸化合物烧成的釉料品	琉璃(liú lí) glaze
Liú ㄌ ㄧ ˊ ㄡ	瀏	浏	很快地閱覽 browse 很快地阅览	瀏覽(liú lǎn) 浏览 browse 瀏陽(liú yáng) 浏阳 Liuyang County in Hunan
Liǔ ㄌ ㄧ ˇ ㄡ	柳	柳	柳樹，落葉喬木，枝細長下垂 willow 柳树，落叶乔木，枝细长下垂	柳樹(liǔ shù) 柳树 willow tree

Liù ㄌ一ㄡˋ	六	六	數目字，在四和五之間 six 数目字，在四和五之间	六神無主(liù shén wú zhǔ) 六神无主 perplexed 六親不認(liù qīn bú rèn) 六亲不认 disown all relatives
Liù liu ㄌ一ㄡˋ ㄌㄡ˙	遛	遛	散步閒逛，緩慢行走 stroll 散步闲逛，缓慢行走	遛達(liù da) 遛达 take a walk 遛狗(liù gǒu) walk a dog
Liù ㄌ一ㄡˋ	餾	馏	第二次重蒸食物 reheat (food)	蒸餾水(zhēng liù shuǐ) 蒸馏水 distilled water
Lóng ㄌㄨㄥˊ	龍	龙	古代傳說中的神奇動物，比喻君主 dragon, refer to the emperor 古代传说中的神奇动物，比喻君主	恐龍(kǒng lóng) 恐龙 dinosaur 龍卷風(lóng juǎn fēng) 龙卷风 tornado
Lóng ㄌㄨㄥˊ	聾	聋	聽不見聲音 deaf 听不见声音	耳聾(ěr lóng) 耳聋 deaf 聾啞人(lóng yǎ rén) 聋哑人 a deaf-mute
Lóng ㄌㄨㄥˊ	隆	隆	凸出，盛大，興盛 bulging, grand, prosperous 凸出，盛大，兴盛	隆重(lóng zhòng) ceremonious 興隆(xīng lóng) 兴隆 prosperous
Lóng ㄌㄨㄥˊ	瓏	珑	精巧 exquisite	玲瓏(líng lóng) 玲珑 good and clever
Lóng ㄌㄨㄥˊ	朧	胧	模糊不清 blurry, hazy	朦朧(méng lóng) 朦胧 hazy

Lóng ㄌㄨㄥˊ	籠	笼	竹子或金屬制成用來養鳥，蟲子或動物的器具 cage 竹子或金属制成用来养鸟，虫子或动物的器具	鳥籠(niǎo lóng) 鸟笼 birdcage
Lǒng ㄌㄨㄥˇ	壟	垄	操縱市場 monopolize 操纵市场	壟斷(lǒng duàn) 垄断 monopolize
Lǒng ㄌㄨㄥˇ	攏	拢	總共，靠近 total, approach 总共，靠近	攏總(lǒng zǒng) 拢总 totaling 拉攏(lā lǒng) 拉拢 win over
Lóu ㄌㄡˊ	婁	娄	姓 Chinese surname	
Lóu ㄌㄡˊ	樓	楼	兩層以上的房子 storied building 两层以上的房子	樓房(lóu fáng) 楼房 storied building 辦公大樓(bàn gōng dà lóu) 办公大楼office building
Lóu ㄌㄡˊ	髏	髅	無毛無皮的屍骨 skeleton 无毛无皮的尸骨	骷髏(kū lóu) 骷髅 skeleton
Lǒu ㄌㄡˇ	摟	搂	擁抱 embrace 拥抱	摟抱(lǒu bào) 搂抱 embrace
Lǒu ㄌㄡˇ	簍	篓	用竹子、柳條等編成的容器 basket 用竹子、柳条等编成的容器	簍子(lǒu zi) 篓子 basket

Lòu ㄌ ㄡˋ	陋	陋	難看的，狹小 ugly, narrow 难看的，狭小	醜陋(chǒu lòu)醜陋 ugly 簡陋(jiǎn lòu)简陋 crude (house)
Lòu ㄌ ㄡˋ	漏	漏	遺落，灌液體到小 口器具裏的用具 omit, funnel 遗落，灌液体到小 口器具里的用具	遺漏(yí lòu)遗漏 omit 漏斗(lòu dǒu) funnel
Lòu Lù ㄌ ㄌ ㄡˋ ㄨˋ	露	露	顯出來 show, expose 显出来	顯露(xiǎn lòu)显露 expose 露面(lòu miàn) appear in public 朝露(zhāo lù)morning dew
Lú ㄌ ㄨˊ	盧	卢	姓 Chinese surname	
Lú ㄌ ㄨˊ	蘆	芦	多年生草本植物， 生長在淺水裏 reed 多年生草本植物， 生长在浅水里	蘆葦(lú wěi)芦苇 reed
Lú ㄌ ㄨˊ	爐	炉	取暖做飯的器具 stove, fireplace 取暖做饭的器具	電爐(diàn lú)电炉 electric range 火爐(huǒ lú)火炉 fireplace
Lú ㄌ ㄨˊ	廬	庐	簡陋的房舍 crude house 简陋的房舍	茅廬(máo lú)茅庐 cottage
Lú ㄌ ㄨˊ	顱	颅	腦蓋，頭骨，頭的 通稱 head 脑盖，头骨，头的 通称	頭顱(tóu lú)头颅 head
Lǔ ㄌ ㄨˇ	滷	卤	用鹽，醬油等制作 食品；濃稠的湯汁 stewed foods, gravy 用盐，酱油等制作 食品；浓稠的汤汁	滷肉(lǔ ròu)卤肉 meat stewed in soy sauce

Pinyin	Traditional	Simplified	Meaning	Examples
Lǔ ㄌㄨˇ	虜	虏	打仗時抓到的敵人 captive 打仗时抓到的敌人	俘虜(fú lǔ) 俘虏 captive
Lǔ ㄌㄨˇ	魯	鲁	愚鈍，冒失 stupid, rash 愚钝，冒失	粗魯(cū lǔ) 粗鲁 rude 魯莽(lǔ mǎng) 鲁莽 rash
Lǔ ㄌㄨˇ	擄	掳	奪取 seize 夺取	擄獲(lǔ huò) 掳获 seize 擄掠(lǔ lüè) 掳掠 plunder
Lù ㄌㄨˋ	陸	陆	高出水面的土地 ，接連不斷 land, continuous 高出水面的土地 ，接连不断	陸地(lù dì) 陆地 land 陸續(lù xù) 陆续 one after another
Lù ㄌㄨˋ	路	路	來往通行的地方， 思想行動的方向 road, line of thought and action 来往通行的地方， 思想行动的方向	公路(gōng lù) highway 路線(lù xiàn) 路线 route
Lù ㄌㄨˋ	鹿	鹿	哺乳動物，腿細長 ，性溫順，雄的頭 上長角 deer 哺乳动物，腿细长 ，性温顺，雄的头 上长角	公鹿(gōng lù) stag 鹿角(lù jiǎo) antler
Lù ㄌㄨˋ	鷺	鹭	水鳥名，有大翼， 頸和腿很長，羽毛 純白 egret 水鸟名，有大翼， 颈和腿很长，羽毛 纯白	白鷺(bái lù) 白鹭 egret
Lù Lòu ㄌㄨˋ ㄌ ㄡˋ	露	露	夜間遇冷凝結的小 水珠，屋外的 dew, outdoors 夜间遇冷凝结的小 水珠，屋外的	露水(lù shuǐ) dew 露天(lù tiān) outdoors
Lù ㄌㄨˋ	錄	录	記載，任用 to record, appoint 记载，任用	記錄(jì lù) 记录 record 錄用(lù yòng) 录用 hire

Lù ㄌㄨˋ	碌	碌	平庸，繁忙 mundane, busy	庸碌(yōng lù) 庸碌 mundane 忙碌(máng lù) 忙碌 busy
Lù ㄌㄨˋ	祿	禄	官吏的俸給 government official's salary 官吏的俸给	俸祿(fèng lù) 俸禄 an official's salary 福祿(fú lù) 福禄 fortune
Lù ㄌㄨˋ	麓	麓	山脚下 at the foot of a mountain 山脚下	山麓(shān lù) foot of a mountain
Lù ㄌㄨˋ	賂	赂	用財物買通人 bribe 用财物买通人	賄賂(huì lù) 贿赂 bribe
Lǘ ㄌㄩˊ	驢	驴	一種家畜，像馬， 能馱東西，供人騎 donkey 一种家畜，像马， 能驮东西，供人骑	驢子(lǘ zi) 驴子 donkey
Lǚ ㄌㄩˇ	閭	闾	巷口的門 gate to an alley 巷口的门	閭里(lǚ lǐ) 闾里 place for town gathering 一閭(yì lǚ) 一闾 25 families
Lǚ ㄌㄩˇ	櫚	榈	常綠喬木，木質堅 硬，可做床 palm 常绿乔木，木质坚 硬，可做床	棕櫚樹(zōng lǚ shù) 棕榈树palm tree
Lǚ ㄌㄩˇ	呂	吕	姓 Chinese surname	
Lǚ ㄌㄩˇ	屢	屡	一再，接連著，經 常 repeatedly, frequently 一再，接连著，经 常	屢次(lǚ cì) 屡次 time and again 屢試(lǚ shì) 屡试 try repeatedly

Lǚ ㄌ ㄩˇ	履	履	鞋子，實行，走過，經歷 shoe, carry out, experience 鞋子，实行，走过，经历	履行合約(lǚ xíng hé yuē) 履行合约 honor a contract 履歷(lǚ lì) 履历 resume
Lǚ ㄌ ㄩˇ	鋁	铝	一種金屬元素，符號Al, 銀白色，質料輕 aluminum 一种金属元素，符号Al, 银白色，质料轻	鋁鍋(lǚ guō) 铝锅 aluminum pan
Lǚ ㄌ ㄩˇ	縷	缕	線 thread 线	一縷炊煙(yì lǚ chuī yān) 一缕炊烟 a column of chimney smoke
Lǚ ㄌ ㄩˇ	褸	褛	衣服破爛 tattered clothes 衣服破烂	襤褸(lán lǚ) 褴褛 tattered clothes
Lǚ ㄌ ㄩˇ	侶	侶	同伴 companion	伴侶(bàn lǚ) 伴侶 companion 情侶(qíng lǚ) 情侶 lovers
Lǚ ㄌ ㄩˇ	旅	旅	出外遊玩，軍隊 travel, troops 出外遊玩，军队	旅行(lǚ xíng) travel 勁旅(jìng lǚ) 劲旅 powerful army
Lǜ ㄌ ㄩˋ	律	律	約束，法令，沒有例外 restrict, law, without exception 约束，法令，没有例外	自律(zì lǜ) self-discipline 律師(lǜ shī) 律师 lawyer
Lǜ ㄌ ㄩˋ	慮	虑	思考，顧忌 consider, misgivings 思考，顾忌	考慮(kǎo lǜ) 考虑 consider 顧慮(gù lǜ) 顾虑 have misgivings

Lǜ ㄌㄩˋ	濾	滤	除去雜質 filter 除去杂质	過濾(guò lǜ) 过滤 filter out 濾嘴(lǜ zuǐ) 滤嘴 filter tip (of cigarette)
Lǜ ㄌㄩˋ	率	率	兩個數的比例相比 rate 两个数的比例相比	增長率(zēng zhǎng lǜ) 增长率 growth rate 利率(lì lǜ) interest rate
Lǜ ㄌㄩˋ	綠	绿	草樹的顏色 green 草树的颜色	綠葉(lǜ yè) 绿叶 green leave 紅綠燈(hóng lǜ dēng) 红绿灯 traffic light
Lǜ ㄌㄩˋ	氯	氯	一種化學元素，符 號Cl，黃綠色有毒 氣體 chlorine 一种化学元素，符 号Cl，黄绿色有毒 气体	氯化(lǜ huà) 氯化 chlorinate
Luán ㄌㄨㄢˊ	巒	峦	小而尖並相互连接 的山 mountain range 小而尖並相互连接 的山	山巒起伏(shān luán qǐ fú) 山峦起伏a range of high and low mountains
Luán ㄌㄨㄢˊ	孿	孪	雙生，一胎生兩個 twin 双生，一胎生两个	攣生子(luán shēng zi) 孪生子 twins
Luán ㄌㄨㄢˊ	攣	挛	意識無法控制的抖 動 cramp 意识无法控制的抖 动	痙攣(jīng luán) 痉挛 cramp
Luǎn ㄌㄨㄢˇ	卵	卵	蛋 egg	排卵(pái luǎn) ovulate 卵巢(luǎn cháo) ovary
Luàn ㄌㄨㄢˋ	亂	乱	沒有秩序，武裝叛 變，隨便 chaos, uprising, unscrupulous 没有秩序，武装叛 变，随便	混亂(hùn luàn) 混乱 in confusion 叛亂(pàn luàn) 叛乱 armed uprising

Lüè ㄌㄩㄝˋ	掠	掠	搶奪，輕輕拂過 plunder, skim over 抢夺，轻轻拂过	掠奪(lüè duó) 掠夺 plunder 掠過(lüè guò) 掠过 skim over
Lüè ㄌㄩㄝˋ	略	略	大概，不詳細，沒注意 sketchy, lose sight of 大概，不详细，没注意	大略(dà lüè) general outline 忽略(hū lüè) lose sight of
Lún ㄌㄨㄣˊ	淪	沦	沈沒，陷落 subside, downfall 沈没，陷落	淪落(lún luò) 沦落 degrade into 淪陷(lún xiàn) 沦陷 fall into enemy's hand
Lún ㄌㄨㄣˊ	倫	伦	長幼尊卑行爲準則 ethics 长幼尊卑行为准则	人倫(rén lún) 人伦 human relationships 倫理(lún lǐ) 伦理 ethics 天倫(tiān lún) 天伦 family love
Lún ㄌㄨㄣˊ	綸	纶	青色的絲線 green silk thread 青色的丝线	經綸(jīng lún) 经纶 arrange silk thread, manage state affairs
Lún ㄌㄨㄣˊ	輪	轮	裝在機器上能旋轉讓機器起動的圓形物體 wheel 装在机器上能旋转让机器起动的圆形物体	車輪(chē lún) 车轮 car wheel 輪胎(lún tāi) 轮胎 tire
Lùn ㄌㄨㄣˋ	論	论	評議，分析 comment, analyze 评议，分析	評論(píng lùn) 评论 commentary 理論(lǐ lùn) 理论 theory
Luō ㄌㄨㄛ	囉	罗	多話 talkative 多话	囉嗦(luō suō) 罗嗦 nagging 哈囉(hā luō) 哈罗 hello
Luō ㄌㄨㄛˊ	羅	罗	捕捉鳥類的網，延攬人才 net for catching birds, recruit 捕捉鸟类的网，延揽人才	羅網(luó wǎng) 罗网 net, trap 羅致(luó zhì) 罗致 recruit talented people

Luó ㄌㄨˊㄛ	螺	螺	有旋紋硬殼的軟體動物 snail 有旋纹硬壳的软体动物	螺絲(luó sī) 螺丝 screw 螺旋槳(luó xuán jiǎng) 螺旋桨 propeller
Luó ㄌㄨˊㄛ	騾	骡	驢和馬交配而生出的家畜，可以馱東西 mule 驴和马交配而生出的家畜，可以驮东西	騾子(luó zi) 骡子 mule
Luó ㄌㄨˊㄛ	邏	逻	巡查 patrol	巡邏(xún luó) 巡逻 patrol
Luó ㄌㄨˊㄛ	鑼	锣	一種盤狀樂器，用槌子敲打可發聲 gong 一种盘状乐器，用槌子敲打可发声	鑼鼓(luó gǔ) 锣鼓 gong and drum
Luǒ ㄌㄨˇㄛ	裸	裸	沒有穿衣服 nude	裸體(luǒ tǐ) 裸体 naked 裸照(luǒ zhào) nude photo
Luò ㄌㄨˋㄛ	洛	洛	洛水 name of river	洛杉磯(luò shān jī) 洛杉矶 Los Angeles
Luò ㄌㄨˋㄛ	落	落	往下降，掉下來，衰敗，不得意 drop, fall, decline 往下降，掉下来，衰败，不得意	落後(luò hòu) 落后 lag behind 沒落(mò luò) 没落 decline (of a nation)
Luò ㄌㄨˋㄛ	絡	络	網狀組織 web-like structure 网状组织	聯絡(lián luò) 联络 connection 網絡(wǎng luò) 网络 network
Luò ㄌㄨˋㄛ	駱	骆	體高家畜，背有一或二個肉峰，能在沙漠中馱貨物 camel 体高家畜，背有一或二个肉峰，能在沙漠中驮货物	駱駝(luò tuó) 骆驼 camel

M

mā ㄇㄚ	媽	妈	母親，對女姓長輩的稱呼 mother, woman of mother's age 母亲，对女姓长辈的称呼	媽媽(mā ma) 妈妈 mother 姨媽(yí mā) 姨妈 auntie (mom's sister) 姑媽(gū mā) 姑妈 auntie (dad's sister)
má ㄇㄚˊ	麻	麻	草本植物，皮可紡織，種子可榨油；肢體無力 hemp, numb 草本植物，皮可纺织，种子可榨油；肢体无力	麻繩(má shéng) 麻绳 rope made of hemp 麻醉(má zuì) anesthesia
má ㄇㄚˊ	痲	痲	一種病名 name of a disease 一种病名	痲瘋(má fēng) 麻风 leprosy 痲臉(má liǎn) 麻脸 pockmarked face
ma ㄇㄚ˙	嗎	吗	表示疑問 used to indicate a question 表示疑问	你好嗎(nǐ hǎo ma) 你好吗 how are you?
má ㄇㄚˊ	蟆	蟆	蛙的一種，暗褐色，背有黑點，生長在水邊 toad 蛙的一种，暗褐色，背有黑点，生长在水边	蛤蟆(há ma) toad
mǎ ㄇㄚˇ	馬	马	哺乳類動物，頸和四肢長，可供騎坐或載貨 horse 哺乳类动物，颈和四肢长，可供骑坐或载货	騎馬(qí mǎ) 骑马 ride a horse 馬上(mǎ shàng) 马上 immediately
mǎ ㄇㄚˇ	碼	码	英制長度單位，一碼是三呎 yard 英制长度单位，一码是三呎	號碼(hào mǎ) 号码 number 碼頭(mǎ tóu) 码头 dock
mǎ ㄇㄚˇ	瑪	玛	瑪瑙：晶瑩光澤的礦物，可做飾物和珠寶 agate 瑪瑙：晶莹光泽的矿物，可做饰物和珠宝	瑪瑙(mǎ nǎo) 玛瑙 agate
mà ㄇㄚˋ	罵	骂	用難聽的話責備人 scold 用难听的话责备人	責罵(zé mà) 责骂 scold 咒罵(zhòu mà) 咒骂 curse

mǎ ㄇㄚˇ	螞	蚂	螞蟻(黑色或褐色 群居小昆蟲) ants 蚂蚁 (黑色或褐色 群居小昆虫)	螞蟻(mǎ yǐ) 蚂蚁 ants
mái mán ㄇㄞˊ ㄇ ㄢˊ ㄐ	埋	埋	把東西放進挖好的 地洞裏,用土蓋上 bury 把东西放进挖好的 地洞里,用土盖上	埋葬(mái zàng) bury 埋怨(mán yuàn) grumble
mái ㄇㄞˊ	霾	霾	大風吹得塵土飛揚 的樣子 dust storm 大风吹得尘土飞扬 的样子	陰霾(yīn mái) 阴霾 gloom
mǎi ㄇㄞˇ	買	买	用錢購物,出代價 讓他人爲自己工作 或利用 buy, buy over 用钱购物,出代价 让他人为自己工作 或利用	買賣(mǎi mài) 买卖 business 收買(shōu mǎi) 收买 buy over
mài ㄇㄞˋ	賣	卖	出售,背地裏害人 ,盡力 sell, betray, do one's best 出售,背地里害人 ,尽力	賣主(mài zhǔ) 卖主 seller 出賣(chū mài) 出卖 betray
mài ㄇㄞˋ	麥	麦	草本植物,中國北 方的重要農產物 wheat and barley 草本植物,中国北 方的重要农产物	麥片(mài piàn) 麦片 oatmeal 小麥(xiǎo mài) 小麦 wheat
mài ㄇㄞˋ	脈	脉	動物的血管,植物 葉上的筋,相連貫 的vein, leaf vein, continuous 动物的血管,植物 叶上的筋,相连贯 的	靜脈(jìng mài) 静脉 vein 山脈(shān mài) 山脉 mountain range
mài ㄇㄞˋ	邁	迈	抬腿向前跨過,衰 老,豪放 stride, old, bold and open 抬腿向前跨过,衰 老,豪放	邁進(mài jìn) 迈进 move ahead in strides 年邁(nián mài) 年迈 of advanced age

mán ㄇㄢˊ	蠻	蛮	粗魯，落後 rude, backward 粗鲁，落后	野蠻(yě mán) 野蛮 savage 蠻荒(mán huāng) 蛮荒 barren land
mán ㄇㄢˊ	饅	馒	饅頭：一種麵食 steamed bread 馒头：一种面食	饅頭(mán tóu) 馒头 steamed bread
mán ㄇㄢˊ	瞞	瞒	隱藏實情 cover up truth 隐藏实情	隱瞞(yǐn mán) 隐瞒 to conceal
mǎn ㄇㄢˇ	滿	满	充實，不缺少，到 了一定限度 full, not lacking 充实，不缺少，到 了一定限度	满足(mǎn zú) 满足 satisfied 满一年(mǎn yì nián) 满一年one full year
màn ㄇㄢˋ	鰻	鳗	背部灰黑色，腹部 白色，形狀如蛇的 魚 eel 背部灰黑色，腹部 白色，形状如蛇的 鱼	鰻魚(màn yú) 鳗鱼 eel
màn ㄇㄢˋ	慢	慢	不快，驕傲，懈怠 slow, arrogant, to neglect 不快，骄傲，懈怠	緩慢(huǎn màn) 缓慢 slowly 傲慢(ào màn) arrogant
màn ㄇㄢˋ	漫	漫	放任不拘，水太滿 向外流 freely, overflow 放任不拘，水太满 向外流	漫畫(màn huà) 漫画 cartoon 水漫出來(shuǐ màn chū lái) water overflows
màn ㄇㄢˋ	幔	幔	帳幕，窗簾 screen, curtain 帐幕，窗帘	布幔(bù màn) cloth screen
màn ㄇㄢˋ	曼	曼	柔美，美好 graceful, beautiful	輕歌曼舞(qīng gē màn wǔ) 轻歌曼舞 beautiful songs and dances

màn mán ㄇㄢˋ ㄇㄢˊ	謾	谩	欺騙，輕視 deceive, rude 欺骗，轻视	謾罵(màn mà) 谩骂 shout abuses 欺謾(qī màn) 欺谩 deceive
màn ㄇㄢˋ	蔓	蔓	細長而攀繞他物 的 植物莖；延伸 vines, spread 细长而攀绕他物 的 植物茎；延伸	蔓生植物(màn shēng zhí wù) 蔓生植物 creeping plant 蔓延(màn yán)蔓延 spread out
máng ㄇㄤˊ	忙	忙	事情繁多，急迫， 趕緊 busy, pressing, hastily 事情繁多，急迫， 赶紧	忙碌(máng lù) 忙碌 busy 急忙(jí máng) hastily
máng ㄇㄤˊ	盲	盲	瞎子，對事物沒有 分辨的能力 blind, lacking in discerning power 瞎子，对事物没有 分辨的能力	文盲(wén máng) illiterate 盲從(máng cóng) 盲从 follow blindly
máng ㄇㄤˊ	氓	氓	不務正業的無賴 hooligan 不务正业的无赖	流氓(liú máng) hooligan
máng ㄇㄤˊ	芒	芒	光線四射；草本植 物，葉細長而尖 radiant, sharp-pointed grass 光线四射；草本植 物，叶细长而尖	光芒(guāng máng) radiating ray 芒果(máng guǒ) mango
máng ㄇㄤˊ	茫	茫	無頭緒，面積大看 不到邊 confounded, boundless 无头绪，面积大看 不到边	茫然(máng rán) confounded 茫茫大海(máng máng dà hǎi) boundless ocean
mǎng ㄇㄤˇ	莽	莽	叢生的草，不細心 ，行動粗野 rank weeds, reckless 丛生的草，不细心 ，行动粗野	草莽(cǎo mǎng) rank weeds 莽撞(mǎng zhuàng) reckless

mǎng ㄇ ㄤˇ	蟒	蟒	一種無毒的大蛇， 背有班紋，捕食小 動物 python 一种无毒的大蛇， 背有班纹，捕食小 动物	蟒蛇(mǎng shé) python
māo ㄇ ㄠ	貓	猫	一種家畜，腳有尖 爪，會捉老鼠 cat 一种家畜，脚有尖 爪，会捉老鼠	熊貓(xióng māo) 熊猫 giant panda 貓頭鷹(māo tóu yīng) 猫头鹰 owl
máo ㄇ ㄠˊ	矛	矛	古代兵器，長柄， 頂端有尖頭 spear, lance 古代兵器，长柄， 顶端有尖头	矛盾(máo dùn) contradiction
máo ㄇ ㄠˊ	毛	毛	動物表皮上長出的 細柔絲狀物；十分 錢 hair, 10 cents 动物表皮上长出的 细柔丝状物；十分 钱	羊毛(yáng máo) wool 一毛(yì máo) 10 cents
máo ㄇ ㄠˊ	錨	锚	一種鐵鉤子，拋入 水中可使船隻停止 不前 anchor 一种铁钩子，抛入 水中可使船隻停止 不前	拋錨(pāo máo) 抛锚 drop the anchor
máo ㄇ ㄠˊ	茅	茅	多年生草本植物， 可用來蓋屋，做繩 子 couch grass 多年生草本植物， 可用来盖屋，做绳 子	茅屋(máo wū) thatched cottage 茅廁(máo cè) 茅厕 lavatory
máo ㄇ ㄠˊ	髦	髦	幼兒垂在前額到眉 毛的短髮 a child's bangs 幼儿垂在前额到眉 毛的短髮	時髦(shí máo) 时髦 fashionable
mǎo ㄇ ㄠˇ	卯	卯	早晨五點到七點 the time between 5 and 7 in the morning 早晨五点到七点	卯時(mǎo shí) 卯时 between 5 and 7 a.m.
mào ㄇ ㄠˋ	茂	茂	草木旺盛 luxuriant	茂盛(mào shèng) luxuriant 茂密(mào mì) dense (forest)

mào ㄇㄠˋ	貿	贸	財物交換，草率地 trading, carelessly 财物交换，草率地	貿易(mào yì)贸易 trading 貿然(mào rán)贸然 carelessly
mào ㄇㄠˋ	冒	冒	勇往直前，充假， 侵犯 forge ahead, feign, offend 勇往直前，充假， 侵犯	冒險(mào xiǎn)冒险 take risk 冒犯(mào fàn) offend
mào ㄇㄠˋ	帽	帽	戴在頭上用來遮太 陽或裝飾的用具 hat, cap 戴在头上用来遮太 阳或装饰的用具	帽子(mào zi) hat, cap 帽檐(mào yán) brim of a hat
mào ㄇㄠˋ	貌	貌	面孔，外表 face, appearance	面貌(miàn mào) the looks 禮貌(lǐ mào)礼貌 courtesy
me ㄇㄜ˙	麼	么	表示疑問的語尾助 詞 used in question 表示疑问的语尾助 词	怎麼(zěn me)怎么 how 什麼(shén me)什么 what
méi mò ㄇㄟˊ ㄇㄛˋ	沒	沒	無，不 no, without 无，不	沒有(méi yǒu) without 沒用(méi yòng) useless 淹沒(yān mò) submerge 沒收(mò shōu) confiscate
méi ㄇㄟˊ	媒	媒	撮合男女結婚 match-making 撮合男女结婚	媒人(méi rén) matchmaker 媒介(méi jiè) media
méi ㄇㄟˊ	玫	玫	玫瑰：落葉灌木， 枝上有刺，花香 rose 玫瑰：落叶灌木， 枝上有刺，花香	玫瑰(méi guī) rose
méi ㄇㄟˊ	枚	枚	小東西一個叫一枚 ，一個一個的 classifier for small objects 小东西一个叫一枚 ，一个一个的	一枚硬幣(yì méi yìng bì) 一枚硬币a coin 不勝枚舉(bú shèng méi jǔ) 不胜枚举countless

méi ㄇㄟˊ	眉	眉	眼睛上面，前額下的毛 eyebrow 眼睛上面，前额下的毛	眉毛(méi máo) eyebrow 眉目(méi mù) leads, clue
méi ㄇㄟˊ	莓	莓	植物名，結紅色小果實 berry 植物名，结红色小果实	草莓(cǎo méi) strawberry
méi ㄇㄟˊ	梅	梅	落葉喬木，五瓣花，果實味酸 plum 落叶乔木，五瓣花，果实味酸	梅花(méi huā) plum blossom 梅毒(méi dú) syphilis
méi ㄇㄟˊ	煤	煤	蘊藏在地底下的黑色礦物，重要的燃料 coal 蕴藏在地底下的黑色矿物，重要的燃料	煤炭(méi tàn) coal 煤礦(méi kuàng) 煤矿 coal mine
méi ㄇㄟˊ	霉	霉	衣服或食物受潮後長的細絲 mildew 衣服或食物受潮后长的细丝	發霉(fā méi) 发霉 turn mouldy 霉爛(méi làn) 霉烂 turn moudly and rot
měi ㄇㄟˇ	每	每	指整體中的任何一個 every 指整体中的任何一个	每天(měi tiān) everyday 每人(měi rén) everybody
měi ㄇㄟˇ	美	美	好，漂亮，稱讚 good, pretty, praise 好，漂亮，称赞	美德(měi dé) virtue 贊美(zàn měi) 赞美 praise
mèi ㄇㄟˋ	妹	妹	同父母比自己年紀小的女性，比自己小的同輩女性 younger sister 同父母比自己年纪小的女性，比自己小的同辈女性	妹妹(mèi mei) younger sister 妹夫(mèi fū) younger sister's husband
mèi ㄇㄟˋ	寐	寐	睡覺 sleep 睡觉	假寐(jiǎ mèi) take a nap 夢寐以求(mèng mèi yǐ qiú) 梦寐以求 yearning for

mèi ㄇㄟˋ	昧	昧	隱藏，不明，愚笨 hidden, dubious, foolish 隐藏，不明，愚笨	曖昧(ài mèi) 暧昧 dubious 愚昧(yú mèi) foolish
mèi ㄇㄟˋ	媚	媚	説好話討人喜歡，令人愛慕的 flatter, charming 说好话讨人喜欢，令人爱慕的	諂媚(chǎn mèi) 谄媚 curry favor with 嫵媚(wǔ mèi) 妩媚 charming
mén ㄇㄣˊ	門	门	建築物的出入口 door 建筑物的出入口	鐵門(tiě mén) 铁门 iron gate 門徒(mén tú) 门徒 disciple
mén ㄇㄣˊ	們	们	人的複數 plural for person 人的复数	我們(wǒ mén) 我们 we 他們(tā mén) 他们 they 你們(nǐ mén) 你们 you (plural form)
mèn ㄇㄣˋ	悶	闷	心煩，不透氣 sullen, muggy 心烦，不透气	煩悶(fán mèn) 烦闷 sulky 悶熱(mèn rè) 闷热 muggy
mèn ㄇㄣˋ	燜	焖	蓋上鍋蓋用小火煮熟 braise 盖上锅盖用小火煮熟	燜飯(mèn fàn) 焖饭 slowly cooked rice
méng ㄇㄥˊ	矇	矇	形象不清楚，天色昏暗 fuzzy, gloomy	矇矓(méng lóng) fuzzy
méng ㄇㄥˊ	朦	朦	不清楚，模糊 not clear, blur	朦朧(méng lóng) 朦胧 blurry
méng ㄇㄥˊ	檬	檬	檸檬：常綠灌木，果實橢圓，果肉黃色，味酸 lemon 柠檬：常绿灌木，果实椭圆，果肉黄色，味酸	檸檬(níng méng) 柠檬 lemon
méng ㄇㄥˊ	萌	萌	發芽，開始發生 to bud, begin to occur 发芽，开始发生	萌芽(méng yá) 萌芽 to bud 萌生(méng shēng) 萌生 begin to occur

méng ㄇㄥˊ	盟	盟	團體與團體，或國 與國之間宣誓締約 alliance 团体与团体，或国 与国之间宣誓缔约	聯盟(lián méng) 联盟 alliance 盟國(méng guó) 盟国 allied nation
méng měng ㄇㄥˊ ㄇㄥˇ	蒙	蒙	欺騙，受到 deceive, receive	蒙蔽(méng bì) 蒙蔽 deceive 蒙受(méng shòu) 蒙受 be subjected to 蒙古(měng gǔ) 蒙古 Mongolia
měng ㄇㄥˇ	猛	猛	健勇，快速，兇惡 vigorous, swift ferocious 健勇，快速，兇惡	猛烈(měng liè) violent 兇猛(xiōng měng) ferocious
měng ㄇㄥˇ	蜢	蜢	蚱蜢：昆蟲名，能 飛會跳 grasshopper 蚱蜢：昆虫名，能 飞会跳	蚱蜢(zhà měng) grasshopper
měng ㄇㄥˇ	錳	锰	金屬元素，Mn， 灰白色，可製合金 manganese 金属元素，Mn， 灰白色，可製合金	錳礦(měng kuàng) 锰矿 manganese ore
mèng ㄇㄥˋ	孟	孟	姓氏 Chinese surname	孟子(mèng zi) Mencius
mèng ㄇㄥˋ	夢	梦	人在睡眠中的幻想 ，空想，不實際 dream, fantasy unrealistic 人在睡眠中的幻想 ，空想，不实际	惡夢(è mèng) 恶梦 nightmare 白日夢(bái rì mèng) 白日梦 daydream 夢遊(mèng yóu)梦遊 sleepwalk
mī ㄇㄧ	咪	咪	形容貓叫，笑的樣 子 mew, smilingly 形容猫叫，笑的样 子	貓咪(māo mī) 猫咪 cat 笑咪咪(xiào mī mī) smilingly

mī ㄇ ㄧ	瞇	眯	眼睛微閉 half-closed eyes 眼睛微闭	瞇著眼睛(mī zhe yǎn jīng) 眯著眼睛with eyes half closed
mí ㄇ ㄧˊ	糜	糜	非常爛，不振作 very rotton, dispirited 非常烂，不振作	糜爛(mí làn) 糜烂 rotten 萎糜(wěi mí) dispirited
mí ㄇ ㄧˊ	迷	迷	不能分辨和判斷， 特別愛好某事物 confused, be obsessed with 不能分辨和判断， 特别爱好某事物	迷信(mí xìn) superstition 沈迷(chén mí) be indulged in 迷人(mí rén) charming 迷路(mí lù) lose one's way 迷宮(mí gōng) maze
mí ㄇ ㄧˊ	彌	弥	填補，滿，充滿 fill up, full of 填补，满，充满	彌補(mí bǔ) 弥补 make up for 彌漫(mí màn) 弥漫 be permeate with
mí ㄇ ㄧˊ	謎	谜	隱含某種意義供人 猜測的詞語，還無 法解釋的事物 riddle, mystery 隐含某种意义供人 猜测的词语，还无 法解释的事物	謎語(mí yǔ) 谜语 a riddle 謎底(mí dǐ) 谜底 answer to a riddle
mǐ ㄇ ㄧˇ	米	米	稻的果實，去殼的 果實 rice 稻的果实，去壳的 果实	稻米(dào mǐ) paddy rice 花生米(huā shēng mǐ) shelled peanut
mǐ ㄇ ㄧˇ	靡	靡	通"糜"，爛，奢 侈，不振作 rotton, dispirited 通"糜"，烂，奢 侈，不振作	靡靡之音(mǐ mǐ zhī yīn) demoralizing music
mì ㄇ ㄧˋ	覓	觅	找，尋求 find, seek 找，寻求	尋覓(xún mì) 寻觅 in search of 覓食(mì shí) 觅食 look for food

mì ㄇㄧˋ	泌	泌	從身體中排出某種液體 secrete 从身体中排出某种液体	分泌(fēn mì) secrete 泌尿科(mì niào kē) urological department
mì ㄇㄧˋ	秘	秘	不讓別人知道，不公開的，稀有的 secret, rare 不让别人知道，不公开的，稀有的	秘書(mì shū) 秘书 secretary 便秘(biàn mì) constipation
mì ㄇㄧˋ	蜜	蜜	蜜蜂採花所釀成的甜汁，甜美 honey, sweet 蜜蜂採花所酿成的甜汁，甜美	蜜蜂(mì fēng) bee 甜蜜(tián mì) sweet
mì ㄇㄧˋ	密	密	"疏"的相反，感情好，不公開 dense, intimate, confidential "疏"的相反，感情好，不公開	親密(qīn mì) 亲密 intimate 保密(bǎo mì) maintain confidentiality
mián ㄇㄧㄢˊ	綿	绵	單薄，延長不斷，親密難分 weak, continuous, intimate 单薄，延长不断，亲密难分	綿薄(mián bó) 绵薄 humble efforts 連綿不斷(lián mián bú duàn) 连绵不断continuous
mián ㄇㄧㄢˊ	棉	棉	一種植物，絮可紡紗織布或做被褥 cotton 一种植物，絮可纺纱织布或做被褥	棉花(mián huā) 棉花 cotton 棉布(mián bù) cotton cloth
mián ㄇㄧㄢˊ	眠	眠	睡覺 sleep 睡觉	睡眠(shuì mián) sleep 安眠藥(ān mián yào) 安眠药 sleeping pill 長眠不起(cháng mián bù qǐ) 长眠不起 rest in peace
miǎn ㄇㄧㄢˇ	免	免	去掉，不被某種事物所牽連 remove, avoid 去掉，不被某种事物所牵连	免費(miǎn fèi) 免费 free of charge 避免(bì miǎn) avoid

miǎn ㄇㄧㄢˇ	緬	缅	遙遠 far away 遥远	緬懷 (miǎn huái) 缅怀 cherish the memory of
miǎn ㄇㄧㄢˇ	娩	娩	婦女生小孩 give birth to 妇女生小孩	分娩(fēn miǎn) childbirth
miǎn ㄇㄧㄢˇ	勉	勉	盡力去做，剛剛夠 do one's best, just enough 尽力去做，刚刚够	勉勵(miǎn lì) 勉励 encourage 勉強(miǎn qián) 勉强 just enough
miǎn ㄇㄧㄢˇ	冕	冕	皇冠 crown	加冕(jiā miǎn) coronate 衛冕(wèi miǎn) 卫冕 defend the title
miàn ㄇㄧㄢˋ	麵	面	用麥或其他穀物磨 成的粉；用麵粉製 成長條食品 flour, noodle 用麦或其他谷物磨 成的粉；用面粉製 成长条食品	麵粉(miàn fěn) 面粉 flour 麵條(miàn tiáo) 面条 noodle 麵包(miàn bāo) 面包 bread
miàn ㄇㄧㄢˋ	面	面	臉，直接接洽 face, personally 脸，直接接洽	面孔(miàn kǒng) face 面談(miàn tán) 面谈 discuss in person
miáo ㄇㄧㄠˊ	苗	苗	初生的動物或植物 ，子孫 seedling, progeny 初生的动物或植物 ，子孙	樹苗(shù miáo) 树苗 sapling 苗裔(miáo yì) progeny 魚苗(yú miáo) fish fry
miáo ㄇㄧㄠˊ	描	描	照樣畫或寫 trace 照样画或写	描寫(miáo xiě) 描写 depict 掃描(sǎo miáo) 扫描 scan

miǎo ㄇㄧㄠˇ	瞄	瞄	注視，把視力集中在一點上 take aim 注視，把视力集中在一点上	瞄準(miáo zhǔn) 瞄准 take aim
miǎo ㄇㄧㄠˇ	秒	秒	時間單位，一分鐘的60分之一 one second 时间单位，一分钟的60分之一	分秒必爭(fēn miǎo bì zhēng) 分秒必争 race against time
miǎo ㄇㄧㄠˇ	渺	渺	微小，看不清楚 tiny, indistinct	渺小(miǎo xiǎo) tiny 渺茫(miǎo máng) uncertain
miǎo ㄇㄧㄠˇ	藐	藐	輕視，小 despise, tiny 轻视，小	藐視(miǎo shì) 藐视 treat with contempt 藐小(miǎo xiǎo) 藐小 tiny
miào ㄇㄧㄠˋ	繆	缪	通謬，錯誤；姓氏 same as "謬", error, Chinese surname 通谬，错误；姓氏	
miào ㄇㄧㄠˋ	妙	妙	美，神奇 beautiful, wonderful	奇妙(qí miào) marvelous 妙計(miào jì) wonderful plan
miào ㄇㄧㄠˋ	廟	庙	供奉神佛或歷史名人的地方 temple, shrine 供奉神佛或历史名人的地方	寺廟(sì miào) 寺庙 temples 廟會(miào huì) 庙会 marketplace at a temple
miè ㄇㄧㄝˋ	滅	灭	使消亡，熄火 destroy, extinguish	消滅(xiāo miè) 消灭 destroy 滅火器(miè huǒ qì) 灭火器 fire extinguisher
miè ㄇㄧㄝˋ	蔑	蔑	輕視，毀壞別人的名譽 despise, slander 轻视，毁坏别人的名誉	蔑視(miè shì) 蔑视 despise 誣蔑(wū miè) 诬蔑 slander

mín ㄇㄧㄣˊ	民	民	百姓，人的通稱 the people 百姓，人的通称	人民(rén mín) the people 公民(gōng mín) citizen
mǐn ㄇㄧㄣˇ	皿	皿	裝食物的容器 container 装食物的容器	器皿(qì mǐn) container
mǐn ㄇㄧㄣˇ	泯	泯	消亡，消失 vanish	難以泯滅(nán yǐ mǐn miè) 难以泯灭 indelible 童心未泯(tóng xīn wèi mǐn) mind is still young
mǐn ㄇㄧㄣˇ	抿	抿	輕輕合起來 slightly closed 轻轻合起来	抿嘴一笑(mǐn zuǐ yí xiào) smile with tightly closed lips
mǐn ㄇㄧㄣˇ	閩	闽	福建省 Fujian Province	閩南(mǐn nán) 闽南 southern Fujian
mǐn ㄇㄧㄣˇ	憫	悯	哀憐 pity 哀怜	悲天憫人(bēi tiān mǐn rén) 悲天悯人 compassion for mankind
mǐn ㄇㄧㄣˇ	敏	敏	靈活，反應迅速 agile, responsive 灵活，反应迅速	敏捷(mǐn jié) agile 靈敏(líng mǐn) 灵敏 keen and sensitive
míng ㄇㄧㄥˊ	名	名	人或事物的稱呼， 有聲望的 name, reputable 人或事物的称呼， 有声望的	名字(míng zì) name 名醫(míng yī) 名医 reputable physician
míng ㄇㄧㄥˊ	明	明	"暗"的相反，亮 ，清楚 bright, clear "暗"的相反，亮 ，清楚	明亮(míng liàng) bright 明天(míng tiān) tomorrow

míng ㄇㄧㄥˊ	鳴	鸣	鳥獸或昆蟲叫聲，表達 sounds of animals, birds, insects; express 鸟兽或昆虫叫声，表达	雞鳴(jī míng) 鸡鸣 cock crow 鳴謝(míng xiè) 鸣谢 express gratitude
míng ㄇㄧㄥˊ	冥	冥	昏暗不明，關於死人的，愚昧， dark, related to the dead, stupid 昏暗不明，关于死人的，愚昧，	冥府(míng fǔ) the underworld 冥頑(míng wán) 冥顽 stupid
míng ㄇㄧㄥˊ	瞑	瞑	閉眼 with eyes closed 闭眼	瞑目(míng mù) with eyes closed
míng ㄇㄧㄥˊ	茗	茗	茶樹的嫩芽 budding tea leaves 茶树的嫩芽	品茗(pǐn míng) 品茗 sip tea 茗具(míng jù) 茗具 tea set
míng ㄇㄧㄥˊ	銘	铭	刻在器物上敘述生平事跡的文字 engraved words 刻在器物上叙述生平事迹的文字	座右銘(zuò yòu míng) 座右铭 a motto 銘記(míng jì) 铭记 be carved in memory
mǐng ㄇㄧㄥˇ	酩	酩	酩酊：爛醉的意思 thoroughly drunk 酩酊：烂醉的意思	酩酊大醉(mǐng dǐng dà zuì) thoroughly drunk
mìng ㄇㄧㄥˋ	命	命	動植物的生活能力；下令 life, order 动植物的生活能力；下令	生命(shēng mìng) life 受命(shòu mìng) receive an order
miù ㄇㄧㄡˋ	謬	谬	錯誤的，不合理的 false, unreasonable 错误的，不合理的	荒謬(huāng miù) 荒谬 absurd 謬誤(miù wù) 谬误 falsehood

mō ㄇㄛ	摸	摸	輕輕用手觸碰，試探，探求 touch, explore 轻轻用手触碰，试探，探求	觸摸(chù mō) 触摸 to touch 摸索(mō suǒ) 摸索 explore
mó ㄇㄛˊ	摹	摹	仿效，通"模"字 imitate, same as "模"	摹仿(mó fǎng) 摹仿 imitate 摹擬(mó nǐ) 摹拟 simulate
mó ㄇㄛˊ	膜	膜	動植物體內像薄皮的組織 membrane 动植物体内像薄皮的组织	薄膜(bó mó) 薄膜 membrane 耳膜(ěr mó) 耳膜 ear drum
mó ㄇㄛˊ	磨	磨	摩擦，消耗 rub, wear away	磨練(mó liàn) 磨练 temper oneself 折磨(zhé mó) torment
mó ㄇㄛˊ	魔	魔	惡鬼，不平常的 devil, unusual 恶鬼，不平常的	魔鬼(mó guǐ) devil 魔術(mó shù) 魔术 magic
mó ㄇㄛˊ	摩	摩	相擦而過，觀察後吸收優點 rub, improve by observing 相擦而过，观察后吸收优点	摩擦(mó cā) rub, friction 觀摩(guān mó) 观摩 improve by observing
mǒ ㄇㄛˇ	抹	抹	涂，擦，除去 apply on surface, rub, erase	抹粉(mǒ fěn) to apply powder 抹殺(mǒ shā) 抹杀 write off
mò ㄇㄛˋ	末	末	最後的，物體的尾端 final, end 最后的，物体的尾端	末了(mò liǎo) finally 末路(mò lù) dead end
mò ㄇㄛˋ	莫	莫	不要，沒有 do not, without	莫要(mò yào) 莫要 do not want 莫須有(mò xū yǒu) 莫须有 groundless (charge)
mò ㄇㄛˋ	陌	陌	田間的小路，生疏 footpath in paddy fields, unfamiliar 田间的小路，生疏	阡陌(qiān mò) crisscross footpaths 陌生(mò shēng) unfamiliar

mò ㄇㄛˋ	脈	脉	用眼神表示愛意 look with affection 用眼神表示爱意	脈脈含情(mò mò hán qíng) 脉脉含情 look with affection
mò ㄇㄛˋ	寞	寞	寂靜，冷清 quiet, lonely 寂静，冷清	寂寞(jí mò) 寂寞 lonely 落寞(luò mò) 落寞 feel left out
mò ㄇㄛˋ	漠	漠	大片由沙所覆蓋的 乾燥地帶，不關心 desert, indifferent 大片由沙所覆盖的 干燥地带，不关心	沙漠(shā mò) 沙漠 desert 冷漠(lěng mò) 冷漠 indifferent
mò ㄇㄛˋ	墨	墨	寫字繪畫用的黑色 顏料 blank ink 写字绘画用的黑色 颜料	墨水(mò shuǐ) ink 墨綠色(mò lǜ sè) 墨绿色 dark green color
mò ㄇㄛˋ	默	默	不出聲，不說話 silently, speechless 不出声，不说话	默認(mò rèn) 默认 acquiesce 默寫(mò xiě) 默写 dictation
móu ㄇㄡˊ	牟	牟	取得 obtain	牟利(móu lì) gain profit 牟取(móu qǔ) obtain
móu ㄇㄡˊ	眸	眸	眼睛，眼珠 eye, pupil	明眸皓齒(míng móu hào chǐ) 明眸皓齿 bright eyes and white teeth
móu ㄇㄡˊ	謀	谋	計劃，尋求，商議 plan, seek, discuss 计划，寻求，商议	計謀(jì móu) 计谋 scheme 謀求(móu qiú) 谋求 seek
mǒu ㄇㄡˇ	某	某	不指明的人或事物 的代稱 a certain person or thing 不指明的人或事物 的代称	某人(mǒu rén) a certain person 某日(mǒu rì) a certain day

mǔ ㄇㄨˇ	畝	亩	中國土地面積單位 mu, Chinese unit of measure for area, about 1/6 acre 中国土地面积单位	英畝(yīng mǔ) acre 畝產(mǔ chǎn) 亩产 per-mu yield
mǔ ㄇㄨˇ	拇	拇	手腳的大指頭 thumb, big toe 手脚的大指头	拇指(mǔ zhǐ) thumb 拇趾(mǔ zhǐ) big toe
mǔ ㄇㄨˇ	姆	姆	負責照顧兒童的女工 nanny 负责照顾儿童的女工	保姆(bǎo mǔ) nanny
mǔ ㄇㄨˇ	母	母	媽媽，女姓長輩，雌性的 mother, motherly female, female 妈妈，女姓长辈，雌性的	母親(mǔ qīn) 母亲 mother 母雞(mǔ jī) 母鸡 hen
mǔ ㄇㄨˇ	牡	牡	雄性的動物 male 雄性的动物	牡牛(mǔ niú) ox 牡蠣(mǔ lì) 牡蛎 oyster
mù ㄇㄨˋ	木	木	樹類的通稱，感覺不靈敏 tree, numb 树类的通称，感觉不灵敏	木材(mù cái) lumber 麻木(má mù) numbness 木瓜(mù guā) papaya
mù ㄇㄨˋ	牧	牧	放養牛羊豬 herd animals 放养牛羊猪	牧羊(mù yáng) tend sheep 牧師(mù shī) 牧师 pastor
mù ㄇㄨˋ	沐	沐	洗頭髮 wash hair 洗头发	沐浴(mù yù) take a bath

mù ㄇㄨˋ	目	目	眼睛，類別，看 eye, category 眼睛，类别，看	目前(mù qián) at present 目錄(mù lù) 目录 catalog 目標(mù biāo) 目标 goal 一目了然(yí mù liǎo rán) easily understood
mù ㄇㄨˋ	幕	幕	帷帳，話劇或歌劇 的一段落 screen, an act of a play 帷帐，话剧或歌剧 的一段落	落幕(luò mù) 落幕 curtain falls 第四幕(dì sì mù) 第四幕 Act 4 內幕(nèi mù) 内幕 inside story
mù ㄇㄨˋ	暮	暮	傍晚，精神不振 sunset, languid	朝朝暮暮(zhāo zhāo mù mù) 朝朝暮暮 day and night 暮氣沈沈(mù qì chén chén) 暮气沈沈 languid
mù ㄇㄨˋ	慕	慕	敬仰 admire	羨慕(xiàn mù) 羡慕 admire 仰慕(yǎng mù) 仰慕 respect and admire
mù ㄇㄨˋ	墓	墓	埋葬死人的地方 cemetery	墳墓(fén mù) 坟墓 cemetery 墓碑(mù bēi) 墓碑 tombstone
mù ㄇㄨˋ	募	募	徵求 solicit 征求	募捐(mù juān) 募捐 raise fund 招募(zhāo mù) 招募 hire, recruit
mù ㄇㄨˋ	睦	睦	和好，親近 harmony, closeness 和好，亲近	和睦(hé mù) in harmony 睦鄰(mù líng) 睦邻 good-neighborliness
mù ㄇㄨˋ	穆	穆	姓氏，恭敬，溫和 Chinese surname, reverence, gentle 姓氏，恭敬，温和	肅穆(sù mù) 肃穆 solemn and revered 穆斯林(mù sī lín) Moslem

N				
ná ㄋㄚˊ	拿	拿	用手抓取 take, hold	拿獲(ná huò) 拿获 arrest 拿手(ná shǒu) expertise
nǎ ㄋㄚˇ	哪	哪	什麼 what 什么	哪裏(nǎ lǐ) 哪里 where? 哪些(nǎ xiē) what kind of ...?
nà nuó ㄋㄚˋ ㄋㄨㄛˊ	娜	娜	翻譯外國人名時用 used in transliterating a foreign name 翻译外国人名时用	安娜(ān nà) Anna
nà ㄋㄚˋ	納	纳	付出 pay	納稅(nà shuì) 纳税 pay taxes 出納(chū nà) 出纳 cashier
nà ㄋㄚˋ	那	那	"這"的相反 that "这"的相反	那裏(nà lǐ) 那里 there 那些(nà xiē) those
nà ㄋㄚˋ	吶	吶	大聲喊叫 yell 大声喊叫	吶喊(nà hǎn) yelling
nǎi ㄋㄞˇ	乃	乃	是，你的 verb to be, your	乃是(nǎi shì) is (was, are, were) 乃兄(nǎi xiōng) your brother
nǎi ㄋㄞˇ	奶	奶	乳房，乳汁，祖母 breast, milk, grandma	奶粉(nǎi fěn) milk powder 奶奶(nǎi nai) grandma
nài ㄋㄞˋ	奈	奈	如何，怎樣處理 how, how to deal with 如何，怎样处理	無奈(wú nài) 无奈 helpless 奈何(nài hé) deal with somebody

nài ㄋㄞ、	耐	耐	不厭倦，忍得住 patient, tolerate 不厌倦，忍得住	忍耐(rěn nài) tolerate 耐心(nài xīn) patience
nán ㄋㄢˊ	男	男	"女"的對稱，兒 子的代稱 man, son "女"的对称，儿 子的代称	男人(nán rén) man 長男(zhǎng nán) 长男 eldest son
nán ㄋㄢˊ	南	南	方向，"北"的相 反 south 方向，"北"的相 反	南極(nán jí) 南极 South Pole 指南針(zhǐ nán zhēn) 指南针 compass
nán nàn ㄋㄢˊㄋㄢ、	難	难	不容易，不大可能 ，不好 hard, not likely, not good	艱難(jiān nán) 艰难 difficult 難看(nán kàn) 难看 unsightly
nàn nán ㄋㄢ、ㄋㄢˊ	難	难	不幸的遭遇 mishap	災難(zāi nàn)灾难disaster 難民(nàn mín) 难民refugee 非難(fēi nàn) 非难reproach
náo ㄋㄠˊ	撓	挠	擾亂，屈服 disturb, surrender 扰乱，屈服	阻撓(zǔ náo) 阻挠 obstruct 不屈不撓(bù qū bù náo) 不屈不挠unyielding
nǎo ㄋㄠˇ	腦	脑	人和動物主管感覺 意識的器官brain 人和动物主管感觉 意识的器官	頭腦(tóu nǎo) 头脑 brain 電腦(diàn nǎo) 电脑 computer
nǎo ㄋㄠˇ	惱	恼	生氣，煩悶 angry, vexed 生气，烦闷	惱恨(nǎo hèn) 恼恨 resent 苦惱(kǔ nǎo) 苦恼 upset
nǎo ㄋㄠˇ	瑙	瑙	瑪瑙：礦物名，可 做飾物或珠寶agate 玛瑙：矿物名，可 做饰物或珠宝	瑪瑙(mǎ nǎo) 玛瑙 agate
nào ㄋㄠ、	鬧	闹	不安靜，發生災害 或疾病 noisy, outbreak 不安静， 发生灾害或疾病	熱鬧(rè nào) 热闹 bustling 鬧水災(nào shuǐ zāi) 闹水灾 flood-stricken
ne ㄋㄜ・	呢	呢	表疑問的助詞 interrogative particle at end of sentence 表疑问的助词	怎麼辦呢？(zěn me bàn ne) 怎么办呢？ What shall we do?

něi ㄋㄟˇ	餒	馁	沒有勇氣 disheartened 沒有勇气	氣餒(qì něi) 气馁 disheartened
nèi ㄋㄟˋ	內	内	"外"的相反,裏 面 inside "外"的相反,里 面	內衣(nèi yī) underwear 內行(nèi háng) expert
nèn ㄋㄣˋ	嫩	嫩	初生而嬌弱,缺乏 經驗 young and tender, inexperienced 初生而娇弱,缺乏 经验	嫩芽(nèn yá) young bud 很嫩(hěn nèn) quite inexperienced
néng ㄋㄥˊ	能	能	本事,會,應該 ability, can, should 本事,会,应该	能力(néng lì) ability 可能(kě néng) possible
ní ㄋㄧˊ	尼	尼	佛家修道的女子 Buddhist nun	尼姑(ní gū) Buddhist nun 仲尼(zhòng ní) Confucius
ní ㄋㄧˊ	呢	呢	低小的聲音 soft voice 低小的声音	呢喃(ní nán) twitter
ní ㄋㄧˊ	倪	倪	姓氏,頭緒 Chinese surname, clue 姓氏,头绪	端倪(duān ní) clue, leads
ní ㄋㄧˊ	霓	霓	彩虹的紫色外圍 purplish outer arc of a rainbow	霓虹燈(ní hóng dēng) 霓虹灯 neon light
ní ㄋㄧˊ	泥	泥	土和水的混合物, 類似這樣的東西 mud, paste 土和水的混合物, 类似这样的东西	水泥(shuǐ ní) cement 蒜泥(suàn ní) mashed garlic
ní ㄋㄧˊ	妮	妮	小女孩,少女 little girl, maiden	小妮子(xiǎo ní zi) little girl

nǐ ㄋ 一ˇ	你	你	稱呼男性對方 you (to male) 称呼男性对方	你是(nǐ shì) you are... 你要(nǐ yào) you want...
nǐ ㄋ 一ˇ	妳	妳	稱呼女性對方 you (to female) 称呼女性对方	妳的(nǐ de) your 妳要去嗎？(nǐ yào qù ma?) 妳要去吗？ Do you want to go?
nǐ ㄋ 一ˇ	擬	拟	打算，模仿，初步設計 plan, simulate, draft 打算，模仿，初步设计	擬訂(nǐ dìng) 拟订 draw up (a plan) 模擬(mó nǐ) 模拟 simulate
nǐ ㄋ 一ˇ	旎	旎	旖旎：美麗風光 scenic 旖旎：美丽风光	旖旎(yǐ nǐ) scenic
nì ㄋ 一ˋ	逆	逆	"順"的相反，方向相反，背叛 go against, betray "顺"的相反，方向相反，背叛	逆流(nì liú) go against the tide 叛逆(pàn nì) betray
nì ㄋ 一ˋ	匿	匿	隱藏，躲避 hide, avoid 隐藏，躲避	藏匿(cáng nì) go into hiding 匿名信(nì míng xìn) anonymous letter
nì ㄋ 一ˋ	膩	腻	油脂，厭煩 oily, fed up with 油脂，厌烦	油膩(yóu nì) 油腻 oily, greasy 吃膩(chī nì) 吃腻 tired of eating
nì ㄋ 一ˋ	溺	溺	沈沒，過分 drown, excessive 沈没，过分	溺斃(nì bì) 溺毙 drowned 溺愛(nì ài) 溺爱 overindulgence
nián ㄋ 一ˊ ㄢ	年	年	365天是一年 a year	年紀(nián jì) 年纪 age 新年(xīn nián) New Year

nián ㄋ 一 ㄢ	黏	粘	具有附著力，使某 物附著在另一物上 sticky, glue onto 具有附著力，使某 物附著在另一物上	黏液(nián yè) 粘液 mucus 黏合(nián hé) 粘合 bond together
niǎn ㄋ 一 ㄢ	捻	捻	用手指搓轉 twist with fingers 用手指搓转	捻繩(niǎn shéng) 捻绳 twisted cord
niǎn ㄋ 一 ㄢ	撵	撵	趕走 chase away 赶走	撵走(niǎn zǒu) 撵走 chase away
niàn ㄋ 一 ㄢ	唸	唸	朗誦，讀 chant, read 朗诵，读	唸經(niàn jīng) 唸经 chant a prayer 唸書(niàn shū) 唸书 study
niàn ㄋ 一 ㄢ	念	念	惦記，想法 remember, idea 惦记，想法	惦念(diàn niàn) remember 念頭(niàn tóu) 念头 idea
niáng ㄋ 一 ㄤ	娘	娘	母親，年輕女子 mother, young girl 母亲，年轻女子	新娘(xīn niáng) bride 姑娘(gū niáng) a girl
niàng ㄋ 一 ㄤ	釀	酿	利用發酵的方法製 造，逐漸演變成 brew, turn into 利用发酵的方法制 造，逐渐演变成	釀酒(niàng jiǔ) 酿酒 brew wine 釀禍(niàng huò) 酿祸 cause a disaster
niǎo ㄋ 一 ㄠ	鳥	鸟	會飛的動物，身上 有羽毛和翅膀 bird 会飞的动物，身上 有羽毛和翅膀	候鳥(hòu niǎo) 候鸟 migrant bird 鳥瞰圖(niǎo kàn tú) 鸟瞰图 bird's-eye view

niǎo ㄋㄧㄠˇ	裊	袅	煙氣繚繞向上 billow 烟气缭绕向上	炊煙裊裊(chuī yān niǎo niǎo) 炊烟袅袅 the billowing chimney smoke
niào ㄋㄧㄠˋ	尿	尿	小便 urine	排尿(pái niào) urinate 尿布(niào bù) diaper
niē ㄋㄧㄝ	捏	捏	用拇指和其他手指夾住，假造 pinch, fabricate 用拇指和其他手指夾住，假造	捏鼻子(niē bí zi) 捏鼻子 hold one's nose 捏造(niē zào) 捏造 fabricate
niè ㄋㄧㄝˋ	孽	孽	惡事 sinful thing 恶事	作孽(zuò niè) 作孽 commit sin 罪孽(zuì niè) 罪孽 crime
nín ㄋㄧㄣˊ	您	您	"你"的尊稱 honorific of "you" "你"的尊称	您府上是(nín fǔ shàng shì) Your native province is ...
níng ㄋㄧㄥˊ	寧	宁	平靜 tranquil 平静	安寧(ān níng) 安宁 peace and quiet 息事寧人(xī shì níng rén) 息事宁人 keep troubles away
níng ㄋㄧㄥˊ	擰	拧	絞 wring 绞	擰毛巾(níng máo jīn) 拧毛巾 wring the towel dry
níng ㄋㄧㄥˊ	嚀	咛	叮嚀：再三囑咐 repeated reminder 叮咛：再三嘱咐	叮嚀(dīng níng) 叮咛 repeated reminder

níng ㄋ 一 ㄥ	凝	凝	液體遇冷變成固體 ，集中 hardening, focus 液体遇冷变成固体 ，集中	凝固(níng gù) harden into solid 凝視(níng shì) 凝视 stare at
niū ㄋ 一 ㄡ	妞	妞	女孩子 girl	胖妞(pàng niū) chubby girl
niú ㄋ 一 ㄡ	牛	牛	家畜，力大能耕田 ，拉車，肉和奶可 食 cattle 家畜，力大能耕田 ，拉车，肉和奶可 食	牛肉(niú ròu) beef 水牛(shuǐ niú) buffalo
niǔ ㄋ 一 ㄡ	扭	扭	轉動，挫傷 twist, sprain 转动，挫伤	扭轉(niǔ zhuǎn) 扭转 turn around 扭到腰(niǔ dào yāo) sprain one's back
niǔ ㄋ 一 ㄡ	忸	忸	忸怩：不好意思， 不大方的樣子 bashful 忸怩：不好意思， 不大方的样子	忸怩(niǔ ní) bashful
niǔ ㄋ 一 ㄡ	紐	纽	可扣合衣服的球狀 物 button 可扣合衣服的球状 物	紐扣(niǔ kòu) 纽扣 button 紐帶(niǔ dài) 纽带 bond, binding force
niù ㄋ 一 ㄡ	拗	拗	不順，固執，反抗 untamed, obstinate, rebellious 不顺，固执，反抗	拗脾氣(niù pí qì) 拗脾气 stubborn 拗不過(niù bú guò) 拗不过 cannot dissuade
nóng ㄋ ㄨ ㄥ	農	农	種田 farming 种田	農業(nóng yè) 农业 agriculture 農民(nóng mín) 农民 peasant

nóng ㄋㄨˊㄥ	濃	浓	"淡"的相反，含某種成份多 dense, thick, concentrated "淡"的相反，含某种成份多	濃煙(nóng yān) 浓烟 thick smoke 興趣濃厚(xìng qù nóng hòu) 兴趣浓厚 have keen interest
nóng ㄋㄨˊㄥ	膿	脓	因發炎而流出的黃白色液體 pus 因发炎而流出的黄白色液体	膿包(nóng bāo) 脓包 pustule, useless man 化膿(huà nóng) 化脓 form or discharge pus
nòng ㄋㄨˋㄥ	弄	弄	用手把玩，做，取得 play with, make, obtain	玩弄(wán nòng) play with 弄清楚(nòng qīng chǔ) make it clear
nú ㄋㄨˊ	奴	奴	供人使喚的人 slave 供人使唤的人	奴隸(nú lì) 奴隶 slave 奴才(nú cái) lackey
nǔ ㄋㄨˇ	努	努	盡力，翹起 exert effort, pout 尽力，翘起	努力(nǔ lì) exert effort 努嘴(nǔ zuǐ) pout one's lips
nù ㄋㄨˋ	怒	怒	生氣，氣憤 angry, indignant 生气，气愤	憤怒(fèn nù) 愤怒 anger 怒吼(nù hǒu) howl
nǚ ㄋㄩˇ	女	女	兩性之一，與"男"相對 female 两性之一，与"男"相对	女兒(nǚ ér) 女儿 daughter 才女(cái nǚ) talented woman
nuǎn ㄋㄨˇㄢ	暖	暖	溫度不冷也不熱 warm 温度不冷也不热	溫暖(wēn nuǎn) warm 暖氣系統(nuǎn qì xì tǒng) 暖气系统heating system

nüè ㄋㄩㄝˋ	虐	虐	殘暴 atrocious 残暴	暴虐(bào nüè) 暴虐 atrocious 虐待(nüè dài) 虐待 abuse
nüè ㄋㄩㄝˋ	瘧	疟	一種由蚊蟲叮咬而 引起的傳染病 malaria 一种由蚊虫叮咬而 引起的传染病	瘧疾(nüè jí) 疟疾 malaria
nuó ㄋㄨㄛˊ	挪	挪	移動，拿 move, take 移动，拿	挪動(nuó dòng) 挪动 move 挪用(nuó yòng) misappropriate (funds)
nuó nà ㄋㄨㄛˊ ㄋㄚˋ	娜	娜	柔美 gentle and pretty	婀娜多姿(ē nuó duō zī) slender and graceful
nuò ㄋㄨㄛˋ	諾	诺	同意，答應 agree, promise 同意，答应	諾言(nuò yán) 诺言 a promise 許諾(xǔ nuò) 许诺 make a promise
nuò ㄋㄨㄛˋ	糯	糯	糯米：一種帶黏性 的稻米 glutinous rice 糯米：一种带黏性 的稻米	糯米(nuò mǐ) glutinous rice
nuò ㄋㄨㄛˋ	懦	懦	軟弱無能 cowardly 软弱无能	懦弱(nuò ruò) cowardly 懦夫(nuò fū) coward

O

ō ㄛ	哦	哦	嘆詞，表示疑問 exclaimation to indicate a question 叹词，表示疑问	哦！是真的嗎？(ō, shì zhēn de ma?) 哦！是真的吗？ Oh, really?
ōu ㄡ	謳	讴	唱歌 sing	謳歌(ōu gē) 讴歌 ode
ōu ㄡ	鷗	鸥	水鳥 gull 水鸟	海鷗(hǎi ōu) 海鸥 sea gull
ōu ㄡ	歐	欧	姓氏 Chinese surname	歐洲(ōu zhōu) 欧洲 Europe 東歐(dōng ōu) 东欧 Eastern Europe
ōu ㄡ	毆	殴	打架 fight	毆打(ōu dǎ) 殴打 fight 毆傷(ōu shāng) 殴伤 beat and injure
ǒu ㄡˇ	偶	偶	用大木或泥土做成 的人像，不常 idol, occasionally	木偶(mù ǒu) idol 偶然(ǒu rán) occasionally
ǒu ㄡˇ	藕	藕	蓮花的莖 lotus root 莲花的茎	蓮藕(lián ǒu) 莲藕 lotus root
ǒu ㄡˇ	嘔	呕	吐 vomit	嘔吐(ǒu tù) 呕吐 vomit 作嘔(zuò ǒu) 作呕 nauseating
òu ㄡˋ	慪	怄	生氣 annoyed 生气	慪氣(òu qì) 怄气 annoyed

pā ㄆㄚ	趴	趴	俯臥 lie on one's stomach 俯卧	趴著睡(pā zhe shuì) 趴著睡 sleep on the stomach 趴在地上(pā zài dì shàng) lie on the ground
pā ㄆㄚ	啪	啪	放炮的響聲 a crackle, a bang 放炮的响声	劈啪響(pī pā xiǎng) 劈啪响 a crackle
pā ㄆㄚ	葩	葩	花，華麗 flower, gorgeous 花，华丽	奇葩(qí pā) phenomenon
pá ㄆㄚˊ	爬	爬	手和腳一起著地走 路 crawl 手和脚一起著地走 路	爬蟲(pá chóng) 爬虫 reptile 爬山(pá shān) mountain climbing
pá ㄆㄚˊ	耙	耙	用來鬆土或掃葉子 的器具 rake 用来松土或扫叶子 的器具	耙子(pá zi) a rake 耙草(pá cǎo) rake the grass
pá ㄆㄚˊ	扒	扒	從別人口袋裏偷取 財物 pick pocket 从别人口袋里偷取 财物	扒手(pá shǒu) pickpocket
pá ㄆㄚˊ	琵	琵	琵琶：長圓形木製 弦樂器 Chinese lute 琵琶：长圆形木制 弦乐器	琵琶(pí pá) Chinese lute
pà ㄆㄚˋ	怕	怕	恐懼，或許 fear, probably 恐惧，或许	害怕(hài pà) fear 恐怕(kǒng pà) probably
pà ㄆㄚˋ	帕	帕	擦手的布 handkerchief	手帕(shǒu pà) handkerchief

pāi ㄆ ㄞ	拍	拍	輕打 pat 轻打	球拍(qiú pāi) racket 拍手(pāi shǒu) clap hands
pái ㄆ ㄞˊ	排	排	編成行列，放出 arrange in rows, discharge 编成行列，放出	排隊(pái duì) 排队 form a line 排除(pái chú) get rid of
pái ㄆ ㄞˊ	徘	徘	徘徊：來回地走 wander about 徘徊：来回地走	徘徊(pái huái) wander about
pái ㄆ ㄞˊ	牌	牌	標誌，娛樂或賭博 用的器具 signboard, playing card 标誌，娱乐或赌博 用的器具	招牌(zhāo pái) signboard 打牌(dǎ pái) play card
pài ㄆ ㄞˋ	派	派	分支系統，指定 faction, assign 分支系统，指定	派別(pài bié) faction 指派(zhǐ pài) assign
pài ㄆ ㄞˋ	湃	湃	澎湃：波浪相衝擊 的聲音 sound of roaring wave 澎湃：波浪相冲击 的声音	澎湃(péng pài) sound of roaring wave
pān ㄆ ㄢ	潘	潘	姓氏 Chinese surname	潘安再世(pān ān zài shì) very handsome face
pān ㄆ ㄢ	攀	攀	抓住東西往上爬， 摘下，拉關係 creep up, pluck 抓住东西往上爬， 摘下，拉关係	攀登(pān dēng) climb up 攀折(pān zhé) pluck
pán ㄆ ㄢˊ	盤	盘	盛放東西的淺器皿 ，檢查 plate, investigate 盛放东西的浅器皿 ，检查	盤子(pán zi) 盘子 plate 盤問(pán wèn) 盘问 interrogate

pán ㄆㄢˊ	磐	磐	大石頭 huge rock 大石头	磐石(pán shí) huge rock
pàn ㄆㄢˋ	判	判	對審理案件做成決定，分辨 to sentence, discern 对审理案件做成决定，分辨	判決(pàn jué) verdict 判斷(pàn duàn) 判断 to pass a judgment
pàn ㄆㄢˋ	畔	畔	田地的分界，邊 boundary of farmland, side 田地的分界，边	河畔(hé pàn) riverside
pàn ㄆㄢˋ	盼	盼	想望，看 yearn for, look	盼望(pàn wàng) earnestly hope for 左顧右盼(zuǎ gù yòu pàn) 左顾右盼look left and right
pàn ㄆㄢˋ	叛	叛	造反，出賣 rebel, betray 造反，出卖	叛亂(pàn luàn) 叛乱 rebellion 叛國(pàn guó) 叛国 treason
pāng ㄆㄤ	乒	乒	開槍，關門或砸東西的聲音 a loud bang 开枪，关门或砸东西的声音	乒乓球(pīng pāng qiú) pingpong ball
pāng ㄆㄤ	滂	滂	水湧出的樣子，雨下得很大 gushing water, downpour 水湧出的样子，雨下得很大	大雨滂沱(dà yǔ pāng tuó) pouring rain
páng ㄆㄤˊ	膀	膀	膀胱：人體內儲存尿液的器官 urinary bladder 膀胱：人体内储存尿液的器官	膀胱(páng guāng) urinary bladder
páng ㄆㄤˊ	彷	彷	彷徨：猶豫不定 vacillating 彷徨：犹豫不定	彷徨(páng huáng) vacillating

páng ㄆ ㄤˊ	旁	旁	邊上，附近 beside, close by 边上，附近	旁邊(páng biān) 旁边 beside 旁觀者(páng guān zhě) 旁观者 spectator
páng ㄆ ㄤˊ	徬	徬	徬徨：遊移不定 wander 徬徨：遊移不定	徬徨(páng huáng) 徬徨 wander
páng ㄆ ㄤˊ	龐	庞	高大，面貌 huge, face	龐大(páng dà) 庞大 huge 面龐(miàn páng) 面庞 the face
pàng ㄆ ㄤˋ	胖	胖	身體肥 fat 身体肥	肥胖(féi pàng) obesity 胖子(pàng zi) fat person
pāo ㄆ ㄠ	拋	抛	扔下，投擲 throw, cast 扔下，投掷	拋棄(pāo qì) 抛弃 discard 拋錨(pāo máo) 抛锚 stalled (car)
páo bào ㄆ ㄠˊ ㄅ ㄠˋ	刨	刨	挖掘，削平表面 dig, to plane a surface	刨地(páo dì) dig the ground 刨木頭(bào mù tóu) 刨木头 to plane wood
páo ㄆ ㄠˊ	咆	咆	怒吼，暴怒叫喊 howl, roar	咆哮(páo xiào) roar
páo ㄆ ㄠˊ	袍	袍	長衣，寬長的外衣 gown, cloak 长衣，宽长的外衣	長袍(cháng páo) 长袍 long gown 戰袍(zhàn páo) 战袍 battle suit
pǎo ㄆ ㄠˇ	跑	跑	快步往前移動 run 快步往前移动	慢跑(màn pǎo) jogging 賽跑(sài pǎo) 赛跑 running race

pào 夂ㄠˋ	砲	炮	軍用火器 artillery 军用火器	大炮(dà pào) artillery 炮彈(pào dàn) 炮弹 cannon ball
pào 夂ㄠˋ	皰	疱	皮膚上長小疙瘩 blister 皮肤上长小疙瘩	面皰(miàn pào) 面疱 acne 水皰(shuǐ pào) 水疱 blister
pào 夂ㄠˋ	泡	泡	浸在水或液體中， 液體含氣鼓起而成 的球狀物 soak, bubble 浸在水或液体中， 液体含气鼓起而成 的球状物	泡水(pào shuǐ) soak in water 泡沫(pào mò) bubble
pēi 夂ㄟ	呸	呸	嘆詞，表示憤怒， 斥責 exclamation to show disdain 叹词，表示愤怒， 斥责	呸！亂説(pēi! luàn shuō) 呸！乱说Pooh! Nonsense
pēi 夂ㄟ	胚	胚	生物體發生的最初 期 embryo 生物体发生的最初 期	胚胎(pēi tāi) embryo 胚芽(pēi yá) sprout
péi 夂ㄟˊ	培	培	訓練教育，照料使 之成長 train, cultivate 训练教育，照料使 之成长	培養(péi yǎng) 培养 cultivate 培訓(péi xùn) 培训 train
péi 夂ㄟˊ	賠	赔	遭受損失，償還 incur losses, pay back 遭受损失，偿还	賠本(péi běn) 赔本 incur losses 賠償(péi cháng) 赔偿 compensate
péi 夂ㄟˊ	陪	陪	在旁邊做伴 accompany 在旁边做伴	陪伴(péi bàn) accompany 陪審員(péi shěn yuán) 陪审员juror
pèi 夂ㄟˋ	珮	佩	古代衣帶上佩帶的 玉飾 jade ornament 古代衣带上佩带的 玉饰	玉珮(yù pèi) 玉佩 jade ornament

pèi ㄆㄟˋ	佩	佩	戴著 wear 戴著	佩帶(pèi dài) 佩带 wear 佩服(pèi fú) admire
pèi ㄆㄟˋ	配	配	兩性結合，調合， 分發 mating, coordinate, distribute 两性结合，调合， 分发	婚配(hūn pèi) marriage 分配(fēn pèi) distribute
pèi ㄆㄟˋ	沛	沛	充足，盛大，辛苦 abundant, distressed	精力充沛(jīng lì chōng pèi) full of energy 顛沛(diān pèi) 颠沛 in distress
pēn ㄆㄣ	噴	喷	很快地射出 spurt	噴水池(pēn shuǐ chí) 喷水池 fountain 噴氣機(pēn qì jī) 喷气机 jet plane
pén ㄆㄣˊ	盆	盆	圓形口大可盛放或 沖洗東西的用具 tub 圆形口大可盛放或 冲洗东西的用具	浴盆(yù pén) bath tub 臨盆(lín pén) 临盆 about to give birth
pēng ㄆㄥ	抨	抨	批評他人錯誤 verbal attack 批评他人错误	抨擊(pēng jí) 抨击 verbally attack
pēng ㄆㄥ	怦	怦	形容心跳 palpitating	怦然心動(pēng rán xīn dòng) 怦然心动palpitate with eagerness
pēng ㄆㄥ	烹	烹	煮 cook	烹調(pēng tiáo) 烹调 cook 烹飪(pēng rèn) 烹饪 art of cooking
péng ㄆㄥˊ	朋	朋	友人，比較 friend, comparison 友人，比较	朋友(péng yǒu) friend 碩大無朋(shuò dà wú péng) 硕大无朋 big beyond compare

péng ㄆㄥˊ	彭	彭	姓氏 Chinese surname	
péng ㄆㄥˊ	篷	篷	遮蓋太陽和風雨的 結構，船帆 awning, sail of a boat 遮盖太阳和风雨的 结构，船帆	帳篷(zhàng péng) 帐篷 tent 敞篷車(chǎng péng chē) 敞篷车a convertible
péng ㄆㄥˊ	蓬	蓬	旺盛，散亂 thriving, dishevelled 旺盛，散乱	蓬勃(péng bó) 蓬勃 thriving 蓬頭散髮(péng tóu sàn fà) 蓬头散发 dishevelled hair
péng ㄆㄥˊ	棚	棚	用竹木搭成的簡單 遮蔽物 shed, shack 用竹木搭成的简单 遮蔽物	草棚(cǎo péng) 草棚 thatched shed 搭棚(dā péng) 搭棚 set up a booth
péng ㄆㄥˊ	鵬	鵬	傳說中的大鳥 legendary big bird 传说中的大鸟	鵬程萬里(péng chéng wàn lǐ) 鹏程万里 used in wishing somebody a brilliant future
péng ㄆㄥˊ	膨	膨	物體加熱體積變大 ，數量增多 expand, increase 物体加热体积变大 ，数量增多	通貨膨脹(tōng huò péng zhàng) 通货膨胀inflation
pěng ㄆㄥˇ	捧	捧	兩手托著，奉承 hold something on open palms, flatter 两手托著，奉承	捧讀(pěng dú) 捧读 be privileged to read 吹捧(chuī péng) extol
pèng ㄆㄥˋ	碰	碰	撞到，遇見 collide with, meet 撞到，遇见	碰撞(pèng zhuàng) collision 碰見(pèng jiàn) 碰见 meet
pī ㄆㄧ	批	批	在公文上寫評語， 大量售貨 write comments, wholesale 在公文上写评语， 大量售货	批評(pī píng) 批评 criticize 批發(pī fā) 批发 wholesale

pī pǐ ㄆ一 ㄆ一ˇ	匹	匹	計算馬的數量 used in counting horses 计算马的数量	一匹馬(yì pī mǎ) 一匹马 a horse 單槍匹馬(dān qiāng pī mǎ) 单枪匹马 single-handedly 匹薩(pī sà) 匹萨 pizza
pī ㄆ一	披	披	覆蓋在肩背上，打開 drape a coat over the shoulders, open 覆盖在肩背上，打开	披肩(pī jiān) cape (outer garment) 披露(pī lù) publicize
pī ㄆ一	劈	劈	用刀、斧等破開，毀壞 chop, damage 用刀、斧等破开，毁坏	劈柴(pī chái) to chop wood 遭雷劈(zāo léi pī) struck by lightning
pī ㄆ一	霹	霹	霹靂：巨大的雷聲 thunderbolt 霹雳：巨大的雷声	霹靂(pī lì) 霹雳 thunderbolt
pí ㄆ一ˊ	皮	皮	動植物表面的一層組織，淘氣 skin, naughty 动植物表面的一层组织，淘气	皮革(pí gé) leather 頑皮(wán pí) 顽皮 naughty
pí ㄆ一ˊ	琵	琵	琵琶：四弦樂器 Chinese lute 琵琶：四弦乐器	琵琶(pí pá) Chinese lute
pí ㄆ一ˊ	啤	啤	啤酒：用大麥釀成的酒 beer 啤酒：用大麦酿成的酒	啤酒(pí jiǔ) beer
pí ㄆ一ˊ	疲	疲	累，倦 exhausted	疲倦(pí juàn) exhausted 疲軟(pí ruǎn) 疲软 sluggish (market)
pí ㄆ一ˊ	枇	枇	枇杷：常綠喬木，開白花，果實長橢圓形，黃色 loquat 枇杷：常绿乔木，开白花，果实长椭圆形，黄色	枇杷(pí pá) loquat

pí ㄆ ㄧˊ	脾	脾	人和動物內臟之一，位於胃的下側 spleen 人和动物内脏之一，位於胃的下側	脾氣(pí qì) 脾气 temper 脾臟(pí zàng) 脾臟 spleen
pǐ pī ㄆㄧˇ ㄆㄧ	匹	匹	計算布帛的單位 used in counting cloth 計算布帛的单位	一匹布(yì pǐ bù) a bolt of cloth 匹配(pǐ pèi) marry 匹夫(pǐ fū) ordinary man
pǐ ㄆㄧˇ	痞	痞	地方無賴，做壞事的人 bum, evildoer 地方无赖，做坏事的人	地痞(dì pǐ) local bum
pǐ ㄆㄧˇ	癖	癖	對事物特別喜好 addiction 对事物特别喜好	癖好(pǐ hào) hobby 潔癖(jié pǐ) 洁癖 obsessed with cleanliness
pǐ ㄆㄧˇ	仳	仳	分離 separated 分离	仳離(pǐ lí) 仳离 divorced
pì ㄆㄧˋ	屁	屁	肛門排出的臭氣 fart 肛门排出的臭气	放屁(fàng pì) fart 屁股(pì gǔ) buttocks
pì ㄆㄧˋ	譬	譬	比方 example	譬如(pì rú) for example 譬喻(pì yù) metaphor
pì ㄆㄧˋ	辟	辟	驅除，迴避，透徹 expel, avoid, thorough 驱除，迴避，透彻	辟邪(pì xié) expel evil 精辟(jīng pì) pithy
pì ㄆㄧˋ	僻	僻	距離市中心較遠地區，性情怪不合群 secluded, a loner 距離市中心較遠地區，性情怪不合群	偏僻(piān pì) out-of-the-way 孤僻(gū pì) a loner
piān biǎn ㄆㄧㄢ ㄅㄧˇ ㄆㄧㄢ ㄅㄧㄢ	扁	扁	體形小的 small 体形小的	扁舟(piān zhōu) small boat

226

piān ㄆ一ㄢ	偏	偏	不正，歪，不在中央 tilt to one side, not centered	偏心(piān xīn) biased toward 偏差(piān chā) deviation
piān ㄆ一ㄢ	篇	篇	頭尾完整的文章，文章的長短 a piece of writing, length of an article 头尾完整的文章，文章的长短	詩篇(shī piān) 诗篇 psalm 篇幅(piān fú) length of an article
piān ㄆ一ㄢ	翩	翩	輕快地飛舞，風流瀟灑 fly swiftly, elegant 轻快地飞舞，风流潇洒	翩翩起舞(piān piān qǐ wǔ) dance gracefully 風度翩翩(fēng dù piān piān) 风度翩翩elegant manners
pián biàn ㄆ一ㄢ ㄅ一ㄢ	便	便	不貴，肚子肥大的樣子 cheap, potbellied 不贵，肚子肥大的样子	便宜(pián yí) cheap 大腹便便(dà fù pián pián) potbellied 糞便(fèn biàn) 粪便 night soil
piàn ㄆ一ㄢ丶	騙	骗	欺蒙 deceive	欺騙(qī piàn) 欺骗 deceive 騙子(piàn zi) 骗子 swindler
piàn ㄆ一ㄢ丶	片	片	平而薄的物體，不全面 a slice, a piece, one-sided 平而薄的物体，不全面	名片(míng piàn) business card 片面(piàn miàn) one-sided, partial 一片葉子(yí piàn yè zi) 一片叶子 a leaf
piāo ㄆ一ㄠ	漂	漂	浮在液體或水面上，流浪 float, wander 浮在液体或水面上，流浪	漂浮(piāo fú) float 漂泊(piāo bó) drift aimlessly
piāo ㄆ一ㄠ	飄	飘	隨風擺動，不穩 flutter, unstable 随风摆动，不稳	飄揚(piāo yáng) 飘扬 flutter 飄雪(piāo xuě) 飘雪 snow falls

227

piāo ㄆ ㄧ ㄠ	剽	剽	搶劫，掠奪 rob, plunder 抢劫，掠夺	剽竊(piāo qiè) 剽窃 plagiarize
piáo ㄆ ㄧ ㄠ	嫖	嫖	招妓女的行爲 visit prostitute 招妓女的行为	嫖妓(piáo jì) visit prostitute 嫖客(piáo kè) whoremaster
piáo ㄆ ㄧ ㄠ	瓢	瓢	舀水或取東西的用 具 ladle 舀水或取东西的用 具	飯瓢(fàn piáo) 饭瓢 rice scoop
piǎo ㄆ ㄧ ㄠ	瞟	瞟	斜眼看 squint	瞟他一眼(piáo tā yì yǎn) take a squint at him
piào ㄆ ㄧ ㄠ	票	票	上面印或寫著價錢 的証件或紙張 ticket 上面印或写著价钱 的証件或纸张	鈔票(chāo piào) 钞票 bank note 火車票(huǒ chē piào) 火车票 train ticket
piào ㄆ ㄧ ㄠ	漂	漂	漂亮：美麗 pretty 漂亮：美丽	漂亮(piào liàng) pretty
piē ㄆ ㄧ ㄝ	撇	撇	丟 discard	撇開(piē kāi) 撇开 put aside 撇棄(piē qì) 撇弃 abandon
piē ㄆ ㄧ ㄝ	瞥	瞥	很快地看一眼 dart at	一瞥(yì piē) a glimpse of

pīn ㄆ一ㄣ	拼	拼	盡力去做，湊合 with all one's might, piece together 尽力去做，凑合	拼命(pīn mìng) with all one's might 拼法(pīn fǎ) spelling
pīn ㄆ一ㄣ	姘	姘	與非配偶發生性關 係 commit adultery 与非配偶发生性关 系	姘婦(pīn fù) 姘妇 adulteress 姘居(pīn jū) cohabit
pín ㄆ一ㄣ	貧	贫	窮，收入少， "富"的相反 poor, low-income 穷，收入少， "富"的相反	貧窮(pín qióng) 贫穷 poverty 貧血(pín xuè) 贫血 anemia
pín ㄆ一ㄣ	頻	频	屢次 repeatedly 屡次	頻繁(pín fán) 频繁 frequently 頻率(pín lù) 频率 frequency
pǐn ㄆ一ㄣ	品	品	東西，等級，種 類 ，細嘗 product, grade, category, taste 东西，等级，种 类 ，细尝	商品(shāng pǐn) commodity 品種(pǐn zhǒng) 品种 variety
pìn ㄆ一ㄣ	聘	聘	請人擔任工作，訂 婚 appoint, engagement 请人担任工作，订 婚	聘請(pìn qǐng) 聘请 employ the service of 聘禮(pìn lǐ) 聘礼 gift for engagement 聘書(pìn shū) 聘书 letter of appointment
pīng ㄆ一ㄥ	乒	乒	槍聲 crack of a rifle 枪声	乒乓(pīng pāng) ping-pong
pīng ㄆ一ㄥ	娉	娉	娉婷：姿態美好的 樣子 graceful manners 娉婷：姿态美好的 样子	娉婷(pīng tíng) graceful manners

píng ㄆ ㄧ ㄥ	平	平	不凹凸，均勻，一般的 level, even, ordinary 不凹凸，均匀，一般的	平地(píng dì) level ground 平常(píng cháng) ordinary
píng ㄆ ㄧ ㄥ	評	评	判斷，論斷 to judge, to comment on 判断，论断	評價(píng jià) 评价 assessment 評論(píng lùn) 评论 commentary
píng ㄆ ㄧ ㄥ	坪	坪	平坦的地方，房屋面積單位 flat ground, a measure of floorspace 平坦的地方，房屋面积单位	草坪(cǎo píng) 草坪 lawn 建坪(jiàn píng) floorspace
píng ㄆ ㄧ ㄥ	萍	萍	浮在水面的多年生草本植物，行蹤不定 duckweed, roving 浮在水面的多年生草本植物，行踪不定	浮萍(fú píng) 浮萍 duckweed 萍蹤(píng zōng) 萍踪 roving
píng ㄆ ㄧ ㄥ	憑	凭	依靠，証據 rely on, evidence 依靠，证据	憑借(píng jiè) 凭借 relying on 憑據(píng jù) 凭据 evidence
píng ㄆ ㄧ ㄥ	瓶	瓶	小口大肚用來裝液體的器皿 bottle 小口大肚用来装液体的器皿	花瓶(huā píng) vase 酒瓶(jiǔ píng) wine bottle
píng ㄆ ㄧ ㄥ	屏	屏	遮擋，遮蔽物 block out, a screen 遮挡，遮蔽物	屏風(píng fēng) 屏风 a screen 屏氣(píng qì) 屏气 hold one's breath
píng ㄆ ㄧ ㄥ	蘋	苹	蘋果：落葉喬木，果實球形，味甜 apple 苹果：落叶乔木，果实球形，味甜	蘋果(píng guǒ) 苹果 apple

pō ㄆㄛ	頗	颇	不正，很 biased, quite	偏頗(piān pō) 偏颇 biased 頗大(pō dà) 颇大 quite big
pō ㄆㄛ	潑	泼	用力把水灑出去， 凶悍的 splash, petulant 用力把水洒出去， 凶悍的	潑冷水(pō lěng shuǐ) 泼冷水 dampen enthusiasm 潑婦(pō fù) 泼妇 a shrew
pō ㄆㄛ	坡	坡	傾斜的地面 slope 倾斜的地面	山坡(shān pō) hillside 陡坡(dǒu pō) steep slope
pō bo ㄆㄛ ㄅㄛ	泊	泊	湖，船靠岸 lake, to berth 湖，船靠岸	湖泊(hú pō) lakes 停泊(tíng bó) to berth
pó ㄆㄛ	婆	婆	老婦人，妻子，丈 夫的母親 old lady, wife, husband's mom 老妇人，妻子，丈 夫的母亲	老太婆(lǎo tài pó) old lady 老婆(lǎo pó) wife
pǒ ㄆㄛ	叵	叵	不可能 impossible	居心叵測 (jū xīn pǒ cè) 居心叵测 with ulterior motive
pò ㄆㄛ	破	破	毀壞，不好的，花 費 destroy, broken, spend money 毁坏，不好的，花 费	破壞(pò huài) 破坏 sabotage 破裂(pò liè) broken
pò ㄆㄛ	迫	迫	強力壓制，急切 coerce, urgent 强力压制，急切	強迫(qiáng pò) 强迫 coerce 緊迫(jǐn pò) 紧迫 urgent

pò ㄆ ㄛ、	魄	魄	精神 spirit	氣魄(qì pò) 气魄 breadth of vision 魄力(pò lì) courage and vigor
pōu ㄆ ㄡ	剖	剖	割開，分析 dissect, analyze 割开，分析	解剖 (jiě pōu) anatomy 剖析 (pōu xī) analyze
pū ㄆ ㄨ	仆	仆	向前倒下 fall headlong	前仆後繼(qián pū hòu jì) 前仆后继one stepping into the breach as the foregoer falls
pū ㄆ ㄨ	撲	扑	輕拍，向前衝 pat, lunge at 轻拍，向前冲	撲粉(pū fěn) 扑粉 powder the nose 撲滅(pū miè) 扑灭 extinguish, wipe out
pú ㄆ ㄨ、	僕	仆	佣人 servant	僕人(pú rén) 仆人 servant 公僕(gōng pú) 公仆 public servant
pú ㄆ ㄨ、	葡	葡	葡萄：藤本植物， 果實可吃也可釀酒 grape 葡萄：藤本植物， 果实可吃也可酿酒	葡萄(pú táo) grape 葡萄牙(pú táo yá) Portugal
pú ㄆ ㄨ、	脯	脯	胸部 chest	胸脯(xiōng pǔ) chest
pú ㄆ ㄨ、	菩	菩	菩薩：佛教中指地 位僅次於佛的人 Budhisattva 菩萨：佛教中指地 位仅次於佛的人	菩薩心肠(pú sà xīn cháng) 菩萨心肠 kind-hearted person

pú ㄆㄨˊ	匍	匍	匍匐：爬行 crawl	匍匐前進(pú fú qián jìn) 匍匐前进 crawl forward
pǔ ㄆㄨˇ	樸	朴	自然的本性，不浮 華，敦厚誠實 natural, simple, honest 自然的本性，不浮 华，敦厚诚实	樸素(pǔ sù) 朴素 plain and simple 樸實(pǔ shí) 朴实 simple and honest
pǔ ㄆㄨˇ	圃	圃	種植蔬菜，花草瓜 果的園子 garden 种植蔬菜，花草瓜 果的园子	花圃(huā pǔ) 花圃 flower nursery 菜圃(cài pǔ) 菜圃 vegetable plot
pǔ ㄆㄨˇ	普	普	一般的，到處 com mon, universal 一般的，到处	普通(pǔ tōng) common, ordinary 普遍(pǔ biàn) universal
pǔ ㄆㄨˇ	譜	谱	照事物類別編成的 書，範圍 manual, scope 照事物类别编成的 书，范围	食譜(shí pǔ) 食谱 cookbook 離譜(lí pǔ) 离谱 far-fetched
pù ㄆㄨˋ	曝	曝	在陽光下曬 expose under the sun 在阳光下晒	曝光(pù guāng) expose 曝曬(pù shài) 曝晒 place under the sun
pù ㄆㄨˋ	鋪	铺	商店，床 store, bed	店鋪(diàn pù) 店铺 store 床鋪(chuáng pù) 床铺 bed
pù ㄆㄨˋ	舖	铺	商店，床 store, bed	當舖(dàng pù) 当铺 pawn shop
pù ㄆㄨˋ	瀑	瀑	水從高處直瀉而下 waterfall 水从高处直泻而下	瀑布(pù bù) waterfall

Q				
qī ㄑ ㄧ	七	七	六和八之間的整數 number 7 六和八之间的整数	七上八下(qī shàng bā xià) nervous 七老八十(qī lǎo bā shí) very old
qī ㄑ ㄧ	柒	柒	"七"的大寫,六 和八之間的整數 word form of the number '7' "七"的大写,六 和八之间的整数	柒圓(qī yuán) 柒圓 seven dollars
qī ㄑ ㄧ	沏	沏	用滾水泡開 steep in hot water 用滚水泡开	沏茶(qī chá) make tea
qī ㄑ ㄧ	漆	漆	落葉喬木,樹脂可 當塗料用;非常黑 lacquer, paint, pitch dark 落叶乔木,树脂可 当涂料用;非常黑	油漆(yóu qī) paint 一片漆黑(yí piàn qī hēi) pitch dark
qī ㄑ ㄧ	妻	妻	男人的配偶 wife	妻子(qī zi) wife 夫妻(fū qī) husband and wife
qī ㄑ ㄧ	棲	栖	停留休息 stop to rest	棲息(qī xí) 栖息 perch on 棲身之處(qī shēn zhī chù) 栖身之处 a place to stay
qī ㄑ ㄧ	悽	凄	悲傷,冷清 sad, lonely 悲伤,冷清	悽涼(qī liáng) 凄凉 miserable 悽慘(qī cǎn) 凄惨 tragic
qī ㄑ ㄧ	戚	戚	有血緣或姻親關係 的人,憂愁 relatives, worried 有血缘或姻亲关系 的人,忧愁	親戚(qīn qī) 亲戚 relatives 憂戚(yōu qī) 忧戚 very worried
qī ㄑ ㄧ	欺	欺	蒙騙,侮辱 deceive, bully 蒙骗,侮辱	欺騙(qī piàn) 欺骗 deceive 欺侮(qī wǔ) 欺侮 bully

qí くˊ一ˊ	齊	齐	不亂，共同，一起 in order, in unison 不乱，共同，一起	整齊(zhěng qí) 整齐 tidy
qí くˊ一ˊ	臍	脐	腹部中央的小孔，是胎兒時期連接臍帶的地方 navel 腹部中央的小孔，是胎儿时期连接脐带的地方	肚臍(dù qí) 肚脐 navel 臍帶(qí dài) 脐带 umbilical cord
qí くˊ一ˊ	祈	祈	向神請求恩賜，請求 pray, request 向神请求恩赐，请求	祈禱(qí dǎo) 祈祷 pray 敬祈(jìng qí) respectively request
qí くˊ一ˊ	歧	歧	分岔，不一樣，不公平 split, different, unfair 分岔，不一样，不公平	歧途(qí tú) off the right path 歧視(qí shì) 歧视 discriminate against
qí くˊ一ˊ	其	其	第三人稱，那個，此外，別的 his, her, its, that, other 第三人称，那个，此外，别的	其他(qí tā) other 其次(qí cì) secondly
qí くˊ一ˊ	期	期	日，希望，界限 day, hope, limit	婚期(hūn qí) wedding day 期待(qí dài) look forward to 星期(xīng qí) week 星期一(xīng qí yī)Monday 星期二(xīng qí èr)Tuesday 星期三(xīng qí sān)Wednesday 星期四(xīng qí sì)Thursday 星期五(xīng qí wǔ)Friday 星期六(xīng qí liù)Saturday 星期日(xīng qí rì)Sunday
qí くˊ一ˊ	奇	奇	特別的，驚訝，出乎意料之外 uncommon, surprise 特别的，惊讶，出乎意料之外	奇怪(qí guài) strange 驚奇(jīng qí) 惊奇 surprise
qí くˊ一ˊ	旗	旗	代表國家或團體的標誌 flag代表国家或团体的标誌	國旗(guó qí) 国旗 national flag 升旗(shēng qí) raise a flag

235

qí く 一 ′	騎	骑	跨坐在牲口或車子上 ride 跨坐在牲口或车子上	騎馬(qí mǎ) 骑马 ride a horse 騎士(qí shì) 騎士 rider
qí く 一 ′	崎	崎	山路高低不平 bumpy road	崎嶇不平(qí qū bù píng) 崎岖不平 bumpy road
qí く 一 ′	琦	琦	美玉，珍奇 fine jade, rare	
qí く 一 ′	琪	琪	美玉 fine jade	
qí く 一 ′	棋	棋	一種娛樂用具 chess 一种娱乐用具	下棋(xià qí) play chess 棋盤(qí pán) 棋盘 chessboard
qí く 一 ′	麒	麒	麒麟：傳說中的好怪獸，有偉人時才出沒 unicorn 麒麟：传说中的好怪兽，有伟人时才出没	麒麟(qí lín) unicorn
qǐ く 一 ˇ	乞	乞	向人請求，討取 beg 向人请求，讨取	乞丐(qǐ gài) beggar 乞靈於(qǐ líng yú) 乞灵於 seek help from
qǐ く 一 ˇ	豈	岂	難道，怎麼，如何 where or how on earth... 难道，怎么，如何	豈有此理(qǐ yǒu cǐ lǐ) 岂有此理 this is absurd 豈敢(qǐ gǎn) 岂敢 I am flattered
qǐ く 一 ˇ	啓	启	打開，開始 open, begin 打开，开始	開啓(kāi qǐ) 开启 open 啓發(qǐ fā) 启发 inspire

qǐ ㄑ一ˇ	起	起	站立，動身出發，產生，發動 stand, set out, give rise to, start 站立，动身出发，产生，发动	起立(qǐ lì) stand up 起飛(qǐ fēi) 起飞 take off 起火(qǐ huǒ) on fire 一起(yì qǐ) together 起草(qǐ cǎo) 起草to draft
qǐ ㄑ一ˇ	綺	绮	有花紋的絲織品，華麗的 patterned silk fabrics, beautiful 有花纹的丝织品，华丽的	綺麗(qǐ lì) 绮丽 beautiful 綺年玉貌(qǐ nián yù mào) 绮年玉貌young and pretty
qì ㄑ一ˋ	企	企	提起腳跟站著，圖謀，希望 stand on toes, attempt, hope 提起脚跟站著，图谋，希望	企鵝(qǐ é) 企鹅 penguin 企業(qì yè) 企业 enterprise
qì ㄑ一ˋ	氣	气	呼吸，不高興，氣體 weather, breath, angry, gas 呼吸，不高兴，气体	天氣(tiān qì) 天气 weather 生氣(shēng qì) 生气 angry
qì ㄑ一ˋ	汽	汽	液體或固體因受熱而變成的氣體 vapor 液体或固体因受热而变成的气体	汽車(qì chē) 汽车 automobile 蒸汽(zhēng qì) steam
qì ㄑ一ˋ	棄	弃	廢除，丟掉 abolish, discard 废除，丢掉	抛棄(pāo qì) 抛弃 discard 棄權(qì quán) 弃权 abstain from voting
qì ㄑ一ˋ	訖	讫	完結 complete 完结	查訖(chá qì) 查讫 finish investigation 收訖(shōu qì) 收讫 payment received
qì ㄑ一ˋ	迄	迄	直到，始終 until, so far 直到，始终	迄今(qì jīn) up till now 迄無音信(qì wú yīn xìn) 迄无音信 no news so far

qì ㄑ一ˋ	泣	泣	哭，流淚不出聲地 哭 cry, sob 哭，流泪不出声地 哭	哭泣(kū qì) sob 飲泣(yǐn qì) 饮泣 shed tears in silence
qì ㄑ一ˋ	砌	砌	用泥灰把磚塊堆 積黏合起來 lay bricks 用泥灰把砖块堆 积黏合起来	砌磚(qì zhuān) 砌砖 lay bricks 砌牆(qì qiáng) 砌墙 build a wall
qì ㄑ一ˋ	器	器	用具，身體內有特 殊功能的部分，才 能 tool, organ, talent 用具，身体内有特 殊功能的部分，才 能	武器(wǔ qì) weapon 器官(qì guān) organ (of body)
qì ㄑ一ˋ	契	契	合同，字據，合約 contract, signed note, agreement 合同，字据，合约	契約(qì yuē) 契约 contract 地契(dì qì) land deed
qì ㄑ一ˋ	憩	憩	休息 rest	小憩片刻(xiǎo qì piàn kè) take a little rest
qiā ㄑ一ㄚ	掐	掐	用手指夾或夾斷， 用手緊緊按著 nip, clutch 用手指夹或夹断， 用手紧紧按著	掐斷(qiā duàn) 掐断 to nip off 掐脖子(qiā bó zi) strangle with hands
qià ㄑ一ㄚˋ	恰	恰	剛剛，合適 just, appropriate 刚刚，合适	恰巧(qià qiǎo) by chance 恰當(qià dàng) 恰当 appropriate
qià ㄑ一ㄚˋ	洽	洽	商量，聯繫 discuss, contact 商量，联系	接洽(jiē qià) get in touch with 洽商(qià shāng) discuss with

qiān ㄑ ㄧ ㄢ	韆	千	一種供人運動娛樂的器具。人站在木板上 swing 一种供人运动娱乐的器具。人站在木板上	秋韆(qiū qiān) 秋千 swing
qiān ㄑ ㄧ ㄢ	千	千	數目，十個一百 thousand 数目，十个一百	一千(yì qiān) one thousand 千萬(qiān wàn) 千万 be sure to, ten million
qiān 千ㄑ ㄧ ㄢ	遷	迁	換住所，搬家 move to another place 换住所，搬家	遷移(qiān yí) 迁移 migrate 遷居(qiān jū) 迁居 move to another place
qiān ㄑ ㄧ ㄢ	簽	签	親自寫姓名，作標誌的紙或其他東西 to sign, a label 亲自写姓名，作标誌的纸或其他东西	簽名(qiān míng) 签名 sign one's name 標簽(biāo qiān) 标签 a label
qiān ㄑ ㄧ ㄢ	籤	签	作標記的片狀物品，尖細物 label, pointed article 作标记的片状物品，尖细物	書籤(shū qiān) 书签 bookmark 牙籤(yá qiān) 牙签 toothpick
qiān ㄑ ㄧ ㄢ	仟	仟	千字的大寫，十個一百 word form of the number 1,000 千字的大写，十个一百	壹仟圓(yì qiān yuán) 壹仟圓 one thousand yuan
qiān ㄑ ㄧ ㄢ	牽	牵	拉，連帶 haul, involved in 拉，连带	牽手(qiān shǒu) 牵手 hold hands 牽連(qiān lián) 牵连 implicated in
qiān ㄑ ㄧ ㄢ	鉛	铅	一種金屬元素，符號Pb，質軟 lead 一种金属元素，符号Pb，质软	鉛筆(qiān bǐ) 铅笔 pencil 推鉛球(tuī qiān qiú) 推铅球 putting the shot
qiān ㄑ ㄧ ㄢ	謙	谦	虛心，不自滿 modest, not conceited 虚心，不自满	謙虛(qiān xū) 谦虚 humble 謙詞(qiān cí) 谦词 humble statement

qián ㄑㄧㄢˊ	前	前	"後"的相反,人臉所面對的那一面,時間過去的 before, prior "后"的相反,人脸所面对的那一面,时间过去的	前面(qián miàn) in front of 前天(qián tiān) day before yesterday
qián ㄑㄧㄢˊ	虔	虔	恭敬 revere	虔誠(qián chēng) 虔诚 devout 虔心(qián xīn) with reverence
qián ㄑㄧㄢˊ	錢	钱	貨幣,費用,財物 money, expense 货币,费用,财物	錢財(qián cái) 钱财 money 花錢(huā qián) 花钱 spend money
qián ㄑㄧㄢˊ	鉗	钳	用東西夾住 clip something 用东西夹住	鉗制(qián zhì) 钳制 impose check on 鉗子(qián zi) 钳子 pliers
qián ㄑㄧㄢˊ	潛	潜	沈在水下活動,隱藏的 submerge, hidden 沈在水下活动,隐藏的	潛水艇(qián shuǐ tǐng) 潜水艇submarine 潛在(qián zài) 潜在 potential
qiǎn ㄑㄧㄢˇ	淺	浅	"深"的相反,程度不深,淡色 shallow, light "深"的相反,程度不深,淡色	淺顯(qiǎn xiǎn) 浅显 easy to understand 淺紅(qiǎn hóng) 浅红 light red
qiǎn ㄑㄧㄢˇ	遣	遣	派,發送,排解 send, transmit, dispel 派,发送,排解	遣返(qiǎn fǎn) repatriate 消遣(xiāo qiǎn) pastime
qiǎn ㄑㄧㄢˇ	譴	谴	責備 denounce 责备	譴責(qiǎn zé) 谴责 denounce

qiàn ㄑ 一 ㄢ	歉	歉	對不起，收成不好 apologize, lean (harvest) 对不起，收成不好	道歉(dào qiàn) apologize 歉收(qiàn shōu) a lean harvest
qiàn ㄑ 一 ㄢ	欠	欠	向人借財物未還，不夠，疲倦時張口吸吐氣 owe, short, yawn 向人借財物未还，不够，疲倦时张口吸吐气	欠錢(qiàn qián) 欠钱 owe money 呵欠(hē qiàn) yawn
qiàn ㄑ 一 ㄢ	倩	倩	美好的 pretty	倩影(qiàn yǐng) pretty figure
qiāng ㄑ 一 ㄤ	槍	枪	發射子彈的武器 gun 发射子弹的武器	手槍(shǒu qiāng) 手枪 pistol 長槍(cháng qiāng) 长枪 rifle
qiāng ㄑ 一 ㄤ	腔	腔	人體中口、胸，腹的中空部分；口音 cavity, accent 人体中口、胸，腹的中空部分；口音	口腔(kǒu qiāng) mouth 腔調(qiāng diào) 腔调 accent
qiāng ㄑ 一 ㄤ	鏹	镪	強酸；硝酸、鹽酸的統稱 corrosive acids 强酸；硝酸、盐酸的统称	硝鏹水(xiāo qiāng shuǐ) 硝镪水 all corrosive acids
qiáng jiàng ㄑ ㄐ 一 一 ㄤ ㄤ	強	强	健壯有力，"弱"的相反，好 strong, good 健壮有力，"弱"的相反，好	強大(qiáng dà) 强大 powerful 強調(qiáng diào) 强调 emphasize
qiáng ㄑ 一 ㄤ	牆	墙	用磚石等砌成的隔屋內外的壁 wall 用砖石等砌成的隔屋内外的壁	磚牆(zhuān qiáng) 砖墙 brick wall 牆壁(qiáng bì) 墙壁 wall

qiáng ㄑ ㄧ ㄤ	薔	蔷	薔薇：落葉灌木， 莖上多刺，有多種 顏色花 rose (flower) 蔷薇：落叶灌木， 茎上多刺，有多种 颜色花	薔薇(qiáng wéi) 蔷薇 rose (flower)
qiǎng ㄑ ㄧ ㄤ	搶	抢	奪，硬拿，趕快 seize, snatch, hurriedly 夺，硬拿，赶快	搶奪(qiǎng duó) 抢夺 seize 搶修(qiǎng xiū) 抢修 emergency repair
qiǎng ㄑ ㄧ ㄤ	襁	襁	襁褓：嬰兒的包被 swaddling clothes 襁褓：婴儿的包被	襁褓(qiǎng bǎo) 襁褓 swaddling clothes
qiàng ㄑ ㄧ ㄤ	嗆	呛	因刺激性氣體或吃 得太快而引起咳嗽 cough from choking 因刺激性气体或吃 得太快而引起咳嗽	嗆到(qiàng dào) 呛到 cough from choking 嗆鼻子(qiàng bí zi) 呛鼻子 pungent smell
qiāo ㄑ ㄧ ㄠ	悄	悄	聲音很低或沒有聲 音 quietly 声音很低或没有声 音	靜悄悄(jìng qiāo qiāo) 静悄悄quietly
qiāo ㄑ ㄧ ㄠ	蹺	跷	抬腳，豎起 lift up, erect 抬脚，竖起	蹺著腿(qiāo zhe tuǐ) 跷著腿 cross one's legs 蹺蹺板(qiāo qiāo bǎn) 跷跷板 a seesaw
qiāo ㄑ ㄧ ㄠ	敲	敲	打 strike	敲打(qiāo dǎ) to strike 敲詐(qiāo zhà) 敲诈 extort money
qiāo ㄑ ㄧ ㄠ	橇	橇	在冰雪上滑行的工 具 sledge	雪橇(xuě qiāo) sledge

qiáo く 一ˊ 幺	喬	乔	高 tall	喬木(qiáo mù) 乔木 trees 喬遷(qiáo qiān) 乔迁 move house
qiáo く 一ˊ 幺	僑	侨	居住在國外，長久 居留國外的本國人 people who live abroad 居住在国外，长久 居留国外的本国人	僑居(qiáo jū) 侨居 live abroad 華僑(huá qiáo) 华侨 overseas Chinese
qiáo く 一ˊ 幺	橋	桥	在水上或空中可通 行的建築物 bridge 在水上或空中可通 行的建筑物	橋樑(qiáo liáng) 桥樑 bridges 過橋(guò qiáo) 过桥 cross a bridge
qiáo く 一ˊ 幺	憔	憔	臉色不好，臉色疲 倦 look washed down 脸色不好，脸色疲 倦	憔悴(qiáo cuì) look washed down
qiáo く 一ˊ 幺	瞧	瞧	看 look	瞧不起(qiáo bù qǐ) look down upon 瞧出(qiáo chū) discern, notice
qiáo く 一ˊ 幺	樵	樵	柴，打柴 firewood, cut wood	樵夫(qiáo fū) woodcutter
qiǎo く 一ˇ 幺	巧	巧	技能好 skillful	技巧(jì qiǎo) skill 靈巧(líng qiǎo) 灵巧 dexterous
qiào く 一ˋ 幺	俏	俏	漂亮 good-looking	俏麗(qiào lì) 俏丽 pretty 俊俏(jùn qiào) handsome

qiào ㄑ一ㄠˋ	竅	窍	孔，事情的主要關鍵 a hole, crux 孔，事情的主要关键	一竅不通(yí qiào bù tōng) 一窍不通 know nothing 竅門(qiào mén) 窍门 tips for doing things
qiào ㄑ一ㄠˋ	撬	撬	用工具把東西敲開 pry open 用工具把东西敲开	撬門(qiào mén) 撬门 pry open the door 撬開(qiào kāi) 撬开 pry open
qiào ㄑ一ㄠˋ	峭	峭	高又陡 tall and steep	峭壁(qiào bì) steep cliff
qiào ㄑ一ㄠˋ	翹	翘	舉起來 perk up 举起来	翹尾巴(qiào wěi ba) 翘尾巴 cocky 翹辮子(qiào biàn zi) 翘辫子 kick the bucket
qiē qiè ㄑ一ㄝˋ ㄑ一ㄝ	切	切	用刀從上往下割 cut 用刀从上往下割	切磋(qiē cuō) learn from each other 切斷(qiē duàn) 切断 cut off
qié ㄑ一ㄝˊ	茄	茄	一年生草本植物，紫色果實可吃 eggplant 一年生草本植物，紫色果实可吃	茄子(qié zi) 茄子 eggplant 番茄(fān qié) 番茄 tomato
qiě ㄑ一ㄝˇ	且	且	暫時，又 for the time being, and 暂时，又	暫且(zhàn qiě) 暂且 for the time being 高且壯(gāo qiě zhuàng) tall and strong
qiè qiē ㄑ一ㄝˋ ㄑ一ㄝ	切	切	所有，緊急，確定 all, urgent, definite 所有，紧急，确定	一切(yí qiè) all 迫切(pò qiè) urgent

qiè ㄑ ㄧ ㄝ	竊	窃	偷，私自 steal, in private	竊取(qiè qǔ) 窃取 steal 竊笑(qiè xiào) 窃笑 laugh in one's sleeve
qiè ㄑ ㄧ ㄝ	妾	妾	男子在妻子以外娶 的女子，古時女子 的自稱 concubine 男子在妻子以外娶 的女子，古时女子 的自称	妻妾(qī qiè) wife and concubine(s) 納妾(nà qiè) 纳妾 take concubine
qiè ㄑ ㄧ ㄝ	怯	怯	膽小 timid 胆小	膽怯(dǎn qiè) 胆怯 timid 怯場(qiè chǎng) 怯场 stage fright
qīn ㄑ ㄧ ㄣ	欽	钦	恭敬 respectful	欽佩(qīn pèi) 钦佩 admire 欽差大臣(qīn chāi dà chén) imperial envoy
qīn ㄑ ㄧ ㄣ	侵	侵	擾亂，奪取別人的 東西，流失 intrude, plunder 扰乱，夺取别人的 东西，流失	侵擾(qīn rǎo) 侵扰 invade and harass 侵略(qīn lüè) aggression
qīn ㄑ ㄧ ㄣ	親	亲	有血統關係，感情 好，本身 kinship, intimate, personally 有血统关係，感情 好，本身	親屬(qīn shǔ) 亲属 dependents 親眼(qīn yǎn) 亲眼 to witness
qín ㄑ ㄧ ㄣ	秦	秦	姓，中國朝代名 Chinese surname, Chinese dynasty name 姓，中国朝代名	秦代(qín dài) Qin Dynasty
qín ㄑ ㄧ ㄣ	琴	琴	一種弦樂器 a kind of string instrument 一种弦乐器	鋼琴(gāng qín) 钢琴 piano 小提琴(xiǎo tí qín) violin

qín ㄑㄧㄣˊ	芹	芹	芹菜：一年或二年生草本植物，可生吃 celery 芹菜：一年或二年生草本植物，可生吃	芹菜(qín cài) 芹菜 celery
qín ㄑㄧㄣˊ	勤	勤	做事盡力，不偷懶 diligent 做事尽力，不偷懒	勤勞(qín láo) 勤劳 hardworking
qín ㄑㄧㄣˊ	禽	禽	鳥類的總稱 birds 鸟类的总称	家禽(jiā qín) poultry 禽獸(qín shòu) 禽兽 beasts
qín ㄑㄧㄣˊ	擒	擒	捕捉 to catch	擒賊(qín zéi) 擒贼 catch a thief
qín ㄑㄧㄣˊ	噙	噙	含在裏面 hold back 含在里面	噙著眼淚(qín zhe yǎn lèi) 噙著眼泪hold back the tears
qǐn ㄑㄧㄣˇ	寢	寝	睡覺 to sleep 睡觉	寢室(qǐn shì) 寝室 bedroom 就寢(jiù qǐn) 就寝 go to bed
qīng ㄑㄧㄥ	青	青	綠色，年輕 green, young 绿色，年轻	青草(qīng cǎo) 青草 green grass 青年(qīng nián) youngster
qīng ㄑㄧㄥ	輕	轻	"重"的相反，不以為重要，隨便 not heavy, take lightly "重"的相反，不以为重要，随便	輕視(qīng shì) 轻视 despise 輕易(qīng yì) 轻易 readily, easily

qīng ㄑ ㄧ ㄥ	傾	倾	歪，斜 lean to the side	傾聽(qīng tīng) 倾听 listen attentively 傾向(qīng xiàng) 倾向 inclination
qīng ㄑ ㄧ ㄥ	清	清	"濁"的相反，純潔沒有污染，不混亂 clear, not tainted "浊"的相反，纯洁没有污染，不混乱	清楚(qīng chǔ) clear 清白(qīng bái) innocent
qīng ㄑ ㄧ ㄥ	蜻	蜻	蜻蜓：會飛的益蟲，肚子細長 dragonfly 蜻蜓：会飞的益虫，肚子细长	蜻蜓(qīng tíng) dragonfly
qíng ㄑ ㄧ ㄥ	情	情	由外界事物引起的心理感覺，狀況 feeling 由外界事物引起的心理感觉，状况	愛情(ài qíng) 爱情 love 情緒(qíng xù) 情绪 emotion
qíng ㄑ ㄧ ㄥ	晴	晴	天空明朗 clear skies	晴天(qíng tiān) clear skies 放晴(fàng qíng) weather clears up
qǐng ㄑ ㄧ ㄥ	請	请	求，用在動詞前表示客氣尊敬，邀 invite, request, please 求，用在动词前表示客气尊敬，邀	請求(qǐng qiú) 请求 request 請問(qǐng wèn) 请问 May I ask ...?
qǐng ㄑ ㄧ ㄥ	頃	顷	田地一百畝叫一頃，短時間 unit measures for area, short time 田地一百亩叫一顷，短时间	頃刻(qǐng kè) 顷刻 instantly
qìng ㄑ ㄧ ㄥ	慶	庆	祝賀某事或人的成功 celebrate 祝贺某事或人的成功	慶祝(qìng zhù) 庆祝 celebrate 慶功(qìng gōng) 庆功 celebrate victory

qìng ㄑ ㄧ ㄥ	罄	罄	用完，用盡，器皿 已空 used up, empty 用完，用尽，器皿 已空	用罄(yòng qìng) used up 罄竹難書(qìng zhú nán shū) 罄竹难书countless
qióng ㄑ ㄩ ㄥ	窮	穷	沒錢，徹底地 poor, thoroughly 没钱，彻底地	窮困(qióng kùn) 穷困 poverty 窮盡(qióng jìn) 穷尽 limit
qióng ㄑ ㄩ ㄥ	瓊	琼	美好的 fine	瓊漿(qióng jiāng) 琼浆 good wine
qiū ㄑ ㄧ ㄡ	秋	秋	四季中的第三季 autumn	秋季(qiū jì) autumn 秋收(qiū shōu) autumn harvest
qiū ㄑ ㄧ ㄡ	鰍	鳅	一種可吃的魚，有 鬚，像小蛇 loach 一种可吃的鱼，有 须，像小蛇	泥鰍(ní qiū) 泥鳅 loach
qiū ㄑ ㄧ ㄡ	丘	丘	土山，土堆 mound	丘陵(qiū líng) hills 沙丘(shā qiū) dune
qiū ㄑ ㄧ ㄡ	邱	邱	通"丘"，姓氏 Chinese surname	
qiū ㄑ ㄧ ㄡ	蚯	蚯	蚯蚓：一種生長在 土裏的環節動物 earthworm 蚯蚓：一种生长在 土里的环节动物	蚯蚓(qiū yǐn) earthworm

248

qiú ㄑ一ㄡˊ	求	求	希望得到 ask for	求學(qiú xué) 求学 receive education 供求(gōng qiú) supply and demand
qiú ㄑ一ㄡˊ	酋	酋	部落的首領 tribal chief 部落的首领	酋長(qiú zhǎng) 酋长 tribal chief 匪酋(fěi qiú) ringleader
qiú ㄑ一ㄡˊ	裘	裘	皮衣 fur coat	狐裘(hú qiú) fox fur coat 皮裘(pí qiú) fur coat
qiú ㄑ一ㄡˊ	球	球	圓形立體 ball 圆形立体	地球(dì qiú) the earth 棒球(bàng qiú) baseball
qiú ㄑ一ㄡˊ	囚	囚	拘禁，被拘禁的人 imprison, prisoner 拘禁，被拘禁的人	囚禁(qiú jìn) imprison 死囚(sǐ qiú) death row inmate
qiǔ ㄑ一ㄡˇ	糗	糗	丟臉，尷尬 shameful, embarrassing 丢脸，尴尬	好糗(hǎo qiǔ) very embarrassing 糗事(qiǔ shì) an embarrassing event
qū ㄑㄩ	區	区	分別，地域 distinguish, territory	區別(qū bié) 区别 distinguish 區區(qū qū) 区区 trivial
qū ㄑㄩ	屈	屈	"伸"的相反，折服，侮辱 bend, surrender, insult	屈辱(qū rǔ) insult 屈服(qū fú) surrender
qū ㄑㄩ	曲	曲	"直"的相反，不公正 not straight, not fair	彎曲(wān qū) 弯曲 winding 曲線(qū xiàn) 曲线 curve

qū ㄑㄩ	軀	躯	身體 body 身体	身軀(shēn qū) 身躯 body 捐軀(juān qū) 捐躯 sacrifice for a cause
qū ㄑㄩ	嶇	岖	崎嶇:山路高低不 平 bumpy (road) 崎岖:山路高低不 平	崎嶇(qí qū) 崎岖 bumpy (road)
qū ㄑㄩ	驅	驱	差遣,趕走 drive, expel 差遣,赶走	驅使(qū shǐ) 驱使 impel 驅除(qū chú) 驱除 expel
qū ㄑㄩ	蛆	蛆	蒼蠅的幼蟲 maggot 苍蝇的幼虫	生蛆(shēng qū) maggoty 長蛆(zhǎng qū) 长蛆 maggoty
qū ㄑㄩ	趨	趋	快走,走勢 walk fast, trend 快走,走势	趨勢(qū shì) 趋势 trend
qú ㄑㄩˊ	渠	渠	人工水道 canal	渠道(qú dào) ditch 幹渠(gàn qú) 干渠 main waterway
qǔ ㄑㄩˇ	取	取	拿,接受 take, receive	取出(qǔ chū) take out 吸取(xī qǔ) absorb
qǔ ㄑㄩˇ	齲	龋	蛀牙 dental caries	齲齒(qǔ chǐ) 龋齿 dental caries
qǔ qū ㄑㄩˇ ㄑㄩ	曲	曲	能唱的詩歌,調子 a verse for singing, tune 能唱的诗歌,调子	歌曲(gē qǔ) song 作曲家(zuò qǔ jiā) composer 曲調(qǔ diào) 曲调 music

qǔ ㄑㄩˇ	娶	娶	男子迎娶女子爲妻 take a wife 男子迎娶女子为妻	娶妻(qǔ qī) take a wife
qù ㄑㄩˋ	去	去	"來"的相反，到 別處，已過的，除 掉 go, past, get rid of "来"的相反，到 別处，已过的，除 掉	去世(qù shì) pass away 去年(qù nián) last year
qù ㄑㄩˋ	趣	趣	使人覺得愉快 interesting 使人觉得愉快	有趣(yǒu qù) interesting 趣事(qù shì) interesting event
quān ㄑㄩㄢ	圈	圈	環形的東西，環形 circle, round-shaped 环形的东西，环形	圓圈(yuán quān) 圆圈 a circle 圈套(quān tào) a trap
quán ㄑㄩㄢˊ	全	全	完整，整個 complete, the whole 完整，整个	完全(wán quán) completely 全國(quán guó) 全国 the whole country
quán ㄑㄩㄢˊ	權	权	有支配和指揮的力 量 power, the right 有支配和指挥的力 量	權利(quán lì) 权利 the rights 政權(zhèng quán) 政权 regime, government
quán ㄑㄩㄢˊ	泉	泉	水源 water source	泉水(quán shuǐ) fountain 溫泉(wēn quán) 温泉 hot spring
quán ㄑㄩㄢˊ	詮	诠	解釋 explain 解释	詮釋(quán shì) 诠释 expound

quán ㄑㄩㄢˊ	痊	痊	病好了，恢復健康 recover from illness 病好了，恢复健康	痊愈(quán yù) be healed
quán ㄑㄩㄢˊ	銓	铨	選拔官吏 select officials 选拔官吏	銓敘(quán xù) 铨叙 select, appoint officials 銓叙部(quán xù bù) 銓叙部 Ministry of Personnel
quán ㄑㄩㄢˊ	拳	拳	彎曲五個指頭向掌 心握緊手 fist 弯曲五个指头向掌 心握紧手	打拳(dǎ quán) play boxing 拳頭(quán tóu) 拳头 fist
quán ㄑㄩㄢˊ	蜷	蜷	身體彎曲 coil up 身体弯曲	蜷曲(quán qū) coil up
quǎn ㄑㄩㄢˇ	犬	犬	狗 dog	小犬(xiǎo quǎn) puppy, my son 犬齒(quǎn chǐ) 犬齿 canine tooth
quǎn ㄑㄩㄢˇ	綣	绻	感情的離不開 feel reluctant to part 感情的离不开	繾綣(qiǎn quǎn) 缱绻 feel reluctant to part
quàn ㄑㄩㄢˋ	勸	劝	说服，勉勵 advice, encourage 说服，勉励	勸告(quàn gào) 劝告 advice 勸勉(quàn miǎn) 劝勉 encourage
quàn ㄑㄩㄢˋ	券	券	做爲憑據的票 coupon 做为凭据的票	獎券(jiǎng quàn) 奖券 lottery ticket 证券(zhèng quàn) 证券 securities

quē ㄑㄩㄝ	缺	缺	不夠，殘破，空額 shortage, incomplete, vacant 不够，残破，空额	殘缺(cán quē) 残缺 incomplete 缺乏(quē fá) lack
qué ㄑㄩˊㄝ	瘸	瘸	腿腳有毛病走路身 體一拐一拐 cripple 腿脚有毛病走路身 体一拐一拐	瘸子(qué zi) cripple
què ㄑㄩˋㄝ	卻	却	不接受，推辭 to decline 不接受，推辞	退卻(tuì què) 退却 retreat 推卻(tuī què) 推却 to decline
què ㄑㄩˋㄝ	確	确	眞實，實在，堅定 real, actual, firm 真实，实在，坚定	正確(zhèng què) 正确 correct 確定(què dìng) 确定 affirm
què ㄑㄩˋㄝ	鵲	鹊	鳥名，嘴尖短尾長 ，吉祥的預兆 magpie 鸟名，嘴尖短尾长 ，吉祥的预兆	喜鵲(xǐ què) 喜鹊 magpie
què ㄑㄩˋㄝ	雀	雀	麻雀：一種羽毛上 有麻點會吃穀類和 小蟲的鳥 sparrow 麻雀：一种羽毛上 有麻点会吃谷类和 小虫的鸟	麻雀(má què) sparrow 孔雀(kǒng què) peacock
qún ㄑㄩˊㄣ	群	群	同類集合在一起， 很多 multitude, many 同类集合在一起， 很多	群眾(qún zhòng) 群众 the masses 群島(qún dǎo) 群岛 archipelago
qún ㄑㄩˊㄣ	裙	裙	圍在腰下的服裝 skirt 围在腰下的服装	裙子(qún zi) skirt 裙帶關係(qún dài guān xì) 裙带关系 nepotism

R

rán ㄖㄢˊ	然	然	是，以後，但是 yes, afterward, however 是，以后，但是	然後(rán hòu) 然后 then 然而(rán ér) however
rán ㄖㄢˊ	燃	燃	燒起火焰，引火點著 burn, set afire 烧起火焰，引火点著	燃燒(rán shāo) 燃烧 burn 燃料(rán liào) fuel
rǎn ㄖㄢˇ	冉	冉	姓。慢慢移動 Chinese surname, move slowly 姓。慢慢移动	冉冉上升(rǎn rǎn shàng shēng) rise slowly
rǎn ㄖㄢˇ	染	染	把東西放在顏料裏變顏色，感受疾病 to dye, contract (disease) 把东西放在颜料里变颜色，感受疾病	染布(rǎn bù) dye the cloth 傳染(chuán rǎn) 传染 infect
rǎng ㄖㄤˇ	壤	壤	鬆軟的土，沒有沙石，柔軟肥沃，適合植物生長的土地 soil 松软的土，没有沙石，柔软肥沃，适合植物生长的土地	土壤(tǔ rǎng) soil 天壤之別(tiān rǎng zhī bié) worlds apart
rǎng ㄖㄤˇ	嚷	嚷	喧鬧，吵鬧 noisy 喧闹，吵闹	喧嚷(xuān rǎng) boisterous 叫嚷(jiào rǎng) shouting
ràng ㄖㄤˋ	讓	让	把東西給別人，不與人爭，隨，任 yield, let 把东西给别人，不与人争，随，任	讓步(ràng bù) 让步 make concession 讓位(ràng wèi) 让位 abdicate
ráo ㄖㄠˊ	饒	饶	富足，多，寬恕 abundant, forgive 富足，多，宽恕	富饒(fù ráo) 富饶 richly endowed 饒恕(ráo shù) 饶恕 forgive

rǎo ㄖㄠˇ	擾	扰	攪亂 disturb 搅乱	打擾(dǎ rǎo)打扰 disturb 騷擾(sāo rǎo)骚扰 harass
rào ㄖㄠˋ	繞	绕	糾纏，圍轉 coil around, go around 纠缠，围转	纏繞(chán rào)缠绕 coil around 繞道(rào dào)绕道 take a detour
rě ㄖㄜˇ	惹	惹	招引，挑起，挑逗 bring about, provoke 招引，挑起，挑逗	惹禍(rě huò) cause trouble 惹人注意(rě rén zhù yì) attract attention
rè ㄖㄜˋ	熱	热	"冷"的相反，高 溫，情意深 hot, passionate	熱飯(rè fàn)热饭 heat the rice 熱心(rè xīn)热心 enthusiastic 熱情(rè qíng)热情passion 熱狗(rè gǒu)热狗 hot dog
rén ㄖㄣˊ	人	人	最有智慧和靈性的 動物 man 最有智慧和灵性的 动物	人類(rén lèi)人类 mankind 人格(rén gé) personality
rén ㄖㄣˊ	仁	仁	同情，友愛，果核 裏的種子 compassion, kernel 同情，友愛，果核 里的种子	仁慈(rén cí) benevolent 杏仁(xìng rén) almond
rěn ㄖㄣˇ	忍	忍	承受 put up with	忍受(rěn shòu) to put up with 殘忍(cán rěn)残忍 cruel
rèn ㄖㄣˋ	刃	刃	刀口 blade of knife	刃具(rèn jù) cutting tool
rèn ㄖㄣˋ	飪	饪	煮熟食物 cooking	烹飪(pēng rèn)烹饪 cooking

rèn ㄖㄣˋ	認	认	知道，分辨，同意 know, discern, agree	認識(rèn shì) 认识 know 認真(rèn zhēn) 认真 conscientious
rèn ㄖㄣˋ	任	任	相信，給予職務， 隨便 to trust, appoint, let 相信，给予职务， 随便	信任(xìn rèn) have trust in 任命(rèn mìng) appoint
rèn ㄖㄣˋ	紉	纫	引線穿針，縫補 sew 引线穿针，缝补	縫紉(féng rèn) 缝纫 sew 縫紉機(féng rèn jī) 缝纫机 sewing machine
rèn ㄖㄣˋ	韌	韧	結實不易斷 not easily broken 结实不易断	韌性(rèn xìng) 韧性 tenacity 堅韌(jiān rèn) 坚韧 tenacious
rēng ㄖㄥ	扔	扔	抛，丟 discard	扔掉(rēng diào) discard 扔球(rēng qiú) pitch a ball
réng ㄖㄥˊ	仍	仍	依然，還是 as usual, still 依然，还是	仍然(réng rán) as usual 仍舊(réng jiù) 仍旧 remain the same
rì ㄖˋ	日	日	太陽，"夜"的相 反，特定的一天 sun, daytime, a day 太阳，"夜"的相 反，特定的一天	日蝕(rì shí) 日蚀 solar eclipse 生日(shēng rì) birthday 日記(rì jì)日记 diary
róng ㄖㄨㄥˊ	榮	荣	好的名聲，繁盛 honor, prosperity 好的名声，繁盛	光榮(guāng róng) 光荣 honor 繁榮(fán róng) 繁荣 prosperity
róng ㄖㄨㄥˊ	熔	熔	固體受熱到一定溫 度時變成液體 smelt 固体受热到一定温 度时变成液体	熔化(róng huà) smelt 熔點(róng diǎn) 熔点 smelting point
róng ㄖㄨㄥˊ	鎔	鎔	鑄造金屬器物的模 型，用火融化金屬 mold for making metal articles, to melt 铸造金属器物的模 型，用火融化金属	鎔鑄(róng zhù) 鎔铸 to cast (metal) 鎔爐(róng lú) 鎔炉 furnace

róng ㄖ ㄨˊ ㄥ	茸	茸	新長的草，帶細毛 才生出來的鹿角 newly grown grass, antler 新长的草，带细毛 才生出来的鹿角	綠茸茸(lǜ róng róng) 绿茸茸 greenish 鹿茸(lù róng) antler 鹿茸
róng ㄖ ㄨˊ ㄥ	戎	戎	軍事 military 军事	戎裝(róng zhuāng) 戎装 military uniform 從戎(cóng róng) 从戎 join the army
róng ㄖ ㄨˊ ㄥ	絨	绒	柔軟細小的毛，柔 細短毛的紡織品 fine hair, down 柔软细小的毛，柔 细短毛的纺织品	鵝絨(é róng) 鹅绒 goose down 絲絨(sī róng) 丝绒 velvet
róng ㄖ ㄨˊ ㄥ	融	融	固體受熱變爲液體 ，流通 melt, circulate 固体受热变为液体 ，流通	融化(róng huà) melt 金融(jīn róng) banking, monetary
róng ㄖ ㄨˊ ㄥ	容	容	容納，對人度量大 ，相貌 contain, generous, looks 容纳，对人度量大 ，相貌	包容(bāo róng) encompass 容貌(róng mào) appearance
róng ㄖ ㄨˊ ㄥ	蓉	蓉	芙蓉：落葉灌木， 有美麗的紅白花 lotus 芙蓉：落叶灌木， 有美丽的红白花	芙蓉(fú róng) lotus
róng ㄖ ㄨˊ ㄥ	溶	溶	在水或其他液體裏 化開 dissolve 在水或其他液体里 化开	溶解(róng jiě) dissolve 溶液(róng yè) solution
róu ㄖ ㄡˊ	柔	柔	軟，溫和 soft, gentle 软，温和	溫柔(wēn róu) 温柔 gentle 柔和(róu hé) soft and gentle

róu ㄖ ㄡˊ	揉	揉	按摩，用手打圓圈地按 massage, rub 按摩，用手打圆圈地按	揉眼(róu yǎn) rub the eye 揉搓(róu cuō) rub, knead
róu ㄖ ㄡˊ	蹂	蹂	侮辱，用暴力侵害 insult, use violence on 侮辱，用暴力侵害	蹂躪(róu lìn) 蹂躏 trample on
ròu ㄖ ㄡˋ	肉	肉	動物肌膚的總稱 meat 动物肌肤的总称	肌肉(jī ròu) muscle 肉體(ròu tǐ) 肉体 body flesh
rú ㄖ ㄨˊ	如	如	就像，假使，依照 just like, if, according to	如今(rú jīn) as of now 如果(rú guǒ) if
rú ㄖ ㄨˊ	儒	儒	古代的讀書人，以孔子、孟子爲代表的學派Confucianism 古代的读书人，以孔子、孟子为代表的学派	儒家(rú jiā) Confucianism 儒生(rú shēng) a Confucian scholar
rú ㄖ ㄨˊ	孺	孺	小孩子，幼兒 little child 小孩子，幼儿	孺子(rú zi) little child
rú ㄖ ㄨˊ	茹	茹	忍 endure	含辛茹苦(hán xīn rú kǔ) endure all hardships
rǔ ㄖ ㄨˇ	乳	乳	分泌奶汁的器官，奶汁，初生的 breast, milk 分泌奶汁的器官，奶汁，初生的	乳房(rǔ fáng) breast 乳豬(rǔ zhū) 乳猪 suckling pig

rǔ rù ㄖㄨˋ	辱	辱	羞恥 disgrace 羞耻	侮辱(wǔ rǔ) insult 辱罵(rǔ mà) 辱骂 shout abuse at
rù ㄖㄨˋ	入	入	"出"的相反，從外面到裏面 inbound "出"的相反，从外面到里面	入口(rù kǒu) entrance 收入(shōu rù) income
rù ㄖㄨˋ	褥	褥	坐或睡時墊在身體下面的東西 mattress 坐或睡时垫在身体下面的东西	被褥(bèi rù) mattress 褥套(rù tào) mattress cover
ruǎn ㄖㄨㄢˇ	軟	软	"硬"的相反，懦弱，沒有力氣 soft, cowardly, lack energy "硬"的相反，懦弱，没有力气	柔軟(róu ruǎn) 柔软 soft 軟弱(ruǎn ruò) 软弱 weak
ruǎn ㄖㄨㄢˇ	阮	阮	姓氏 Chinese surname	阮囊羞澀(ruǎn náng xiū sè) 阮囊羞涩 very poor
ruǐ ㄖㄨㄟˇ	蕊	蕊	植物的生殖器官，還沒有開放的花苞 pistil 植物的生殖器官，还没有开放的花苞	花蕊(huā ruǐ) pistil
ruì ㄖㄨㄟˋ	瑞	瑞	吉祥，好預兆 lucky, auspicious 吉祥，好预兆	人瑞(rén ruì) propitious old person 瑞雪(ruì xuě) timely snow
ruì ㄖㄨㄟˋ	銳	锐	鋒利 sharp 锋利	敏銳(mǐn ruì) 敏锐 keen 銳利(ruì lì) 锐利 sharp

rùn ㄖ ㄨ ㄣˋ	閏	闰	地球公轉所累積的 多餘時間 leap (year or month) 地球公转所累积的 多馀时间	閏月(rùn yuè) 闰月 leap month 閏年(rùn nián) 闰年 leap year
rìn ㄖ ㄨ ㄣˋ	潤	润	不乾枯，利益 moist, profit 不乾枯，利益	濕潤(shī rùn) 湿润 moist 利潤(lì rùn) 利润 profit
ruò ㄖ ㄨ ㄛˋ	若	若	如果，好像，多少 if, resemble, several	若是(ruò shì) if 若干(ruò gān) several
ruò ㄖ ㄨ ㄛˋ	弱	弱	"強"的相反，力 氣小 weak "强"的相反，力 气小	懦弱(nuò ruò) cowardly 弱小(ruò xiǎo) weak and small

S

sā ㄙㄚ	撒	撒	放開，排泄，施展 release, dispense, perform 放开，排泄，施展	撒尿(sā niào) urinate 撒嬌(sā jiāo) 撒娇 act like a spoiled child
sǎ ㄙㄚˇ	撒	撒	散布 spread	撒種(sǎ zhǒng) 撒种 sow seed 撒農藥(sǎ nóng yào) 撒农药 spray insecticide
sǎ ㄙㄚˇ	灑	洒	把水散布在地上， 東西散落，不拘束 sprinkle, scatter, carefree 把水散布在地上， 东西散落，不拘束	灑水(sǎ shuǐ) 洒水 spray water 灑淚(sǎ lèi) 洒泪 shed tears
sà ㄙㄚˋ	薩	萨	姓氏 Chinese surname	菩薩(pú sà) 菩萨 Bodhisattva 拉薩(lā sà) 拉萨 Lhasa (capital of Tibet)
sāi ㄙㄞ	塞	塞	堵，填滿空隙，堵 住器物口的東西 clog, fill up, stopper 堵，填满空隙，堵 住器物口的东西	塞子(sāi zi) stopper 瓶塞(píng sāi) cork
sài ㄙㄞˋ	塞	塞	邊界上險要的地方 strategic border location 边界上险要的地方	要塞(yào sài) fortress 塞外(sài wài) beyond the Great Wall
sài ㄙㄞˋ	賽	赛	比較好壞，勝負， 強弱 compete 比较好坏，胜负， 强弱	賽跑(sài pǎo) 赛跑 running race 比賽(bǐ sài) 比赛 competition
sān ㄙㄢ	三	三	數目字，在二之後 表示多數 three 数目字，在二之后 表示多数	再三(zài sān) time and again 三角形(sān jiǎo xíng) triangle
sǎn ㄙㄢˇ	傘	伞	擋雨或遮太陽的用 具 umbrella 挡雨或遮太阳的用 具	雨傘(yǔ sǎn) 雨伞 umbrella 降落傘(jiàng luò sǎn) 降落伞 parachute

sǎn ㄙㄢˇ	散	散	鬆開的，不集中的 scattered, not packed 松开的，不集中的	散光(sǎn guāng) astigmatism 散貨(sǎn huò) 散货 loose cargo
sàn ㄙㄢˋ	散	散	分開，遊玩解悶 separate, stroll 分开，遊玩解闷	分散(fēn sàn) scatter 散步(sàn bù) take a walk
sāng sàng ㄙㄤ ㄙㄤˋ	喪	丧	跟死人有關的事 funeral 跟死人有关的事	喪事(sāng shì) 丧事 funeral matter 喪禮(sāng lǐ) 丧礼 funeral ceremony
sāng ㄙㄤ	桑	桑	落葉喬木，果實叫 桑，味甜可吃 mulberry 落叶乔木，果实叫 桑，味甜可吃	桑樹(sāng shù) 桑树 mulberry tree
sǎng ㄙㄤˇ	嗓	嗓	喉嚨 throat, larynx 喉咙	嗓子(sǎng zi) voice 啞嗓(yǎ sǎng) 哑嗓 hoarse voice
sāo ㄙㄠ	搔	搔	用指甲輕抓 scratch 用指甲轻抓	搔癢(sāo yǎng) 搔痒 scratch the itchy part
sāo sào ㄙㄠ ㄙㄠˋ	臊	臊	難聞腥臭氣味 foul smell 难闻腥臭气味	尿臊(niào sāo) smell of urine 狐臊(hú sāo) fox odor
sāo ㄙㄠ	騷	骚	不安定，擾亂，舉 止輕佻 unstable, harass frivolous 不安定，扰乱，举 止轻佻	騷動(sāo dòng) 骚动 commotion 騷客(sāo kè) 骚客 poet
sǎo sào ㄙㄠˇ ㄙㄠˋ	掃	扫	除去灰塵或髒東西 ，很快地掠過 sweep, skim over 除去灰尘或脏东西 ，很快地掠过	掃地(sǎo dì) 扫地 sweep the floor 掃除(sǎo chú) 扫除 sweep away 掃把(sào bǎ) 扫把 broom

sǎo ㄙㄠˇ	嫂	嫂	哥哥的妻子 elder brother's wife	嫂嫂(sǎo sao) elder brother's wife
sào sāo ㄙㄠˋ ㄙㄠ	臊	臊	害羞 shy	害臊(hài sào) shy
sè ㄙㄜˋ	色	色	眼睛對照射在物體 上的光的一種感覺 ，性慾 color, lust 眼睛对照射在物体 上的光的一种感觉 ，性慾	顏色(yán sè) 颜色 color 色情(sè qíng) pornographic
sè ㄙㄜˋ	澀	涩	不好受的滋味，文 章難讀難懂 distasteful, hard to understand 不好受的滋味，文 章难读难懂	艱澀(jiān sè) 艰涩 difficult to understand 青澀(qīng sè)青涩 slightly bitter taste of unripened fruit
sēn ㄙㄣ	森	森	樹木眾多，深密 forest 树木众多，深密	森林(sēn lín) forest 陰森森(yīn sēn sēn) 阴森森spooky
sēng ㄙㄥ	僧	僧	佛教指出家修行 的男子 monk	高僧(gāo sēng) senior monk 僧侶(sēng lǚ) 僧侣 monk
shā ㄕㄚ	紗	纱	用棉花，麻等紡成 的細縷，可織成布 ，有小孔的織品 yarn, gauze 用棉花，麻等纺成 的细缕，可织成布 ，有小孔的织品	紗布(shā bù) 纱布 gauze 紡紗(fǎng shā) 纺纱 spin cotton to make yarn
shā ㄕㄚ	殺	杀	使生物失去生命， 消滅 kill, destroy 使生物失去生命， 消灭	謀殺(móu shā) 谋杀 murder 殺價(shā jià) 杀价 haggle for lower price
shā ㄕㄚ	沙	沙	非常細碎的石粒， 海邊的土地 sand 非常细碎的石粒， 海边的土地	沙灘(shā tān) 沙滩 the beaches 沙漠(shā mò) 沙漠 desert

shā ㄕㄚ	莎	莎	多用於人名，地名 a word used mainly in names	
shā ㄕㄚ	鯊	鲨	生長在海洋中的凶 猛魚類　shark 生长在海洋中的凶 猛鱼类	鯊魚(shā yú)　鲨鱼 shark
shā ㄕㄚ	裟	裟	袈裟：和尚，尼姑 所穿的衣服 Buddhist monk's robe	袈裟(jiā shā) Buddhist monk's robe
shā ㄕㄚ	砂	砂	細碎小石粒 fine sand 细碎小石粒	砂紙(shā zhǐ)　砂纸 sand paper 砂眼(shā yǎn) trachoma
shā ㄕㄚ	煞	煞	停止 stop	煞車(shā chē)　煞车 brake
shá ㄕㄚˊ	啥	啥	什麼 (比較粗的口 語) what 什么 (比较粗的口 语)	幹啥？(gàn shá)　干啥？ what for?
shǎ ㄕㄚˇ	傻	傻	笨，愚蠢 foolish	傻瓜(shǎ guā) fool 傻話(shǎ huà)　傻话 foolish remark
shà ㄕㄚˋ	煞	煞	很，凶惡的 very, fiendish 很，凶恶的	煞費苦心 (shà fèi kǔ xīn) 煞费苦心 take great pains 惡煞(è shà)　恶煞 fiendish person
shà xià ㄕㄚˋ ㄒㄧㄚˋ	廈	厦	大屋子 big building	高樓大廈(gāo lóu dà shà) 高楼大厦　highrises

264

shà ㄕㄚˋ	霎	霎	很短時間 a short time 很短时间	霎時(shà shí) 霎时 momentarily 一霎那(yí shà nà) in a wink
shāi ㄕㄞ	篩	筛	有很多小孔可以漏 下細小東西的器具 sieve 有很多小孔可以漏 下细小东西的器具	篩子(shāi zi) 筛子 sieve 篩米(shāi mǐ) 筛米 sift the rice
shài ㄕㄞˋ	曬	晒	把東西放在陽光下 任其乾燥 expose to the sun 把东西放在阳光下 任其干燥	曬太陽(shài tài yáng) 晒太阳 expose to the sun 曬衣服(shài yī fú) 晒衣服 hang clothes under sun
shān ㄕㄢ	山	山	地面上由土、石、 小樹集成並隆起的 地方 hill, mountain 地面上由土、石、 小树集成并隆起的 地方	高山(gāo shān) high mountain 山頂(shān dǐng) 山顶 summit 火山(huǒ shān) volcano
shān ㄕㄢ	衫	衫	上衣 upper garment	衣衫(yī shān) dress 襯衫(chèn shān) 衬衫 shirt
shān ㄕㄢ	杉	杉	常綠喬木，木材可 以用來蓋房子 fir 常绿乔木，木材可 以用来盖房子	杉木(shān mù) fir tree
shān ㄕㄢ	煽	煽	搖動扇子或其他東 西 to fan 摇动扇子 或其他东西	煽動(shān dòng) 煽动 incite 煽火(shān huǒ) fan the fire
shān ㄕㄢ	刪	删	除去，去掉文字中 不妥當的部分 delete 除去，去掉文字中 不妥当的部分	刪改(shān gǎi) correct by deletion 刪去(shān qù) delete
shān ㄕㄢ	珊	珊	珊瑚：在海底狀似 樹枝的東西 coral 珊瑚：在海底状似 树枝的东西	珊瑚(shān hú) coral
shān ㄕㄢ	蹣	蹒	蹣跚：一拐一拐地走 hobble along 蹒跚：一拐一拐地走	蹣跚(pán shān) 蹒跚 hobble along

shān ㄕ ㄢ	姍	姗	走路慢 walk slowly	姍姍來遲(shān shān lái chí) 姗姗来迟 come late
shǎn ㄕ ㄢˇ	閃	闪	光一亮一暗 blinking	閃光(shǎn guāng) 闪光 flashing light 閃電(shǎn diàn) 闪电 lightning
shàn shan ㄕ ㄕ ㄢˋㄢ	訕	讪	譏笑 jeer 讥笑	訕笑(shàn xiào) 讪笑 deride 搭訕(dā shan) 搭讪 start a conversation with
shàn ㄕ ㄢˋ	扇	扇	搖動生風使人涼快 的用具 a fan 摇动生风使人凉快 的用具	扇子(shàn zi) fan 電扇(diàn shàn) 电扇 electric fan
shàn ㄕ ㄢˋ	贍	赡	提供生活費 provide living expenses for 提供生活费	贍養(shàn yǎng) 赡养 provide for 贍養費(shàn yǎng fèi) 赡养费 alimony
shàn ㄕ ㄢˋ	擅	擅	專長，獨斷獨行 expertise, unilaterally 专长，独断独行	擅自(shàn zì) unilaterally 擅長(shàn cháng) 擅长 skilled in
shàn ㄕ ㄢˋ	疝	疝	病名 hernia	疝氣(shàn qì) 疝气 hernia
shàn ㄕ ㄢˋ	善	善	心地好，容易 kind, prone to	善良(shàn liáng) kind 善變(shàn biàn) 善变 prone to changes
shāng ㄕ ㄤ	傷	伤	身體受到損壞，得 罪，悲哀 injure, hurt, sad 身体受到损坏，得 罪，悲哀	傷害(shāng hài) 伤害 injury 傷心(shāng xīn) 伤心 sad

shāng ㄕㄤ	殤	殇	還沒有到二十歲就死去 die young 还没有到二十岁就死去	國殤(guó shāng) 国殇 national martyr 國殤日(guó shāng rì) 国殇日 Memorial Day
shāng ㄕㄤ	商	商	做買賣，討論，使用除法得的結果 do business, discuss, quotient 做买卖，讨论，使用除法得的结果	商人(shāng rén) businessman 商量(shāng liáng) discuss
sháng ㄕㄤˊ	裳	裳	衣裙 skirt	衣裳(yī sháng) clothes
shǎng ㄕㄤˇ	賞	赏	把財物給有功勞的人，讚美 reward, praise 把财物给有功劳的人，赞美	獎賞(jiǎng shǎng) 奖赏 reward 讚賞(zàn shǎng) 赞赏 show appreciation for
shàng ㄕㄤˋ	上	上	"下"的相反，對於尊貴或高位的通稱 up, refer to the higher-up "下"的相反，对於尊贵或高位的通称	山上(shān shàng) up the hill 皇上(huáng shàng) His Majesty
shàng ㄕㄤˋ	尚	尚	重視 attach importance to	高尚(gāo shàng) noble 和尚(hé shàng) Buddhish monk
shāo ㄕㄠ	稍	稍	略微，小小一點 a little 略微，小小一点	稍微(shāo wéi) a little bit 稍候(shāo hòu) wait a moment
shāo ㄕㄠ	燒	烧	熱，用火烹煮，焚 heat, cook, burn 热，用火烹煮，焚	發燒(fā shāo) 发烧 have fever 燒飯(shāo fàn) 烧饭 cook rice
sháo ㄕㄠˊ	勺	勺	舀液體的器具 ladle 舀液体的器具	勺子(sháo zi) ladle 湯勺(tāng sháo) 汤勺 soup ladle

shǎo ㄕㄠˇ	少	少	不夠，不多 not enough, little 不够，不多	缺少(quē shǎo) short of 多少(duō shǎo) how many, how much
shào ㄕㄠˋ	少	少	年輕 young 年轻	少女(shào nǚ) maiden 少年(shào niān) young man
shào ㄕㄠˋ	邵	邵	姓氏 Chinese surname	
shào ㄕㄠˋ	哨	哨	口中吹出的聲音， 軍隊所設置的警衛 whistle, sentry 口中吹出的声音， 军队所设置的警卫	口哨(kǒu shào) whistle 崗哨(gǎng shào) 岗哨 sentry post
shē ㄕㄜ	賒	赊	買東西暫時不付錢 ，以後再付on credit 买东西暂时不付钱 ，以后再付	賒帳(shē zhàng) 赊帐 buy things on credit 賒欠(shē qiàn) 赊欠 owe
shē ㄕㄜ	奢	奢	浪費，過分的 wasteful, excessive 浪费，过分的	奢侈(shē chǐ) extravagant 奢望(shē wàng) wishful thinking
shé ㄕㄜˊ	舌	舌	口腔裏分辨味道和 幫助咀嚼和發聲的 器官 tongue 口腔里分辨味道和 帮助咀嚼和发声的 器官	舌頭(shé tóu) 舌头 tongue 舌戰(shé zhàn) 舌战 heated argument
shé ㄕㄜˊ	蛇	蛇	有鱗的爬行動物 snake 有鳞的爬行动物	蟒蛇(mǎng shé) python 毒蛇(dú shé) poisonous snake
shě ㄕㄜˇ	捨	舍	放棄 abandon 放弃	捨不得(shě bù dé) 舍不得 reluctant to part with 捨棄(shě qì) 舍弃 abandon

shè shě ㄕ ㄕ ㄜˋ ㄜˇ	舍	舍	賓客休息的房屋， 對人謙稱自己輩份 較低的親屬 inn, my 宾客休息的房屋， 对人谦称自己辈份 较低的亲属	宿舍(sù shè) dormitory 舍弟(shè dì) my younger brother 舍我其誰(shě wǒ qí shuí) 舍我其谁who else but me?
shè ㄕ ㄜˋ	社	社	有組織的團體 association 有组织的团体	社會(shè huì) 社会 society 社論(shè lùn) 社论 editorial
shè ㄕ ㄜˋ	設	设	建立，佈置 establish, arrange 建立，佈置	設立(shè lì) 设立 establish 設計(shè jì) 设计 design
shè ㄕ ㄜˋ	射	射	發箭，用推力送出 子彈，液體受壓力 很快地流出 shoot 发箭，用推力送出 子弹，液体受压力 很快地流出	發射(fā shè) 发射 launch (rocket) 反射(fǎn shè) reflect
shè ㄕ ㄜˋ	涉	涉	徒步經過，經歷， 牽連 walk past, to experience, involve in 徒步经过，经历， 牽连	牽涉(qiān shè) 牵涉 complicate 涉嫌(shè xián) be considered a suspect
shè ㄕ ㄜˋ	攝	摄	收，取 receive, take in	攝影(shè yǐng) 摄影 photography 攝取(shè qǔ) 摄取 absorb
shè ㄕ ㄜˋ	赦	赦	寬免罪行 absolve 宽免罪行	大赦(dà shè) amnesty 赦免(shè miǎn) absolve
shè ㄕ ㄜˋ	懾	慑	恐懼，害怕 fear 恐惧，害怕	懾服(shè fú) 慑服 surrender due to fear 威懾(wēi shè) 威慑 deter

shéi shuí ㄕ ㄕ ㄟˊ ㄨˊ ㄟ	誰	谁	什麼人，任何人 who, whom 什么人，任何人	是誰？(shì shéi) 是谁？ Who is it? 誰的？(shéi de) 谁的？ Whose? 給誰？(gěi shéi) 给谁？ give to whom?
shēn ㄕ ㄣ	申	申	说明，陈述 explain, make a statement 说明，陈述	申請(shēn qǐng) 申请 apply for 申明(shēn míng) declare
shēn ㄕ ㄣ	伸	伸	舒展開 stretch out 舒展开	伸手(shēn shǒu) stretch out hand 伸縮(shēn suō) 伸缩 expand and contract
shēn ㄕ ㄣ	紳	绅	稱有地位穿著整齊 的男子，地方上有 地位的人 gentleman 称有地位穿着整齐 的男子，地方上有 地位的人	紳士(shēn shì) 绅士 gentleman 富紳(fù shēn) 富绅 wealthy gentleman
shēn ㄕ ㄣ	呻	呻	哼哼聲，痛苦時發 出的聲音 groan, moan 哼哼声，痛苦时发 出的声音	呻吟(shēn yín) moan
shēn ㄕ ㄣ	身	身	軀體 body 躯体	身體(shēn tǐ) 身体 body 身分(shēn fèn) identification
shēn cān cēn ㄕ ㄘ ㄣ ㄢ ㄥ	參	参	人參 ginseng 人参	人參(rén shēn) 人参 ginseng
shēn ㄕ ㄣ	深	深	"淺"的相反，非 常 deep, very "浅"的相反，非 常	深山(shēn shān) deep in the mountain 深信(shēn xìn) deeply believe 深度(shēn dù) depth 深刻(shēn kè) profound 深夜(shēn yè) late at night

shēn xīn ㄕㄣ ㄒㄧㄣ	莘	莘	多年生草本植物，開紫色花，根可做菜，很多 a plant, many 多年生草本植物，开紫色花，根可做菜，很多	莘莘學子(shēn shēn xué zi) 莘莘学子 the numerous students
shén shí ㄕㄣˊ ㄕˊ	什	什	同"甚"，疑問代名詞 what 同"甚"，疑问代名词	什麼?(shén me) 什么? What?
shén ㄕㄣˊ	神	神	天地萬物的創造者，不平凡的 God, unusual 天地万物的创造者，不平凡的	神話(shén huà) 神话 myth 神祕(shén mì) mysterious
shěn ㄕㄣˇ	審	审	仔細思考，詢問案件 ponder, try a case 仔细思考，询问案件	審查(shěn chá) 审查 investigate 審判(shěn pàn) 审判 conduct a trial
shěn ㄕㄣˇ	嬸	婶	叔叔的妻子，尊稱已婚的長輩女性 auntie 叔叔的妻子，尊称已婚的长辈女性	嬸嬸(shěn shen) 婶婶 auntie 王嬸(wáng shěn) 王婶 Auntie Wang
shèn ㄕㄣˋ	甚	甚	"甚麼"同"什麼"，連接詞表示更進一層 what "甚么"同"什么"，连接词表示更进一层	甚多(shèn duō) quite many 甚至於(shèn zhì yú) 甚至於 so much so that
shèn ㄕㄣˋ	腎	肾	濾出尿液的主要器官 kidney 滤出尿液的主要器官	腎臟(shèn zàng) 肾脏 kidney 腎結石(shèn jié shí) 肾结石 kidney stone
shèn ㄕㄣˋ	滲	渗	液體慢慢地漏出或進入 permeate, seep through 液体慢慢地漏出或进入	滲透(shèn tòu) 渗透 permeate, infiltrate 滲出(shèn chū) 渗出 ooze from
shèn ㄕㄣˋ	慎	慎	小心 cautious	謹慎(jǐn shèn) 谨慎 discreet 慎重(shèn zhòng) cautious

shēng ㄕ ㄥ	生	生	"死"的相反，產下，出現 alive, born, occur "死"的相反，产下，出现	出生(chū shēng) be born 發生(fā shēng) 发生 occur
shēng ㄕ ㄥ	昇	昇	上揚，提高 rise up, raise 上扬，提高	升旗(shēng qí) raise flag 升級(shēng jí) promote to higher level
shēng ㄕ ㄥ	聲	声	物體振動而產生的音響，說出讓人知道 sound, announce 物体振动而产生的音响，说出让人知道	聲音(shēng yīn) 声音 sound 聲張(shēng zhāng) 声张 publicize
shēng ㄕ ㄥ	牲	牲	指牛，馬，驢等家畜 draft animals 指牛，马，驴等家畜	牲口(shēng kǒu) draft animals 牲畜(shēng chù) livestock
shēng ㄕ ㄥ	甥	甥	姊妹的孩子 sister's child	外甥(wài shēng) nephew 外甥女(wài shēng nǚ) niece
shéng ㄕ ㄥˊ	繩	绳	用兩股以上的線，棉等編成的長條物 rope 用两股以上的线，棉等编成的长条物	繩子(shéng zi) 绳子 rope 準繩(zhǔn shéng) 准绳 yardstick
shěng xing ㄕ ㄒ ㄥˇ ㄥ	省	省	全國第一級地方行政組織，節約，簡略 province, save, abbreviate 全国第一级地方行政组织，节约，简略	省份(shěng fèn) province 省錢(shěng qián) 省钱 save money
shèng ㄕ ㄥˋ	聖	圣	崇高的 sacred	聖人(shèng rén) 圣人 saint 聖經(shèng jīng) 圣经 Bible
shèng ㄕ ㄥˋ	勝	胜	贏，承受，風景優美的地方 win, undertake, scenic place 赢，承受，风景优美的地方	勝利(shèng lì) 胜利 victory 名勝(míng shèng) 名胜 tourist attraction

shèng chéng ㄕㄥˋ ㄔㄥˊ	盛	盛	興旺，豐富，深厚 flourishing, abundant, grand 兴旺，丰富，深厚	茂盛(mào shèng) luxuriant 盛會(shèng huì) 盛会 grand gathering
shèng ㄕㄥˋ	剩	剩	留下來的，餘下的 remaining 留下来的，餘下的	剩餘(shèng yú) 剩餘 residual 剩下(shèng xià) remaining
shī ㄕ	失	失	丟，找不到，沒有 達到目的 lost, misplaced, fall short of 丢，找不到，没 有达到目的	遺失(yí shī) lose something 失敗(shī bài) 失败 defeat 失望(shī wàng) disappointed 失明(shī míng) become blind 失業(shī yè) 失业 jobless
shī ㄕ	師	师	教導學生的人，對 有技能者的稱呼 teacher, master 教导学生的人，对 有技能者的称呼	老師(lǎo shī) 老师 teacher 技師(jì shī) 技师 technician
shī ㄕ	詩	诗	用有押韻的詞句來 表達情感的文體 poetry 用有押韵的词句来 表达情感的文体	詩歌(shī gē) 诗歌 poetry 作詩(zuò shī) 作诗 compose a poem
shī ㄕ	蝨	虱	寄生在人，家畜身 上的一種會吸血的 蟲子 louse 寄生在人，家畜身 上的一种会吸血的 虫子	蝨子(shī zi) 虱子 louse 頭蝨(tóu shī) 头虱 lice on the hair
shī ㄕ	獅	狮	一種兇猛的野獸， 毛黃褐色 lion 一种兇猛的野兽， 毛黃褐色	獅子(shī zi) 狮子 lion 母獅(mǔ shī) 母狮 lioness 獅子狗(shī zi gǒu) 狮子狗 pug-dog
shī ㄕ	屍	尸	死人的身體 corpse 死人的身体	屍首(shī shǒu) 尸首 corpse 僵屍(jiāng shī) 僵尸 zombi 屍袋(shī dài) 尸袋 body bag 屍體(shī tǐ) 尸体 dead body

shī ㄕ	濕	湿	"乾"的相反,含 有水份或沾水了 wet "干"的相反,含 有水份或沾水了	潮濕(cháo shī) 潮湿 wet 打濕(dǎ shī) 打湿 to wet
shī ㄕ	施	施	給予,實行 give, implement 给予,实行	施捨(shī shě) give alms 施工(shī gōng) construction
shí ㄕˊ	石	石	由礦物集結而成的 堅硬塊狀物 stone, rock 由矿物集结而成的 坚硬块状物	石頭(shí tóu) 石头 rock 石油(shí yóu) petroleum
shí ㄕˊ	時	时	一小時是六十分鐘 hour 一小时是六十分钟	時間(shí jiān) 时间 time 時代(shí dài) 时代 era
shí shìh ㄕˊㄕˋ	識	识	見解,知道 opinion, know 见解,知道	認識(rèn shì) 认识 know 知識(zhī shì) 知识 knowledge
shí ㄕˊ	實	实	充滿,不虛 full, not empty 充满,不虚	誠實(chéng shí)诚实honest 實在(shí zài) 实在realistic 事實(shì shí) 事实 fact 現實(xiàn shí) 现实 reality
shí ㄕˊ	拾	拾	撿,"十"字的大 寫 word form of number "10" 捡,"十"字的大 写	收拾(shōu shí) tidy up, pack up 拾荒(shí huāng) scavenge
shí ㄕˊ	食	食	吃 eat	食言(shí yán) fail to keep promise 零食(líng shí) snack 食指(shí zhǐ) index finger

shí shén ㄕ˙ ㄕ ㄣˊ	什	什	多而雜，數目名同 "十" miscellaneous, same as "十" 多而杂，数目名同 "十"	什锦(shí jǐn) 什锦 a hodgepodge
shí ㄕˊ	十	十	九之後的數目，同 "拾" ten 九之后的数目，同 "拾"	十分(shí fēn) very 11十一, 12十二, 13十三, 14十四, 15十五, 16十六, 17十七, 18十八, 19十九, 20二十, 30三十, 40四十, 50五十, 60六十, 70七十, 80八十, 90九十
shí ㄕˊ	蝕	蚀	剝落，損壞，虧損 peel off, damage, loss 剥落，损坏，亏损	蝕本(shí běn) 蚀本 operating at a loss 月蝕(yuè shí) 月蚀 lunar eclipse
shǐ ㄕˇ	史	史	過去事跡的記載 history 过去事迹的记载	歷史(lì shǐ) 历史 history 史學家(shǐ xué jiā) 史学家 historian
shǐ ㄕˇ	使	使	派遣，命令，駐外 國的外交長官 send, order, emissary 派遣，命令，驻外 国的外交长官	使用(shǐ yòng) use 大使(dà shǐ) ambassador 使節(shǐ jié) 使节 emissary
shǐ ㄕˇ	始	始	最初 the beginning	開始(kāi shǐ) 开始 begin 始終(shǐ zhōng) 始终 from beginning to end
shǐ ㄕˇ	駛	驶	操作交通工具 drive	駕駛(jià shǐ) 驾驶 drive, driver 駛向(shǐ xiàng) 驶向 drive (or sail) toward
shǐ ㄕˇ	屎	屎	糞便，耳、眼的分 泌物 excrement, secretion from ears, eyes 粪便，耳、眼 的分泌物	拉屎(lā shǐ) excrete 耳屎(ěr shǐ) ear wax
shì ㄕˋ	士	士	古代的讀書人 old-time scholar 古代的读书人	學士(xué shì) 学士 bachelor's degree 士兵(shì bīng) soldier

shì ㄕˋ	市	市	做生意的地方，人口密集的地方 market, city	市場(shì chǎng) 市场 market 城市(chéng shì) city
shì ㄕˋ	示	示	告訴，表明，給人看 tell, express, show 告诉，表明，给人看	表示(biǎo shì) express, indicate 暗示(àn shì) hint
shì ㄕˋ	仕	仕	做官 to become official	仕途(shì tú) career of an official
shì ㄕˋ	柿	柿	落葉喬木，開黃花，果實可食 persimmon 落叶乔木，开黄花，果实可食	柿子(shì zi) persimmon
shì sì ㄕˋ、ㄙˋ	似	似	同某種情況相像 similar to 同某种情况相像	像雪似的那麼白(xiàng xuě shì de nà me bái) 像雪似的那么白 as white as snow
shì ㄕˋ	勢	势	權力，威力 power, force 权力，威力	勢力(shì lì) 势力 influence 姿勢(zī shì) 姿势 posture 優勢(yōu shì) 优势 advantage
shì ㄕˋ	事	事	人的所作所爲，工作，做 work, do 人的所作所为，工作，做	事情(shì qíng) matter, affair 故事(gù shì) story 事先(shì xiān) beforehand 事故(shì gù) accident
shì ㄕˋ	世	世	時代，世界，人的一生 era, world, lifetime 时代，世界，人的一生	世界(shì jiè) world 世紀(shì jì) 世纪 century

shì ㄕˋ	氏	氏	古代族號的分出 a division of ancient clan 古代族号的分出	姓氏(xìng shì) family name 張氏(zhāng shì) 张氏 Mrs. Zhang
shì ㄕˋ	式	式	特定的規格 format 特定的规格	格式(gé shì) format 公式(gōng shì) formula
shì ㄕˋ	恃	恃	依賴 rely 依赖	有恃無恐(yǒu shì wú kǒng) 有恃无恐unafraid due to strong backing
shì ㄕˋ	誓	誓	表示決心，依照所 說的話實行 promise 表示决心，依照所 说的话实行	宣誓(xuān shì) take oath 誓言(shì yán) promise, oath
shì ㄕˋ	室	室	屋子，機關團體的 工作單位 room, a work unit of an organization 屋子，机关团体的 工作单位	室內(shì nèi) indoor 教室(jiào shì) 教室 classroom
shì ㄕˋ	侍	侍	隨時替人服務的人 ，晚輩陪伴在旁 waiter, serve 随时替人服务的人 ，晚辈陪伴在旁	服侍(fú shì) to wait on, serve 侍者(shì zhě) waiter
shì ㄕˋ	視	视	看見，觀察 watch, observe 看见，观察	近視(jìn shì) 近视 shortsighted 視察(shì chá) 视察 inspect
shì ㄕˋ	飾	饰	裝修，打扮，穿戴 的用品 decorate, dress up, ornament 装修，打扮，穿戴 的用品	裝飾(zhuāng shì) 装饰 decorate 首飾(shǒu shì) 首饰 ornament

shì ㄕˋ	是	是	"非"的相反，對 ，這 yes, this "非"的相反，对 ，这	國是(guó shì) 国是 important state affairs 是否(shì fǒu) whether or not
shì ㄕˋ	適	适	相合，舒服，剛巧 match, comfortable, just 相合，舒服，刚巧	合適(hé shì) 合适 suitable 不適(bú shì) 不适 feel discomfort
shì ㄕˋ	逝	逝	過去 past 过去	逝世(shì shì) pass away 病逝(bìng shì) die of illness
shì ㄕˋ	釋	释	解說，放下 explain, release 解说，放下	解釋(jiě shì) 解释 explain 釋放(shì fàng) 释放 release
shì ㄕˋ	嗜	嗜	喜好，沈迷 hobby, indulge in	嗜好(shì hào) hobby 嗜酒(shì jiǔ) indulge in drinking
shì ㄕˋ	拭	拭	擦 rub	拭目以待(shì mù yǐ dài) wait and see 擦拭(cā shì) wipe
shì ㄕˋ	試	试	測驗，探測，先做 做看 test, probe, try 测验，探测，先做 做看	考試(kǎo shì) 考试 examination 試探(shì tàn) 试探 test
shì ㄕˋ	弒	弒	地位低的人殺了地 位高的人 slaying one's superior 地位低的人杀了地 位高的人	弒君(shì jūn) murdering the king 弒父(shì fù) patricide
shì ㄕˋ	軾	轼	古時車前可依靠的 橫木 horizontal bar in front of ancient carriage 古时车前 可依靠的横木	蘇軾(sū shì) 苏轼 famous Chinese scholar of the Song Dynasty

shi chi ˊ ㄕ ˙ ㄔ	匙	匙	可開鎖的東西，可以舀取流質的用具 key, spoon 可开锁的东西，可以舀取流质的用具	鑰匙(yào shi)钥匙 key 湯匙(tāng chí)汤匙 tablespoon
shōu ㄕ ㄡ	收	收	接受，招回，結束 accept, recall, end 接受，招回，结束	收到(shōu dào) receive 豐收(fēng shōu) 丰收 bumper harvest
shóu ㄕ ㄡ ˊ	熟	熟	不陌生，食物煮到可以吃，有經驗 acquainted, ripe, skilled 不陌生，食物煮到可以吃，有经验	熟悉(shóu xī) familiar 熟練(shóu liàn)熟练 skilled
shǒu ㄕ ㄡ ˇ	手	手	人體上肢前端拿東西的部分，有專長的人 hand 人体上肢前端拿东西的部分，有专长的人	右手(yòu shǒu) right hand 高手(gāo shǒu) master in a field
shǒu ㄕ ㄡ ˇ	首	首	頭，領導人 head, leader 头，领导人	昂首(áng shǒu) hold one's head high 首次(shǒu cì) for the first time
shǒu ㄕ ㄡ ˇ	守	守	看管，保持，依照，防禦 look after, keep, defend 看管，保持，依照，防禦	保守(bǎo shǒu) conservative 守時(shǒu shí)守时 punctual
shòu ㄕ ㄡ ˋ	受	受	接收，遭到 receive, sustain	接受(jiē shòu) accept 受害(shòu hài) victimized
shòu ㄕ ㄡ ˋ	授	授	給予，教 give, teach 给予，教	授權(shòu quán)授权 authorize 人工授精(rén gōng shòu jīng) artificial insemination

shòu ㄕ ㄡˋ	售	售	賣 sell 卖	售票(shòu piào) sell ticket 零售(líng shòu) retail sale
shòu ㄕ ㄡˋ	狩	狩	打獵 hunt 打猎	狩獵(shòu liè) 狩猎 hunting 巡狩(xún shòu) imperial inspection trip
shòu ㄕ ㄡˋ	壽	寿	生命的長短 lifespan 生命的长短	長壽(cháng shòu) 长寿 longevity 壽命(shòu mìng) 寿命 lifespan
shòu ㄕ ㄡˋ	獸	兽	有四條腿的哺乳動 物，野蠻，下流 beast, savage, basely 有四条腿的哺乳动 物，野蛮，下流	野獸(yě shòu) 野兽 beasts 獸行(shòu xíng) 兽行 brutal act
shòu ㄕ ㄡˋ	瘦	瘦	"肥"的相反 thin	瘦長(shòu cháng) 瘦长 slender 瘦弱(shòu ruò) thin and weak
shū ㄕ ㄨ	書	书	有文字或圖畫的冊 子　book 有文字或图画的册 子	証書(zhèng shū) 证书 certificate 書信(shū xìn) 书信 letters
shū ㄕ ㄨ	抒	抒	發表，解除 express, lift 发表，解除	抒情(shū qíng) express one's feelings 抒發(shū fā) 抒发 give expression to
shū shú ㄕ ㄕ ㄨ ㄨˊ	淑	淑	品德好，美善 virtuous	嫻淑(xián shū) virtuous (woman)

shū ㄕㄨ	舒	舒	伸開，愉快，安適 stretch, happy, comfortable 伸开，愉快，安适	舒展(shū zhǎn) 舒展 stretch out 舒服(shū fú) comfortable
shū shú ㄕㄨ ㄕㄨˊ	叔	叔	父親的弟弟 father's younger brother 父亲的弟弟	叔叔(shū shu) father's younger brother
shū ㄕㄨ	樞	枢	重要的關鍵，中心 部分 crux, core 重要的关键，中心 部分	樞紐(shū niǔ) 枢纽 pivot 中樞(zhōng shū) 中枢 central government
shū ㄕㄨ	殊	殊	不同，特別 different, special	特殊(tè shū) special 殊榮(shū róng) 殊荣 special honor
shū ㄕㄨ	疏	疏	不親近，開通 not close, unclog 不亲近，开通	疏遠(shū yuǎn) 疏远 estrange from 生疏(shēng shū) unfamiliar
shū ㄕㄨ	蔬	蔬	可吃的植物或菜 vegetables	蔬菜(shū cài) 蔬菜 vegetables 蔬果(shū guǒ) vegetables and fruits
shū ㄕㄨ	姝	姝	美貌的女子 pretty girl	名姝(míng shū) famous, pretty lady
shū ㄕㄨ	梳	梳	整理頭髮的用具 comb 整理头发的用具	梳子(shū zi) comb 梳頭(shū tóu) 梳头 comb hair

shū ㄕ ㄨ	輸	输	從一地到另一地， 敗 from one place to another, lose 从一地到另一地， 败	輸血(shū xuè) 输血 blood transfusion 輸出(shū chū) 输出 export
shú ㄕ ㄨˊ	贖	赎	用行動或財物來免 除刑罰或抵銷罪過 atone 用行动或财物来免 除刑罚或抵销罪过	贖回(shú huí) 赎回 redeem 贖金(shú jīn) 赎金 ransom money
shǔ ㄕ ㄨˇ	暑	暑	熱 hot 热	中暑(zhòng shǔ) heat stroke 暑假(shǔ jià) summer vacation
shǔ ㄕ ㄨˇ	薯	薯	多年生草本植物， 延地面生長，塊根 付食 tuber 多年生草本植物， 延地面生长，块根 可食	番薯(fān shǔ) 番薯 sweet potato 薯條(shǔ tiáo) 薯条 French fry
shǔ ㄕ ㄨˇ	署	署	辦公的處所，簽名 an office, sign one's name 办公的处所，签名	部署(bù shǔ) make arrangements 署名(shǔ míng) signed (article)
shǔ ㄕ ㄨˇ	屬	属	同一家族的，類 from the same family, group 同一家族的，类	家屬(jiā shǔ) 家属 dependents 屬實(shǔ shí) 属实 authenticated
shǔ ㄕ ㄨˇ	鼠	鼠	哺乳動物，身體小 ，牙齒發達 rodent 哺乳动物，身体小 ，牙齿发达	老鼠(lǎo shǔ) rat 鼠輩(shǔ bèi) 鼠辈 mean fellows
shǔ ㄕ ㄨˇ	曙	曙	天剛亮 dawn 天刚亮	曙光(shǔ guāng) dawn

shǔ shù ㄕ ㄕ ㄨ ㄨ	數	数	一個一個地計算 count 一个一个地计算	數一數(shǔ yì shǔ) 数一数 count 倒數計時(dào shǔ jì shí) 倒数计时 countdown
shù ㄕ ㄨ	術	术	技能 skill	技術(jì shù) 技术 technology 術語(shú yǔ) 术语 terminology
shù ㄕ ㄨ	述	述	訴說，陳說 tell, make a statement 诉说，陈说	敘述(xù shù) describe 口述(kǒu shù) narrate
shù ㄕ ㄨ	漱	漱	含水清洗口腔 rinse (mouth) 含水清洗口腔	漱口(shù kǒu) rinse the mouth 漱口水(shù kǒu shuǐ) mouthwash 漱口杯(shù kǒu bēi) mug for rinsing mouth
shù shǔ ㄕ ㄕ ㄨ ㄨ	數	数	計算東西多少 number 计算东西多少	數目(shù mù) 数目 number 單數(dān shù) 单数 odd number
shù ㄕ ㄨ	束	束	捆住，一捆 bundle up, a bundle	束縛(shù fù) 束缚 restriction 花束(huā shù) 花束 boutique
shù ㄕ ㄨ	恕	恕	原諒 forgive 原谅	寬恕(kuān shù) forgive 恕罪(shù zuì) pardon a sin
shù ㄕ ㄨ	樹	树	有枝幹的植物，木 本的總稱， 建立 tree, establish 有枝干的植物，木 本的总称· 建立	樹林(shù lín) 树林 woods 樹立(shù lì) 树立 establish

283

shù ㄕ ㄨˋ	墅	墅	住宅以外供遊玩的 房屋 villa 住宅以外供遊玩的 房屋	別墅(bié shù) villa
shù ㄕ ㄨˋ	庶	庶	眾多，一般的 many, ordinary 众多，一般的	富庶(fù shù) richly endowed 庶民(shù mín) common people
shù ㄕ ㄨˋ	豎	竖	直立，從上而下 erect, vertically 直立，从上而下	豎立(shù lì) 竖立 erect 豎寫(shù xiě) 竖写 write vertically
shuā ㄕ ㄨ ㄚ	刷	刷	除去污垢的用具 brush	牙刷(yá shuā) tooth brush 印刷(yìn shuā) printing
shuǎ ㄕ ㄨ ㄚˇ	耍	耍	玩，戲弄 play 玩，戏弄	玩耍(wán shuǎ) play 耍手段(shuǎ shǒu duàn) play tricks
shuāi ㄕ ㄨ ㄞ	衰	衰	彎弱，不強健，由 興盛而衰微沒落 weaken, decline 弯弱，不强健，由 兴盛而衰微没落	衰弱(shuāi ruò) frail 衰退(shuāi tuì) degenerate
shuāi ㄕ ㄨ ㄞ	摔	摔	用力往下扔，跌 throw off, fall	摔跤(shuāi jiāo) trip and fall 摔角(shuāi jiǎo) wrestling
shuǎi ㄕ ㄨ ㄞˇ	甩	甩	拋棄，搖擺，理會 throw away, shake, take heed 抛弃，摇摆，理会	甩掉(shuǎi diào) throw away 不甩他(bù shuǎi tā) pay no attention to him

shuài ㄕㄨㄞˋ	帥	帅	最高指揮官，俊美 supreme commander, handsome 最高指挥官，俊美	元帥(yuán shuài) 元帅 generalissimo 帥氣(shuài qì) 帅气 handsome
shuài ㄕㄨㄞˋ	率	率	帶領，輕易，爽直 lead, readily, straightforward 带领，轻易，爽直	率領(shuài lǐng) 率领 to lead 率直(shuài zhí) 率直 straightforward
shuài ㄕㄨㄞˋ	蟀	蟀	蟋蟀：很會跳的昆蟲，雄性常在晚間發聲求偶 cricket (insect) 蟋蟀：很会跳的昆虫，雄性常在晚间发声求偶	蟋蟀(xī shuài) cricket (insect)
shuān ㄕㄨㄢ	閂	闩	橫插在門後使門推不開的棍子 door bolt 横插在门后使门推不开的棍子	閂門(shuān mén) 闩门 bolt the door 門閂(mén shuān) 门闩 door bolt
shuān ㄕㄨㄢ	拴	拴	綁 tie up 绑	拴馬(shuān mǎ) 拴马 hitch a horse
shuān ㄕㄨㄢ	栓	栓	瓶塞，器物上可開關的活門 stopper, valve 瓶塞，器物上可开关的活门	消防栓(xiāo fáng shuān) fire hydrant
shuāng ㄕㄨㄤ	雙	双	兩個，一對 a pair 两个，一对	一雙鞋(yì shuāng xié) 一双鞋 a pair of shoes 雙生子(shuāng shēng zi) 双生子 twins
shuāng ㄕㄨㄤ	霜	霜	水蒸汽冷至零度以下凝結附在地上的微細冰粒 frost 水蒸汽冷至零度以下凝结附在地上的微细冰粒	白霜(bái shuāng) white frost

shuāng ㄕ ㄨ ㄤ	孀	孀	死了丈夫的婦人 widow 死了丈夫的妇人	遺孀(yí shuāng)遗孀 widow 富孀(fù shuāng) rich widow
shuǎng ㄕ ㄨ ㄤ	爽	爽	舒服，率直，違背 comfortable, straightforward, go against 舒服，率直，违背	涼爽(liáng shuǎng)凉爽 cool 爽約(shuǎng yuē)爽约 stand somebody up
shuǐ ㄕ ㄨ ㄟ	水	水	一種無色無味的液 體 water 一种无色无味的液 体	冷水(lěng shuǐ) cold water 水份(shuǐ fèn) water content
shuì ㄕ ㄨ ㄟ	睡	睡	閉眼休息 sleep 闭眼休息	睡覺(shuì jiào)睡觉 sleep 睡衣(shuì yī) pajamas
shuì ㄕ ㄨ ㄟ	稅	税	政府向人民徵收的 錢 tax 政府向人民征收的 钱	稅金(shuì jīn) tax payment 納稅(nà shuì)纳税 pay taxes
shuì shuō ㄕ ㄕ ㄨ ㄨ ㄟ ㄛ	説	说	用言語使他人聽從 自己的意見 persuade, convince 用言语使他人听从 自己的意见	游説(yóu shuì)游说 lobby 説服(shuì fú)说服 persuade
shǔn ㄕ ㄨ ㄣ	吮	吮	用嘴吸 suck	吮乳(shǔn rǔ) suck the breast 吮指頭(shǔn zhǐ tóu) 吮指头 suck the thumb
shùn ㄕ ㄨ ㄣ	順	顺	向著相同的方向， 沿著 go with the flow, along 向著相同的方向， 沿著	順流(shùn liú)顺流 go with the flow 順序(shùn xù)顺序 sequentially
shùn ㄕ ㄨ ㄣ	瞬	瞬	轉眼，很短的時間 momentarily 转眼，很短的时间	瞬間(shùn jiān)瞬间 split second

shuō shuì ㄕㄨ ㄕㄨㄟˋ ㄕㄨㄛ	說	说	言語，解釋，責備 speak, explain, criticize 言语，解释，责备	演說(yǎn shuō)演说 public speaking 說話(shuō huà)说话 speaking
shuò ㄕㄨㄛˋ	爍	烁	光亮 bright	閃爍(shǎn shuò)闪烁 twinkle
shuò ㄕㄨㄛˋ	朔	朔	陰曆每月初一，北 方 first day of lunar month, north 阴历每月初一，北 方	朔望(shuò wàng) 1st and 15th of lunar month 朔風(shuò fēng) 朔风 north wind
shuò ㄕㄨㄛˋ	碩	硕	大，學識廣博 big, profound knowledge 大，学识广博	碩士(shuò shì)硕士 Master's degree
sī ㄙ	絲	丝	蠶吐出來的東西， 一點 silk, a little bit 蚕吐出来的东西， 一点	絲綢(sī chóu)丝绸 silk 絲毫不(sī háo bù)丝毫不 not in the least
sī ㄙ	思	思	想，考慮，想念 think, consider, miss (someone) 想，考虑，想念	思想(sī xiǎng) thought 相思(xiāng sī) miss somebody
sī ㄙ	司	司	政府機關的單位， 主管 a government agency, in charge 政府机关的单位， 主管	司法(sī fǎ) judicial 公司(gōng sī) company
sī ㄙ	私	私	"公"的相反，個 人的private, personal "公"的相反，个 人的	自私(zì sī) selfish 私利(sī lì) selfish interest
sī ㄙ	鷥	鸶	鷺鷥：白色水鳥， 頸和腿很長 egret 鹭鸶：白色水鸟， 颈和腿很长	鷺鷥(lù sī)鹭鸶 egret

sī ㄙ	斯	斯	這，這個，這裏 this 这，这个，这里	斯時(sī shí) 斯时 this time 斯文(sī wén) look educated
sī ㄙ	撕	撕	用手分開，分裂 tear, split 用手分开，分裂	撕裂(sī liè) tear apart 撕開(sī kāi) 撕开 tear open
sī ㄙ	廝	厮	僕役，對人輕視的 稱呼 servant, fellow 仆役，对人轻视的 称呼	這廝(zhè sī) 这厮 this fellow 廝守(sī shǒu) 厮守 stick together
sǐ ㄙˇ	死	死	失去生命，堅決的 ，不靈活的 die, doggedly, rigid 失去生命，坚决的 ，不灵活的	死亡(sǐ wáng) death 死守(sǐ shǒu) doggedly defend 死心(sǐ xīn) give up hope 死板(sǐ bǎn) rigid
sì ㄙˋ	肆	肆	"四"的大寫，不 顧一切 word form of number '4', willful "四"的大写，不 顾一切	放肆(fàng sì) unbridled 肆意(sì yì) willfully
sì ㄙˋ	寺	寺	教徒禮拜的地方， 和尚或尼姑住的地 方 temple 教徒礼拜的地方， 和尚或尼姑住的地 方	寺廟(sì miào) 寺庙 temples 佛寺(fó sì) Buddhist temple
sì shì ㄙˋㄕˋ	似	似	像，好像 resemble, as if	相似(xiāng sì) resemble 似乎(sì hū) as if 如花似玉(rú huā sì yù) 如花似玉 very beautiful (like flower and jade)
sì ㄙˋ	四	四	數目字，阿拉伯數 字"4" four 数目字，阿拉伯数 字"4"	四面(sì miàn) all around 四季(sì jì) the four seasons
sì cì ㄙˋㄘˋ	伺	伺	守候 wait for	伺機而動(sì jī ér dòng) 伺机而动 wait for the right moment to take action 伺服器(sì fú qì) server
sì ㄙˋ	駟	驷	四匹一組的馬 a four-horse team 四匹一组的马	一言既出，駟馬難追(yì yán jì chū, sì mǎ nán zhuī) 一言既出，驷马难追 what is said cannot be unsaid

sì ㄙˋ	俟	俟	等待 wait	俟時(sì shí) 俟时 by that time
sì ㄙˋ	飼	饲	餵養動物 feed animal 喂养动物	飼養(sì yǎng) 饲养 raise animals 飼料(sì liào) 饲料 animal feeds
sōng ㄙㄨㄥ	松	松	常綠喬木，葉呈針狀，木質堅硬 pine tree 常绿乔木，叶呈针状，木质坚硬	松樹(sōng shù) 松树 pine tree 松鼠(sōng shù) squirrel
sōng ㄙㄨㄥ	鬆	松	不緊，放開 loose, relax 不紧，放开	放鬆(fàng sōng) 放松relax 鬆緊帶(sōng jǐn dài) 松紧带 elastic band 肉鬆(ròu sōng)肉松 dried meat floss
sōng ㄙㄨㄥ	忪	忪	還沒完全清醒的樣子not fully awake yet 还没完全清醒的样子	惺忪(xīng sōng) eyes not yet fully open on waking up
sōng ㄙㄨㄥ	嵩	嵩	高，巨大而高聳 tall, huge 高，巨大而高耸	嵩山(sōng shān) Song mountain
sǒng ㄙㄨㄥˇ	悚	悚	恐懼，害怕 fear 恐惧，害怕	悚然(sǒng rán) terrified
sǒng ㄙㄨㄥˇ	慫	怂	鼓動，唆使 instigate, abet 鼓动，唆使	慫恿(sǒng yǒng) 怂恿 instigate
sǒng ㄙㄨㄥˇ	聳	耸	驚動，使人吃驚，高高的 surprising, high rising 惊动，使人吃惊，高高的	聳肩(sǒng jiān) 耸肩 shrug the shoulders 高聳(gāo sǒng) 高耸 very tall
sòng ㄙㄨㄥˋ	宋	宋	姓氏，朝代名 Chinese surname, dynasty name	宋朝(sòng cháo) Song Dynasty 宋體(sòng tǐ) 宋体 Song-type font

sòng ㄙ ㄨ ㄥˋ	送	送	將東西給人，傳遞 deliver, pass on to 将东西给人，传递	送禮(sòng lǐ) 送礼 present gift 送信(sòng xìn) deliver letter
sòng ㄙ ㄨ ㄥˋ	誦	诵	述說，大聲念 chant, read aloud 述说，大声念	誦經(sòng jīng) 诵经 chant prayers 朗誦(lǎng sòng) 朗诵 read aloud
sòng ㄙ ㄨ ㄥˋ	訟	讼	打官司 file a lawsuit	訴訟(sù sòng) 诉讼 lawsuit
sòng ㄙ ㄨ ㄥˋ	頌	颂	贊揚別人的好處 praise 赞扬别人的好处	頌揚(sòng yáng) 颂扬 eulogize 歌頌(gē sòng) 歌颂 sing praise to
sōu ㄙ ㄡ	搜	搜	尋找 search 寻找	搜集(sōu jí) collect 搜查(sōu chá) search
sōu ㄙ ㄡ	餿	馊	食物因受熱太久而 變質發出酸臭味 rotten smell 食物因受热太久而 变质发出酸臭味	餿主意(sōu zhǔ yì) 馊主意 lousy idea
sōu ㄙ ㄡ	艘	艘	指船隻的量詞 classifier for ships 指船只的量词	一艘船(yì sōu chuán) a ship
sǒu ㄙ ㄡˇ	叟	叟	老頭 an old man 老头	童叟無欺(tóng sǒu wú qī) 童叟无欺 honest deal with both young and old

sòu ㄙ ㄡˋ	嗽	嗽	呼吸器官因受刺激 而呼出氣 cough 呼吸器官因受刺激 而呼出气	咳嗽(ké sòu) cough
sū ㄙ ㄨ	蘇	苏	植物名，假死而再 活 a plant, revive 植物名，假死而再 活	死而復蘇(sǐ ér fù sū) 死而复苏come back to life
sū ㄙ ㄨ	穌	稣	同“蘇” same as “蘇”	耶穌基督(yē sū jī dū) 耶稣基督 Jesus Christ
sū ㄙ ㄨ	酥	酥	鬆脆，軟弱 crispy, soft 松脆，软弱	酥糖(sū táng) crunchy candy 酥軟(sū ruǎn) 酥软 soft and weak
sú ㄙ ㄨˊ	俗	俗	社會上的習慣，大 眾化，不文雅 social customs, popular, vulgar 社会上的习惯，大 众化，不文雅	風俗(fēng sú) 风俗 social customs 粗俗(cū sú) vulgar
sù ㄙ ㄨˋ	夙	夙	早晨 morning	夙興夜寐(sù xīng yè mèi) 夙兴夜寐 work hard all day
sù ㄙ ㄨˋ	素	素	單純，本來的，東 西的基本部分 simple, original, essence 单纯，本来的，东 西的基本部分	色素(sè sù) pigment 吃素(chī sù) vegetarian
sù ㄙ ㄨˋ	訴	诉	敘說，控告 narrate, sue 叙说，控告	告訴(gào sù) 告诉 tell 訴訟(sù sòng) 诉讼 lawsuit

sù ㄙ ㄨˋ	肅	肃	恭敬 respectful	嚴肅(yán sù) 严肃 stern-looking 肅立(sù lì) 肃立 stand to show respect
sù ㄙ ㄨˋ	速	速	快，邀請 rapid, invite 快，邀请	快速(kuài sù) rapid 不速之客(bú sù zhī kè) uninvited guest
sù ㄙ ㄨˋ	宿	宿	住，過夜 live, stay over 住，过夜	住宿(zhù sù) stay over 歸宿(guī sù) 归宿 home
sù ㄙ ㄨˋ	塑	塑	由泥土做成的形象 statue, mould	塑像(sù xiàng) statue 塑造(sù zào) to mould
suān ㄙ ㄨㄢ	酸	酸	像醋的味道，微痛 無力，悲痛 sour 像醋的味道，微痛 无力，悲痛	酸味(suān wèi) sour taste 心酸(xīn suān) feel sad and hurt
suàn ㄙ ㄨㄢˋ	蒜	蒜	多年生草本植物， 是調味品 garlic 多年生草本植物， 是调味品	大蒜(dà suàn) garlic
suàn ㄙ ㄨㄢˋ	算	算	核計，計劃，當做 calculate, plan, consider 核计，计划，当做	計算(jì suàn) 计算 calculate 打算(dǎ suàn) intend to, plan to
suī ㄙ ㄨㄟ	雖	虽	連接詞，即使 although 连接词，即使	雖然(suī rán) 虽然 although

suí ㄙㄨㄟˊ	隨	随	順從，跟著，順便 compliant, follow, do while 顺从，跟著，顺便	隨從(suí cóng) 随从 entourage 隨和(suí hé) 随和 easygoing
suǐ ㄙㄨㄟˇ	髓	髓	骨頭裏脂肪的東西，事物的精華 marrow, quintessence 骨头里脂肪的东西，事物的精华	骨髓(gǔ suǐ) bone marrow 精髓(jīng suǐ) quintessence
suì ㄙㄨㄟˋ	歲	岁	計算年齡的單位，年 age, year 计算年龄的单位，年	歲月(suì yuè) 岁月 the time 歲數(suì shù) 岁数 age
suì ㄙㄨㄟˋ	碎	碎	破成幾塊，零星，不完整 broken pieces, piecemeal, incomplete 破成几块，零星，不完整	碎片(suì piàn) broken pieces 瑣碎(suǒ suì) 琐碎 trivialities
suì ㄙㄨㄟˋ	祟	祟	鬼神所降的災禍，行動不光明 disaster caused by devils, sneaky 鬼神所降的灾祸，行动不光明	鬼鬼祟祟(guǐ guǐ suì suì) sneaky 作祟(zuò suì) cause trouble
suì ㄙㄨㄟˋ	穗	穗	植物上成串的花和果實，結扎成的裝飾品 ears of crops 植物上成串的花和果实，结扎成的装饰品	稻穗(dào suì) ears of rice 穗子(suì zi) tassel
suì ㄙㄨㄟˋ	邃	邃	深遠，精通，遠古 far-reaching, expert, remote past 深远，精通，远古	深邃(shēn suì) profound 邃古(suì gǔ) the remote past
suì ㄙㄨㄟˋ	隧	隧	地下道路 tunnel	隧道(suì dào) tunnel

sūn ㄙㄨㄣ	孫	孙	子女所生的子女，兒子以後的時代 grand children 子女所生的子女，儿子以后的时代	孫子(sūn zi)孫子 grandson 子孫(zǐ sūn)子孙 posterity
sǔn ㄙㄨㄣˇ	損	损	減少，破壞，虧 reduce, damage, loss 减少，破坏，亏	損失(sǔn shī)損失 loss 破損(pò sǔn)破损 damage
sǔn ㄙㄨㄣˇ	筍	笋	竹子地下莖所長出的可吃嫩芽 bamboo shoot 竹子地下茎所长出的可吃嫩芽	竹筍(zhú sún)竹笋 bamboo shoot 筍乾(sǔn gān)笋干 dried bamboo shoot
suō ㄙㄨㄛ	娑	娑	婆娑：跳舞的樣子 like dancing 婆娑：跳舞的样子	婆娑起舞(pó suō qǐ wǔ) begin to dance
suō ㄙㄨㄛ	梭	梭	古時織布機上拉著橫線穿過直線的工具 shuttle 古时织布机上拉著横线穿过直线的工具	穿梭(chuān suō) go back and forth 梭子(suō zi) shuttle
suō ㄙㄨㄛ	縮	缩	不伸開，向後退，由大變小，節約 shrink, retreat, practice frugality 不伸开，向后退，由大变小，节约	畏縮(wèi suō)畏缩 withdrawn 縮短(suō duǎn)缩短 shorten
suō ㄙㄨㄛ	唆	唆	誘使別人做壞事 incite 诱使别人做坏事	教唆(jiào suō)教唆 instigate 唆使(suō shǐ) incite
suō ㄙㄨㄛ	嗦	嗦	發抖 shiver 发抖	哆嗦(duō suō)shiver 囉嗦(luō suō)罗嗦 nagging
suǒ ㄙㄨㄛˇ	所	所	地方，機關或辦事的地方 location, office 地方，机关或办事的地方	住所(zhù suǒ) residence 所以(suǒ yǐ) therefore 研究所(yán jiū suǒ) graduate school

294

suǒ ㄙㄨㄛˇ	索	索	粗繩，尋求 rope, search 粗绳，寻求	繩索(shéng suǒ)绳索 rope 索引(suǒ yǐn) index 索取(suǒ qǔ) ask for 索然(suǒ rán) boring
suǒ ㄙㄨㄛˇ	鎖	锁	加在門上或箱子上 的不能隨便打開的 器具 lock 加在门上或箱子上 的不能随便打开的 器具	上鎖(shàng suǒ)上锁 lock up 門鎖(mén suǒ)门锁 door lock
suǒ ㄙㄨㄛˇ	瑣	琐	零碎，細小的 trivialities 零碎，细小的	瑣事(suǒ shì) 琐事 trivialities 繁瑣(fán suǒ)繁琐 detail oriented 瑣碎(suǒ suì) 琐碎trifling

T				
tā ㄊㄚ	塌	塌	倒下 collapse	倒塌(dǎo tā) collapse
tā ㄊㄚ	踏	踏	踩，切實 step on, solidly 踩，切实	踏實(tā shí) 踏实 down to earth 腳踏車(jiǎo tā chē) 脚踏车 bicycle
tā ㄊㄚ	她	她	女性第三人稱 she 女性第三人称	她們(tā mén) 她们 they (for female) 聽她的(tīng tā de) 听她的 listen to her
tā ㄊㄚ	他	他	男性第三人稱 he 男性第三人称	他人(tā rén) others 他們(tā mén) 他们 they (for male) 他日(tā rì) some other day
tā ㄊㄚ	它	它	指事物 it (refers to a thing)	其它(qí tā) others 它的(tā de) its
tā ㄊㄚ	牠	牠	指事物或動物 it (refers to a thing or an animal) 指事物或动物	牠們(tā mén) 牠们 they (animals)
tǎ ㄊㄚˇ	塔	塔	一種高而頂尖的佛 教建築物，高聳尖 形的建築 tower 一种高而顶尖的佛 教建筑物，高耸尖 形的建筑	寶塔(bǎo tǎ) 宝塔 pagoda 燈塔(dēng tǎ) 灯塔 lighthouse
tǎ ㄊㄚˇ	獺	獺	四肢短小，住在水 裏的哺乳類動物， 皮可做皮衣 otter 四肢短小，住在水 里的哺乳类动物， 皮可做皮衣	水獺(shuǐ tǎ) 水獭 otter
tāi ㄊㄞ	胎	胎	在母體中的幼體 fetus 在母体中的幼体	胎兒(tāi ér) 胎儿 fetus 輪胎(lún tāi) 轮胎 tire

296

tāi ㄊㄞ	苔	苔	舌頭上的垢，可幫 助診斷病症 tongue's coating 舌头上的垢，可帮 助诊断病症	舌苔(shé tāi) tongue's coating
tái ㄊㄞˊ	抬	抬	提高，推崇 lift, speak highly of	抬頭(tái tóu) 抬头 lift up the head 抬價(tái jià) 抬价 raise the price
tái ㄊㄞˊ	台	台	對人的尊稱 honorific "you" 对人的尊称	台端(tái duān) you (honorific) 兄台(xiōng tái) you (a man)
tái ㄊㄞˊ	臺	台	高出地面供人表演 或演講的平板 stage, platform 高出地面供人表演 或演讲的平板	講臺(jiǎng tái) 讲台 podium 電臺(diàn tái) 电台 radio station
tái ㄊㄞˊ	颱	台	發生在熱帶海洋上 的一種風暴 typhoon 发生在热带海洋上 的一种风暴	颱風(tái fēng) 台风 typhoon
tài ㄊㄞˋ	太	太	很 very	太陽(tài yáng) 太阳 sun 太平(tài píng) peace 太太(tài tai) wife 太美了 !(tài měi le) how beautiful!
tài ㄊㄞˋ	態	态	形狀，樣子，情況 ，人的舉止動作 shape, posture, status, attitude 形状，样子，情况 ，人的举止动作	變態(biàn tài) 变态 abnormal 態度(tài dù) 态度 attitude
tài ㄊㄞˋ	泰	泰	平安，安定 peace, stability	泰然(tài rán) take it easy 泰半(tài bàn) more than half

tān ㄊㄢ	坍	坍	建築物或堆起來的 東西倒塌 collapse 建筑物或堆起来的 东西倒塌	坍方(tān fāng) collapse
tān ㄊㄢ	貪	贪	求多而不滿足，愛 財 greedy 求多而不满足，爱 财	貪心(tān xīn) 贪心 greedy 貪污(tān wū) 贪污 corruption
tān ㄊㄢ	攤	摊	擺開來 lay out 摆开来	攤位(tān wèi) 摊位 booth 攤牌(tān pái) 摊牌 showdown
tān ㄊㄢ	灘	滩	河海邊的平地 beach 河海边的平地	海灘(hǎi tān) 海滩 beach 灘頭(tān tóu) 滩头 beachhead
tān ㄊㄢ	癱	瘫	神經機能失去功用 ，肢體不能活動 paralyzed 神经机能失去功用 ，肢体不能活动	癱瘓(tān huàn) 瘫痪 paralyzed
tán ㄊㄢˊ	談	谈	説，對話 talk, converse 说，对话	談話(tán huà) 谈话 talk 面談(miàn tán) 面谈 interview
tán ㄊㄢˊ	壇	坛	祭典用的高台，文 藝或體育界 platform, circles 祭典用的高台，文 艺或体育界	祭壇(jì tán) 祭坛 altar 文壇(wén tán) 文坛 literary circles
tán ㄊㄢˊ	檀	檀	植物名，木質堅硬 sandalwood 植物名，木质坚硬	檀香山(tán xiāng shān) Honolulu 檀木(tán mù) sandalwood
tán dàn ㄊㄢˊㄉㄢˋ	彈	弹	放開壓緊的東西， 撥弄bounce at sudden release of pressure, flick 放开压紧的东 西，撥弄	彈性(tán xìng) 弹性 elasticity 彈劾(tán hé) 弹劾 impeach 彈簧(tán huáng) 弹簧 a spring

tán ㄊㄢˊ	潭	潭	深水池，小湖 deep pool of water, small lake	潭水(tán shuǐ) lake water 龍潭虎穴(lóng tán hǔ xuè) 龙潭虎穴 dangerous area
tán ㄊㄢˊ	曇	昙	常綠灌木，花開花 謝同在一個晚上 a night-blooming plant 常绿灌木，花开花 谢同在一个晚上	曇花一現(tán huā yí xiàn) 昙花一现transient event
tán ㄊㄢˊ	痰	痰	由喉管内分泌出的 黏液 sputum 由喉管内分泌出的 粘液	吐痰(tǔ tán) spit out sputum 痰盂(tán yú) spittoon
tǎn ㄊㄢˇ	忐	忐	心神不安 ill at ease	忐忑不安(tǎn tè bù ān) feel ill at ease
tǎn ㄊㄢˇ	坦	坦	寬平，心地平靜， 沒有隱藏直說 broad and level, candid 宽平，心地平静， 没有隐藏直说	平坦(píng tǎn) flat 坦白(tǎn bái) frank, candid
tǎn ㄊㄢˇ	毯	毯	有毛絨的紡織品 carpet 有毛绒的纺织品	毛毯(máo tǎn) blanket 地毯(dì tǎn) carpet
tàn ㄊㄢˋ	嘆	叹	因悲哀而發出的聲 音，稱贊 sigh, praise 因悲哀而发出的声 音，称赞	感嘆(gǎn tàn) 感叹 sigh 嘆為觀止(tàn wéi guān zhǐ) 叹为观止marvel at
tàn ㄊㄢˋ	歎	叹	因悲傷煩悶而呼氣 sigh 因悲伤烦闷而呼气	歎氣(tàn qì) 叹气 sigh
tàn ㄊㄢˋ	炭	炭	將木材做成的黑色 燃料 charcoal 将木材做成的黑色 燃料	木炭(mù tàn) charcoal 煤炭(méi tàn) coal

tàn ㄊㄢˋ	探	探	尋求，暗中考察 search, secretly investigate 寻求，暗中考察	探索(tàn suǒ) explore 偵探(zhēn tàn) 侦探 detective
tāng ㄊㄤ	湯	汤	把菜或肉加水煮成的可喝液體 soup 把菜或肉加水煮成的可喝液体	湯匙(tāng chí) 汤匙 tablespoon 雞湯(jī tāng) 鸡汤 chicken soup
táng ㄊㄤˊ	唐	唐	誇大，冒犯，姓 exaggerate, offensive, Chinese surname 夸大，冒犯，姓	荒唐(huāng táng) absurd 唐突(táng tū) blunt
táng ㄊㄤˊ	糖	糖	從甘蔗提煉出來的甜東西 sugar 从甘蔗提炼出来的甜东西	糖果(táng guǒ) candy 蔗糖(zhè táng) cane sugar
táng ㄊㄤˊ	堂	堂	高大的屋子，同祖父的親戚 tall building, of the same grandpa 高大的屋子，同祖父的亲戚	禮堂(lǐ táng) 礼堂 auditorium 堂兄(táng xiōng) son of father's brother
táng ㄊㄤˊ	搪	搪	敷衍，隨便地應付 evade, act perfunctorily 敷衍，随便地应付	搪塞(táng sè) evade the issue 搪瓷(táng cí) enamel
táng ㄊㄤˊ	膛	膛	體腔，器物中空的部分 chest, cavity 体腔，器物中空的部分	胸膛(xiōng táng) chest 槍膛(qiāng táng) 枪膛 barrel of a gun
táng ㄊㄤˊ	塘	塘	水池，隄岸 pond, dike	池塘(chí táng) pond 魚塘(yú táng) fish pond 河塘(hé táng) river dike 海塘(hǎi táng) seawall
tǎng ㄊㄤˇ	倘	倘	假如，如果 if	倘若(tǎng ruò) if

300

tǎng ㄊ ㄤ ˇ	躺	躺	身體睡下 lie down 身体睡下	平躺(píng tǎng) lie flat 躺椅(tǎng yǐ) recliner
tàng ㄊ ㄤ ˋ	燙	烫	溫度高，用熱的物體使另一物體起變化 very hot, apply heat on 溫度高，用熱的物體使另一物體起變化	燙手(tàng shǒu) 烫手 tricky (issue) 燙髮(tàng fǎ) 烫发 have a perm
tàng ㄊ ㄤ ˋ	趟	趟	來回的次數 frequency 来回的次数	一趟(yí tàng) one time
tāo ㄊ ㄠ	濤	涛	大波浪 big wave	波濤(bō tāo) 波涛 big waves 松濤(sōng tāo) 松涛 wind's blow in the pines
tāo ㄊ ㄠ	滔	滔	充滿，大水漫流 filled with, surging water 充满，大水漫流	滔滔不絕(tāo tāo bù jué) 滔滔不绝eloquent 浪滔滔(làng tāo tāo) the rolling waves
tāo ㄊ ㄠ	掏	掏	挖，伸手進去拿東西 dig, with a hand reaching in to take something 挖，伸手进去拿东西	掏腰包(tāo yāo bāo) foot the bill 掏耳朵(tāo ěr duō) pick the ears
táo ㄊ ㄠ ˊ	淘	淘	用水沖洗，除掉不要的部分 to pan for 用水冲洗，除掉不要的部分	淘金(táo jīn) pan for gold 淘氣(táo qì) 淘气 mischievous
táo ㄊ ㄠ ˊ	陶	陶	瓦器，教化 pottery, educate 瓦器，教化	陶器(táo qì) pottery 陶冶(táo yě) mould character
táo ㄊ ㄠ ˊ	萄	萄	葡萄：蔓生木本植物，果實可吃也可釀酒 grape 葡萄：蔓生木本植物，果实可吃也可酿酒	葡萄(pú táo) grape

táo ㄊㄠˊ	桃	桃	桃樹，落葉喬木 peach 桃树，落叶乔木	桃子(táo zi) peach 桃花(táo huā) peach blossom
tóo ㄊㄠˊ	逃	逃	因害怕或為了避開 而跑走　run away 因害怕或为了避开 而跑走	逃避(táo bì) dodge 逃稅(táo shuì) evade taxes
tǎo ㄊㄠˇ	討	讨	發動攻擊，研究， 惹 attack, study, incur 发动攻击，研究， 惹	討厭(tǎo yàn)　讨厌 disgusting 研討會(yán tǎo huì) 研讨会　seminar
tào ㄊㄠˋ	套	套	罩在外面的東西 cover 罩在外面的东西	外套(wài tào) overcoat 手套(shǒu tào) gloves
tè ㄊㄜˋ	忑	忑	心神不定 ill at ease	忐忑不安(tǎn tè bù ān) feel ill at ease
tè ㄊㄜˋ	特	特	不平常的 special	特別(tè bié) special 特務(tè wù)　特务 secret agent
téng ㄊㄥˊ	疼	疼	因生病或受傷而有 難受感覺，寵愛 painful, show affection for 因生病或受伤而有 难受感觉，宠爱.	疼痛(téng tòng) pain 疼愛(téng ài)　疼爱 show affection for
téng ㄊㄥˊ	騰	腾	奔跑，跳躍，上升 gallop, leap, soar 奔跑，跳跃，上升	奔騰(bēn téng)　奔腾 gallop forward 騰空(téng kōng)　腾空 shoot up into the sky
téng ㄊㄥˊ	藤	藤	蔓生木本植物，生 在岩壁或樹上，可 以編成物品　rattan 蔓生木本植物，生 在岩壁或树上，可 以编成物品	藤椅(téng yǐ) rattan chair 瓜藤(guā téng) melon vine

302

Pinyin	Traditional	Simplified	Meaning	Examples
tī ㄊㄧ	梯	梯	爬高用的器具 ladder	梯子(tī zi) ladder 電梯(diàn tī) 电梯 elevator
tī ㄊㄧ	踢	踢	抬腳撞擊東西 kick 抬脚撞击东西	踢球(tī qiú) kick ball 踢毽子(tī jiàn zi) play shuttlecock
tī ㄊㄧ	剔	剔	把肉從骨頭上刮下 來，挑出不好的 remove the bad 把肉从骨头上刮下 来，挑出不好的	挑剔(tiāo tī) picky 剔除(tī chú) discard
tí ㄊㄧ	提	提	垂手拿東西，說出 ，舉出 hold in hand, say, suggest 垂手拿 东西，说出，举出	提醒(tí xǐng) remind 提議(tí yì)提议 suggestion
tí ㄊㄧ	堤	堤	防水的建築物 dyke, embankment 防水的建筑物	堤防(tí fáng) dyke 河堤(hé tí) river embankment
tí ㄊㄧ	啼	啼	哭出聲，鳥獸鳴叫 cry 哭出声，鸟兽鸣叫	啼哭(tí kū) cry 雞啼(jī tí) 鸡啼 cock's crow
tí ㄊㄧ	蹄	蹄	牛羊等趾端的角質 保護物 hoof 牛羊等趾端的角质 保护物	馬蹄(mǎ tí) horse's hoof 口蹄疫(kǒu tí yì) foot-and-mouth disease
tí ㄊㄧ	題	题	考試時要求解答的 ，寫作內容 test questions考试时要求 解答的，写作内容	考題(kǎo tí) 考题 test question 問題(wèn tí) 问题problem
tǐ ㄊㄧˇ	體	体	全身，全部，親身 whole body, the whole, personally 全身，全部，亲身	人體(rén tǐ) 人体 human body 全體(quán tǐ) 全体 the whole
tì ㄊㄧˋ	屜	屉	可拿出放東西的分 層的格架 drawer 可拿出放东西的分 层的格架	抽屜(chōu tì) 抽屉 drawer
tì ㄊㄧˋ	剃	剃	用刀刮去毛髮 shave 用刀刮去毛发	剃頭(tī tóu) 剃头 shave the head 剃鬍子(tī hú zi) 剃胡子 shave the face

303

tì ㄊㄧˋ	惕	惕	小心謹慎，警覺 cautious, alert 小心谨慎，警觉	警惕(jǐng tì) guard against
tì ㄊㄧˋ	涕	涕	眼淚，鼻子裏分泌 的液體 tear, nasal mucus 眼泪，鼻子 里分泌的液体	哭涕(kū tì) tearful cry 鼻涕(bí tì) nasal mucus
tì ㄊㄧˋ	替	替	代理，代換，為 substitute, replace, for 代理，代换，为	代替(dài tì) replace 替身(tì shēn) a substitute
tì ㄊㄧˋ	嚔	嚔	受刺激的鼻子發出 猛烈噴氣的現象 sneeze 受刺激的鼻子发出 猛烈喷气的现象	噴嚔(pēn tì) sneeze
tiān ㄊㄧㄢ	天	天	空中 sky	天氣(tiān qì) 天气 climate 天然(tiān rán) natural
tiān ㄊㄧㄢ	添	添	增加 add to	增添(zēng tiān) add to 添丁(tiān dīng) give birth to a boy
tián ㄊㄧㄢ	田	田	可種植農作物的土 地 farmland 可种植农作物的土 地	田地(tián dì) farmland 田徑(tián jìng) 田径 track and field
tián ㄊㄧㄢˊ	甜	甜	像糖的滋味，使人 覺得舒服 sweet 像糖的滋味，使人 觉得舒服	甜密(tián mì) sweet, pleasant 甜言(tián yán) honeyed words
tián ㄊㄧㄢˊ	填	填	把空缺的地方補起 來，在空白的表格 上照項目寫 fill in 把空缺的地方补起 来，在空白的表格 上照项目写	填平(tián píng) 填平 level off 填寫(tián xiě) 填写 fill in (a form)

tián ㄊ ㄧ ㄢ	恬	恬	安靜 quiet 安静	恬靜(tián jìng) 恬静 peaceful 安恬(ān tián) peaceful
tiǎn ㄊ ㄧ ㄢ	舔	舔	用舌頭嘗或取東西 lick 用舌头尝或取东西	舔嘴唇(tiǎn zuǐ chún) 舔一舔(tiǎn yì tiǎn) give it a lick
tiāo tiǎo ㄊ ㄊ ㄧ ㄧ ㄠ ㄠ	挑	挑	用肩膀擔著，選 carry on shoulder, choose 用肩膀担著，选	挑毛病(tiāo máo bìng) find fault with 挑選(tiāo xuǎn) 挑选 choose
tiāo ㄊ ㄧ ㄠ	佻	佻	輕薄，不莊重 frivolous 轻薄，不庄重	輕佻(qīng tiāo) 轻佻 frivolous
tiáo ㄊ ㄧ ㄠ	條	条	細長的東西，秩序 ，項目 long, thin stetch, order, item 细长的东西，秩序 ，项目	麵條(miàn tiáo) 面条 noodle 條件(tiáo jiàn) 条件 condition
tiáo ㄊ ㄧ ㄠ	迢	迢	遠 far 远	千里迢迢(qiān lǐ tiáo tiáo) from faraway
tiáo diào ㄊ ㄉ ㄧ ㄠ ㄠ	調	调	配合均勻 do something to achieve balance	調整(tiáo zhěng) 调整 readjust 調解(tiáo jiě) 调解 mediate
tiǎo tiao ㄊ ㄊ ㄧ ㄧ ㄠ ㄠ	挑	挑	引起 cause	挑戰(tiǎo zhàn) 挑战 challenge 挑釁(tiǎo xìn) 挑衅 provoke

tiǎo ㄊㄧㄠˇ	窕	窕	女子文静幽雅美好 的樣子 graceful 女子文静幽雅美好 的样子	窈窕(yǎo tiǎo) graceful (lady)
tiào ㄊㄧㄠˋ	跳	跳	雙腳離地讓身體往 上或往前的動作 jump 双脚离地让身体往 上或往前的动作	跳遠(tiào yuǎn)跳远 long jump 跳水(tiào shuǐ) diving
tiào ㄊㄧㄠˋ	眺	眺	往遠的地方看 peer into the distance 往远的地方看	眺望(tiào wàng) peer into the distance
tiē ㄊㄧㄝ	貼	贴	黏，靠近，補助 stick to, draw near, subsidize 粘，靠近，补助	貼紙(tiē zhǐ)贴纸 sticker 津貼(jīn tiē)津贴 subsidy
tiē ㄊㄧㄝ	帖	帖	便條，邀請客人的 紙片 note, invitation card 便条，邀请客人的 纸片	謝帖(xiè tiē)谢帖 thank-you note 請帖(qǐng tiē)请帖 invitation card
tiě ㄊㄧㄝˇ	鐵	铁	一種金屬元素，符 號Fe，可製用具； 意志堅定 iron, iron will 一种金属元素，符 号Fe，可制用具； 意志坚定	鋼鐵(gāng tiě)钢铁 iron and steel 鐵匠(tiě jiàng)铁匠 blacksmith
tīng tìng ㄊㄧㄥ ㄊㄧㄥˋ	聽	听	耳朵接受聲音，順 從，接受 listen, comply with, accept 耳朵接受声音，顺 从，接受	聽從(tīng cóng)听从 follow the order 聽筒(tīng tǒng)听筒 stethoscope 聽其自然(tìng qí zì rán) 听其自然 let nature take its course
tīng ㄊㄧㄥ	廳	厅	聚會或招待客人的 大房間 hall 聚会或招待客人的 大房间	客廳(kè tīng)客厅 living room 辦公廳(bàn gōng tīng) 办公厅 office

tíng ㄊㄧㄥˊ	亭	亭	在路肩或花圍裏可作休息用的建築物 pavilion 在路肩或花园里可作休息用的建筑物	涼亭(liáng tíng) 涼亭 pavilion 售票亭(shòu piào tíng) ticket booth
tíng ㄊㄧㄥˊ	停	停	中止不動，暫時擱置 stop, put aside 中止不动，暂时搁置	停止(tíng zhǐ) stop 停火(tíng huǒ) truce
tíng ㄊㄧㄥˊ	婷	婷	直立的樣子，美好 gracefully stand erect 直立的样子，美好	婷婷玉立(tíng tíng yù lì) stand erect and gracefully
tíng ㄊㄧㄥˊ	廷	廷	古代帝王接受群臣朝見的地方 central government in ancient China 古代帝王接受群臣朝见的地方	宮廷(gōng tíng) the imperial court
tíng ㄊㄧㄥˊ	庭	庭	院子，廳堂 courtyard, hall 院子，厅堂	家庭(jiā tíng) family 法庭(fǎ tíng) court of law
tíng ㄊㄧㄥˊ	霆	霆	突然的雷聲 thunderbolt 突然的雷声	雷霆(léi tíng) thunderbolt
tǐng ㄊㄧㄥˇ	挺	挺	直立而高聳，不顧一切向前 high rise, forge ahead 直立而高耸，不顾一切向前	挺拔(tǐng bá) tall and straight 挺進(tǐng jìn) 挺进 move ahead
tǐng ㄊㄧㄥˇ	艇	艇	輕便的小船 small boat 轻便的小船	遊艇(yóu tǐng) 遊艇 yacht 汽艇(qì tǐng) motorboat

tōng ㄊㄨㄥ	通	通	穿過去，專精， 傳達 pass through, specialize in, deliver 穿过去，专精， 传达	通車(tōng chē) 通车 open to traffic 精通(jīng tōng) specialized in
tóng ㄊㄨㄥˊ	同	同	沒有差別，一樣， 和 same as, and 没有差别，一样， 和	相同(xiāng tóng) same as 同時(tóng shí) 同时 at the same time
tóng ㄊㄨㄥˊ	銅	铜	一種金屬元素，符 號Cu, 可製合金、 器皿 copper 一种金属元素，符 号Cu, 可制合金、 器皿	銅器(tóng qì) 铜器 bronze 銅板(tóng bǎn) 铜板 coin
tóng ㄊㄨㄥˊ	童	童	小孩子 child	兒童(ér tóng) 儿童 child 童年(tóng nián) childhood
tóng ㄊㄨㄥˊ	瞳	瞳	眼球中央的小孔， 可隨光線的強弱縮 小或擴大 pupil (of the eye) 眼球中央的小孔， 可随光线的强弱缩 小或扩大	瞳孔(tóng kǒng) pupil (of the eye)
tǒng ㄊㄨㄥˇ	統	统	總管，世代相繼不 斷的體系，合 command, system, unify 总管，世代相继不 断的体系·合	系統(xì tǒng) 系统 system 統一(tǒng yī) 统一 unification
tǒng ㄊㄨㄥˇ	桶	桶	深度較大的盛水或 東西的器具 bucket, barrel 深度较大的盛水或 东西的器具	水桶(shuǐ tǒng) bucket 飯桶(fàn tǒng) 饭桶 useless person
tǒng ㄊㄨㄥˇ	筒	筒	中空的器物 hollow appliance	郵筒(yóu tǒng) 邮筒 mail box 電筒(diàn tǒng) 电筒 flash light

tòng ㄊㄨㄥˋ	痛	痛	疼，悲傷，深切地 painful, sad, deeply 疼，悲伤，深切地	痛苦(tòng kǔ) suffering 痛恨(tòng hèn) deep hatred
tòng ㄊㄨㄥˋ	慟	恸	很悲哀，大哭 grieve, cry out loud	慟哭(tòng kū) 恸哭 sorrowful cry 悲慟(bēi tòng) 悲恸 sorrow
tōu ㄊㄡ	偷	偷	竊取，抽出 steal, take off 窃取，抽出	小偷(xiǎo tōu) thief 偷空(tōu kòng) find time to do ...
tóu ㄊㄡˊ	頭	头	人或動物的頂部 ，物品的殘餘部分 head, remnant 人或动物的顶部 ，物品的残馀部分	頭腦(tóu nǎo) 头脑 brain 煙頭(yān tóu) 烟头 cigarette butt
tóu ㄊㄡˊ	投	投	放進去 pitch in 放进去	投票(tóu piào) to vote 投資(tóu zī) 投资 invest
tòu ㄊㄡˋ	透	透	穿過，超過 pass through, exceed 穿过，超过	透明(tòu míng) transparent 透支(tòu zhī) overdraft
tū ㄊㄨ	凸	凸	高出，突出 protrude, bulging	凸出(tū chū) bulging
tū ㄊㄨ	禿	秃	頭上沒有毛髮 bald 头上没有毛发	禿頭(tū tóu) 秃头 bald-headed 禿子(tū zi) bald-headed person

tū tú ㄊㄨ ㄊㄨ ㄨ ㄨ	突	突	衝破，凸出，忽然 break out of, bulge, suddenly 冲破，凸出，忽然	突圍(tū wéi) 突围 break out of a siege 突然(tū rán) suddenly
tú ㄊㄨ ㄨ	途	途	道路，路線 road, route 道路，路线	路途(lù tú) journey 前途(qián tú) the future
tú ㄊㄨ ㄨ	徒	徒	白白地，步行 in vain, walk	徒然(tú rán) in vain 徒步(tú bù) to walk
tú ㄊㄨ ㄨ	圖	图	繪畫，謀取 draw, plot for 绘画，谋取	繪圖(huì tú) 绘图 drawing 圖謀(tú móu) 图谋 scheme, plot
tú ㄊㄨ ㄨ	塗	涂	使顏色，油漆等附 在表面上 to paint on 使颜色，油漆等附 在表面上	塗鴉(tú yā) 涂鸦 scribble 塗料(tú liào) 涂料 paint, coating
tú ㄊㄨ ㄨ	屠	屠	宰殺牲畜 slaughter 宰杀牲畜	屠夫(tú fū) butcher 屠殺(tú shā) 屠杀 massacre
tǔ ㄊㄨ ㄨ	土	土	地面上的沙，泥等 混合物，不時髦 earth, rustic 地面上的沙，泥等 混合物，不时髦	土壤(tǔ rǎng) soil 領土(lǐng tǔ) 领土 territory 土地(tǔ dì) land 土著(tǔ zhù) aborigines 土產(tǔ chǎn) 土产 local produce 土裏土氣(tǔ lǐ tǔ qì) 土里土气 rustic
tǔ tù ㄊㄨ ㄊㄨ ㄨ ㄨ	吐	吐	使東西從嘴裏出來 ，説出 spit out, speak out 使东西从嘴里出来 ，说出	吞吞吐吐(tūn tūn tǔ tǔ) mumble 吐露(tǔ lù) disclose

tù tǔ ㄊ ㄨˇ ㄨˇ	吐	吐	東西從胃裏嘔出来 vomit 东西从胃里呕出来	嘔吐(ǒu tù) 呕吐 vomit 吐血(tù xiě) cough up blood
tù ㄊ ㄨˋ	兔	兔	長耳尾短的哺乳動 物 rabbit 长耳尾短的哺乳动 物	兔子(tù zi) rabbit 兔唇(tù chún) cleft lip 野兔(yě tù) hare 養兔場(yǎng tù chǎng) 养兔场 rabbitry
tuān ㄊ ㄨ ㄢ	湍	湍	急流的水 rapids	急湍(jí tuān) rapids
tuán ㄊ ㄨˊ ㄢ	團	团	球形體 ball-shaped mass 球形体	團結(tuán jié) 团结 unite 團圓(tuán yuán) 团圆 reunion
tuī ㄊ ㄨ ㄟ	推	推	用力使物體移動， 使事情開展，進一 步想 push, unfold 用力使物体移动， 使事情开展，进一 步想	推銷(tuī xiāo) 推销 push a sale 推翻(tuī fān) 推翻 overthrow
tuí ㄊ ㄨˊ ㄟ	頹	颓	精神萎靡不振 disheartened	頹廢(tuí fèi) 颓废 down and out 頹唐(tuí táng) 颓唐 dispirited
tuǐ ㄊ ㄨˇ ㄟ	腿	腿	人體的下肢，有大 腿和小腿之分 thigh, leg 人体的下肢，有大 腿和小腿之分	大腿(dà tuǐ) thigh 火腿(huǒ tuǐ) ham
tuì ㄊ ㄨˋ ㄟ	退	退	向後移動，送還 retreat, return 向后移动，送还	後退(hòu tuì) 后退 retreat 退步(tuì bù) lag behind

tuì ㄊㄨㄟˋ	褪	褪	顏色變淡 discolor 颜色变淡	褪色(tuì sè) discolor
tuì ㄊㄨㄟˋ	蛻	蜕	蟲、蛇類脫下來的 皮，脫落 molting 虫、蛇类脱下来的 皮，脱落	蛻變(tuì biàn) 蜕变 transmute 蛻皮(tuì pí) molting
tūn ㄊㄨㄣ	吞	吞	不經咀嚼整個嚥下 去，侵占，忍受 swallow, annex, endure 不经咀嚼整个咽下 去，侵占，忍受	併吞(bìng tūn) to annex 吞吐量(tūn tǔ liàng) cargo handling capacity
tún ㄊㄨㄣˊ	屯	屯	村莊，軍隊駐守， 儲存 village, garrison, hoard up 村庄，军队驻守， 储存	屯兵(tún bīng) garrison 屯糧(tún liáng) 屯粮 hoard up grain
tún ㄊㄨㄣˊ	囤	囤	積聚 hoard up 积聚	囤積(tún jī) 囤积 hoard up goods
tún ㄊㄨㄣˊ	飩	饨	餛飩：用麵粉做成 薄皮，裏面包餡的 食品 wonton 馄饨：用面粉做成 薄皮，里面包馅的 食品	餛飩(hún tún) 馄饨 wonton
tún ㄊㄨㄣˊ	豚	豚	小豬 suckling pig 小猪	海豚(hǎi tún) dolphin 河豚(hé tún) globefish
tún ㄊㄨㄣˊ	臀	臀	屁股，大腿以上與 腰相連的部分 hip 屁股，大腿以上与 腰相连的部分	臀部(tún bù) hip 臀圍(tún wéi) 臀围 hip measurement

tuō ㄊㄨㄛ	托	托	手捧東西，求人代勞，從旁陪襯 hold in open palms, entrust 手捧东西，求人代劳，从旁陪衬	托兒所(tuō ér suǒ) nursery 襯托(chèn tuō) 衬托 show by contrast
tuō ㄊㄨㄛ	託	托	暫寄，推卸 entrust, offer an excuse 暂寄，推卸	寄託(jì tuō) 寄托 to pin hope on 託詞(tuō cí) 托词 an excuse
tuō ㄊㄨㄛ	拖	拖	牽引，拉長時間 drag on, to delay 牵引，拉长时间	拖延(tuō yán) delay 拖拉(tuō lā) sluggish
tuō ㄊㄨㄛ	脫	脱	離開，落掉，去掉 to separate, take off, remove 离开，落掉，去掉	脫皮(tuō pí) molting 擺脫(bǎi tuō) 摆脱 shake off
tuó ㄊㄨㄛˊ	馱	驮	用背載人或物 carry load on back 用背载人或物	馱馬(tuó mǎ) 驮马 pack horse
tuó ㄊㄨㄛˊ	駝	驼	身體向前，背脊突出 camel 身体向前，背脊突出	駱駝(luò tuó) 骆驼 camel 駝背(tuó bèi) 驼背 hunchback
tuó ㄊㄨㄛˊ	鴕	鸵	鴕鳥：鳥類中最大的一種，頸長翅小，不能飛 ostrich 鸵鸟：鸟类中最大的一种，颈长翅小，不能飞	鴕鳥(tuó niǎo) 鸵鸟 ostrich
tuǒ ㄊㄨㄛˇ	妥	妥	適當，合適 proper, suitable 适当，合适	妥協(tuǒ xié) compromise 妥善(tuǒ shàn) properly
tuǒ ㄊㄨㄛˇ	橢	椭	長圓形 oval 长圆形	橢圓(tuǒ yuán) 椭圆 oval

313

tuò ㄊㄨㄛˋ	拓	拓	開展，開墾 develop, reclaim 开展，开垦	開拓(kāi tuò) 开拓 open up 拓寬(tuò kuān) 拓宽 widen
tuò ㄊㄨㄛˋ	唾	唾	口腔分泌的消化液 ；口液；從嘴裏吐 出來 saliva, to spit 口腔分泌的消化液 ；口液；从嘴里吐 出来	唾液(tuò yè) saliva 唾沫(tuò mò) spittle 唾棄(tuò qì) 唾弃 spurn 唾罵(tuò mà) 唾骂 spit on and curse

wā ㄨㄚ	挖	挖	掘 dig	挖洞(wā dòng) dig hole 挖苦(wā kǔ) speak sarcastically of
wā ㄨㄚ	蛙	蛙	兩棲類動物，很會 跳躍 frog 两栖类动物，很会 跳跃	青蛙(qīng wā) frog 蛙式(wā shì) breaststroke
wā ㄨㄚ	哇	哇	表示驚嘆，小孩哭 聲 cry 表示惊叹，小孩哭 声	哇哇叫(wā wā jiào) cry aloud
wá ㄨㄚˊ	娃	娃	小孩 child	男娃(nán wá) baby boy 嬌娃(jiāo wá) 娇娃 charming lady
wǎ ㄨㄚˇ	瓦	瓦	用陶土燒成的器物 ，蓋在屋頂上用來 蔽雨的薄片 tile 用陶土烧成的器物 ，盖在屋顶上用来 蔽雨的薄片	屋瓦(wū wǎ) roof tile
wà ㄨㄚˋ	襪	袜	穿在腳上的東西 socks 穿在脚上的东西	襪子(wà zi) 袜子 socks 絲襪(sī wà) 丝袜 panty hose
wāi ㄨㄞ	歪	歪	傾斜，偏向一邊， 不正當 crooked, lean to one side, improper 倾斜，偏向一边， 不正当	歪曲(wāi qū) distort 歪風(wāi fēng) 歪风 unhealthy trend
wài ㄨㄞˋ	外	外	"內"的相反，缺 乏經驗 outside, lacking experience "内"的相反，缺 乏经验	外國(wài guó) 外国 foreign country 外行(wài háng) outsider

wān ㄨㄢ	彎	弯	屈曲不直 bend 屈曲不直	彎曲(wān qū) 弯曲 bend 轉彎(zhuǎn wān) 转弯 circle around
wān ㄨㄢ	灣	湾	水流彎曲的地方 curved part of a stream 水流弯曲的地方	海灣(hǎi wān) 海湾 gulf 港灣(gǎng wān) 港湾 estuary
wān ㄨㄢ	豌	豌	一年或二年生草本 植物，種子和嫩莖 可吃 pea 一年或二年生草本 植物，种子和嫩茎 可吃	豌豆(wān dòu) pea
wán ㄨㄢˊ	丸	丸	小而圓的東西 small ball 小而圆的东西	彈丸(dàn wán) 弹丸 bullet 肉丸(ròu wán) meat dumpling
wán ㄨㄢˊ	完	完	齊全，沒有了，做 成了 complete, finish, accomplish 齐全，没有了，做 成了	完全(wán quán) completely 完成(wán chéng) accomplish
wán ㄨㄢˊ	頑	顽	愚蠢無知，固執 ignorant, stubborn 愚蠢无知，固执	頑固(wán gù) 顽固 stubborn 頑抗(wán kàng) 顽抗 doggedly resist
wán ㄨㄢˊ	玩	玩	遊戲 play 游戏	遊玩(yóu wán) play 玩具(wán jù) toy
wǎn ㄨㄢˇ	晚	晚	太陽下山的時候， 夜間 night 太阳下山的时候， 夜间	晚飯(wǎn fàn) 晚饭 dinner 晚年(wǎn nián) old age

wǎn ㄨㄢˇ	碗	碗	盛食物，湯水的器具 bowl 盛食物，汤水的器具	飯碗(fàn wǎn) 饭碗 rice bowl 碗盤(wǎn pán) 碗盘 bowls and plates
wǎn ㄨㄢˇ	惋	惋	感嘆，嘆惜 sigh, regret 感叹，叹惜	惋惜(wǎn xí) regret
wǎn ㄨㄢˇ	婉	婉	溫和，和順 gentle, docile 温和，和顺	委婉(wěi wǎn) indirectly 婉轉(wǎn zhuǎn) 婉转 tactful
wàn ㄨㄢˋ	萬	万	十個一千，多 ten thousand, many 十个一千，多	一萬(yí wàn) 一万 ten thousand 萬一(wàn yī) 万一 in case
wàn ㄨㄢˋ	腕	腕	手臂下端和手掌相連的部分 wrist 手臂下端和手掌相连的部分	手腕(shǒu wàn) tact 腕力(wàn lì) wrist strength
wāng ㄨㄤ	汪	汪	深廣，狗叫聲 vast, dog bark 深广，狗叫声	汪洋(wāng yáng) vast ocean 汪汪叫(wāng wāng jiào) dog barks
wáng ㄨㄤˊ	王	王	姓氏，統治者 Chinese surname, ruler 姓氏，统治者	王牌(wáng pái) ace 國王(guó wáng) 国王 king
wáng ㄨㄤˊ	亡	亡	死，逃 die, escape	死亡(sǐ wáng) death 逃亡(táo wáng) escape

wǎng ㄨㄤˇ	枉	枉	曲解，違反，白費 distort, violate, in vain 曲解，违反，白费	枉然(wǎng rán) in vain 冤枉(yuān wǎng) to wrong a person
wǎng ㄨㄤˇ	往	往	去到，過去 go to, the past 去到，过去	往返(wǎng fǎn) round trip 往事(wǎng shì) past events
wǎng ㄨㄤˇ	罔	罔	冤枉人，無，不 to wrong people, without, not 冤枉人，无，不	罔顧(wǎng gù) 罔顾 disregard 欺罔(qī wǎng) deceive
wǎng ㄨㄤˇ	網	网	用線，繩等結成的有孔用具，捕捉 net 用线，绳等结成的有孔用具，捕捉	漁網(yú wǎng) 渔网 fishing net 法網(fǎ wǎng) 法网 net of justice 網際網路(wǎng jì wǎng lù) the Internet 网际网路 網路(wǎng lù) network 网路
wǎng ㄨㄤˇ	惘	惘	失意，不如意的樣子 disappointed, frustrated 失意，不如意的样子	惘然(wǎng rán) a blank expression 迷惘(mí wǎng) bewildered
wàng ㄨㄤˋ	旺	旺	興盛 prosperous 兴盛	旺盛(wàng shèng) full of vigor 旺季(wàng jì) peak season 燒得很旺(shāo de hěn wàng) 烧得很旺 blazing
wàng ㄨㄤˋ	忘	忘	不記得，遺漏 forget, leave out 不记得，遗漏	忘記(wàng jì) 忘记 forget 難忘(nán wàng) 难忘 unforgettable
wàng ㄨㄤˋ	望	望	看，往遠處看，拜訪，向 look, look afar, visit, face toward 看，往远处看，拜访，向	希望(xī wàng) hope, wish 絕望(jué wàng) 绝望 despair 探望(tàn wàng) visit 望遠鏡(wàng yuǎn jìng) 望远镜 telescope

wàng ㄨ ㅊˋ	妄	妄	狂亂的，胡亂的 deranged, wild 狂乱的，胡乱的	狂妄(kuáng wàng) arrogant 妄動(wàng dòng) 妄动 reckless action
wēi wéi ㄨ ㄨ ㄟ ㄟˊ	危	危	傷害，損害，不安 全 injure, damage, dangerous 伤害，损害，不安 全	危險(wéi xiǎn) 危险 danger 病危(bìng wéi) be critically ill
wēi ㄨ ㄟ	威	威	使人敬畏的 awe-inspiring	示威(shì wēi) hold demonstration 威力(wēi lì) power
wēi ㄨ ㄟ	偎	偎	緊挨的，親密地依 靠著 lean closely upon a person 紧挨的，亲密地依 靠著	依偎(yī wēi) lean on a person
wēi wéi ㄨ ㄨ ㄟ ㄟˊ	微	微	細小，稍，少 tiny, a little 细小，稍，少	微小(wéi xiǎo) tiny 微笑(wéi xiào) smile
wēi wéi ㄨ ㄨ ㄟ ㄟˊ	薇	薇	薔薇：一年或二年 生草本植物，可供 觀賞和製香水 rose (flower) 薔薇：一年或二年 生草本植物，可供 观赏和制香水	薔薇(qiáng wéi) rose (flower)
wéi ㄨ ㄟˊ	圍	围	環繞，四周擋起來 around, encircle 环绕，四周挡起来	周圍(zhōu wéi) 周围 surrounding 圍巾(wéi jīn) 围巾 scarf 包圍(bāo wéi) 包围 surround, encircle
wéi ㄨ ㄟˊ	桅	桅	船上掛帆的杆子 mast 船上挂帆的杆子	桅杆(wéi gān) mast

wéi ㄨㄟˊ	維	维	保護，設法使繼續存在 protect, sustain 保护，设法使继续存在	維持(wéi chí)维持 maintain 維護(wéi hù)维护 defend, protect
wéi ㄨㄟˊ	違	违	不遵守，分離 go against, separate 不遵守，分离	違背(wéi bèi)违背 violate 違憲(wéi xiàn)违宪 unconstitutional
wéi wèi ㄨㄟˊ ㄨㄟˋ	爲	为	做，變成 do, become 做，变成	作爲(zuò wéi)作为 acting as 成爲(chéng wéi)成为 become
wéi ㄨㄟˊ	唯	唯	單單 only 单单	唯一(wéi yī) the only 唯物論(wéi wù lùn) 唯物论 materialism
wéi ㄨㄟˊ	惟	惟	只是 only	惟恐(wéi kǒng) for fear, lest
wěi ㄨㄟˇ	韋	韦	姓氏，去毛加工鞣制的獸皮 Chinese surname, hide 姓氏，去毛加工鞣制的兽皮	
wěi ㄨㄟˇ	緯	纬	織物上的橫線 woof 织物上的横线	北緯(běi wěi)北纬 north latitude 緯度(wěi dù)纬度 latitude
wěi ㄨㄟˇ	偉	伟	大，壯，人的品格事跡有大貢獻者 great 大，壮，人的品格事迹有大贡献者	偉大(wěi dà)伟大 great 雄偉(xióng wěi)雄伟 magnificent
wěi ㄨㄟˇ	僞	伪	假的 false	僞造(wěi zào)伪造 forgery 僞裝(wěi zhuāng)伪装 camouflage
wěi ㄨㄟˇ	尾	尾	鳥獸身體末端突出的部分，在後面 tail 鸟兽身体末端突出的部分，在后面	尾巴(wěi ba) the tail 尾隨(wěi suí)尾随 to tail a person

wěi ㄨㄟˇ	委	委	派任，推卸 appoint	委任(wěi rèn) appoint to office 推委(tuī wěi) shift responsibility
wěi ㄨㄟˇ	萎	萎	乾枯衰弱 wither 干枯衰弱	萎縮(wěi suō) 萎缩 wither 枯萎(kū wěi) fade away
wěi ㄨㄟˇ	猥	猥	鄙陋，下流 nasty	猥褻(wěi xiè) 猥亵 obscene
wèi wéi ㄨㄟˋ ㄨㄟˊ	爲	为	替，給，幫助 do for, give, help 替，给，帮助	爲何(wèi hé) 为何 why 因爲(yīn wèi) 因为 because
wèi ㄨㄟˋ	喂	喂	打招呼時用 hello 打招呼时用	喂！你是誰？(wèi, nǐ shì shéi?) 喂！你是谁？ Hello, who is it? 喂！你好嗎？(wèi, nǐ hǎo ma?) 喂！你好吗？Hello, how are you?
wèi ㄨㄟˋ	餵	喂	把東西送嘴裏，給動物吃東西 feed 把东西送嘴里，给动物吃东西	餵飯(wèi fàn)喂饭 feed 餵豬(wèi zhū)喂猪 feed the pig
wèi ㄨㄟˋ	位	位	所在的地方 location	位置(wèi zhì) 位置 location 地位(dì wèi) position, status
wèi ㄨㄟˋ	胃	胃	動物消化器官 stomach 动物消化器官	腸胃(cháng wèi)肠胃 stomach 胃病(wèi bìng) stomach trouble

wèi ㄨㄟˋ	謂	谓	说，意義 say, meaning 说，意义	所謂(suǒ wèi) 所谓 the so-called 無謂(wú wèi) 无谓 meaningless
wèi ㄨㄟˋ	畏	畏	怕，敬佩 fear, admire	可畏(kě wèi) awesome 敬畏(jìng wèi) revere and fear
wèi ㄨㄟˋ	尉	尉	官名 rank of officer	上尉(shàng wèi) captain 少尉(shào wèi) second lieutenant
wèi ㄨㄟˋ	慰	慰	使別人安心，心安 console, find solace	慰勞(wèi láo) 慰劳 extend comfort to 安慰(ān wèi) console
wèi ㄨㄟˋ	未	未	沒有，不 not yet, no	未成年(wèi chéng nián) underaged 未知數(wèi zhī shù) 未知数 the unknown factor
wèi ㄨㄟˋ	味	味	舌頭嘗東西的感覺 ，鼻子聞東西的感 覺，體會taste, smell 舌头尝东西的感觉 ，鼻子闻东西的感 觉，体会	味道(wèi dào) taste 氣味(qì wèi) 气味 odor
wèi ㄨㄟˋ	衛	卫	保護 protect 保护	保衛(bǎo wèi) 保卫 defend 衛生(wèi shēng) 卫生 hygiene
wèi ㄨㄟˋ	魏	魏	姓氏，古代國名 Chinese surname, name of ancient state 姓氏，古代国名	
wēn ㄨㄣ	溫	温	不冷不熱，性情柔 和 warm, gentle 不冷不热，性情柔 和	溫度(wēn dù) 温度 temperature 溫和(wēn hé) 温和 mild

wēn ㄨㄣ	瘟	瘟	流行急性傳染病 pestilence 流行急性传染病	瘟疫(wēn yì) 瘟疫 pestilence
wén ㄨㄣˊ	文	文	記錄語言的符號 written script 记录语言的符号	文字(wén zì) written script 文學(wén xué) 文学 literature 作文(zuò wén) composition
wén ㄨㄣˊ	紋	纹	物體上縐起的痕跡 ，皺痕 crease, wrinkle 物体上绉起的痕迹 ，皱痕	指紋(zhǐ wén) 指纹 fingerprint 皺紋(zhòu wén) 皱纹 wrinkle
wén ㄨㄣˊ	蚊	蚊	叮咬人畜，吸血並 傳染疾病的飛蟲 mosquito 叮咬人畜，吸血並 传染疾病的飞虫	蚊子(wén zi) mosquito
wén ㄨㄣˊ	聞	闻	聽見，用鼻子嗅氣 味 hear, smell 听见，用鼻子嗅气 味	新聞(xīn wén) 新闻news 奇聞(qí wén) 奇闻 exotic story 耳聞目睹(ěr wén mù dǔ) 耳闻目睹 to witness
wén ㄨㄣˊ	雯	雯	美麗的雲彩 beautiful cloud 美丽的云彩	
wěn ㄨㄣˇ	穩	稳	沈著 steady 沈著	穩定(wěn dìng) 稳定 stable 穩當(wěn dàng) 稳当 sound and proper
wěn ㄨㄣˇ	吻	吻	親嘴 kiss 亲嘴	接吻(jiē wěn) kiss 吻合(wěn hé) match
wěn ㄨㄣˇ	刎	刎	割脖子 slit throat	自刎(zì wěn) slit one's throat to commit suicide
wěn ㄨㄣˇ	紊	紊	亂 disorderly 乱	紊亂(wěn luàn) 紊乱 chaos 有條不紊(yǒu tiáo bù wěn) 有条不紊orderly

wèn ㄨㄣˋ	問	问	請人解答不明白的地方，追究 ask, look into 请人解答不明白的地方，追究	問題(wèn tí) 问题 question 問候(wèn hòu) 问候 send regards to
wēng ㄨㄥ	翁	翁	老頭，對男性年長者的稱呼 old man 老头，对男性年长者的称呼	老翁(lǎo wēng) old man 尊翁(zūn wēng) your father
wēng ㄨㄥ	嗡	嗡	聲音，蜜蜂叫聲，飛機聲 buzzing sound 声音，蜜蜂叫声，飞机声	蜜蜂嗡嗡嗡(mì fēng wēng wēng wēng) bee buzzes
wō ㄨㄛ	倭	倭	矮小，古代稱日本 short, ancient name for Japan 矮小，古代称日本	倭寇(wō kòu) Japanese pirates
wō ㄨㄛ	蝸	蜗	蝸牛：軟體有螺旋形硬殼的害蟲 snail 蜗牛：软体有螺旋形硬壳的害虫	蝸牛(wō niú) 蜗牛 snail
wō ㄨㄛ	窩	窝	動物的巢穴 den, nest 动物的巢穴	鳥窩(niǎo wō) 鸟窝 bird's nest 賊窩(zéi wō) 贼窝 bandits' hideout
wǒ ㄨㄛˇ	我	我	稱自己 I, me 称自己	自我(zì wǒ) ego, self 我們(wǒ mén) we 我軍(wǒ jūn)我军our army 我的(wǒ de) my 我們的(wǒ mén de) our
wò ㄨㄛˋ	臥	卧	睡，躺 lie down	臥病(wò bìng) 卧病 sick in bed 臥室(wò shì) 卧室 bedroom
wò ㄨㄛˋ	沃	沃	土地肥 fertile	肥沃(féi wò) fertile 沃土(wò tǔ) fertile soil

wò ㄨㄛˋ	握	握	手指彎曲來拿 grasp 手指弯曲来拿	把握(bǎ wò) to master 握手(wò shǒu) shake hands
wò ㄨㄛˋ	幄	幄	帳幕 tent 帐幕	運籌帷幄(yùn chóu wéi wò) 运筹帷幄 map out a strategy
wò ㄨㄛˋ	齷	龌	骯髒，不乾淨 filthy, unclean 肮脏，不干净	齷齪(wò chuò)龌龊 filthy
wò ㄨㄛˋ	斡	斡	旋轉，調停 turn around, mediate 旋转，调停	斡旋(wò xuán) to mediate
wū ㄨ	烏	乌	黑色的 black	烏鴉(wū yā) 乌鸦 crow 烏龜(wū guī) 乌龟 tortoise
wū ㄨ	誣	诬	硬說別人 slander 硬说别人	誣告(wū gào) 诬告 slander 誣賴(wū lài) 诬赖 shift blame on
wū ㄨ	污	污	骯髒，不廉潔，用無禮言行給人難堪 dirty, corrupt, insult 肮脏，不廉洁，用无礼言行给人难堪	貪污(tān wū) 贪污 corruption 污辱(wū rǔ) insult
wū ㄨ	屋	屋	房子 house	房屋(fáng wū) house 屋頂(wū dǐng) 屋顶 roof
wū ㄨ	巫	巫	替人求鬼神賜福的人 wizard, witch	巫師(wū shī) 巫师 wizard 巫婆(wū pó) witch
wū ㄨ	嗚	呜	哭泣，表示悲傷的詞 cry, to show sadness 哭泣，表示悲伤的词	嗚咽(wū yīn) 呜咽 sob 嗚呼(wū hū) 呜呼 alas
wú ㄨˊ	無	无	沒有，不 without, no	無妨(wú fáng) 无妨 does not matter 無非(wú fēi) 无非 nothing but

wú ㄨˊ	蕪	芜	滿處亂草 shaggy 满处乱草	荒蕪(huāng wú)荒芜 barren
wú ㄨˊ	吾	吾	我，我的 me, my	吾愛(wú ài) 吾爱 my love 吾師(wú shī) 吾师 my teacher
wú ㄨˊ	吳	吴	姓氏 Chinese surname	
wú ㄨˊ	蜈	蜈	多環節的節肢動物 ，能分泌毒液 centipede 多环节的节肢动物 ，能分泌毒液	蜈蚣(wú gōng) 蜈蚣 centipede
wǔ ㄨˇ	午	午	白天十一點到一點 的時間 noon 白天十一点到一点 的时间	午時(wǔ shí) 午时 at noon 午飯(wǔ fàn) 午饭 lunch
wǔ ㄨˇ	武	武	軍事，技藝，功夫 military force, skill 军事，技艺，功夫	武器(wǔ qì) weapon 武裝(wǔ zhuāng) 武装 armed
wǔ ㄨˇ	五	五	數目字，在四和六 之間 five 数目字，在四和六 之间	五官(wǔ guān) the five senses 五臟(wǔ zàng) five internal organs
wǔ ㄨˇ	伍	伍	同 "五" same as "五"	隊伍(duì wǔ) 队伍 contingent 伍長(wǔ zhǎng) 伍长 corporal
wǔ ㄨˇ	忤	忤	不順從的，違背 intractable, turn against 不顺从的，违背	忤逆(wǔ nì) violate
wǔ ㄨˇ	侮	侮	欺負，侵略，輕賤 bully, invade, slight 欺负，侵略，轻贱	侮辱(wǔ rǔ) insult 欺侮(qī wǔ) bully
wǔ ㄨˇ	舞	舞	配合音樂轉動身體 表演各種姿勢 dance 配合音乐转动身体 表演各种姿势	跳舞(tiào wǔ) dance 編舞(biān wǔ) 编舞 choreography
wǔ ㄨˇ	嫵	妩	美好姿態 charming 美好姿态	嫵媚(wǔ mèi) 妩媚 charming
wǔ ㄨˇ	鵡	鹉	見，鸚， see "鸚(yīng)" 见，鹦，	鸚鵡(yīng wǔ) 鹦鹉 parrot

326

wù ㄨˋ	務	务	事情，從事，必須 matters, engage in, must 事情，从事，必须	公務(gōng wù) 公务 official business 務必(wù bì) 务必 it is imperative that
wù ㄨˋ	霧	雾	水蒸汽遇冷凝結後 飄浮在空中的小水 滴 mist 水蒸汽遇冷凝结后 飘浮在空中的小水 滴	噴霧(pēn wù) 喷雾 spray 霧氣(wù qì) 雾气 mist
wù ㄨˋ	誤	误	差錯，妨害 error, interfere 差错，妨害	錯誤(cuò wù) 错误 mistake 誤會(wù huì) 误会 misunderstanding
wù ě è ㄨˋ ㄜˋ ㄜˋ	惡	恶	討厭，憎恨 disgusting, hate 讨厌，憎恨	可惡(kě wù) 可恶 abominable 深惡痛絕(shēn wù tòng jué) 深恶痛绝hate bitterly
wù ㄨˋ	勿	勿	別，不要 do not	勿失良機(wù shī liáng jī) 勿失良机 don't miss the good opportunity
wù ㄨˋ	物	物	東西 thing 东西	物質(wù zhí) 物质 matter 物價(wù jià) 物价 commodity price
wù ㄨˋ	悟	悟	理解，明白，覺醒 understand, realize 理解，明白，觉醒	覺悟(jué wù) 觉悟 come to the senses 悟性(wù xìng) comprehension
wù ㄨˋ	晤	晤	見面 meet 见面	會晤(huì wù) 会晤meet 晤談(wù tán) 晤谈 discuss in person
wù ㄨˋ	塢	坞	小堡壘 fortress-like structure 小堡垒	船塢(chuán wù)船坞dock 好萊塢(hǎo lái wù)好莱坞 Hollywood
wù ㄨˋ	騖	骛	力求 strive for	好高騖遠(hào gāo wù yuǎn) 好高骛远 over-ambitious

X				
xī ㄒㄧ	吸	吸	"呼"的相反，從口或鼻子把氣體引入體內 inhale "呼"的相反，从口或鼻子把气体引入体内	吸水(xī shuǐ) absorb water 吸收(xī shōu) absorb
xī ㄒㄧ	析	析	分開 separate 分开	分析(fēn xī) analyze
xī ㄒㄧ	犀	犀	犀牛：哺乳動物，形狀如牛，皮粗厚，鼻上有角 rhinoceros 犀牛：哺乳动物，形状如牛，皮粗厚，鼻上有角	犀牛(xī niú) rhinoceros
xī ㄒㄧ	希	希	盼望，少 hope, rare	希望(xī wàng) hope, wish 希奇(xī qí) peculiar
xī ㄒㄧ	稀	稀	"密"的相反，含水分多的，少 not dense, diluted rare	稀薄(xī bó) 稀薄 thin, not dense 稀有(xī yǒu) rare
xī ㄒㄧ	淅	淅	淅瀝：象聲詞，雨聲 the patter of rain 淅沥：象声词，雨声	淅瀝(xī lì) 淅沥 the patter of rain
xī xí ㄒㄧ ㄒㄧˊ	息	息	鼻子呼吸氣，音信，停止 breath, news, stop 鼻子呼吸气，音信，停止	消息(xiāo xí) news 息怒(xí nù) don't be angry
xī xí ㄒㄧ ㄒㄧˊ	昔	昔	從前 the past 从前	今昔(jīn xí) past and present 昔日(xí rì) in the past

xī xí ㄒ ㄒ ー ー、	惜	惜	重視，捨不得，覺 得遺憾 to treasure, reluctant to part 重视，舍不得，觉 得遗憾	愛惜(ài xí) 爱惜 to treasure 惜別(xí bié) part reluctantly
xī xí ㄒ ㄒ ー ー、	熄	熄	把火滅掉 put out fire 把火灭掉	熄燈(xí dēng) 熄灯 turn off the light 熄滅(xí miè) 熄灭 extinguish
xī ㄒ ー	悉	悉	全，知道 all, know	悉數(xī shù) 悉数 everything, all 熟悉(shóu xī) familiar
xī ㄒ ー	奚	奚	爲什麼，譏笑，嘲 弄 why, jeer 为什么，讥笑，嘲 弄	奚落(xī luò) 奚落 scorn
xī ㄒ ー	溪	溪	小河 creek	溪流(xī liú) creek 小溪(xiǎo xī) brook
xī xì ㄒ ㄒ ー ー、	夕	夕	日落的時候，夜 sunset, evening 日落的时候，夜	夕陽(xī yáng) 夕阳 sunset 前夕(qián xī) eve
xī ㄒ ー	西	西	"東"的相反，太 陽升起的一邊，屬 歐美地區的 west, western "东"的相反，太 阳升起的一边，属 欧美地区的	西部(xī bù) the West 西化(xī huà) Westernize 西裝(xī zhuāng) 西装 Western-style suit 西班牙(xī bān yá) Spain 西醫(xī yī) 西医 Western medicine
xī ㄒ ー	犧	牺	犧牲：爲正義而獻 出自己生命sacrifice 牺牲：为正义而献 出自己生命	犧牲(xī shēng) 牺牲 sacrifice

xī ㄒㄧ	熙	熙	光明，和樂，形容人來人往非常熱鬧 bright, merry, bustling 光明，和乐，形容人来人往非常热闹	熙攘(xī rǎng) bustling with activity
xī ㄒㄧ	嬉	嬉	遊戲，玩耍 play 遊戏，玩耍	嬉笑(xī xiào) playful
xī ㄒㄧ	曦	曦	陽光 sunlight 阳光	晨曦(chén xī) morning sun
xī ㄒㄧ	嘻	嘻	喜笑的樣子，笑的聲音 grin 喜笑的样子，笑的声音	笑嘻嘻(xiào xī xī) grin 嘻皮笑臉(xī pí xiào liǎn) 嘻皮笑脸 mischievous grin
xī ㄒㄧ	膝	膝	大腿和小腿相連可以彎曲的關節的前面部位 knee 大腿和小腿相连可以弯曲的关节的前面部位	膝蓋(xī gài) 膝盖 knee 屈膝(qū xī) kneel down
xī ㄒㄧ	晰	晰	清楚，明白 clear, understand	清晰(qīng xī) crispy clear
xí ㄒㄧˊ	習	习	學過後反覆再讀，長期重複地做成不自覺的動作 practice, habit 学过后反复再读，长期重复地做成不自觉的动作	習慣(xí guàn) 习惯 habit 溫習(wēn xí) 温习 review (lesson)
xí ㄒㄧˊ	席	席	到場，議會的座位，成桌的菜 present, seat 到场，议会的座位，成桌的菜	出席(chū xí) attend 席位(xí wèi) seat

xí ㄒ一ˊ	媳	媳	兒子的妻子 daughter-in-law 儿子的妻子	媳婦(xí fù) 媳妇 daughter-in-law
xí ㄒ一ˊ	襲	袭	趁人不注意而攻擊 ，照樣做 surprise attack, copy 趁人不注意而攻击 ，照样做	空襲(kōng xí) 空袭 air raid 世襲(shì xí) 世袭 hereditary
xǐ ㄒ一ˇ	洗	洗	用水去掉骯髒部分 to wash 用水去掉肮脏部分	洗衣(xǐ yī) do laundry 洗澡(xǐ zǎo) take a bath
xǐ ㄒ一ˇ	璽	玺	印，皇帝的印 imperial seal	玉璽(yù xǐ) 玉玺 imperial seal
xǐ ㄒ一ˇ	喜	喜	高興，快樂；愛好 happy, like to 高兴，快乐；爱好	喜好(xǐ hào) like 歡喜(huān xǐ) 欢喜happy 喜歡(xǐ huān) 喜欢 fond of
xǐ ㄒ一ˇ	徙	徙	遷移 move (from one place to another) 迁移	遷徙(qiān xǐ) 迁徙 move
xǐ ㄒ一ˇ	禧	禧	福，吉祥 happiness, luck	恭賀新禧(gōng hè xīn xǐ) 恭贺新禧 wishing you a happy New Year
xì ㄒ一ˋ	係	係	關聯 connection 关联	關係(guān xì) 关系 relationship 沒關係(méi guān xì) 没关系 it does not matter
xì ㄒ一ˋ	系	系	聯屬的關係，大學 的學科 system, field of study in college 联属的关系，大学 的学科	系統(xì tǒng) 系统 system 系列(xì liè) series
xì ㄒ一ˋ	繫	系	聯絡，維持，綁 to contact, maintain, fasten 联络，维持，绑	聯繫(lián xì) 联系 contact 繫鞋帶(xì xié dài) 系鞋带 tie shoelace
xì ㄒ一ˋ	戲	戏	玩耍 play	戲劇(xì jù) 戏剧 drama 戲弄(xì nòng) 戏弄 make fun of

xì ㄒㄧˋ	細	细	"粗"的相反，顆粒小的，周密 refined "粗"的相反，颗粒小的，周密	細小(xì xiǎo) 细小 tiny 細心(xì xīn) 细心 careful
xì ㄒㄧˋ	隙	隙	裂縫，機會 crack, opportunity 裂缝，机会	墻隙(qiáng xì) 墙隙 crack in the wall 空隙(kòng xì) break time
xì ㄒㄧˋ	鬩	阋	爭吵 quarrel 争吵	鬩牆(xì qiáng) 阋墙 internal strife
xiā ㄒㄧㄚ	蝦	虾	節肢有殼動物，生活在水裏，可吃 shrimp, prawn 节肢有壳动物，生活在水里，可吃	龍蝦(lóng xiā) 龙虾 lobster 蝦仁(xiā rén) 虾仁 shrimp
xiā ㄒㄧㄚ	瞎	瞎	眼睛看不見 blind 眼睛看不见	瞎子(xiā zi) blind person 瞎扯(xiā chě) talk nonsense
xiá ㄒㄧㄚˊ	匣	匣	放東西的小箱子或盒子 small box 放东西的小箱子或盒子	話匣子(huà xiá zi) 话匣子 chatterbox 木匣(mù xiá) wooden box
xiá ㄒㄧㄚˊ	俠	侠	見義勇爲，扶持弱小的人 man with chivalrous qualities 见义勇为，扶持弱小的人	俠客(xiá kè) 侠客 chivalrous man 劍俠(jiàn xiá) 剑侠 swordsman
xiá ㄒㄧㄚˊ	峽	峡	兩山夾著水道的地方，兩大陸地中間的狹長水道 gorge 两山夹著水道的地方，两大陆地中间的狭长水道	三峽(sān xiá) 三峡 the Three Gorges 海峽(hǎi xiá) 海峡 straits

xiá ㄒ ㄧ ㄚ	狹	狭	窄，不寬 narrow 窄，不宽	狹窄(xiá zhǎi) 狭窄 narrow 狹義(xiá yì) 狭义 in a narrow sense
xiá ㄒ ㄧ ㄚ	霞	霞	太陽光照射在雲層 上所映出的紅色光 彩 rosy clouds 太阳光照射在云层 上所映出的红色光 彩	晚霞(wǎn xiá) rosy clouds at sunset 彩霞(cǎi xiá) colorful clouds
xiá ㄒ ㄧ ㄚ	暇	暇	空閒 leisure 空闲	閒暇(xián xiá) 闲暇 leisure 無暇(wú xiá) 无暇 do not have time to
xiá ㄒ ㄧ ㄚ	遐	遐	遠處，長久的 faraway place, long time 远处，长久的	遐思(xiá sī) fantasy
xiá ㄒ ㄧ ㄚ	轄	辖	管理 manage	管轄(guǎn xiá) 管辖 have jurisdiction over 直轄(zhí xiá) 直辖 directly governed by
xiá ㄒ ㄧ ㄚ	黠	黠	聰明而狡猾 smark and cunning 聪明而狡猾	狡黠(jiǎo xiá) cunning 黠慧(xiá huì) clever
xiá ㄒ ㄧ ㄚ	瑕	瑕	玉上的斑點，比喻 缺點 defect 玉上的斑点，比喻 缺点	瑕疵(xiá cī) defect
xiá ㄒ ㄧ ㄚ	下	下	位置在低處的，降 落，次序後的 down, drop, next 位置在低处的，降 落，次序后的	山下(shān xià) foot of a hill 下雨(xià yǔ) to rain

xià hè ㄒㄧㄚˋ ㄏㄜˋ	嚇	吓	害怕，使人害怕 scare, frighten	嚇人(xià rén) 吓人 scare others 嚇呆了(xià dāi le) 吓呆了 be scared stiff 恐嚇(kǒng hè) 恐吓 threaten
xià ㄒㄧㄚˋ	夏	夏	四季中第二季 summer	夏天(xià tiān) summer 入夏(rù xià) beginning of summer
xià shà ㄒㄧㄚˋ	廈	厦	高大的房屋 tall, big house	大廈(dà shà) 大厦 high rise 廈門(xià mén) 厦门 Xiamen City (in Fujian Province)
xiān ㄒㄧㄢ	纖	纤	細小的 tiny 细小的	纖細(xiān xì) 纤细 slim, fine 纖維(xiān wéi) 纤维 fiber
xiān ㄒㄧㄢ	仙	仙	有特殊神力長生不老的人 immortals 有特殊神力长生不老的人	仙女(xiān nǚ) fairy 神仙(shén xiān) immortals
xiān ㄒㄧㄢ	先	先	祖宗，已死的，時間秩序在前面的 ancestor, deceased, before 祖宗，已死的，时间秩序在前面的	祖先(zǔ xiān) ancestor 先天(xiān tiān) hereditary
xiān ㄒㄧㄢ	掀	掀	打開，發動，興起 open, initiate, whip up 打开，发动，兴起	掀開(xiān kāi) 掀开 uncover 掀起(xiān qǐ) whip up
xiān ㄒㄧㄢ	鮮	鲜	新的，滋味美的，有光彩的 fresh, taste good, bright-colored 新的，滋味美的，有光彩的	鮮花(xiān huā) 鲜花 fresh flower 新鮮(xīn xiān) 新鲜 fresh

334

xián 丁一ㄢˊ	閑	闲	沒有事情做，不使用 idle, not being used	閑暇(xián xiá) 闲暇 leisure 閑話(xián huà) 闲话 gossip
xián 丁一ㄢˊ	賢	贤	有道德才能者 virtuous and capable	賢能(xián néng) 贤能 virtuous and capable 賢妻(xián qī) 贤妻 good wife
xián 丁一ㄢˊ	弦	弦	張在弓或樂器上的 線 string on bow or musical instrument 张在弓或乐器上的 线	弓弦(gōng xián) bowstring 續弦(xù xián) 续弦 remarry after wife's death
xián 丁一ㄢˊ	嫻	娴	沈靜，文雅，熟練 demure, refined, skilled 沈静，文雅，熟练	嫻淑(xián shú) 娴淑 demure 嫻熟(xián shú) 娴熟 skilled
xián 丁一ㄢˊ	涎	涎	口水 saliva	垂涎三尺(chuí xián sān chǐ) cast a covetous eye at
xián 丁一ㄢˊ	嫌	嫌	厭惡，懷疑，可疑 detest, suspect, suspicious 厌恶，怀疑，可疑	嫌棄(xián qì) 嫌弃 avoid in disgust 嫌疑(xián yí) a suspect
xián 丁一ㄢˊ	鹹	咸	鹽的滋味，含有鹽 分的 salty 盐的滋味，含有盐 分的	鹹肉(xián ròu) 咸肉 salted meat 鹹水(xián shuǐ) 咸水 salt water
xián 丁一ㄢˊ	銜	衔	用嘴啥著，官吏的 階級，連接 hold in mouth, title, hook up 用嘴含著，官吏的 阶级，连接	頭銜(tóu xián) 头衔 title 銜接(xián jiē) 衔接 tie in with

xiǎn ㄒ一ㄢˇ	顯	显	露在外面容易看出來，表現 show, express 露在外面容易看出来，表现	明顯(míng xiǎn) 明显 obvious 顯出(xiǎn chū) 显出 show
xiǎn ㄒ一ㄢˇ	險	险	可能發生的災難，重要的，幾乎 danger, important, almost 可能发生的灾难，重要的，几乎	危險(wéi xiǎn) 危险 danger 保險(bǎo xiǎn) 保险 insurance
xiàn ㄒ一ㄢˋ	限	限	指定的範圍 limit 指定的范围	限制(xiàn zhì) restriction 期限(qí xiàn) time limit
xiàn ㄒ一ㄢˋ	現	现	顯露 show 显露	出現(chū xiàn) 出现 appear 實現(shí xiàn) 实现 materialize
xiàn ㄒ一ㄢˋ	縣	县	省以下鄉鎮以上的行政區域 county 省以下乡镇以上的行政区域	縣長(xiàn zhǎng) 县长 county head 縣城(xiàn chéng) 县城 county seat
xiàn ㄒ一ㄢˋ	線	线	細長的東西，細小的 line, thread 细长的东西，细小的	打毛線(dǎ máo xiàn) 打毛线 to knit 光線(guāng xiàn) 光线 ray of light
xiàn ㄒ一ㄢˋ	陷	陷	沈下，掉進，設計害人 sink, fall into, plot against 沈下，掉进，设计害人	淪陷(lún xiàn) 沦陷 fall into enemy's hands 陷阱(xiàn jǐng) a trap
xiàn ㄒ一ㄢˋ	憲	宪	國家最高的法律 constitution 国家最高的法律	憲法(xiàn fǎ) 宪法 the constitution 修憲(xiū xiàn) 修宪 revise the constitution

xiàn ㄒㄧㄢˋ	羨	羡	仰慕，愛慕，喜愛 而希望得到 admire, love, yearn for 仰慕，爱慕，喜爱 而希望得到	羨慕(xiàn mù) 羡慕 admire 稱羨(chēng xiàn) 称羡 praise in admiration
xiàn ㄒㄧㄢˋ	獻	献	恭敬地送給，表現 出來 offer 恭敬地送给，表现 出来	奉獻(fèng xiàn) 奉献 sacrifice 獻禮(xiàn lǐ) 献礼 offer a gift
xiàn ㄒㄧㄢˋ	腺	腺	身體中能分泌的組 織 gland 身体中能分泌的组 织	汗腺(hàn xiàn) sweat gland 分泌腺(fēn mì xiàn) secreting gland
xiāng ㄒㄧㄤ	香	香	"臭"的相反，氣 味好聞 fragrant "臭"的相反，气 味好闻	香水(xiāng shuǐ) perfume 香花(xiāng huā) fragrant flower 蚊香(wén xiāng) mosquito- repellent incense 香料(xiāng liào) spice
xiāng ㄒㄧㄤ	鄉	乡	城市外的區域 countryside 城市外的区域	鄉下(xiàng xià) 乡下 countryside 故鄉(gù xiāng) 故乡 hometown
xiāng ㄒㄧㄤ	相	相	交互，彼此，等於 mutual, equal 交互，彼此，等於	互相(hù xiāng) mutual 相當(xiāng dāng) 相当 equivalent to
xiāng ㄒㄧㄤ	廂	廂	正房前面兩旁的房 屋，容納人或東西 的地方 chamber 正房前面两旁的房 屋，容纳人或东西 的地方	包廂(bāo xiāng) reserved box (in theater) 車廂(chē xiāng) 车厢 train car
xiāng ㄒㄧㄤ	箱	箱	可儲存東西的有蓋 器具 box 可储存东西的有盖 器具	箱子(xiāng zi) box 信箱(xìn xiāng) mailbox

xiáng ㄒㄧㄤˊ	詳	详	完備 complete, detailed 完备	詳情(xiáng qíng) 详情 detailed information 詳談(xiáng tán) 详谈 discuss in detail
xiáng ㄒㄧㄤˊ	祥	祥	能帶好運的 auspicious 能带好运的	吉祥(jí xiáng) auspicious
xiáng ㄒㄧㄤˊ	翔	翔	在空中轉圈飛行 circle in the air 在空中转圈飞行	飛翔(fēi xiáng) 飞翔 fly 滑翔(huá xiáng) glide
xiáng jiàng ㄒㄧㄤˊ ㄐㄧㄤˋ	降	降	屈服，制服對方， 歸順 surrender, subdue 屈服，制服 对方，归顺	投降(tóu xiáng) surrender 降服(xiáng fú) subdue 降低(jiàng dī) to lower 降雨量(jiàng yǔ liàng) precipitation (rainfall)
xiǎng ㄒㄧㄤˇ	享	享	受用，消受快樂 enjoy 受用，消受快乐	享受(xiǎng shòu) enjoy 共享(gòng xiǎng) share the joy
xiǎng ㄒㄧㄤˇ	餉	饷	軍警的薪水，軍糧 police, military pay; army ration 军警的薪水，军粮	發餉(fā xiǎng) 发饷 pay out salary 糧餉(liáng xiǎng) 粮饷 food ration
xiǎng ㄒㄧㄤˇ	想	想	念頭，思考，打算 idea, thought, intention 念头，思考，打算	想念(xiǎng niàn) miss a person 料想(liào xiǎng) expect
xiǎng ㄒㄧㄤˇ	響	响	聲音大 loud noise 声音大	音響(yīn xiǎng) 音响 sound, stereo 響亮(xiǎng liàng) 响亮 loud
xiǎng ㄒㄧㄤˋ	嚮	向	引導，勸勉，接近 guide, encourage, approach 引导，劝勉，接近	嚮導(xiàng dǎo) 向导 a guide 嚮往(xiàng wǎng) 向往 yearn for
xiàng ㄒㄧㄤˋ	巷	巷	大街或大路旁的小 路 alley 大街或大路旁的小 路	巷子(xiàng zi) alley 巷戰(xiàng zhàn) 巷战 street battle

338

xiàng ㄒ 一 ㄤ	項	项	事物的種類或條目 ，脖子的後部 item, neck 事物的种类或条目 ，脖子的后部	項目(xiàng mù) 项目 item, project 項鍊(xiàng liàn) 项链 necklace
xiàng xiāng ㄒ ㄒ 一 一 ㄤ ㄤ	相	相	形貌，樣子，神情 looks, appearance 形貌，样子，神情	相貌(xiàng mào) appearance, looks 真相(zhēn xiàng) the truth 相同(xiāng tóng) same 相信(xiāng xìn) believe
xiàng ㄒ 一 ㄤ	象	象	哺乳動物，鼻子可 伸卷，有一對白色 門牙 elephant 哺乳动物，鼻子可 伸卷，有一对白色 门牙	大象(dà xiàng) elephant 象徵(xiàng zhēng) 象征 symbol
xiàng ㄒ 一 ㄤ	像	像	相似，按照人物做 成的東西 resemble, portrait or statue 相似，按照人物做 成的东西	好像(hǎo xiàng) resemble 畫像(huà xiàng) 画像 portrait
xiàng ㄒ 一 ㄤ	向	向	方位，對著，傾於 某一方面 direction, facing, lean toward 方位，对著，倾於 某一方面	方向(fāng xiàng) direction 一向(yí xiàng) always
xiāo ㄒ 一 ㄠ	硝	硝	白色透明的結晶礦 物，可以製火藥和 玻璃 nitre 白色透明的结晶矿 物，可以制火药和 玻璃	硝酸(xiāo suān) nitric acid
xiāo ㄒ 一 ㄠ	銷	销	燒掉，出賣貨物 burn, sell 烧掉，出卖货物	銷毀(xiāo huǐ) 销毁 destroy 銷售(xiāo shòu) 销售 sell

xiāo ㄒ 一 ㄠ	削	削	用刀斜切掉外面的 皮 slice off 用刀斜切掉外面的 皮	削鉛筆(xiāo qiān bǐ) 削铅笔 sharpen pencil 削果皮(xiāo guǒ pí) peel fruit
xiāo ㄒ 一 ㄠ	宵	宵	夜 night	通宵(tōng xiāo) throughout the night 宵禁(xiāo jìn) curfew
xiāo ㄒ 一 ㄠ	逍	逍	逍遙：自由自在， 無拘無束 carefree 逍遥：自由自在， 无拘无束	逍遙(xiāo yáo) carefree
xiāo ㄒ 一 ㄠ	消	消	除去，散去，把時 間渡過 remove, vanish, kill time 除去，散去，把时 间渡过	消毒(xiāo dú) sterilize 消化(xiāo huà) digest
xiāo ㄒ 一 ㄠ	蕭	萧	冷落，不興旺 desolate, not prosperous 冷落，不兴旺	蕭條(xiāo tiáo) 萧条 desolate 風蕭蕭(fēng xiāo xiāo) 风萧萧 wind's soughing
xiāo ㄒ 一 ㄠ	簫	箫	直吹的管樂 vertical flute 直吹的管乐	吹簫(chuī xiāo) 吹箫 play vertical flute
xiāo ㄒ 一 ㄠ	瀟	潇	瀟灑：行動大方爽 朗 elegant and graceful 潇洒：行动大方爽 朗	瀟灑(xiāo sǎ) 潇洒 elegant and graceful
xiǎo ㄒ 一 ㄠ	小	小	"大·的相反，壞 人，年紀輕 small, mean "大·的相反，坏 人，年纪轻	小人(xiǎo rén) a mean person 小費(xiǎo fèi) 小费 tip (for service)

xiǎo ㄒ一ˇ ㄠ	曉	晓	早晨天剛亮時，知道 dawn 早晨天刚亮时，知道	破曉(pò xiǎo)破晓 dawn 曉得(xiǎo dé)晓得 know
xiào ㄒ一ˋ ㄠ	肖	肖	像，相似 resemble 像，相似	肖像(xiào xiàng) portrait
xiào ㄒ一ˋ ㄠ	笑	笑	露出愉快的表情，輕視，譏諷 laugh, slight 露出愉快的表情，轻视，讥讽	笑容(xiào róng) smile 笑話(xiào huà)笑话 joke
xiào ㄒ一ˋ ㄠ	孝	孝	盡心奉養父母 filial piety 尽心奉养父母	孝子(xiào zi) dutiful son 帶孝(dài xiào)带孝 mourn parent's death
xiào jiào ㄒ ㄐ一 ㄠˋ ㄠˋ	校	校	研究傳授學問的地方，官階名 school, rank of officer 研究传授学问的地方，官阶名	學校(xué xiào)学校 school 上校(shàng xiào) colonel
xiào ㄒ一ˋ ㄠ	嘯	啸	拉長聲音叫，飛機，子彈飛過的聲音 howl, whizz 拉长声音叫，飞机，子弹飞过的声音	虎嘯(hǔ xiào)虎啸 tiger's roar 呼嘯而過(hū xiào ér guò) 呼啸而过 whizz past
xiào ㄒ一ˋ ㄠ	效	效	摹仿，成果，功用 imitate, result, effect	仿效(fǎng xiào) imitate 效率(xiào lǜ) efficiency
xiào ㄒ一ˋ ㄠ	酵	酵	有機物受細菌等作用而發生分解 ferment 有机物受细菌等作用而发生分解	發酵(fā xiào)发酵 ferment 酵母(xiào mǔ) yeast
xiāo ㄒ一 ㄠ	哮	哮	吼叫 roar	咆哮(páo xiāo) roar 哮喘(xiāo chuǎn) asthma
xiē ㄒ一 ㄝ	些	些	量詞，表示不定的數量 some 量词，表示不定的数量	一些(yì xiē) some 多些(duō xiē) a little more

xiē ㄒ 一 ㄝ	歇	歇	休息，停止 rest, stop	歇業(xiē yè) 歇业 business closedown 歇腳(xiē jiǎo) 歇脚 take a rest
xié ㄒ 一 ㄝ	協	协	共同合作 cooperate	協調(xié tiáo) 协调 coordinate 協會(xié huì) 协会 association
xié ㄒ 一 ㄝ	邪	邪	不正當，怪異的事 evil, sinister 不正当，怪异的事	邪惡(xié è) 邪恶 evil 邪教(xié jiào) 邪教 cult
xié ㄒ 一 ㄝ	斜	斜	位置或姿勢不正 tilted to one side, not erect 位置或姿势不正	斜眼(xié yǎn) squint 斜坡(xié pō) slope
xié ㄒ 一 ㄝ	鞋	鞋	穿在腳上的東西 shoe 穿在脚上的东西	皮鞋(pí xié) leather shoe 鞋底(xié dǐ) sole
xié ㄒ 一 ㄝ	諧	谐	配合適當，滑稽 harmony, humorous 配合适当，滑稽	和諧(hé xié) 和谐 harmony 詼諧(huī xié) 诙谐 humorous
xié ㄒ 一 ㄝ	攜	携	帶，合作 bring, cooperate 带，合作	攜伴(xié bàn) 携伴 bring a partner 攜帶(xié dài) 携带 bring along
xié ㄒ 一 ㄝ	挾	挟	夾在胳膊底下，強 迫人服從，心裏懷 恨 squeeze under one's arm 夹在胳膊 底下，强迫人服从 ，心里怀恨	挾持(xié chí) 挟持 force a person to yield 要挾(yāo xié) 要挟 coerce

xié ㄒㄧㄝˊ	脅	胁	逼迫恐嚇 threaten 逼迫恐吓	威脅(wēi xié)威胁 threaten 脅迫(xié pò)胁迫 coerce
xiě ㄒㄧㄝˇ	寫	写	拿筆作書畫 write 拿笔作书画	寫字(xiě zì)写字 write 寫信(xiě xìn)写信 write letter
xiě ㄒㄧㄝˇ	血	血	動物脈管裏所含的 紅色流體 blood 动物脉管里所含的 红色流体	血液(xiě yè) blood 流血(liú xiě) bleed
xiè ㄒㄧㄝˋ	泄	泄	透露，發散 disclose, release 透露，发散	排泄(pái xiè) excrete 泄洪(xiè hóng) flood discharge
xiè ㄒㄧㄝˋ	瀉	泻	水向下流得很快， 拉肚子 swift fall of water, diarrhea 水向下流得很快， 拉肚子	瀉肚(xiè dù)泻肚 have diarrhea 瀉藥(xiè yào)泻药 diarrhea medicine
xiè ㄒㄧㄝˋ	屑	屑	碎末，甘願，細碎 sawdust, willing, pieces 碎末，甘愿，细碎	木屑(mù xiè) sawdust 不屑(bú xiè) disdain
xiè ㄒㄧㄝˋ	謝	谢	表示感激，凋落 thank, wither	感謝(gǎn xiè)感谢 thank 凋謝(diāo xiè)凋谢 wither
xiè ㄒㄧㄝˋ	懈	懈	疏懶，怠惰 lax, lazy 疏懒，怠惰	懈怠(xiè dài) to slacken 不懈的努力(bú xiè de nǔ lì) unremitting efforts
xiè ㄒㄧㄝˋ	邂	邂	邂逅：沒約會而遇 到 meet by chance 邂逅：没约会而遇 到	邂逅(xiè hòu) meet by chance

xiè ㄒㄧㄝˋ	械	械	機器，武器 machinery, weapon 机器，武器	機械(jī xiè) 机械 machinery 槍械(qiāng xiè) 枪械 firearms
xiè ㄒㄧㄝˋ	蟹	蟹	全身有甲殼水陸兩 棲動物，前面一對 腳成鉗狀，橫著走 crab 全身有甲壳水陆两 栖动物，前面一对 脚成钳状，横著走	螃蟹(páng xiè) crab 蟹肉(xiè ròu) crab meat 蟹黃(xiè huáng) crab eggs
xīn ㄒㄧㄣ	新	新	"舊"的相反，沒 有用過的 new, unused "旧"的相反，没 有用过的	新年(xīn nián) New Year 新郎(xīn láng) bridegroom
xīn ㄒㄧㄣ	薪	薪	木柴，工作的酬勞 firewood, salary 木柴，工作的酬劳	薪水(xīn shuǐ) 薪水 salary 薪火(xīn huǒ) 薪火 firewood
xīn ㄒㄧㄣ	欣	欣	喜歡，快樂，生機 旺盛 happy, energetic 喜欢，快乐，生机 旺盛	欣喜(xīn xǐ) happy 欣賞(xīn shǎng) 欣赏 appreciate
xīn ㄒㄧㄣ	心	心	專管血液流通的內 臟 heart 专管血液流通的内 脏	心臟(xīn zàng) 心脏 heart 小心(xiǎo xīn) careful
xīn ㄒㄧㄣ	辛	辛	勞苦 toil 劳苦	辛苦(xīn kǔ) toilsome 辛勤(xīn qín) diligence
xīn ㄒㄧㄣ	鑫	鑫	興盛，有財富 prosperous, wealthy 兴盛，有财富	
xīn ㄒㄧ	馨	馨	香氣 fragrance 香气	溫馨(wēn xīn) 温馨 warmth 馨香(xīn xiāng) fragrance

xìn ㄒㄧㄣ	信	信	誠實，不欺騙，不懷疑 honest, trust 诚实，不欺骗，不怀疑	信用(xìn yòng) credibility 宗教信仰(zōng jiào xìn yǎng) 宗教信仰 religious belief
xìn ㄒㄧㄣ	釁	衅	爭端 dispute 争端	挑釁(tiǎo xìn)挑衅 provoke
xīng xìng ㄒㄧㄥ	興	兴	旺盛 prosperous	興盛(xīng shèng) 兴盛 prosperous 興奮(xìng fèn) 兴奋 excited
xīng ㄒㄧㄥ	星	星	夜間天空中閃爍發光的天體，影藝界的名人 star 夜间天空中闪烁发光的天体，影艺界的名人	星星(xīng xīng) stars 明星(míng xīng) movie star
xīng ㄒㄧㄥ	猩	猩	一種大猴子，深紅色的 gorilla 一种大猴子，深红色的	猩猩(xīng xīng) gorilla 猩紅(xīng hóng) scarlet
xīng ㄒㄧㄥ	腥	腥	像魚的氣味 smell of fish 像鱼的气味	血腥(xuè xīng) bloody 腥臭(xīng chòu) stench
xíng háng ㄒㄧㄥ	行	行	作為，走，能幹 action, walk, capable 作为，走，能干	行為(xíng wéi) 行为 behavior 遠行(yuǎn xíng)远行 travel afar 行業(háng yè) 行业 profession
xíng ㄒㄧㄥ	刑	刑	處罰罪犯 criminal punishment 处罚罪犯	死刑(sǐ xíng) death penalty 刑罰(xíng fá)刑罚 criminal punishment
xíng ㄒㄧㄥ	邢	邢	姓氏 Chinese surname	

xíng ㄒㄧㄥˊ	型	型	製造器物所用的模子，樣式 model 制造器物所用的模子，样式	模型(mó xíng) model 髮型(fǎ xíng) 发型 hairstyle
xíng ㄒㄧㄥˊ	形	形	樣子 shape 样子	形狀(xíng zhuàng) shape 形勢(xíng shì) 形势 situation
xǐng ㄒㄧㄥˇ	醒	醒	沒睡，睡起來了，由迷惑變清楚 not asleep, wake up, sober 没睡，睡起来了，由迷惑变清楚	睡醒(shuì xǐng) awake 清醒(qīng xǐng) sober
xǐng ㄒㄧㄥˇ	擤	擤	捏住鼻子用氣排出鼻涕 blow one's nose 捏住鼻子用气排出鼻涕	擤鼻涕(xǐng bí tì) blow one's nose
xǐng shěng ㄒㄧㄥˇ ㄕㄥˇ	省	省	檢討，知覺 examine, perception 检讨，知觉	反省(fǎn xǐng) look into oneself 不省人事(bù xǐng rén shì) lose consciousness 省略(shěng lüè) omit
xìng ㄒㄧㄥˋ	杏	杏	落葉喬木，果實可吃也可製藥 apricot 落叶乔木，果实可吃也可制药	杏仁(xìng rén) apricot
xìng ㄒㄧㄥˋ	幸	幸	福氣，過分的喜愛 luck, bliss 福气，过分的喜爱	幸福(xìng fú) happiness, bliss 幸運(xìng yùn) 幸运 lucky 不幸(bú xìng) misfortune
xìng ㄒㄧㄥˋ	姓	姓	代表家族的字 family name	姓名(xìng míng) name 貴姓？(guì xìng) 贵姓？ What's your name?

xìng xìng ㄒ ㄒ 一 一 ∠ ∠	興	兴	愛好 enthusiasm 爱好	興趣(xìng qù) 兴趣 interest 高興(gāo xìng) 高兴 happy
xìng ㄒ 一 、 ∠	性	性	男女的特質，個人 思想行動上的特點 gender, trait 男女的特质，个人 思想行动上的特点	性別(xìng bié) gender 個性(gè xìng) 个性 personality
xiōng ㄒ ㄩ ∠	兄	兄	哥哥，對哥哥輩份 的人的尊稱 elder brother 哥哥，对哥哥辈份 的人的尊称	兄弟(xiōng dì) brothers 長兄(zhǎng xiōng) 长兄 eldest brother
xiōng ㄒ ㄩ ∠	凶	凶	不幸的，惡，殺傷 misfortune, evil, assault 不幸的，恶，杀伤	凶暴(xiōng bào) violent 凶手(xiōng shǒu) murderer
xiōng ㄒ ㄩ ∠	洶	汹	水勢猛烈向上湧 tempestuous 水势猛烈向上涌	洶湧(xiōng yǒng) 汹涌 turbulent 洶洶(xiōng xiōng) 汹汹 in a violent manner
xiōng ㄒ ㄩ ∠	兇	兇	殺人，強不講理 murder, ferocious 杀人，强不讲理	行兇(xíng xiōng) 行兇 commit murder 兇惡(xiōng è) 兇恶 ferocious
xiōng ㄒ ㄩ ∠	胸	胸	身體前面脖子以下 肚子以上的部分 chest 身体前面脖子以下 肚子以上的部分	胸部(xiōng bù) chest 胸襟(xiōng jīn) breadth of vision
xióng ㄒ ㄩ ´ ∠	雄	雄	公的，強有力的 male 公的，强有力的	英雄(yīng xióng) hero 雄心(xióng xīn) ambition
xióng ㄒ ㄩ ´ ∠	熊	熊	體大四肢粗短的哺 乳動物 bear 体大四肢粗短的哺 乳动物	熊掌(xióng zhǎng) a bear's paw 熊貓(xióng māo) 熊猫 giant panda
xiū ㄒ 一 ㄡ	休	休	歇息，停止 rest, stop	休息(xiū xí) to rest 休假(xiū jià) on vacation

xiū ㄒㄧㄡ	修	修	恢復完美，研究， 建造 restore, study, build 恢复完美，研究， 建造	修飾(xiū shì) 修饰 decorate, dress up 修理(xiū lǐ) repair
xiū ㄒㄧㄡ	羞	羞	感到恥辱，難為情 feel ashamed, shy 感到耻辱，难为情	羞辱(xiū rǔ) insult 害羞(hài xiū) shy
xiǔ ㄒㄧㄡˇ	朽	朽	木頭腐爛 rotten 木头腐烂	不朽(bù xiǔ) live forever 腐朽(fǔ xiǔ) rotten
xiù ㄒㄧㄡˋ	秀	秀	才智傑出的，美好 的outstanding, pretty, handsome 才智杰出的，美好 的	優秀(yōu xiù) 优秀 outstanding 秀麗(xiù lì) 秀丽 beautiful
xiù ㄒㄧㄡˋ	袖	袖	衣服從肩膀到手腕 的部分 sleeve 衣服从肩膀到手腕 的部分	長袖(cháng xiù) 长袖 long sleeve 袖珍(xiù zhēn) miniature
xiù ㄒㄧㄡˋ	嗅	嗅	用鼻子辨別氣味， 聞 smell 用鼻子辨别气味， 闻	嗅覺(xiù jué) 嗅觉 sense of smell
xiù ㄒㄧㄡˋ	銹	锈	金屬表面所生的氧 化物 rust 金属表面所生的氧 化物	鐵銹(tiě xiù) 铁锈 iron rust 生銹(shēng xiù) 生锈 to rust
xiù ㄒㄧㄡˋ	繡	绣	刺有五彩花紋的絲 織品 embroidery 刺有五彩花纹的丝 织品	繡花(xiù huā) 绣花 to embroider

xū ㄒㄩ	須	须	應當 must 应当	必須(bì xū) 必须 must 須知(xū zhī) 须知 things to know
xū ㄒㄩ	需	需	必得用的財物，費 用，欲求 necessities, expenses, needs 必得用的财物，费 用，欲求	需求(xū qiú) demand 軍需(jūn xū) 军需 military supplies
xū ㄒㄩ	虛	虚	空的，不真實的 empty, not realistic 空的，不真实的	空虛(kōng xū) empty 虛偽(xū wèi) 虚伪 hypocritical
xū ㄒㄩ	鬚	须	長在下巴或嘴巴的 毛，植物的細絲細 根 beard, feeler 長 在下巴或嘴巴的毛 ，植物的细丝细根	鬍鬚(hú xū) 胡须 beard, mustache
xū ㄒㄩ	噓	嘘	慢慢把氣從嘴裏吐 出來，說好話 exhale slowly, boast 慢慢把气从嘴里吐 出来，说好话	噓氣(xū qì) 嘘气 exhale 吹噓(chuī xū) boast
xū ㄒㄩ	墟	墟	有人住過現已荒廢 的地方 ruins 有人住过现已荒废 的地方	廢墟(fèi xū) 废墟 the ruins
xú ㄒㄩˊ	徐	徐	慢慢地 slowly	徐徐(xú xú) slowly
xǔ ㄒㄩˇ	栩	栩	生動的樣子 lively 生动的样子	栩栩如生(xǔ xǔ rú shēng) vivid, lively

xǔ ㄒㄩˇ	許	许	同意，很，可能 agree, very, probably	允許(yǔn xǔ) 允许 permit 許多(xǔ duō) 许多 many
xù ㄒㄩˋ	旭	旭	剛升起的太陽 rising sun 刚升起的太阳	旭日(xù rì) rising sun 朝旭(zhāo xù) morning sun
xù ㄒㄩˋ	序	序	排列，在正式内容 之前的文字 order, foreword	順序(shùn xù) 顺序 sequential order 序文(xù wén) preface
xù ㄒㄩˋ	婿	婿	女兒的丈夫，女人 稱自己的丈夫 son-in-law 女儿的丈夫，女人 称自己的丈夫	女婿(nǚ xù) son-in-law 夫婿(fū xù) husband
xù ㄒㄩˋ	畜	畜	飼養禽獸 raise domestic animal 饲养禽兽	畜牧(xù mù) animal husbandry 畜養(xù yǎng) 畜养 raise animals
xù ㄒㄩˋ	蓄	蓄	儲藏，聚積，保存 store, gather, conserve 储藏，聚积，保存	儲蓄(chú xù) 储蓄 savings 蓄水池(xù shuǐ chí)蓄水池 reservoir
xù ㄒㄩˋ	酗	酗	沈迷於喝酒 alcoholic 沈迷於喝酒	酗酒(xù jiǔ) alcoholic
xù ㄒㄩˋ	緒	绪	絲的頭，心情思想 thread end, mood, thought 丝的头，心情思想	情緒(qíng xù) 情绪 emotion 思緒(sī xù) 思绪 train of thought
xù ㄒㄩˋ	敘	叙	述說，陳述 describe, narrate 述说，陈述	敘述(xù shù) 叙述 describe 敘舊(xù jiù) 叙旧 talk about the old days

xù ㄒㄩˋ	續	续	連接，接下去，補充 reconnect, continue, supplement 连接，接下去，补充	繼續(jì xù) 继续 continue 續約(xù yuē) 续约 renew contract
xù ㄒㄩˋ	恤	恤	憐憫，救濟 compassion, give relief 怜悯，救济	體恤(tǐ xù) 体恤 show consideration for 撫恤金(fǔ xù jīn) 抚恤金 pension for the disabled
xù ㄒㄩˋ	絮	絮	彈過後的鬆棉花，輕柔似棉的花 wadding 弹过后的松棉花，轻柔似棉的花	棉絮(mián xù) cotton wadding 花絮(huā xù) tidbits
xù xǔ ㄒㄩˋ ㄒㄩˇ	煦	煦	暖和的，溫暖的 warm	和煦(hé xù) warm (sunlight or breeze)
xuān ㄒㄩㄢ	宣	宣	公開發表，公布，散布，發揚 declare, publicize, spread 公开发表，公布，散布，发扬	宣布(xuān bù) declare 宣誓(xuān shì) take oath
xuān ㄒㄩㄢ	喧	喧	大聲說話，聲音雜亂 speak loudly, noisy 大声说话，声音杂乱	喧鬧(xuān nào) 喧闹 boisterous 喧天(xuān tiān) deafening sound
xuán ㄒㄩㄢˊ	玄	玄	深奧不容易理解的，不真實 incomprehensible, unrealistic 深奥不容易理解的，不真实	玄妙(xuán miào) mysterious 玄孫(xuán sūn) 玄孙 great great grandson
xuán ㄒㄩㄢˊ	懸	悬	掛著，沒有著落 hanging, unsettled 挂著，没有著落	懸疑(xuán yí) 悬疑 unsolved mysteries 懸案(xuán àn) 悬案 unsettled case

xuán ㄒㄩㄢˊ	漩	漩	水流轉動或螺形 whirl 水流转动或螺形	漩渦(xuán wō) 漩涡 whirlpool 迴漩(huí xuán) be in a whirl
xuán ㄒㄩㄢˊ	旋	旋	轉動，馬上 revolve, soon 转动，马上	旋轉(xuán zhuǎn) 旋转 revolve, rotate 凱旋(kǎi xuán) 凯旋 victory
xuǎn ㄒㄩㄢˇ	選	选	挑揀，擇取 choose, select 挑拣，择取	選擇(xuǎn zé) 选择 select 選舉(xuǎn jǔ) 选举 election
xuǎn ㄒㄩㄢˇ	癬	癬	皮膚病，患處常發 癢 ringworm 皮肤病，患处常发 痒	牛皮癬(niú pí xuǎn) 牛皮癬psoriasis
xuàn ㄒㄩㄢˋ	炫	炫	誇耀，照耀 praise, shine on 夸耀，照耀	炫耀(xuàn yào) 炫耀 show off 炫目耀眼(xuàn mù yào yǎn) bright
xuàn ㄒㄩㄢˋ	渲	渲	類似水彩的畫法 watercolor-type drawing 类似水彩的画法	渲染(xuàn rǎn) exaggerate
xuàn ㄒㄩㄢˋ	絢	绚	美好的文采，光彩 奪目的樣子 brilliant 美好的文采，光彩 夺目的样子	絢爛(xuàn làn) 绚烂 splendid
xuàn ㄒㄩㄢˋ	眩	眩	眼睛昏花看不清楚 dazzling 眼睛昏花看不清楚	目眩(mù xuàn) dizzy

xuē ㄒㄩㄝ	削	削	除 cut	削減(xuē jiǎn) 削减 reduce 剝削(bō xuē) 剥削 exploit
xuē ㄒㄩㄝ	靴	靴	長筒鞋 boots 长筒鞋	皮靴(pí xuē) leather boots 馬靴(mǎ xuē) 马靴 riding boots
xué ㄒㄩㄝˊ	學	学	研習，知識 study, knowledge 研习，知识	學習(xué xí) 学习 learn, study 科學(kē xué) 科学 science
xuě xuè ㄒㄩㄝˇ ㄒㄩㄝˋ	雪	雪	冷天天空落下的白 色晶體，洗去 snow, wash away 冷天天空落下的白 色晶体，洗去	白雪(bái xuě) white snow 雪恥(xuě chǐ) 雪耻 avenge an insult 雪白(xuè bái) white as snow
xuè ㄒㄩㄝˋ	血	血	動物脈管裏所含的 紅色流體 blood 动物脉管里所含的 红色流体	血液(xuè yè) blood 流血(liú xuè) bleed
xuè ㄒㄩㄝˋ	穴	穴	動物的窩，人居住 的石洞 den, cave 动物的窝，人居住 的石洞	穴居(xuè jū) living in cave 墓穴(mù xuè) grave
xūn ㄒㄩㄣ	勛	勋	特殊功勞 meritorious service 特殊功劳	功勛(gōng xūn) 功勋 meritorious service 勛章(xūn zhāng) 勋章 medal
xūn ㄒㄩㄣ	燻	熏	用煙烤食物，氣味 刺激人 to expose to smoke 用烟烤食物，气味 刺激人	燻魚(xūn yú) 熏鱼 smoked fish 燻黑(xūn hēi) 熏黑 blackened by smoke
xūn ㄒㄩㄣ	醺	醺	醉的樣子 drunk 醉的样子	醉醺醺(zuì xūn xūn) completely drunk

xún ㄒㄩㄣˊ	旬	旬	十天叫一旬，十歲 是一旬 10 days, 10 years 十天叫一旬，十岁 是一旬	上旬(shàng xún) first 10 days of a month 下旬(xià xún) last 10 days of a month
xún ㄒㄩㄣˊ	詢	询	查問 inquire 查问	詢問(xún wèn) 询问 inquire 質詢(zhí xún) 质询 interpellate
xún ㄒㄩㄣˊ	尋	寻	找 find	找尋(zhǎo xún) 找寻 search 尋求(xún qiú) 寻求 pursue
xún ㄒㄩㄣˊ	循	循	依照，順著 according to, following 依照，顺著	循環(xún huán) 循环 circulation 循序(xún xù) in proper order
xún ㄒㄩㄣˊ	巡	巡	往來查看，按一定 路線到各處走 patrol, make the round 往来查看，按一定 路线到各处走	巡邏(xún luó) 巡逻 patrol 巡迴(xún huí) itinerant
xún ㄒㄩㄣˊ	馴	驯	順從，訓練野獸使 能順從人意 tractable, tame 顺从，训练野兽使 能顺从人意	馴服(xún fú) 驯服 to tame 馴馬(xún mǎ) 驯马 tame a horse
xùn ㄒㄩㄣˋ	訓	训	教導，可以作爲法 則的話 teach, motto 教导，可以作为法 则的话	教訓(jiào xùn) 教训 a lesson 訓練(xùn liàn) 训练 train
xùn ㄒㄩㄣˋ	迅	迅	快 swift	迅速(xùn sù) rapid 迅雷(xùn léi) sudden clap of thunder
xùn ㄒㄩㄣˋ	遜	逊	謙虛 humble 谦虚	謙遜(qiān xùn) 谦逊 humility

xùn xún ㄒㄩㄣˋ ㄒㄩㄣˊ	訊	讯	消息，音信，問 news, ask 消息，音信，问	資訊(zī xùn) 资讯 information 通訊(tōng xùn) 通讯 newsletter
xùn ㄒㄩㄣˋ	殉	殉	爲某事業而犧牲生 命 dies for a cause 为某事业而牺牲生 命	殉國(xùn guó) 殉国 die for one's country 殉情(xùn qíng) die for love

Y				
yā 一丫	壓	压	加重力，威力制服 exert pressure, hold down	壓力(yā lì) 压力 pressure 壓迫(yā pò) 压迫 oppression
yā 一丫	押	押	把財物交出作擔保 ，拘留 mortgage, detain 把財物交出作担保 ，拘留	押金(yā jīn) security deposit 收押(shōu yā) detain
ya 一丫	呀	呀	嘆詞，表示驚疑 exclamation to show surprise 叹词，表示惊疑	哎呀(āi ya) Oh, dear!
yā 一丫	鴨	鸭	嘴扁腿短，喜歡游 泳的家禽 duck 嘴扁腿短，喜欢游 泳的家禽	鴨子(yā zi) 鸭子 duck 烤鴨(kǎo yā) 烤鸭 roast duck
yā 一丫	鴉	鸦	大嘴黑色的鳥 crow 大嘴黑色的鸟	烏鴉(wū yā) 乌鸦 crow 鴉雀無聲(yā què wú shēng) 鸦雀无声 dead silence
yá 一丫ˊ	牙	牙	口腔裏白色咬食物 的器官 tooth 口腔里白色咬食物 的器官	牙齒(yá chǐ) 牙齿 tooth 牙醫(yá yī) 牙医 dentist
yá 一丫ˊ	崖	崖	山邊，高地的邊 cliff, precipice 山边，高地的边	懸崖(xuán yá) 悬崖 cliff
yá 一丫ˊ	衙	衙	古代官吏辦公的地 方 government office in ancient China 古代官吏办公的地 方	衙門(yá mén) 衙门 government office 衙役(yá yì) office worker

356

yá ㄧㄚˊ	芽	芽	植物初生的嫩苗， 事物的開頭 bud, beginning 植物初生的嫩苗， 事物的开头	嫩芽(nèn yá) budlet 豆芽(dòu yá) bean sprout
yá ㄧㄚˊ	涯	涯	水邊 water margin 水边	天涯海角(tiān yá hǎi jiǎo) everywhere 生涯(shēng yá) lifetime
yǎ ㄧㄚˇ	啞	哑	聲帶有毛病，不能 發出聲音 mute 声带有毛病，不能 发出声音	啞吧(yǎ ba) 哑吧 a mute 啞謎(yǎ mí) 哑谜 riddle
yǎ ㄧㄚˇ	雅	雅	清高不俗氣，優美 的，正常的 elegant, normal 清高不俗气，优美 的，正常的	文雅(wén yǎ) elegant 雅觀(yǎ guān) 雅观 nice-looking
yà yǎ ㄧㄚˋㄧㄚˇ	亞	亚	第二的，次等的 secondary 第二的，次等的	亞軍(yà jūn) 亚军 runner-up 亞洲(yà zhōu) 亚洲 Asia
yà ㄧㄚˋ	訝	讶	奇怪，驚異 surprise 奇怪，惊异	驚訝(jīng yà) 惊讶 surprise 訝異(yà yì) 讶异 astonished
yān ㄧㄢ	淹	淹	浸沒 flooded	淹沒(yān mò) inundated 淹水(yān shuǐ) waterlogged
yān ㄧㄢ	醃	腌	用鹽，醬油浸漬食 品 treat food with salt 用盐，酱油浸渍食 品	醃肉(yān ròu) salted meat

yān 一 ㄢ	奄	奄	快斷氣了 dying 快断气了	奄奄一息(yān yān yì xí) dying
yān 一 ㄢ	閹	阉	割去生殖腺 castrate 割去生殖腺	閹割(yān gē) 阉割 castrate
yān 一 ㄢ	湮	湮	埋沒 to obscure	湮沒(yān mò) fall into oblivion
yān 一 ㄢ	煙	烟	物質燃燒時冒出的氣體，山水雲霧等氣 smoke 物质燃烧时冒出的气体，山水云雾等气	香煙(xiāng yān) 香烟 cigarette 抽煙(chōu yān) 抽烟 to smoke cigarette
yān 一 ㄢ	咽	咽	口腔和食道中間的區域，聲音堵塞 throat 口腔和食道中间的区域，声音堵塞	鼻咽(bí yān) nasopharynx 咽喉(yān hóu) throat
yān 一 ㄢ	胭	胭	婦女化妝用的一種紅色顏料 rouge 妇女化妆用的一种红色颜料	胭脂(yān zhī) rouge
yán 一 ㄢˊ	延	延	引長，展緩 extend, postpone 引长，展缓	延長(yán cháng) 延长 extend 延期(yán qí) postpone
yán 一 ㄢˊ	嚴	严	不放鬆，認真，屬害的 strict, earnest, severe 不放松，认真，厉害的	嚴格(yán gé) 严格 strict 嚴寒(yán hán) 严寒 bitter cold

yán 一ㄢˊ	筵	筵	酒席 feast	筵席(yán xí) feast
yán 一ㄢˊ	炎	炎	熱，身體某部因感 染而發腫 inflammation 热，身体某部因感 染而发肿	炎熱(yán rè) 炎热 hot (day) 發炎(fā yán) 发炎 inflammation
yán 一ㄢˊ	言	言	說話 speak 说话	發言(fā yán) 发言 deliver a speech 謠言(yáo yán) 谣言 rumor
yán 一ㄢˊ	研	研	細磨，深入地探求 grind, deeply explore 细磨，深入地探求	研究(yán jiù) research 研討會(yán tǎo huì) 研讨会 seminar
yán 一ㄢˊ	鹽	盐	食品中鹹味的原料 salt 食品中咸味的原料	食鹽(shí yán) 食盐 salt 鹽分(yán fèn) 盐分 salinity
yán 一ㄢˊ	顏	颜	臉色，色彩，面子 face, color 脸色，色彩，面子	笑顏(xiào yán) 笑颜 smiling face 顏色(yán sè) 颜色 color
yán 一ㄢˊ	沿	沿	順著，照著 along, according to 顺著，照著	沿途(yán tú) along the way 沿海(yán hǎi) coastal
yán 一ㄢˊ	岩	岩	石頭 rock 石头	岩石(yán shí) rock 岩洞(yán dòng) grotto

yǎn ㄧㄢˇ	掩	掩	遮蔽 cover up	遮掩(zhē yǎn) cover up 掩護(yǎn hù) 掩护 provide cover
yǎn ㄧㄢˇ	眼	眼	視覺器官 eye 视觉器官	眼睛(yǎn jīng) eye 眼淚(yǎn lèi) 眼泪 tears 眼科(yǎn kē) ophthalmology
yǎn ㄧㄢˇ	演	演	練習，表演技藝 practice, perform 练习，表演技艺	演戲(yǎn xì) 演戏 act in a show 演出(yǎn chū) performance
yǎn ㄧㄢˇ	衍	衍	延伸，擴展 extend, expand 延伸，扩展	敷衍(fū yǎn) do half-heartedly 繁衍(fán yǎn) proliferate
yàn ㄧㄢˋ	厭	厌	煩，滿足 bored, satisfaction 烦，满足	討厭(tǎo yàn) 讨厌 disgusting 厭倦(yàn juàn) 厌倦 fed up with
yàn ㄧㄢˋ	宴	宴	以食物飲料款待客 人 feast 以食物饮料款待客 人	宴客(yàn kè) throw a party 宴會(yàn huì) 宴会 banquet
yàn ㄧㄢˋ	晏	晏	姓氏，晚，太平 Chinese surname, late, peace	晏子(yàn zi) famous statesman in Ancient China
yàn ㄧㄢˋ	艷	艳	光彩，美麗豐滿 colorful, beautiful 光彩，美丽丰满	艷麗(yàn lì) 艳丽 charming 鮮艷(xiān yàn) 鲜艳 bright colored
yàn ㄧㄢˋ	驗	验	証明，功效，檢查 verify, effect, inspect 证明，功效，检查	體驗(tǐ yàn) 体验 to experience 經驗(jīng yàn) 经验 the experience

yàn ㄧㄢˋ	雁	雁	身體和鵝很相似的 鳥，喜群飛 wild goose 身体和鹅很相似的 鸟，喜群飞	孤雁(gū yàn) lone wild goose 雁行(yàn xíng) brothers
yàn ㄧㄢˋ	燕	燕	身體小、翅膀大、 尾巴像剪刀的鳥 swallow 身体小、翅膀大、 尾巴像剪刀的鸟	燕子(yàn zi) swallow 燕尾服(yàn wěi fú) tailcoat
yàn ㄧㄢˋ	焰	焰	物體燃燒時發出的 火光　flame 物体燃烧时发出的 火光	火焰(huǒ yàn) flame 焰火(yàn huǒ) fireworks
yàn ㄧㄢˋ	焱	焱	火花 spark	火焱(huǒ yàn) spark
yāng ㄧㄤ	央	央	懇求，中間 beg, center 恳求，中间	央求(yāng qiú) beseech 中央(zhōng yāng) central
yāng ㄧㄤ	秧	秧	初生的稻苗 rice seedling	秧苗(yāng miáo) rice seedling 樹秧(shù yāng) 树秧 sapling
yāng ㄧㄤ	殃	殃	災禍，危害 disaster, danger 灾祸，危害	遭殃(zāo yāng) meet with disaster 災殃(zāi yāng) 灾殃 disaster
yāng ㄧㄤ	鴦	鸯	鴛鴦：鳥名，常常 雌雄成對游泳 mandarin duck 鸳鸯：鸟名，常常 雌雄成对遊泳	鴛鴦(yuān yāng) 鸳鸯 mandarin duck

yáng 一ˊ 尢	揚	扬	高舉，傳開 raise, spread 高举，传开	表揚(biǎo yáng) 表扬 commend 揚言(yáng yán) 扬言 threaten
yáng 一ˊ 尢	楊	杨	姓氏，落葉喬木， 有些可做器物poplar 姓氏，落叶乔木， 有些可做器物	楊樹(yáng shù) 杨树 poplar tree
yáng 一ˊ 尢	瘍	疡	潰爛 ruptured 溃烂	胃潰瘍(wèi kuì yáng) 胃溃疡 stomach ulcer
yáng 一ˊ 尢	陽	阳	日，男性的，正的 sun, masculine, positive	太陽(tài yáng) 太阳 sun 陽性(yáng xìng) 阳性 positive, masculine
yáng 一ˊ 尢	羊	羊	家畜名，有山羊， 綿羊兩種goat, sheep 家畜名，有山羊， 绵羊两种	山羊(shān yáng) goat 綿羊(mián yáng) 绵羊 sheep
yáng 一ˊ 尢	洋	洋	地球上最大的水域 ，外國的 ocean, foreign 地球上最大 的水域，外国的	海洋(hǎi yáng) ocean 洋人(yáng rén) Westerner
yǎng 一ˇ 尢	仰	仰	抬頭向上，傾慕， raise one's head, admire 抬头向上，倾慕	仰頭(yǎng tóu) 仰头 raise one's head 仰慕(yǎng mù) look upon with respect
yang 一ˇ 尢	氧	氧	動植物必須呼吸的 氣體 oxygen 动植物必须呼吸的 气体	氧氣(yǎng qì) 氧气 oxygen 氧化(yǎng huà) oxidize
yǎng 一ˇ 尢	養	养	照顧，扶育，休息 ，康復 take care of, rear, rest, recuperate 照顾，扶育，休息 ，康复	養老金(yǎng lǎo jīn) 养老金 pension 扶養(fú yǎng) 扶养 to provide for
yǎng 一ˇ 尢	癢	痒	皮膚受刺激想抓了 才舒服的感覺 itch 皮肤受刺激想抓了 才舒服的感觉	抓癢(zhuā yǎng) 抓痒 scratch the itchy part 技癢(jì yǎng) 技痒 eager to show one's skill
yàng 一ˋ 尢	樣	样	形狀，做標準的東 西 shape, sample 形状，做标准的东 西	樣子(yàng zi) 样子manner 樣品(yàng pǐn) 样品 sample

yàng 一ˋ 尢	漾	漾	水波搖動 ripple 水波摇动	蕩漾(dàng yàng)荡漾 ripple
yàng 一ˋ 尢	恙	恙	災禍，疾病 disaster, sickness 灾祸，疾病	無恙(wú yàng) safe and sound
yàng yáng 一ˋ 一ˊ 尢 尢	烊	烊	打烊：商店晚上關 門停止營業 closed for business 打烊：商店晚上关 门停止营业	打烊(dǎ yàng) closed for business
yāo 一 幺	么	么	小，排行最小的 small, the youngest child	么兒(yāo ér) youngest son 么妹(yāo mèi) youngest sister
yāo 一 幺	吆	吆	大聲喊叫 yell 大声喊叫	吆喝(yāo he) yell
yāo yào 一 一ˋ 幺 幺	要	要	求 ask, demand	要求(yāo qiú) ask, demand
yāo 一 幺	殀	夭	未成年就死亡 premature death	殀折(yāo zhé) 夭折 die a premature death
yāo 一 幺	妖	妖	可怕的怪物，打扮 艷麗不莊重 goblin, gaudy 可怕的怪物，打扮 艳丽不庄重	妖怪(yāo guài) goblin 妖艷(yāo yàn)妖艳 gaudy
yāo 一 幺	腰	腰	身體的中部兩旁， 事物的中段 waist 身体的中部两旁， 事物的中段	彎腰(wān yāo)弯腰 bend over 山腰(shān yāo) hillside
yāo 一 幺	邀	邀	請 invite	邀請(yāo qǐng)邀请 invite
yáo 一ˊ 幺	餚	肴	煮熟好吃的魚肉菜 dishes 煮熟好吃的鱼肉菜	佳餚(jiā yáo) 佳肴 fine dishes

yáo 一ˊ ㄠ	遙	遙	遠 far 远	遙望(yáo wàng) look from afar 遙控(yáo kòng) remote control
yáo 一ˊ ㄠ	搖	摇	擺動，不堅定 sway, not firm 摆动，不坚定	搖頭(yáo tóu)摇头 shake one's head 動搖(dòng yáo)动摇 wavering
yáo 一ˊ ㄠ	謠	谣	憑空捏造的話，隨口唱的歌 rumor, song 凭空捏造的话，随口唱的歌	謠言(yáo yán)谣言 rumor 童謠(tóng yáo)童谣 children's songs
yáo 一ˊ ㄠ	窯	窑	燒磚瓦等的建築物，陶瓷器 kiln, ceramic 烧砖瓦等的建筑物，陶瓷器	瓦窯(wǎ yáo)瓦窑 kiln 窯洞(yáo dòng)窑洞 cave dwelling
yǎo 一ˇ ㄠ	咬	咬	用牙齒切斷或夾住東西，發音 bite, pronounce 用牙齿切断或夹住东西，发音	咬定(yǎo dìng) insist 咬字(yǎo zì) pronunciation
yǎo 一ˇ ㄠ	舀	舀	用湯匙，勺等用具取東西 scoop up 用汤匙，勺等用具取东西	舀水(yǎo shuǐ) scoop up water
yǎo 一ˇ ㄠ	窈	窈	窈窕：女子文靜美好 graceful 窈窕：女子文静美好	窈窕(yǎo tiǎo) graceful (lady)
yào 一ˋ ㄠ	藥	药	可以治病的東西，有一定作用的化學物品 medicine 可以治病的东西，有一定作用的化学物品	藥品(yào pǐn)药品 medicine 火藥(huǒ yào)火药 gun powder
yào yāo ㄠˋ ㄠ	要	要	希望得到，重大 want	重要(zhòng yào) important 要素(yào sù) essential element

yào 一ˋ ㄠ	鑰	钥	鑰匙：開鎖的器具 key 钥匙：开锁的器具	鑰匙(yào shi) 钥匙 key
yào 一ˋ ㄠ	耀	耀	光線強烈的照射， 光榮，顯示出來 shine on, glory, show 光线强烈的照射， 光荣，显示出来	耀眼(yào yǎn) dazzling 榮耀(róng yào) 荣耀 glory
yē 一 ㄝ	椰	椰	椰樹：產於熱帶常 綠喬木，果實有汁 可解暑 coconut 椰树：产于热带常 绿乔木，果实有汁 可解暑	椰樹(yē shù) 椰树 coconut tree
yē 一 ㄝ	噎	噎	食物塞住食道 choke 食物塞住食道	因噎廢食(yīn yē fèi shí) 因噎废食 stop eating for fear of choking
yē yé 一 一 ㄝ ㄝ	耶	耶	放在句尾表示疑問 used at end of sentence to ask question 放在句尾表示疑问	耶穌(yē sū) Jesus 耶誕節(yē dàn jié) 耶诞节 Christmas 是耶非耶？(shì yé fēi yé) Is it or is it not?
yé 一 ㄝ	爺	爷	祖父，稱老人 grandpa, an old man 祖父，称老人	爺爺(yé ye) 爷爷 grandpa 老爺(lǎo yé) 老爷 master
yě 一ˇ ㄝ	也	也	同樣，或許 also, probably 同样，或许	也許(yě xǔ) 也许 probably 也要(yě yào) also want
yě 一ˇ ㄝ	冶	冶	把金屬鎔化鑄成東 西 smelt and forge 把金属熔化铸成东 西	陶冶(táo yě) mould character 冶金(yě jīn) metallurgy

yě ㄧㄝˇ	野	野	粗鄙無禮 rude 粗鄙无礼	野心(yě xīn) ambition 野獸(yě shòu) 野兽 beasts
yè ㄧㄝˋ	頁	页	書或印刷品的單張 或一面 page 书或印刷品的单张 或一面	頁數(yè shù) 页数 page number 活頁(huó yè) 活页 loose leaf
yè ㄧㄝˋ	業	业	從事的工作，各種 職業 occupation 从事的工作，各种 职业	職業(zhí yè) 职业 occupation 工業(gōng yè) 工业 industry
yè ㄧㄝˋ	葉	叶	植物的器官，長在 枝莖上，主管呼吸 leaf 植物的器官，长在 枝茎上，主管呼吸	綠葉(lǜ yè) 绿叶 green leaf 樹葉(shù yè) 树叶 tree leaf
yè ㄧㄝˋ	夜	夜	日落以後到日出前 的時間 night 日落以后到日出前 的时间	夜晚(yè wǎn) night 深夜(shēn yè) late at night
yè ㄧㄝˋ	液	液	能流動沒有一定形 狀的物質 liquid 能流动没有一定形 状的物质	液體(yè tǐ) 液体 liquid 血液(xuè yè) blood
yè ㄧㄝˋ	腋	腋	肩和手臂相連的部 份 armpit 肩和手臂相连的部 份	腋下(yè xià) armpit 腋窩(yè wō) armpit
yè ㄧㄝˋ	謁	谒	進見，拜見尊長 meet with one's superior 进见，拜见尊长	謁見(yè jiàn) 谒见 have an audience with
yè ㄧㄝˋ	靨	靥	臉上的小渦 dimple 脸上的小涡	笑靨(xiào yè) 笑靥 dimple

yī 一	一	一	數目，阿拉伯數字 '1'，單個，相同 one 数目，阿拉伯数字 '1'，单个，相同	一樣(yí yàng) 一样 the same 一條心(yì tiáo xīn) 一条心 of one heart
yī 一	衣	衣	披或包在物體外面 的東西 clothes 披或包在物体外面 的东西	衣服(yī fú) dress 糖衣(táng yī) sugarcoat
yī 一	依	依	倚靠，按照，仍然 depend on, according to, still	依照(yī zhào) according to 依靠(yī kào) depend on
yī 一	醫	医	替人治病，治病的 人 treat illness, physician	醫生(yī shēng) 医生 medical doctor 醫院(yī yuàn) 医院 hospital
yī 一	揖	揖	拱手敬禮 bow and cup hands to salute 拱手敬礼	揖客(yī kè) bow to visitor 長揖(cháng yī) 长揖 make a deep bow
yí 一´	儀	仪	舉止，容貌，程序 ，形式 manners, looks, ceremony, form 举止，容貌，程序 ，形式	儀式(yí shì) 仪式 ceremony 儀器(yí qì) 仪器 equipment
yí 一´	姨	姨	母親的姊妹，妻子 的姊妹 auntie 母亲的姊妹，妻子 的姊妹	姨媽(yí mā) 姨妈 auntie 小姨子(xiǎo yí zi) wife's sister
yí 一´	怡	怡	快樂 happy 快乐	怡然(yí rán) feel contented 心曠神怡(xīn kuàng shén yí) 心旷神怡 relaxed, happy
yí 一´	宜	宜	適合，和睦相處 suitable, harmonious 适合，和睦相处	適宜(shì yí) 适宜 suitable 宜人(yí rén) agreeable

yí ㄧˊ	夷	夷	中國古代稱東部的民族，平安 Eastern nations in ancient China, safety 中国古代称东部的民族，平安	蠻夷(mán yí) 蛮夷 the barbarous East 化險爲夷(huà xiǎn wéi yí) 化险为夷 turn danger into safety
yí ㄧˊ	痍	痍	傷，創傷 wound 伤，创伤	瘡痍滿目(chuāng yí mǎn mù) 疮痍满目 scenes of devastation everywhere
yí ㄧˊ	移	移	挪動，變動 move, shift 挪动，变动	移動(yí dòng) 移动 move 轉移(zhuǎn yí) 转移 to shift
yí ㄧˊ	遺	遗	丟失，漏，留下 lose, omit, leave behind	遺失(yí shī) 遗失 lose 遺忘(yí wàng) 遗忘 forget
yí ㄧˊ	疑	疑	不信而猜想，不能解決的 doubt, unsolved	懷疑(huái yí) 怀疑 suspect 疑問(yí wèn) 疑问 a doubt
yǐ ㄧˇ	已	已	過去，完成，停止 the past, already, stop 过去，完成，停止	已經(yǐ jīng) 已经 already 悲痛不已(bēi tòng bù yǐ) extreme grief
yǐ ㄧˇ	以	以	用，因爲，表示空間或時間之後或之前 use, because 用，因为，表示空间或时间之后或之前	所以(suǒ yǐ) therefore 以後(yǐ hòu) 以后 in the future
yǐ ㄧˇ	蟻	蚁	在地下成群做窩分工合作的小昆蟲 ant 在地下成群做窝分工合作的小昆虫	螞蟻(mǎ yǐ) 蚂蚁 ant
yǐ ㄧˇ	倚	倚	依靠，依賴 depend, rely 依靠，依赖	倚靠(yǐ kào) lean against 倚賴(yǐ lài) 倚赖 rely on

yǐ 一 ˇ	椅	椅	有四隻腳和靠背的 坐具 chair 有四隻脚和靠背的 坐具	椅子(yǐ zi) chair 椅墊(yǐ diàn) 椅垫 chair cushion
yǐ 一 ˇ	乙	乙	第二，人或地的代 稱 second, substitute for person, place 第二，人或地的代 称	乙等(yǐ děng) second grade 乙方(yǐ fāng) party B
yì 一 ˋ	議	议	意見，商量，評論 opinion, discuss, comment 意见，商量，评论	建議(jiàn yì) 建议 suggestion 議論(yì lùn) 议论 deliberation
yì 一 ˋ	藝	艺	才能，技術 skills, technique 才能，技术	工藝(gōng yì) 工艺 technique 藝術(yì shù) 艺术 art
yì 一 ˋ	憶	忆	想念，牢記不忘 miss, remember 想念，牢记不忘	回憶(huí yì) 回忆 reminisce 記憶(jì yì) 记忆 memory
yì 一 ˋ	億	亿	一萬萬 100 million 一万万	一億(yí yì) 一亿 100 million
yì 一 ˋ	亦	亦	也，又 also, too	不亦樂乎(bú yì yuè hū) 不亦乐乎 Isn't it pleasant to...
yì 一 ˋ	奕	奕	精神煥發的樣子 energetic 精神焕发的样子	神采奕奕(shén cǎi yì yì) in good spirit
yì 一 ˋ	裔	裔	後代子孫 descendent 后代子孙	後裔(hòu yì) 后裔 descendent 華裔(huá yì) 华裔 of Chinese origin
yì 一 ˋ	羿	羿	后羿：夏朝有窮國 國王 a legendary monarch 后羿：夏朝 有穷国国王	后羿(hòu yì) legendary monarch

yì 一、	異	异	不同的，奇怪的 different, strange	異議分子(yì yi fen zi) 异议分子 dissident 特異(tè yì) 特异 extraordinary
yì 一、	抑	抑	壓制，煩悶 repress, bored 压制，烦闷	抑制(yì zhì) repress 抑鬱(yì yù) 抑郁 depressed
yì 一、	役	役	事件，戰爭，差遣 event, war, dispatch 事件，战争，差遣	服役(fú yì) join the military 戰役(zhàn yì) 战役 battle
yì 一、	疫	疫	流行性傳染病 disease 流行性传染病	瘟疫(wēn yì) 瘟疫 pestilence 疫苗(yì miáo) vaccine
yì 一、	毅	毅	意志堅定 firm will 意志坚定	毅力(yì lì) perseverance 剛毅(gāng yì) 刚毅 firm and persistent
yì 一、	譯	译	用一種語言說出或 寫出另一種語言的 意義 translate, interpret 用一种语言说出或 写出另一种语言的 意义	翻譯(fān yì) 翻译 translation, translator 譯文(yì wén) 译文 translated passage
yì 一、	益	益	有利，有好處，增 加，更 beneficial, advantageous 有利，有好处，增 加，更	益處(yì chù) 益处 benefit 有益(yǒu yì) beneficial
yì 一、	易	易	不費力，交換 easy, exchange 不费力，交换	容易(róng yì) easy 貿易(mào yì) 贸易 trade

yì ㄧˋ	意	意	心思，見解，看法 idea, opinion, view 心思，见解，看法	意思(yì si) meaning 意見(yì jiàn) 意见 opinion
yì ㄧˋ	誼	谊	交情 friendship	友誼(yǒu yì) 友谊 friendship
yì ㄧˋ	翼	翼	翅膀，左右的一側 wing 翅膀，左右的一侧	雙翼(shuāng yì) 双翼 both wings 展翼(zhǎn yì) 展翼 spread the wings
yì ㄧˋ	逸	逸	安閒 relaxation 安闲	逸事(yì shì) anecdote 逃逸(táo yì) flee
yì ㄧˋ	詣	诣	造詣：學問或技術 達到的程度 accomplishment 造诣：学问或技术 达到的程度	造詣(zào yì) 造诣 accomplishment
yīn ㄧㄣ	音	音	物體受振動後由空 氣傳播而發出的聲 響，消息 sound, news 物体受振动后由空 气传播而发出的声 响，消息	音樂(yīn yuè)·音乐 music 音信(yīn xìn) news
yīn ㄧㄣ	陰	阴	"陽"的相反，暗 ，隱密 negative, gloomy, covert "阳"的相反，暗 ，隐密	陰天(yīn tiān) 阴天 gloomy day 陰性(yīn xìng) 阴性 negative, feminine
yīn ㄧㄣ	蔭	荫	又涼又潮，保佑 cool and humid, blessing 又凉又潮，保佑	樹蔭(shù yīn) 树荫 shade under a tree 庇蔭(bì yīn) 庇荫 under the blessing
yīn ㄧㄣ	殷	殷	朝代名，富足 name of dynasty, rich	殷商(yīn shāng) rich merchant 殷實(yīn shí) 殷实 well off

yīn 一 ㄣ	因	因	事情的起源，經由 cause, because 事情的起源，经由	因爲(yīn wèi) 因为 because 因果(yīn guǒ) cause and effect
yīn 一 ㄣ	姻	姻	婚配 marriage	婚姻(hūn yīn) marriage 姻親(yīn qīn) 姻亲 relative by marriage
yīn 一 ㄣ	慇	殷	深厚，豐盛，盡心 profound, abundant, devoted 深厚，丰盛，尽心	慇切(yīn qiè) 殷切 eager 慇勤(yīn qín) 殷勤 hospitable
yín 一ˊ ㄣ	銀	银	金屬元素，容易傳 熱導電，可用來做 貨幣，器皿和飾物 silver 金属元素，容易传 热导电，可用来做 货币，器皿和饰物	白銀(bái yín) 白银 silver 銀行(yín háng) 银行 bank
yín 一ˊ ㄣ	吟	吟	拉長聲音的誦讀， 因痛而叫嘆 recite, moan 拉长声音的诵读， 因痛而叫叹	吟詩(yín shī) 吟诗 recite poem 呻吟(shēn yín) moan
yín 一ˊ ㄣ	齦	龈	牙根肉 gum (of teeth)	牙齦(yá yín) 牙龈 gum (of teeth)
yín 一ˊ ㄣ	淫	淫	男女間不正常的性 關係，浪蕩的 lewd 男女间不正常的性 关系，浪荡的	賣淫(mài yín) 卖淫 be a prostitute 淫穢(yín huì) obscene
yǐn 一ˇ ㄣ	引	引	領導，招徠，承認 to lead, solicit, admit 领导，招徕，承认	引導(yǐn dǎo) 引导 guide 引起(yǐn qǐ) bring about
yǐn 一ˇ ㄣ	飲	饮	喝，可喝的東西 drink, drinks 喝，可喝的东西	飲水(yǐn shuǐ) 饮水 drink water 冷飲(lěng yǐn) 冷饮 cold drinks

yǐn 一ˇ ㄣ	隱	隐	藏，不顯露 concealed 藏，不显露	隱藏(yǐn cáng) 隐藏 hide 隱私(yǐn sī) 隐私 privacy
yǐn 一ˇ ㄣ	癮	瘾	特別深的嗜好 addiction 特别深的嗜好	上癮(shàng yǐn) 上瘾 addicted 毒癮(dú yǐn) 毒瘾 drug addiction
yǐn 一ˇ ㄣ	蚓	蚓	蚯蚓：一種生長在 土裏的蟲子，對農 作物有益 earthworm 蚯蚓：一种生长在 土里的虫子，对农 作物有益	蚯蚓(qiū yǐn) earthworm
yìn 一ˋ ㄣ	印	印	圖章，留下痕跡 seal, mark 图章，留下痕迹	印章(yìn zhāng) seal, chop 印象(yìn xiàng) impression
yīng yìng 一ˉˋ ㄥ ㄥ	應	应	該當 ought to 该当	應該(yīng gāi) 应该 should, ought to 應允(yìng yǔn) 应允 promise
yīng 一ˉ ㄥ	英	英	精萃部分，才能出 眾，容貌俊秀 cream of the crop, talented 精萃部分，才能出 众，容貌俊秀	英俊(yīng jùn) handsome 英雄(yīng xióng) hero
yīng 一ˉ ㄥ	鶯	莺	叫聲清脆好聽的小 鳥 oriole 叫声清脆好听的小 鸟	黃鶯(huáng yīng) 黄莺 oriole
yīng 一ˉ ㄥ	嬰	婴	才生下來的小孩子 baby	嬰兒(yīng ér) 婴儿 baby 女嬰(nǚ yīng) 女婴 baby girl

yīng 一 ∠	櫻	樱	落葉喬木，木質硬可做傢俱，果實可吃 cherry 落叶乔木，木质硬可做傢俱，果实可吃	櫻桃(yīng táo) 樱桃 cherry 櫻花(yīng huā) 樱花 cherry blossom
yīng 一 ∠	鸚	鹦	鸚鵡：彎嘴能模仿人說話的鳥 parrot 鹦鹉：弯嘴能模仿人说话的鸟	鸚鵡(yīng wǔ) 鹦鹉 parrot
yīng 一 ∠	膺	膺	胸，接受，承當 chest, receive, assume 胸，接受，承当	義憤填膺(yì fèn tián yīng) 义愤填膺 be filled with righteous indignation
yīng 一 ∠	鷹	鹰	嘴彎而尖銳的兇猛的肉食鳥類 eagle 嘴弯而尖锐的兇猛的肉食鸟类	老鷹(lǎo yīng) 老鹰 eagle 秃鷹(tū yīng) 秃鹰 vulture
yīng 一 ∠	盈	盈	充滿，多餘 full, surplus 充满，多余	盈利(yíng lì) profit 盈餘(yíng yú) 盈余 surplus
yíng 一 ∠	迎	迎	接，向著 receive, facing 接，向著	歡迎(huān yíng) 欢迎 welcome 迎面(yíng miàn) face to face, oncoming
yíng 一 ∠	營	营	軍隊駐札的地方，管理 barrack, manage 军队驻札的地方，管理	軍營(jūn yíng) 军营 barrack 營業(yíng yè) 营业 business
yíng 一 ∠	蠅	蝇	會傳染疾病的害蟲 housefly 会传染疾病的害虫	蒼蠅(cāng yíng) 苍蝇 housefly 蚊蠅(wén yíng) 蚊蝇 mosquitos and flies
yíng 一 ∠	瑩	莹	光潔象玉的石頭，透明光潔 jade-like stone, clear 光洁象玉的石头，透明光洁	晶瑩(jīng yíng) 晶莹 crystal clear

yíng 一ˊ ㄥ	縈	萦	圍繞 linger 围绕	縈繞(yíng rào) 萦绕 linger 瑣事縈身(suǒ shì yíng shēng) 琐事萦身 be tied up by trifles
yíng 一ˊ ㄥ	螢	萤	一種尾部會發閃光 的昆蟲 firefly 一种尾部会发闪光 的昆虫	螢火蟲(yíng huǒ chóng) 萤火虫 firefly 螢光屏(yíng guāng píng) 萤光屏 TV screen
yíng 一ˊ ㄥ	贏	赢	勝，獲得，賺得 win, obtain, earn 胜，获得，赚得	贏錢(yíng qián) 赢钱 win money 贏取(yíng qǔ) 赢取 obtain
yǐng 一ˇ ㄥ	影	影	光線被遮擋而形成 的陰暗部分，人或 物的形象 shadow, image 光线被遮挡而形成 的阴暗部分，人或 物的形象	電影(diàn yǐng)电影movie 影印(yǐng yìn) photocopy 電影院(diàn yǐng yuàn) 电影院 cinema theater 影響(yǐng xiǎng) 影响 influence
yìng 一ˋ ㄥ	映	映	照射而顯出 to mirror 照射而显出	放映機(fàng yìng jī) 放映机 projector 反映(fǎn yìng) reflect
yìng 一ˋ ㄥ	硬	硬	"軟"的相反，物 體堅固，剛強有力 hard, insist on "软"的相反，物 体坚固，刚强有力	堅硬(jiān yìng) 坚硬 hard 硬要(yìng yào) insist on wanting
yìng yīng 一ˋ一 ㄥ ㄥ	應	应	回答，接受，對待 reply, receive, treat 回答，接受，对待	答應(dá yìng) 答应 promise 應付(yìng fù) 应付 deal with
yo 一 ㄛ	喲	哟	嘆詞和疑問詞 used in exclamation and question 叹词和疑问词	你一定要來喲！ (nǐ yí dìng yào lái yo!) 你一定要来哟 You must come!
yōng ㄩㄥ	庸	庸	平常 mediocre	庸俗(yōng sú) mundane 庸才(yōng cái) mediocre person

yōng ㄩㄥ	傭	佣	被人雇用的人 hired hand	女傭(nǚ yōng) 女佣 housemaid 雇傭(gù yōng) 雇佣 hire
yǒng ㄩㄥˇ	永	永	長久 forever 长久	永遠(yǒng yuǎn) 永远 forever 永生(yǒng shēng) eternal life
yǒng ㄩㄥˇ	泳	泳	在水裏游動 swim 在水里游动	游泳(yóu yǒng) swim 蛙泳(wā yǒng) breast stroke
yǒng ㄩㄥˇ	湧	湧	水由下往上冒出來 ，像水冒出來一樣 gush out 水由下往上冒出来 ，像水冒出来一样	湧出(yǒng chū) 湧出 gush out 湧現(yǒng xiàn) 湧现 emerge
yǒng ㄩㄥˇ	擁	拥	抱，持有，聚到一 起 embrace, possess, gather	擁有(yǒng yǒu) 拥有 possess 擁抱(yǒng bào) 拥抱 embrace
yǒng ㄩㄥˇ	勇	勇	有膽量 brave 有胆量	勇敢(yǒng gǎn) brave 英勇(yīng yǒng) heroic
yòng ㄩㄥˋ	用	用	操作，效果，功能 to use, effect, the use	使用(shǐ yòng) use 費用(fèi yòng) 费用 expenses
yòng ㄩㄥˋ	佣	佣	買賣東西時給介紹 人的錢 commission payment 买卖东西时给介绍 人的钱	佣金(yòng jīn) commission

yōu 一 又	優	优	美好的 excellent	優良(yōu liáng) 优良 good 優勢(yōu shì) 优势 advantage
yōu 一 又	悠	悠	長久，閒適 long time, leisurely 长久，闲适	悠久(yōu jiǔ) date back a long time 悠閒(yōu xián) 悠闲 leisurely
yōu 一 又	幽	幽	光線暗，很清靜， 秘密的 dark, quiet, private 光线暗，很清静， 秘密的	幽靜(yōu jìng) 幽静 quiet 幽魂(yōu hún) ghost
yōu 一 又	憂	忧	發愁，擔心 worried 发愁，担心	憂慮(yōu lǜ) 忧虑 worries 憂傷(yōu shāng) 忧伤 sorrow
yóu 一′ 又	游	游	浮行於水上，江河 的段落 swim, sections of a river 浮行於水上，江河 的段落	游泳(yóu yǒng) swim 下游(xià yóu) lower reaches
yóu 一′ 又	遊	遊	閒逛，從容地走 stroll 闲逛，从容地走	遊戲(yóu xì) 遊戏 game 郊遊(jiāo yóu) 郊遊 field trip
yóu 一′ 又	尤	尤	格外，更，怨恨 especially, more, complaint	尤其(yóu qí) especially 怨尤(yuàn yóu) complaint
yóu 一′ 又	猶	犹	好像，還 just like, also 好像，还	猶如(yóu rú) 犹如 just like 猶豫(yóu yú) 犹豫 hesistate
yóu 一′ 又	由	由	自從，原因，任憑 ，因為 from, reason, let, due to 自从，原因，任凭 ，因为	自由(zì yóu) freedom 理由(lǐ yóu) reason

yóu 一ˊ ㄡ	油	油	動植物體内的脂肪，狡猾 oil, cunning 动植物体内的脂肪，狡猾	豬油(zhū yóu) 猪油 lard 石油(shí yóu) petroleum
yóu 一ˊ ㄡ	郵	邮	傳遞信件，有關傳遞信件的機關和事物 postal 传递信件，有关传递信件的机关和事物	郵局(yóu jú) 邮局 post office 郵差(yóu chāi) 邮差 postman
yóu yòu 一ˊ 一ˋ ㄡ ㄡ	柚	柚	柚木:木材堅硬可用來造船 teak 柚木:木材坚硬可用来造船	柚木(yóu mù) teak
yóu 一ˊ ㄡ	鈾	铀	一種放射性元素，符號U，是產生原子能的重要元素 uranium 一种放射性元素，符号U，是产生原子能的重要元素	鈾礦(yóu kuàng) 铀矿 uranium mine
yǒu 一ˇ ㄡ	有	有	"無"的相反，表示事物存在 have, exist "无"的相反，表示事物存在	富有(fù yǒu) rich 有害(yǒu hài) harmful
yǒu 一ˇ ㄡ	友	友	有交情的人，親愛和睦 friend, harmonious 有交情的人，亲爱和睦	朋友(péng yǒu) friend 友善(yǒu shàn) friendly
yòu 一ˋ ㄡ	右	右	"左"的相對，表示方向，位置 right-hand side "左"的相对，表示方向，位置	左右(zuǒ yòu) about, around 右翼(yòu yì) right wing
yòu 一ˋ ㄡ	幼	幼	年紀小，初生的 young, newborn 年纪小，初生的	幼兒(yòu ér) 幼儿 little child 幼稚(yòu zhì) childish
yòu 一ˋ ㄡ	釉	釉	以石英等原料涂在陶瓷器外面，燒制後光澤較亮 glaze 以石英等原料涂在瓷器，陶器外面，烧制后光泽较亮	彩釉(cǎi yòu) colored glaze

yòu 一ˋ ㄡ	誘	诱	吸引，教導 attract, guide 吸引，教导	誘惑(yòu huò) 诱惑 temptation 誘導(yòu dǎo) 诱导 guide
yòu 一ˋ ㄡ	又	又	重複，加重語氣， 連續 again, used in emphasis 重复，加重语气， 连续	又來了(yòu lái le) 又来了 here he goes again! 又高又大(yòu gāo yòu dà) big and tall
yòu yóu 一ˋ ㄡˊ ㄡ ㄡ	柚	柚	常綠喬木，葉子圓 大，果實叫柚子 grapefruit 常绿乔木，叶子圆 大，果实叫柚子	葡萄柚(pú táo yòu) grapefruit
yū ㄩ	迂	迂	路曲折，言行固執 ，不實際 detour, stubborn, unrealistic 路曲折，言行固执 ，不实际	迂迴(yū huí) indirect 迂腐(yū fǔ) pedantic
yū ㄩ	淤	淤	水道被泥沙阻塞 clogged waterway	淤塞(yū sāi) clogged 淤泥(yū ní) sediment
yú ㄩˊ	於	於	在，比較連詞，到 at, conjunction, until 在，比较连词，到	等於(děng yú) 等於 equal to 由於(yóu yú) 由於 because of
yú ㄩˊ	愚	愚	笨，傻，謙虛之辭 foolish, humble expression 笨，傻，谦虚之辞	愚笨(yú bèn) foolish 愚見(yú jiàn) 愚见 my opinion
yú ㄩˊ	愉	愉	歡喜快樂 glad 欢喜快乐	愉快(yú kuài) glad

yú ㄩˊ	娛	娱	使人快樂 entertaining 使人快乐	娛樂(yú lè) 娱乐 recreation 娛興(yú xìng) 娱兴 entertainment
yú ㄩˊ	輿	舆	公眾的 public 公众的	輿論(yú lùn) 舆论 public opinion
yú ㄩˊ	諛	谀	奉承討好 flatter 奉承讨好	阿諛(ē yú) 阿谀 curry favor with 諂諛(chǎn yú) 谄谀 flatter
yú ㄩˊ	餘	余	剩下，多出的，殘 ，將盡 remaining, surplus, balance 剩下，多出的，残 ，将尽	多餘(duō yú) 多余 extraneous 餘額(yú é) 余额 remaining sum
yú ㄩˊ	魚	鱼	生活在水中有鱗和 鰭的脊椎動物 fish 生活在水中有鳞和 鳍的脊椎动物	金魚(jīn yú) 金鱼 gold fish 鯨魚(jīng yú) 鲸鱼 whale
yú ㄩˊ	漁	渔	捕魚，謀取不應得 的東西 to fish, seek undeserved gains 捕鱼，谋取不应得 的东西	漁船(yú chuán) 渔船 fishing boat 漁人(yú rén) 渔人 fisherman
yú ㄩˊ	逾	逾	超過，更 exceed, even more 超过，更	逾期(yú qí) past due 逾權(yú quán) 逾权 overstep one's authority
yǔ ㄩˇ	雨	雨	大氣水氣遇冷凝結 成水滴後落在地面 上的水珠 rain 大气水气遇冷凝结 成水滴后落在地面 上的水珠	下雨(xià yǔ) to rain 雨衣(yǔ yī) raincoat
yǔ ㄩˇ	予	予	許可，賜，贊許 permit, give, praise 许可，赐，赞许	給予(gěi yǔ) 给予 give 准予(zhǔn yǔ) permit

yǔ ㄩˇ	宇	宇	房屋，上下四方所有的空間，人的儀表 building, space, bearing 房屋，上下四方所有的空間，人的仪表	宇宙(yǔ zhòu) cosmos 氣宇(qì yǔ) 气宇 bearing, manners
yǔ ㄩˇ	羽	羽	鳥毛，同黨 feather, cohort 鸟毛，同党	羽毛(yǔ máo) feather 黨羽(dǎng yǔ) 党羽 cohort
yǔ ㄩˇ	與	与	和，給 and, to 和，给	贈與(zèng yǔ) 赠与 gift 與其(yǔ qí) 与其 rather than...
yǔ ㄩˇ	語	语	話，說，鳥蟲的鳴聲，代表語言的信號 word, say, sign 话，说，鸟虫的鸣声，代表语言的信号	語言(yǔ yán) 语言 language 手語(shǒu yǔ) 手语 sign language
yǔ ㄩˇ	禹	禹	夏朝的開國君主，治洪水有功勞 founder of the Hsia Dynasty 夏朝的开国君主，治洪水有功劳	大禹(dà yǔ) one of China's earliest emperors
yǔ ㄩˇ	嶼	屿	海中的小島 island 海中的小岛	島嶼(dǎo yǔ) 岛屿 islands
yù ㄩˋ	玉	玉	半透明有光澤的美麗石頭，漂亮的，珍貴的 jade 半透明有光泽的美丽石头，漂亮的，珍贵的	玉石(yù shí) jade 玉米(yù mǐ) corn
yù ㄩˋ	馭	驭	控制車、馬，管理，統治 drive a carriage, manage, control 控制车、马，管理，统治	駕馭(jià yù) 驾驭 to control, manage 馭眾(yù zhòng) 驭众 control the masses

yù ㄩˋ	籲	吁	請求，呼告 urge, appeal 请求，呼告	呼籲(hū yù) 呼吁 appeal to 籲請(yù qǐng) 吁请 request
yù ㄩˋ	裕	裕	豐富，富足 abundant, rich 丰富，富足	富裕(fù yù) wealthy 充裕(chōng yù) plenty
yù ㄩˋ	浴	浴	洗澡 take a bath	沐浴(mù yù) take a bath 浴室(yù shì) bathroom
yù ㄩˋ	慾	慾	想得到某種東西或 達到某種目的 desire 想得到某种东西或 达到某种目的	慾望(yù wàng) 慾望 desire 性慾(xìng yù) 性慾 sexual desire
yù ㄩˋ	鬱	郁	憂愁，不快樂 depressed, unhappy 忧愁，不快乐	憂鬱(yōu yù) 忧郁 depressed 鬱積(yù jī) 郁积 pent-up (emotions)
yù ㄩˋ	育	育	生養，培育 nurture, educate 生养，培育	教育(jiào yù) 教育 education 生育(shēng yù) childbearing
yù ㄩˋ	獄	狱	監禁囚犯的地方 prison 监禁囚犯的地方	牢獄(láo yù) 牢狱 prison 越獄(yuè yù) 越狱 escape prison
yù ㄩˋ	遇	遇	碰到，機會 meet, opportunity 碰到，机会	遇見(yù jiàn) meet with 際遇(jì yù) 际遇 opportunity 遇難(yù nàn) 遇难 die in an accident, murdered

yù ㄩˋ	愈	愈	病好了，更 healed, even more	痊愈(quán yù) healed 愈加(yù jiā) even more
yù ㄩˋ	諭	谕	告訴，使人知道 tell, announce 告诉，使人知道	手諭(shǒu yù) 手谕 letter from one's superior
yù ㄩˋ	喻	喻	比方，知道 for instance, know	比喻(bǐ yù) metaphor 家喻戶曉(jiā yù hù xiǎo) 家喻户晓 widely known
yù ㄩˋ	預	预	事前，加入 beforehand, get involved	干預(gān yù) 干预 intervene 預報(yù bào) 预报 forecast
yù ㄩˋ	譽	誉	名聲 reputation 名声	名譽(míng yù) 名誉 reputation 榮譽(róng yù) 荣誉 honor
yù ㄩˋ	寓	寓	居住，住的地方， 包含 live, residence, contain 居住，住的地方， 包含	公寓(gōng yù) apartment 寓言(yù yán) fable
yù ㄩˋ	御	御	駕駛，尊稱和帝王 有關的事物 drive, related to the emporer 驾驶，尊称和帝王 有关的事物	駕御(jià yù) 驾御 control, manage 御醫(yù yī) 御医 imperial physician
yù ㄩˋ	禦	禦	防備，抗拒敵人 defense against, resist enemy 防备，抗拒敌人	防禦(fáng yù) 防禦 defense
yù ㄩˋ	域	域	有一定範圍的地方 region 有一定范围的地方	水域(shuǐ yù) territorial waters 區域(qū yù) 区域 region

yuān ㄩㄢ	鴛	鸳	鴛鴦：水鳥名，雄雌鳥常成對游泳 mandarin duck 鸳鸯：水鸟名，雄雌鸟常成对游泳	鴛鴦(yuān yāng) 鸳鸯 mandarin duck
yuān ㄩㄢ	冤	冤	無辜受誣告或誤解，仇恨 injustice, hatred 无辜受诬告或误解，仇恨	冤枉(yuān wǎng) injustice 冤家(yuān jiā) enemy
yuān ㄩㄢ	淵	渊	深水，潭 abyss	深淵(shēn yuān) 深渊 abyss 淵博(yuān bó) 渊博 profound (knowledge)
yuán ㄩㄢˊ	袁	袁	姓氏 Chinese surname	
yuán ㄩㄢˊ	原	原	最初的，開始的，沒有經過加工的 original, initial, raw 最初的，开始的，没有经过加工的	原來(yuán lái) 原来 original 原料(yuán liào) raw material
yuán ㄩㄢˊ	源	源	水流出之處，事物的根本，連續不斷 source, continuous 水流出之处，事物的根本，连续不断	源頭(yuán tóu) 源头 river source 來源(lái yuán) 来源 source
yuán ㄩㄢˊ	圓	圆	像球的形狀 circle 像球的形状	圓圈(yuán quān) 圆圈 circle 團圓(tuán yuán) 团圆 reunion
yuán ㄩㄢˊ	園	园	種植花果蔬菜之處 garden 种植花果蔬菜之处	公園(gōng yuán)公园park 花園(huā yuán) 花园 garden
yuán ㄩㄢˊ	元	元	開始的，第一的 beginning, first 开始的，第一的	元素(yuán sù) element 元旦(yuán dàn) New Year's day
yuán ㄩㄢˊ	員	员	團體中的一分子 member 团体中的一分子	會員(huì yuán)会员 member 演員(yǎn yuán)演员actor
yuán ㄩㄢˊ	媛	媛	美女 beautiful lady	名媛(míng yuán) renowned beauty

yuán ㄩㄢˊ	援	援	幫助 aid 帮助	援助(yuán zhù) assistance 援救(yuán jiù) rescue
yuán ㄩㄢˊ	猿	猿	比猴子大，形狀像 人的哺乳動物 ape 比猴子大，形状像 人的哺乳动物	猿猴(yuán hóu) ape 人猿(rén yuán) man ape
yuán ㄩㄢˊ	緣	缘	人和人的情份，原 因 predestined relationship, reason	姻緣(yīn yuán) 姻缘 marriage 緣故(yuán gù) 缘故 reason
yuǎn ㄩㄢˇ	遠	远	空間，時間距離大 ，不親切 far, remote, not familiar 空间，时间距离大 ，不亲切	遠程(yuǎn chéng) 远程 long-range 疏遠(shū yuǎn) 疏远 alienate
yuàn ㄩㄢˋ	怨	怨	仇恨，表示不滿 hate, resent 仇恨，表示不满	怨恨(yuàn hèn) to resent 埋怨(mán yuàn) to blame, complain
yuàn ㄩㄢˋ	願	愿	希望，樂意 hope, willing to 希望，乐意	願意(yuàn yì) 愿意 willing to 自願(zì yuàn) 自愿 voluntarily
yuàn ㄩㄢˋ	院	院	房屋四周的空地， 場所 courtyard, place 房屋四周的空地， 场所	院子(yuàn zi) courtyard 學院(xué yuàn) 学院 college
yuē ㄩㄝ	約	约	預先說定，邀請， 共同訂立條文 set appointment, invite, agreement 预先说定，邀请， 共同订立条文	約會(yuē huì) 约会 appointment, date 大約(dà yuē) 大约 about, around

yuè 凵ˋ せ	月	月	绕地球轉的衛星，一年有十二個月 moon, month 绕地球转的卫星，一年有十二个月	月亮(yuè liàng) moon 月經(yuè jīng) 月经 menstruation 一月 January, 二月 February, 三月 March, 四月 April, 五月 May, 六月 June, 七月 July, 八月 August, 九月 September, 十月 October, 十一月 November, 十二月 December
yuè 凵ˋ せ	嶽	岳	高大的山 high mountain	山嶽(shān yuè) 山岳 mountain
yuè 凵ˋ せ	岳	岳	妻子的父母親 wife's parents 妻子的父母亲	岳父(yuè fù) father-in-law 岳母(yuè mǔ) mother-in-law
yuè 凵ˋ せ	樂	乐	和諧而有規律的聲音 music 和谐而有规律的声音	音樂(yīn yuè) 音乐 music 樂器(yuè qì) 乐器 musicial instrument
yuè 凵ˋ せ	悦	悦	愉快 happy	悦耳(yuè ěr) pleasing to the ears 喜悦(xǐ yuè) pleasant
yuè 凵ˋ せ	閱	阅	看，檢驗，經歷 read, inspect, experience 看，检验，经历	閱兵(yuè bīng) 阅兵 military parade 閱讀(yuè dú) 阅读 read
yuè 凵ˋ せ	越	越	度過，超出範圍，程度加大 cross over, exceed, even 度过，超出范围，程度加大	越過(yuè guò) 越过 cross over 越來越好(yuè lái yuè hǎo) 越来越好 become better
yuè 凵ˋ せ	粤	粤	廣東省的別稱 Guangdong Province 广东省的别称	粤語(yuè yǔ) 粤语 Cantonese

yuè ㄩㄝˋ	躍	跃	跳，生氣勃勃的樣子 jump, vibrant 跳，生气勃勃的样子	躍過(yuè guò) 跃过 jump over 跳躍(tiào yuè) 跳跃 leap, jump
yūn ㄩㄣ	暈	晕	昏迷，頭腦不清 faint, giddy 昏迷，头脑不清	暈車(yūn chē) 晕车 car-sick 頭暈(tóu yūn) 头晕 feel giddy
yún ㄩㄣˊ	雲	云	地面水蒸汽上升，遇冷結成細微的，在空中浮遊的水點 cloud 地面水蒸汽上升，遇冷结成细微的，在空中浮游的水点	采雲(cǎi yún) 采云 colorful clouds 白雲(bái yún) 白云 white cloud
yún ㄩㄣˊ	勻	匀	平均，分讓 even, share 平均，分让	均勻(jūn yún) even, well-balanced 攪勻(jiǎo yún) 搅匀 stir well
yún ㄩㄣˊ	耘	耘	除草 to weed	耕耘(gēng yún) till the land
yǔn ㄩㄣˇ	允	允	答應，認可，適當 agree, approve, appropriate 答应，认可，适当	允許(yǔn xǔ) 允许 permit 應允(yìng yǔn) 应允 to promise
yùn ㄩㄣˋ	熨	熨	燙平衣服 to iron clothes 烫平衣服	熨斗(yùn dǒu) iron (for ironing clothes)
yùn ㄩㄣˋ	運	运	命中注定的遭遇，使用，搬送 fate, apply, transport	運氣(yùn qì) 运气 luck 運輸(yùn shū) 运输 transport
yùn ㄩㄣˋ	韻	韵	和諧的聲音，讀音時收音部分，風格 rhyme, style 和谐的声音，读音时收音部分，风格	韻母(yùn mǔ) 韵母 vowel 押韻(yā yùn) 押韵 rhyme

yùn ㄩㄣˋ	孕	孕	懷胎，培養 pregnant, cultivate 怀胎，培养	懷孕(huái yùn) 怀孕 pregnant 孕婦(yùn fù) 孕妇 pregnant woman
yùn ㄩㄣˋ	醞	酝	釀酒 brew wine 酿酒	醞釀(yùn niàng) 酝酿 ferment
yùn ㄩㄣˋ	慍	愠	生氣 unhappy 生气	慍怒(yùn nù) 愠怒 silent anger 慍色(yùn sè) 愠色 unhappy expression

Z

zā ㄗㄚ	扎	扎	捆，束 bundle	扎辮子(zā biàn zi) 扎辮子 plait the hair
zá ㄗㄚˊ	雜	杂	多種多樣的，不單純的 mixed, not pure 多种多样的，不单纯的	複雜(fù zá) 复杂 complicated 雜技(zá jì) 杂技 acrobatics
zá ㄗㄚˊ	砸	砸	打 smash	砸破(zá pò) smash 搞砸(gǎo zá) a blunder
zāi ㄗㄞ	災	灾	禍害，個人不幸的遭遇 disaster 祸害，个人不幸的遭遇	水災(shuǐ zāi) 水灾 flood 災禍(zāi huò) 灾祸 disaster
zāi ㄗㄞ	栽	栽	種植 plant 种植	盆栽(pén zāi) potted plant 栽花(zāi huā) plant flower
zǎi ㄗㄞˇ	宰	宰	主管，主持 in charge of, preside over	宰相(zǎi xiàng) prime minister 主宰(zhǔ zǎi) mastermind
zǎi ㄗㄞˇ	崽	崽	小孩子，幼獸 child, young animal 小孩子，幼兽	狗崽子(gǒu zǎi zi) son of a bitch
zài ㄗㄞˋ	再	再	重複地，更加 again, even 重复地，更加	再三(zài sān) time and again 再版(zài bǎn) reprint

zài ㄗㄞˋ	在	在	生存，表示事情發生的時間地點情況 exist, at 生存，表示事情发生的时间地点情况	存在(cún zài) exist 在家(zài jiā) at home
zài ㄗㄞˋ	載	载	用交通工具裝，充滿，記錄 load on vehicle, fill with, to record 用交通工具装，充满，记录	載貨(zài huò) 载货 carry cargo 記載(jì zài) 记载 to record
zān ㄗㄢ	簪	簪	頭飾 hairpin 头饰	簪子(zān zi) hairpin
zán ㄗㄢˊ	咱	咱	我們 we (you and me) 我们	咱們(zán mén) 咱们 we 咱倆(zán liǎ) 咱俩 both of us
zǎn ㄗㄢˇ	攢	攒	聚集，積蓄 gather, accumulate 聚集，积蓄	攢錢(zǎn qián) 攒钱 save up money
zàn ㄗㄢˋ	贊	赞	幫助，表示同意 assist, agree 帮助，表示同意	贊同(zàn tóng) 赞同 agree with 贊助(zàn zhù) 赞助 sponsor
zàn ㄗㄢˋ	讚	赞	誇獎，稱揚 praise, commend 夸奖，称扬	稱讚(chēng zàn) 称赞 praise 讚頌(zàn sòng) 赞颂 sing praise to
zàn ㄗㄢˋ	暫	暂	短時間內 short time 短时间内	暫緩(zàn huǎn) 暂缓 put off temporarily 暫時(zàn shí) 暂时 temporary

zāng ㄗ ㄤ	贓	赃	偷來的錢和貨 stolen money and goods 偷来的钱和货	分贓(fēn zāng) 分赃 divide up the spoils 贓物(zāng wù) 赃物 the spoils
zāng ㄗ ㄤ	髒	脏	不乾淨 dirty 不乾净	骯髒(āng zāng) 肮脏 dirty 髒亂(zāng luàn) 脏乱 filthy and chaotic
zàng ㄗ ㄤ、	葬	葬	掩埋 bury	火葬(huǒ zàng) cremation 埋葬(mái zàng) bury
zàng cang ㄗ ㄤ、ㄘ 尢、	藏	藏	躲起來，儲存 hide, store 躲起来，储存	寶藏(bǎo zàng) 宝藏 treasure 西藏(xī zàng) Tibet
zàng ㄗ ㄤ、	臟	脏	胸腹內各器官的總 稱 internal organs 胸腹内各器官的总 称	心臟(xīn zàng) heart 肝臟(gān zàng) liver
zāo ㄗ ㄠ	遭	遭	遇到 encounter	遭遇(zāo yù) encounter 遭殃(zāo yāng) stricken by disaster
záo ㄗ ㄠ、	鑿	凿	穿孔，挖掘 punch hole, dig	鑿孔(záo kǒng) 凿孔 punch hole
zǎo ㄗ ㄠˇ	早	早	太陽出來的時候 morning 太阳出来的时候	早安(zǎo ān) Good morning! 早晨(zǎo chén) morning
zǎo ㄗ ㄠˇ	棗	枣	棗樹，枝有刺，果 實可吃 date (fruit) 枣树，枝有刺，果 实可吃	棗樹(zǎo shù) 枣树 date tree

zǎo ㄗㄠˇ	澡	澡	沐浴，洗身 take a bath	洗澡(xǐ zǎo) take a bath 澡盆(zǎo pén) bath tub
zào ㄗㄠˋ	噪	噪	許多鳥或蟲子亂叫 ，吵鬧 noisy 许多鸟或虫子乱叫 ，吵闹	噪音(zào yīn) noise 鼓噪(gǔ zào) kick up a fuss
zào ㄗㄠˋ	燥	燥	天氣乾熱 dry, arid 天气干热	燥熱(zào rè) 燥热 hot 乾燥(gān zào) 干燥 dry
zào ㄗㄠˋ	灶	灶	用磚土等疊成的生 火做飯的設備stove 用砖土等叠成的生 火做饭的设备	爐灶(lú zào) 炉灶 stove 灶神(zào shén) god of kitchen
zào ㄗㄠˋ	造	造	製作，成就 make, accomplishment 制作，成就	創造(chuàng zào) 创造 create 造詣(zào yì) 造诣 accomplishment
zào ㄗㄠˋ	皂	皂	黑色 black	肥皂(féi zào) soap 不分皂白(bù fēn zào bái) indiscriminately
zé ㄗㄜˊ	責	责	分內應做的事 duty 分内应做的事	責備(zé bèi) 责备 scold 責任(zé rèn) 责任 responsibility
zé ㄗㄜˊ	則	则	模範，制度，就 model, system, then 模范，制度，就	原則(yuán zé) 原则 principle 規則(guī zé) 规则rules 以身作則(yǐ shēn zuò zé) 以身作则 set an example for others to follow

zé ㄗㄜˊ	澤	泽	水積聚的地方，光 亮 marsh, bright 水积聚的地方，光 亮	沼澤(zhǎo zé) 沼泽marsh 光澤(guāng zé) 光泽gloss 色澤(sè zé) 色泽 tinge 恩澤(ēn zé) 恩泽 kindness
zé ㄗㄜˊ	擇	择	挑選 choose 挑选	選擇(xuǎn zé) 选择 select 擇友(zé yǒu) 择友 choose a friend
zéi ㄗㄟˊ	賊	贼	偷東西的人，盜匪 thief, bandit 偷东西的人，盗匪	盜賊(dào zéi) 盗贼 thief 賣國賊(mài guó zéi) 卖国贼 traitor
zěn ㄗㄣˇ	怎	怎	如何 how	怎樣(zěn yàng) 怎样 how? 怎麼辦(zěn me bàn) 怎么办 What should we do?
zeng céng ㄗㄥ ㄘㄥˊ	曾	曾	間隔兩代的親屬關 係；姓氏 a relative three generations older or younger; Chinese surname 间隔两代的亲属关 系；姓氏	曾孫(zēng sūn) 曾孙 great grandson 曾祖父(zēng zǔ fù) great grandfather
zēng ㄗㄥ	增	增	加多，添加 add, increase	增加(zēng jiā) increase 增多(zēng duō) add
zèng ㄗㄥˋ	贈	赠	把東西送给别人 give to others 把东西送给别人	贈品(zèng pǐn) 赠品 gift 贈送(zèng sòng) 赠送 present a gift to
zhá ㄓㄚˊ	閘	闸	可以開關的水門 floodgate 可以开关的水门	水閘(shuǐ zhá) 水闸 floodgate
zhá ㄓㄚˊ	紮	扎	屯駐軍隊 station (army) 屯驻军队	紮營(zhá yíng) 扎营 station army 結紮(jié zhá) 结扎 ligation
zhá zhà ㄓㄚˊ ㄓㄚˋ	炸	炸	把食物放入多量的 沸油中烹熟deep fry 把食物放入多量的 沸油中烹熟	炸雞(zhà jī) 炸鸡 fried chicken 炸魚(zhà yú) 炸鱼 fried fish

393

zhá ㄓㄚˊ	扎	扎	掙扎：用力抗拒 struggle 挣扎：用力抗拒	掙扎(zhēng zhá) 挣扎 struggle
zhǎ ㄓㄚˇ	眨	眨	眼睛一閉一開 wink 眼睛一闭一开	眨眼(zhǎ yǎn) wink 一眨眼(yì zhǎ yǎn) in a wink
zhà zhá ㄓㄚˋ、ㄓㄚˊ	炸	炸	突然破裂 explode	炸彈(zhà dàn) 炸弹 bomb 炸藥(zhà yào) 炸药 dynamite
zhà ㄓㄚˋ	榨	榨	用力擠出 squeeze 用力挤出	壓榨(yā zhà) 压榨 exploit 榨油(zhà yóu) extract oil
zhà ㄓㄚˋ	柵	栅	用竹、木、鐵等做 成的阻攔物，籬笆 fence 用竹、木、铁等做 成的阻拦物，篱笆	鐵柵(tiě zhà) 铁栅 iron fence 欄柵(lán zhà) 栏栅 railing
zhà ㄓㄚˋ	詐	诈	欺騙，假裝 defraud, feign 欺骗，假装	欺詐(qī zhà) 欺诈 swindle 詐騙(zhà piàn) 诈骗 defraud
zhāi ㄓㄞ	齋	斋	書房或學舍 study room 书房或学舍	齋戒(zhāi jiè) 斋戒 practice abstinence 吃齋(chī zhāi) 吃斋 be a vegetarian
zhāi ㄓㄞ	摘	摘	採取，拿下，選取 pluck, take down, choose 采取，拿下，选取	摘要(zhāi yào) excerpts 文摘(wén zhāi) summary of article 採摘(cǎi zhāi)采摘 pluck (fruits)

zhái ㄓ ㄞˊ	宅	宅	住所，存 residence	住宅(zhù zhái) residence 宅基地(zhái jī dì) homestead 宅心善良 (zhái xīn shàn liáng) kindhearted
zhǎi ㄓ ㄞˇ	窄	窄	不寬 narrow 不宽	狹窄(xiá zhǎi) narrow 窄小(zhǎi xiǎo) small and narrow
zhài ㄓ ㄞˋ	債	债	欠別人的錢財 debt 欠别人的钱财	債務(zhài wù) 债务 debt 借債(jiè zhài) 借债 be in debt
zhài ㄓ ㄞˋ	寨	寨	防守的障礙物，村 子 stockade, village 防守的障碍物，村 子	山寨(shān zhài) fortified village
zhān ㄓ ㄢ	粘	粘	附著 stick to 附著	粘接(zhān jiē) to splice
zhān ㄓ ㄢ	氈	毡	防寒用品 felt (cloth)	毛氈(máo zhān) 毛毡 felt
zhān ㄓ ㄢ	霑	沾	浸濕，借某種關係 而得到好處 moisten, benefit from a relationship 浸湿，借某种关系 而得到好处	霑光(zhān guāng)沾光 benefit from a relationship
zhān ㄓ ㄢ	瞻	瞻	往上或往前看 look forward or upward 往上或往前看	瞻仰(zhān yǎng) look to with reverence 前瞻(qián zhān) prospect

zhǎn ㄓ ㄢˇ	斬	斩	砍斷 chop off 砍断	斬首(zhǎn shǒu) 斩首 decapitate 斬斷(zhǎn duàn) 斩断 chop off
zhǎn ㄓ ㄢˇ	盞	盏	小杯子，量詞，一 盞燈 small cup, classifier for lamp 小杯子，量詞，一 盏灯	兩盞燈(liǎng zhǎn dēng) 兩盏灯 two lamps
zhǎn ㄓ ㄢˇ	展	展	張開，施展 unfold, apply 张开，施展	發展(fā zhǎn) 发展 development 展翅(zhǎn chì) spread the wings
zhǎn ㄓ ㄢˇ	輾	辗	轉，來回轉動 roll back and forth 转，来回转动	輾轉(zhǎn zhuǎn) 辗转 toss and turn
zhàn ㄓ ㄢˋ	戰	战	打仗 battle	戰爭(zhàn zhēng) 战争 war 戰略(zhàn lüè) 战略 strategy
zhàn ㄓ ㄢˋ	棧	栈	儲存貨物或可供旅 客住宿的小房屋 inn 储存货物或可供旅 客住宿的小房屋	客棧(kè zhàn) 客栈 inn 貨棧(huò zhàn) 货栈 warehouse
zhàn ㄓ ㄢˋ	佔	占	據有，用強力取得 occupy, seize 据有，用强力取得	佔領(zhàn lǐng) 占领 occupy (territory) 佔上風(zhàn shàng fēng) 占上风 on the upper hand
zhàn ㄓ ㄢˋ	站	站	立，乘客搭車停靠 的地方 stand, waiting station 立，乘客搭車停靠 的地方	站立(zhàn lì) stand 火車站(huǒ chē zhàn) 火车站 railway station
zhàn ㄓ ㄢˋ	顫	颤	因寒冷，氣憤，害 怕而發抖，物體振 動 shudder, vibrate 因寒冷，气愤，害 怕而发抖，物体振 动	顫抖(zhàn dǒu) 颤抖 shudder 顫動(zhàn dòng) 颤动 vibrate

zhāng ㄓㄤ	張	张	打開，計算物品的 單位 open up, classifier for flat, thin objects 打开，计算物品的 单位	張口(zhāng kǒu)张口 open the mouth 緊張(jǐn zhāng)紧张 nervous 一張桌子(yì zhāng zhuō zi)一张桌子 a table, desk
zhāng ㄓㄤ	章	章	成篇的文字，小説 的段落 written passage 成篇的文字，小说 的段落	文章(wén zhāng) article 圖章(tú zhāng)图章 seal, chop
zhāng ㄓㄤ	樟	樟	樟樹：常綠喬木， 可做箱子 camphor tree 樟树：常绿乔木， 可做箱子	樟腦(zhāng nǎo)樟脑 camphor
zhāng ㄓㄤ	彰	彰	明顯，顯著，讚揚 conspicious, remarkable, commend 明显，显著，赞扬	彰顯(zhāng xiǎn)彰显 publicize 表彰(biǎo zhāng) commend
zhāng ㄓㄤ	蟑	蟑	蟑螂：一種黑褐色 害蟲，常在深夜偷 吃東西 cockroach 蟑螂：一种黑褐色 害虫，常在深夜偷 吃东西	蟑螂(zhāng láng) cockroach
zhǎng cháng ㄓㄤˇㄔ ˊㄤ	長	长	發育，負責人 grow, responsible person 发育，负责人	長大(zhǎng dà)长大 grow up 校長(xiào zhǎng)校长 school principal
zhǎng ㄓㄤˇ	漲	涨	水量增加，價格增 加 rising water level, price hike 水量增加，价格增 加	水漲(shuǐ zhǎng)水涨 water level rises 漲價(zhǎng jià)涨价 raise the price
zhǎng ㄓㄤˇ	掌	掌	手腳的裏面，把握 ，用手打 palm, strike with hand 手脚的里面，把握 ，用手打	手掌(shǒu zhǎng) palm 掌握(zhǎng wò) master

zhàng ㄓ ㄤ、	丈	丈	長度單位，女人的配偶，大男子 measure of length, husband 长度单位，女人的配偶，大男子	丈夫(zhàng fū) husband 大丈夫(dà zhàng fū) true man
zhàng ㄓ ㄤ、	仗	仗	戰爭，依靠 battle, rely on 战争，依靠	打仗(dǎ zhàng) at war 倚仗(yǐ zhàng) rely on
zhàng ㄓ ㄤ、	杖	杖	扶著走路的棍子 walking stick 扶著走路的棍子	拐杖(guǎi zhàng) walking stick 手杖(shǒu zhàng) cane
zhàng ㄓ ㄤ、	脹	胀	體積變大 expand, inflate 体积变大	通貨膨脹(tōng huò péng zhàng)通货膨胀 inflation
zhàng ㄓ ㄤ、	帳	帐	用布或其他材料做成的帷幕，會計科目 curtain, account 用布或其他材料做成的帷幕，会计科目	蚊帳(wén zhàng)蚊帐 mosquito net 做帳(zuò zhàng)做帐 do bookkeeping
zhàng ㄓ ㄤ、	障	障	阻隔，用作防衛的東西 barrier 阻隔，用作防卫的东西	屏障(píng zhàng) protective screen 障礙(zhàng ài)障碍 obstacle
zhāo ㄓ ㄠ	朝	朝	早晨，向上發展的氣勢 morning, momentum to move up 早晨，向上发展的气势	朝氣(zhāo qì)朝气 full of vigor 朝陽(zhāo yáng)朝阳 morning sun 綽綽記記(zhāo zhāo mù mù) day and night
zhāo zháo zhe zhù zhuó ㄓ ㄓ ㄠ ㄠˊ ㄓ ㄓˋ ㄜ˙ ㄨˋ ㄓ ㄨˊ ㄛˊ	著	著	一步棋 one move in a chess game	棋差一著(qí chā yì zháo) 棋差一著lose a chess game by one move (meaning not as good)

zhāo ㄓㄠ	招	招	打手勢叫人來，召喚 beckon 打手势叫人来，召唤	招攬(zhāo lǎn) 招揽 solicit (customers) 招募(zhāo mù) to recruit
zháo zhāo zhe zhù zhuó ㄓㄠˊ ㄓㄠ ㄓㄜ˙ ㄓㄨˋ ㄓㄨㄛˊ	著	著	接觸，受到 touch, affected by 接触，受到	著陸(zháo lù) 著陆 landing 著涼(zháo liáng) 著凉 catch cold
zhǎo ㄓㄠˇ	找	找	尋求，退回 seek, give back 寻求，退回	尋找(xún zhǎo) 寻找 search 找麻煩(zhǎo má fán) 找麻烦 look for trouble
zhǎo ㄓㄠˇ	爪	爪	鳥獸的腳指 claw 鸟兽的脚指	爪牙(zhǎo yá) underlings
zhǎo ㄓㄠˇ	沼	沼	池子 pond	沼澤(zhǎo zé) 沼泽 marsh 沼氣(zhǎo qì) 沼气 marsh gas
zhào ㄓㄠˋ	召	召	呼喚 call up 呼唤	召開(zhào kāi) 召开 convene (a meeting) 召回(zhào huí) recall (an official)
zhào ㄓㄠˋ	照	照	光線射在物體上 shine on 光线射在物体上	照射(zhào shè) shine on 照相(zhào xiàng) take photos
zhào ㄓㄠˋ	詔	诏	皇帝的命令文告 imperial order 皇帝的命令文告	詔書(zhào shū) 诏书 imperial order

zhào ㄓㄠˋ	兆	兆	事情發生前的信號 ，一萬億 omen, one trillion 事情发生前的信号 ，一万亿	預兆(yù zhào) 預兆 omen 一兆(yí zhào) one trillion
zhào ㄓㄠˋ	趙	赵	姓氏 Chinese surname	
zhào ㄓㄠˋ	罩	罩	覆蓋在物體上的東 西 cover 覆盖在物体上的东 西	口罩(kǒu zhào) mask 罩衫(zhào shān) blouse
zhào ㄓㄠˋ	肇	肇	開始，發生 begin, occur 开始，发生	肇禍(zhào huò) 肇禍 cause disaster 肇事者(zhào shì zhě) the perpetrator
zhē ㄓㄜ	遮	遮	掩蔽，掩蓋 cover up 掩蔽，掩盖	遮掩(zhē yǎn) cover up 遮擋(zhē dǎng) 遮挡 block
zhē ㄓㄜ	螫	螫	蟲子用尾針刺人畜 sting 虫子用尾针刺人畜	被蜜蜂螫(bèi mì fēng zhē) stung by a bee
zhé ㄓㄜˊ	哲	哲	有智慧 wise	哲學(zhé xué) 哲学 philosophy 哲人(zhé rén) sage
zhé ㄓㄜˊ	蜇	蜇	海蜇：一種形狀像 傘，身體透明的腔 腸動物 jellyfish 海蜇：一种形状像 伞，身体透明的腔 肠动物	海蜇(hǎi zhé) jellyfish
zhé ㄓㄜˊ	摺	摺	折疊 to fold 折叠	摺紙(zhé zhǐ) 摺纸 origami

zhe zhāo zháo zhù zhuó ㄓㄜ ㄓㄠ ㄓㄠˊ ㄓㄨˋ ㄓㄨㄛˊ	著	着	表示動作正進行 used to show continuous action 表示动作正进行	走著(zǒu zhe) 走着 walking 看著(kàn zhe) 看着 looking at
zhě ㄓㄜˇ	者	者	人或事物的代稱 pronouns "who" and "which" 人或事物的代称	仁者(rén zhě) the benevolent person 死者(sǐ zhě) the dead
zhè ㄓㄜˋ	這	这	"那"的相反，指 較近的人，事物， 立刻 his, right away "那"的相反，指 较近的人，事物， 立刻	這是(zhè shì) 这是 this is 這樣(zhè yàng) 这样 like this
zhè ㄓㄜˋ	蔗	蔗	多年生草本植物， 有甜汁，可以制糖 sugarcane 多年生草本植物， 有甜汁，可以制糖	甘蔗(gān zhè) sugarcane 蔗糖(zhè táng) cane sugar
zhè ㄓㄜˋ	浙	浙	浙江省的簡稱 Zhejiang Province 浙江省的简称	浙江(zhè jiāng) Zhejiang Province
zhēn ㄓㄣ	珍	珍	寶貴，重視 precious, to treasure 宝贵，重视	珍貴(zhēn guì) 珍贵 precious 珍惜(zhēn xí) to treasure
zhēn ㄓㄣ	眞	真	不假，實在的 true, real 不假，实在的	天眞(tiān zhēn) 天真naive 傳眞(chuán zhēn)传真 fax 眞理(zhēn lǐ) 真理 truth 寫眞(xiě zhēn) 写真portrait
zhēn ㄓㄣ	針	针	縫紉，刺繡或編結 的工具 needle 缝纫，刺绣或编结 的工具	打針(dǎ zhēn) 打针 get an injection 針灸(zhēn jiǔ) 针灸 acupuncture

zhēn ㄓ ㄣ	甄	甄	審查選拔 select by examination 审查选拔	甄選(zhēn xuǎn) 甄选 select
zhēn ㄓ ㄣ	貞	贞	意志操守堅定不移 faithful 意志操守坚定不移	忠貞(zhōng zhēn) 忠贞 loyal 貞節(zhēn jié) 贞节 chastity
zhēn ㄓ ㄣ	偵	侦	查看 detect	偵察(zhēn chá) 侦察 reconnaissance 偵探(zhēn tàn) 侦探 detective
zhēn ㄓ ㄣ	箴	箴	勸導性的言詞 proverb 劝导性的言词	箴言(zhēn yán) proverb
zhěn ㄓ ㄣˇ	疹	疹	病人皮膚上起的小 顆粒，通常是紅色 rash 病人皮肤上起的小 颗粒，通常是红色	痲疹(má zhěn) measle 湿疹(shī zhěn) rash
zhěn ㄓ ㄣˇ	診	诊	檢驗判斷 diagnose 检验判断	診斷(zhěn duàn) 诊断 diagnose 診所(zhěn suǒ) 诊所 clinic
zhěn ㄓ ㄣˇ	枕	枕	躺下用的頭墊 pillow 躺下用的头垫	枕頭(zhěn tóu) 枕头 pillow
zhèn ㄓ ㄣˋ	陣	阵	一段時間，軍隊作 戰布置隊伍排列 for a time, battle formation 一段时间，军队作 战布置队伍排列	陣雨(zhèn yǔ) 阵雨 occasional rain 陣地(zhèn dì) 阵地 battleground
zhèn ㄓ ㄣˋ	振	振	揮動，奮發 shake, brace oneself up 挥动，奋发	振蕩(zhèn dàng) 振荡 vibrate 振奮(zhèn fèn) 振奋 brace oneself up

zhèn ㄓㄣˋ	震	震	激烈動盪，驚動 jolt, commotion 激烈动荡，惊动	地震(dì zhèn) earthquake 震驚(zhèn jīng) 震惊 shocking
zhèn ㄓㄣˋ	朕	朕	皇帝自稱，先兆 I (used by emperor to refer to himself), omen 皇帝自称，先兆	朕兆(zhèn zhào) omen
zhèn ㄓㄣˋ	鎮	镇	縣以下的地方行政區域單位，壓制 township, suppress 县以下的地方行政区域单位，压制	城鎮(chéng zhèn) 城镇 urban area 鎮壓(zhèn yā) 镇压 suppress
zhēng ㄓㄥ	爭	争	努力取得 strive for	爭奪(zhēng duó) 争夺 vie for 爭取(zhēng qǔ) 争取 strive for
zhēng ㄓㄥ	掙	挣	掙扎：用力抗拒 struggle 挣扎：用力抗拒	掙扎(zhēng zhá) 挣扎 struggle
zhēng ㄓㄥ	睜	睁	張著眼睛 with eyes open 张著眼睛	眼睜睜(yǎn zhēng zhēng) 眼睁睁 with eyes open 睜開(zhēng kāi) 睁开 open (the eyes)
zhēng ㄓㄥ	猙	狰	猙獰：樣子凶惡 hideous 狰狞：样子凶恶	猙獰面目(zhēng níng miàn mù) 狰狞面目 hideous looks
zhēng ㄓㄥ	箏	筝	古代弦樂器，玩具的一種 25-string musical instrument 古代弦乐器，玩具的一种	風箏(fēng zhēng) 风筝 kite

zhēng zhèng ㄓ ㄥ ㄥˋ	正	正	正月：農曆每年的 第一個月 1st month of lunar year 正月：农历每年的 第一个月	正月(zhēng yuè) first month of lunar year
zhēng ㄓ ㄥ	征	征	出兵攻打，收取 military expedition, collect	征服(zhēng fú) conquer 征兵(zhēng bīng) conscription
zhēng ㄓ ㄥ	徵	征	現象，求，收稅 symbol, solicit, collect tax 现象，求，收税	象徵(xiàng zhēng) 象征 symbolize 徵求(zhēng qiú) 征求 ask for
zhēng ㄓ ㄥ	癥	症	腹中有硬塊，比喻 困難的問題 abdomenal mass, crux 腹中有硬块，比喻 困难的问题	癥結(zhēng jié) 症结 crux 病癥(bìng zhēng) 病症 symptom
zhēng ㄓ ㄥ	蒸	蒸	熱氣上升，向上發 展的勢頭 evaporate, flourishing 热气上升，向上发 展的势头	蒸發(zhēng fā) 蒸发 evaporate 蒸餾水(zhēng liù shuǐ) 蒸馏水distilled water
zhěng ㄓ ㄥˇ	拯	拯	救援 rescue	拯救(zhěng jiù) rescue
zhěng ㄓ ㄥˇ	整	整	沒有零頭的數目， 完全的，使事物有 條理whole, complete 没有零头的数目， 完全的，使事物有 条理	完整(wán zhěng) complete 整理(zhěng lǐ) tidy up
zhěng ㄓ ㄥˋ	掙	挣	用力擺脫，努力賺 取 struggle to get away, make money 用力摆脱，努力赚 取	掙錢(zhèng qián) 挣钱 make money 掙脫(zhèng tuō) 挣脱 struggle to get away

zhèng ㄓ ㄥˋ	證	证	表明事實的憑據，用事實來表明 evidence, prove 表明事实的凭据，用事实来表明	證人(zhèng rén) 证人 a witness 證明(zhèng míng) 证明 proof, prove
zhèng ㄓ ㄥˋ	鄭	郑	姓氏，審慎 Chinese surname, serious 姓氏，审慎	鄭重(zhèng zhòng) 郑重 sternly
zhèng zhēng ㄓ ㄓ ㄥˋ ㄥ	正	正	不偏斜，恰好，合規則 upright, just as, conform to rules 不偏斜，恰好，合规则	立正(lì zhèng) stand attention 正常(zhèng cháng) normal 正式(zhèng shì) formal 正好(zhèng hǎo) just in time 糾正(jiū zhèng)纠正 to rectify, to set right
zhèng ㄓ ㄥˋ	政	政	機關學校辦的事 administration 机关学校办的事	政府(zhèng fǔ) government 行政(xíng zhèng) administration
zhī ㄓ	汁	汁	水果，蔬菜中所榨出的液體 juice 水果，蔬菜中所榨出的液体	果汁(guǒ zhī) fruit juice
zhī ㄓ	織	织	用絲，麻，棉，毛等物編製物品 weave 用丝，麻，棉，毛等物编制物品	紡織(fǎng zhī) 纺织 textile 組織(zǔ zhī) 组织 organization
zhī ㄓ	之	之	在，這，的 on, this, of 在，这，的	之前(zhī qián) before 好自爲之(hǎo zì wéi zhī) 好自为之 do your best
zhī ㄓ	芝	芝	寄生在枯木上象徵吉祥的菌類 a parasitic fungus 寄生在枯木上象征吉祥的菌类	芝麻(zhī má) sesame 靈芝(líng zhī) 灵芝 a healing fungus

zhī ㄓ	脂	脂	油性物質 fat, greese 油性物质	脂肪(zhī fáng) fat 脱脂奶粉(tuō zhī nǎi fěn) skim milk
zhī ㄓ	支	支	给，分散 give, dispense 给，分散	支持(zhī chí) support 支出(zhī chū) expenditure
zhī ㄓ	枝	枝	從樹幹旁生出的細 條，量詞 branch, classifier for long thin object 从树干旁生出的细 条，量词	樹枝(shù zhī) 树枝 tree branch 一枝筆(yì zhī bǐ) 一枝笔 a pen
zhī ㄓ	肢	肢	手腳 limb 手脚	上肢(shàng zhī) arms 四肢(sì zhì) the four limbs
zhī ㄓ	隻	只	單個，量詞，計算 物體的件數 alone, classifier for birds 单个，量词，计算 物体的件数	一隻鳥(yì zhī niǎo) 一只鸟　a bird 隻字不提(zhī zì bù tí) 只字不提 make no mention about it
zhī ㄓ	知	知	懂得，察覺 know, perceive 懂得，察觉	知道(zhī dào) know 知識(zhī shì) 知识 knowledge
zhī ㄓ	蜘	蜘	蜘蛛：有四對腳會 抽絲織網捕食動物 的昆蟲　spider 蜘蛛：有四对脚会 抽丝织网捕食动物 的昆虫	蜘蛛(zhī zhū) spider
zhí ㄓˊ	值	值	當班，價錢 on duty, value 当班，价钱	值班(zhí bān) 值班 be on duty 價值(jià zhí) 价值 value

zhí 业ˊ	執	执	堅持，守，拿著 adhere to, guard, hold 坚持，守，拿著	固執(gù zhí) 固执 stubborn 執行(zhí xíng) 执行 execute
zhí 业ˊ	職	职	官位，專業，工作 official post, profession, work 官位，专业，工作	職業(zhí yè) 职业 occupation 辭職(cí zhí) 辞职 resign
zhí 业ˊ	直	直	不歪曲，性格爽快，連續不斷 straight, candid, continuous 不歪曲，性格爽快，连续不断	正直(zhèng zhí) 正直 upright 直到(zhí dào) 直到 until
zhí 业ˊ	植	植	草木的總稱，栽種 plant 草木的总称，栽种	植物(zhí wù) 植物 plant 培植(péi zhí) 培植 cultivate
zhí 业ˊ	殖	殖	生，種植，樹立 reproduce, plant, set up 生，种植，树立	生殖(shēng zhí) reproduce 殖民地(zhí mín dì) colony
zhí 业ˊ	姪	侄	兄弟的子女，對父親輩的自稱 brother's children 兄弟的子女，对父亲辈的自称	姪女(zhí nǚ) 侄女 niece 姪子(zhí zi) 侄子 nephew
zhí 业ˊ	質	质	物的本性，抵押 essence, mortgage	質料(zhí liào) 质料 texture 人質(rén zhí) 人质 hostage
zhí 业ˊ	擲	掷	投，拋 throw, pitch	擲鐵餅(zhí tiě bǐng) 掷铁饼 discus throw 投擲(tóu zhí) 投掷 to throw

zhǐ ㄓˇ	只	只	僅僅，惟一 only 仅仅，惟一	只有(zhǐ yǒu) only 只要(zhǐ yào) as long as
zhǐ ㄓˇ	止	止	停，禁阻 stop, block	停止(tíng zhǐ) stop 止血(zhǐ xuè) stop bleeding
zhǐ ㄓˇ	址	址	所在地 address	地址(dì zhǐ) address
zhǐ ㄓˇ	趾	趾	腳指頭 toe 脚指头	腳趾(jiǎo zhǐ) 脚趾 toe
zhǐ ㄓˇ	旨	旨	用意，意思 purpose, intention	旨意(zhǐ yì) intention 主旨(zhǔ zhǐ) main purpose
zhǐ ㄓˇ	指	指	手掌或腳掌前端的 部分，向著 finger, point to 手掌或脚掌前端的 部分，向著	手指(shǒu zhǐ) finger 指示(zhǐ shì) instruct, instruction
zhǐ ㄓˇ	紙	纸	用植物纖維製成用 來寫字，畫圖，包 裝，印刷的東西 paper 用植物纤维制成用 来写字，画图，包 装，印刷的东西	紙巾(zhǐ jīn) 纸巾 napkin 紙張(zhǐ zhāng) 纸张 paper 報紙(bào zhǐ) 报纸 newspaper 衛生紙(wèi shēng zhǐ) 卫生纸 toilet paper
zhì ㄓˋ	幟	帜	直長條旗用來做標 識 banner 直长条旗用来做标 识	旗幟(qí zhì) 旗帜 banner 標幟(biāo zhì) 标帜 mark, symbol
zhì ㄓˋ	致	致	表示 express	致意(zhì yì) convey regards 致歉(zhì qiàn) apologize

zhì ㄓˋ	炙	炙	烤 roast	炙熱(zhì rè) 炙热 sizzling hot 膾炙人口(kuài zhì rén kǒu) 脍炙人口 very popular
zhì ㄓˋ	志	志	意念，心意所向 intention	志願(zhì yuàn) 志愿 volunteer 志向(zhì xiàng) aspiration
zhì ㄓˋ	秩	秩	次序 order	秩序(zhì xù) order
zhì ㄓˋ	制	制	系統，壓抑 system, suppress 系统，压抑	制服(zhì fú) uniform, to subdue 制度(zhì dù) system
zhì ㄓˋ	製	制	做 make	製造(zhì zào) 制造 manufacture 訂製(dìng zhì) 订制 custom made
zhì ㄓˋ	置	置	購買，安放 purchase, place 购买，安放	處置(chǔ zhì) 处置 dispose of 置產(zhì chǎn) 置产 buy property
zhì ㄓˋ	治	治	管理，醫療 manage, treat illness 管理，医疗	治理(zhì lǐ) govern 治病(zhì bìng) cure disease
zhì ㄓˋ	智	智	才識，謀略 intellect, stratagem 才识，谋略	理智(lǐ zhì) faculty of reason 智慧(zhì huì) wisdom
zhì ㄓˋ	稚	稚	幼小 young	幼稚(yòu zhì) childish 稚子(zhì zi) small child

zhì ㄓˋ	滯	滞	停留，不流通 stay over, stagnant	停滯(tíng zhì) 停滞 stoppage 呆滯(dāi zhì) 呆滞 sluggish
zhì ㄓˋ	摯	挚	誠懇 sincere 诚恳	摯友(zhì yǒu) 挚友 bosom friend 摯誠(zhì chéng) 挚诚 sincere
zhì ㄓˋ	至	至	最，到來，直到 the most, arrive, until 最，到来，直到	至此(zhì cǐ) at this point 至親(zhì qīn) 至亲 the dearest
zhì ㄓˋ	桎	桎	腳鐐 fetters 脚镣	桎梏(zhì gù) shackles
zhì ㄓˋ	窒	窒	阻塞，障礙 block, blockade 阻塞，障碍	窒息(zhì xí) suffocate 窒礙(zhì ài) 窒碍 obstacles
zhì ㄓˋ	痔	痔	直腸下端的靜脈擴 張長成的瘤 hemorrhoids 直肠下端的静脉扩 张长成的瘤	痔瘡(zhì chuāng) 痔疮 hemorrhoids
zhōng ㄓㄨㄥ	鐘	钟	銅製中空樂器，可 敲打發出聲音，計 算時間的器具 bell, clock 铜制中空乐器，可 敲打发出声音，计 算时间的器具	鐘聲(zhōng shēng) 钟声 sound of bell 時鐘(shí zhōng) 时钟 clock
zhōng ㄓㄨㄥ	鍾	钟	姓氏，集中 (情感) Chinese surname, concentrate (affection) on	鍾愛(zhōng ài)钟爱 beloved 一見鍾情(yí jiàn zhōng qíng) 一见钟情 love at first sight
zhōng ㄓㄨㄥ	終	终	完畢 the end 完毕	終結(zhōng jié) 终结 the end 終於(zhōng yú) 终於 finally

zhōng ㄓ ㄨ ㄥ	衷	衷	好心意 good intention	衷心(zhōng xīn) sincerely 初衷(chū zhōng) original intention
zhōng zhòng ㄓ ㄓ ㄨ ㄨ、 ㄥ ㄥ	中	中	距離四週，兩邊都 相同 center 距离四周，两边都 相同	中間(zhōng jiān) 中间 the middle 中等(zhōng děng) medium 中國(zhōng guó) China 中國人(zhōng guó rén) Chinese
zhōng ㄓ ㄨ ㄥ	忠	忠	盡自己心力待人處 事 loyal, faithful 尽自己心力待人处 事	忠心(zhōng xīn) loyal 忠言(zhōng yán) earnest advice
zhōng ㄓ ㄨ ㄥ	盅	盅	小杯子 small cup	一盅酒(yì zhōng jiǔ) a cup of wine 酒盅(jiǔ zhōng) wine cup
zhǒng ㄓ ㄨ ㄥˇ	腫	肿	皮膚發紅而浮脹， 粗胖 swell, obese 皮肤发红而浮胀， 粗胖	臃腫(yōng zhǒng) 臃肿 obese 紅腫(hóng zhǒng) 红肿 red and swollen
zhǒng ㄓ ㄨ ㄥˇ	種	种	類別，植物的籽 variety, seed 类别，植物的籽	種類(zhǒng lèi) 种类 variety 種子(zhǒng zi) 种子 seed
zhòng ㄓ ㄨ、 ㄥ	種	种	栽植 plant 栽植	種菜(zhòng cài) 种菜 grow vegetables 種田(zhòng tián) 种田 till the land
zhòng ㄓ ㄨ、 ㄥ	眾	众	人、事、物的多數 ，平常 many, ordinary 人、事、物的多数 ，平常	大眾(dà zhòng) 大众 the public 出眾(chū zhòng) 出众 extraordinary
zhòng ㄓ ㄔ ㄨ、ㄨˊ ㄥ ㄥ	重	重	物體的分量，緊要 heavy, important 物体的分量，紧要	重量(zhòng liàng) weight 重要(zhòng yào) important

zhòng zhòng ㄓ ㄓ ㄨˋ ㄨˋ ㄥ ㄥ	中	中	正確，適合，打到 目標 correct, suitable, right on target 正确，适合，打到 目标	中的(zhòng dì) hit the target 中意(zhòng yì) like, prefer
zhòng ㄓ ㄨˋ ㄥ	仲	仲	兄弟排行第二，居 中的 second in sibling order, middle	伯仲之間(bó zhòng zhī jiān) 伯仲之间 almost the same 仲裁(zhòng cái) arbitrate 仲夏(zhòng xià) midsummer
zhōu ㄓ ㄡ	州	州	行政區域名 a state 行政区域名	州立(zhōu lì) state-run 加州(jiā zhōu) California
zhōu ㄓ ㄡ	洲	洲	水中的大陸，大陸 continent 水中的大陆，大陆	亞洲(yà zhōu) Asia 洲際(zhōu jì) 洲际 intercontinental
zhōu ㄓ ㄡ	舟	舟	小船 small boat	輕舟(qīng zhōu) 轻舟 small boat 龍舟(lóng zhōu) 龙舟 dragon boat
zhōu ㄓ ㄡ	周	周	朝代名，圓形的外 圍 dynasty name, circumference 朝代名，圆形的外 围	圓周(yuán zhōu) 圆周 circumference 周圍(zhōu wéi) 周围 surrounding
zhōu ㄓ ㄡ	週	週	一星期，走圓圈一 圈 one week, walk one round 一星期，走圆圈一 圈	一週(yì zhōu) 一週 one week 週年(zhōu nián) 週年 anniversary
zhōu ㄓ ㄡ	粥	粥	米加很多水煮得很 稀的飯 porridge 米加很多水煮得很 稀的饭	米粥(mǐ zhōu) rice soup
zhóu ㄓ ㄡˊ	妯	妯	妯娌：兄弟的妻子 間相互的稱呼 sisters-in-law 妯娌：兄弟的妻子 间相互的称呼	妯娌(zhóu lǐ) sisters-in-law

zhóu ㄓㄡˊ	軸	轴	控制車輪轉動，貫穿車輪中心的橫杆 axle, shaft 控制车轮转动，贯穿车轮中心的横杆	車軸(chē zhóu) 车轴 car axle 輪軸(lún zhóu) 轮轴 wheel shaft
zhóu ㄓㄡˇ	肘	肘	人的上臂和下臂相接連的外關節 elbow 人的上臂和下臂相接连的外关节	手肘(shǒu zhóu) elbow
zhòu ㄓㄡˋ	宙	宙	從古到今 time (from the past to the present) 从古到今	宇宙(yǔ zhòu) cosmos
zhòu ㄓㄡˋ	晝	昼	白天，從日出到日落 daytime 白天，从日出到日落	晝夜(zhòu yè) 昼夜 day and night 白晝(bái zhòu) 白昼 daytime
zhòu ㄓㄡˋ	皺	皱	面部所生的紋，物體的摺痕 wrinkle, crease 面部所生的纹，物体的摺痕	皺紋(zhòu wén) 皱纹 wrinkle 皺折(zhòu zhé) 皱折 crease
zhòu ㄓㄡˋ	紂	纣	商朝的最後一位皇帝，非常暴虐 Shang Dynasty's last emperor 商朝的最后一位皇帝，非常暴虐	紂王(zhòu wáng) 纣王 the Emperor Zhou
zhòu ㄓㄡˋ	咒	咒	驅鬼除妖魔邪怪的話或口訣，講惡毒的話希望對方不利 curse 驱鬼除妖魔邪怪的话或口诀，讲恶毒的话希望对方不利	詛咒(zǔ zhòu) 诅咒 lay a curse upon (a person) 咒罵(zhòu mà) 咒骂 to curse 詛咒語(zǔ zhòu yǔ) 诅咒语 cussword
zhòu ㄓㄡˋ	冑	冑	古時兵士作戰時所戴的頭盔 helmet 古时兵士作战时所戴的头盔	冑甲(zhòu jiǎ) helmet and armor

zhū ㄓ ㄨ	朱	朱	深紅色 bright red 深红色	朱唇(zhū chún) red lips 朱門(zhū mén) 朱门 red-lacquered doors
zhū ㄓ ㄨ	侏	侏	矮小，短小 short	侏儒(zhū rú) dwarf
zhū ㄓ ㄨ	珠	珠	打開蛤類中有白色 圓形帶光澤的東西 pearl 打开蛤类中有白色 圆形带光泽的东西	珍珠(zhēn zhū) pearl 珠寶(zhū bǎo) 珠宝 jewelry
zhū ㄓ ㄨ	株	株	樹木露在地面上的 根部，樹木一棵 stub, a tree 树木露在地面上的 根部，树木一棵	一株樹(yì zhū shù) 一株树 a tree
zhū ㄓ ㄨ	誅	诛	殺，責備 kill, criticize 杀，责备	天誅地滅(tiān zhū dì miè) 天诛地灭condemned by all
zhū ㄓ ㄨ	諸	诸	表示不知道多少的 多數 many 表示不知道多少的 多数	諸位(zhū wèi) 诸位 everyone 諸侯(zhū hóu) 诸侯 feudal prince
zhū ㄓ ㄨ	豬	猪	四條腿鼻孔朝上可 以吃的家畜 pig 四条腿鼻孔朝上可 以吃的家畜	養豬(yǎng zhū) 养猪 hog raising 小豬(xiǎo zhū) 小猪 suckling pig
zhū ㄓ ㄨ	蛛	蛛	蜘蛛：有四對腳會 抽絲織網捕食動物 的昆蟲 spider 蜘蛛：有四对脚会 抽丝织网捕食动物 的昆虫	蜘蛛(zhī zhū) spider
zhú ㄓ ㄨˊ	竹	竹	多年生中空有節可 做笛，簫樂器的植 物 bamboo 多年生中空有节可 做笛，箫乐器的植 物	竹林(zhú lín) bamboo grove 竹籃(zhú lán) 竹篮 bamboo basket

zhú ㄓㄨˊ	逐	逐	在後面追趕，趕走，依照秩序進行 chase, chase away, one by one 在后面追赶，赶走，依照秩序进行	追逐(zhuī zhú) chase after 逐步(zhú bù) gradually
zhú ㄓㄨˊ	築	筑	建造，修蓋 build, construct 建造，修盖	建築物(jiàn zhú wù) 建筑物 architecture 建築師(jiàn zhú shī) 建筑师 architect
zhú ㄓㄨˊ	燭	烛	蠟，油製成可點火發光的東西 candle 蜡，油制成可点火发光的东西	燭火(zhú huǒ) 烛火 candle light 蠟燭(là zhú) 蜡烛 candle
zhǔ ㄓㄨˇ	主	主	家長，有事權或物權的人 master 家长，有事权或物权的人	主人(zhǔ rén) master 主要(zhǔ yào) primary
zhǔ ㄓㄨˇ	煮	煮	把食物放在有水或湯的鍋中，再加火燒熱 cook 把食物放在有水或汤的锅中，再加火烧热	煮飯(zhǔ fàn) 煮饭 cook rice 煮熟(zhǔ shóu) well cooked
zhǔ ㄓㄨˇ	囑	嘱	託付，叮嚀 entrust, remind 托付，叮咛	遺囑(yí zhǔ) 遗嘱 last will 囑咐(zhǔ fù) 嘱咐 reminder
zhù ㄓㄨˋ	住	住	居留，歇宿，牢固 live, stay, firmly	居住(jū zhù) reside 記住(jì zhù) 记住 keep in mind
zhù ㄓㄨˋ	助	助	幫忙，對人有益處 help, beneficial 帮忙，对人有益处	助手(zhù shǒu) assistant 互助(hù zhù) mutual assistance
zhù ㄓㄨˋ	祝	祝	姓，希望，頌賀 Chinese surname, wish, celebrate 姓，希望，颂贺	祝福(zhù fú) give blessing 祝賀(zhù hè) 祝贺 congratulate

zhù 业 ㄨˋ	駐	驻	停留，停止 station, stop	駐防(zhù fáng) 驻防 station army 駐軍(zhù jūn) 驻军 garrison
zhù 业 ㄨˋ	柱	柱	屋子中用來支撐樑 的粗木，支持 pillar, support 屋子中用来支撑梁 的粗木，支持	支柱(zhī zhù) pillar 脊柱(jǐ zhù) spine
zhù 业 ㄨˋ	蛀	蛀	蟲子咬壞 damaged by borer 虫子咬坏	蛀牙(zhù yá) dental caries 蛀蟲(zhù chóng) 蛀虫 borer
zhù 业 ㄨˋ	注	注	賭博時所賭下的財 物，灌入，專心 stakes, pour 赌博时所赌下的财 物，灌入，专心	賭注(dǔ zhù) 赌注 stakes 注意(zhù yì) pay attention, beware
zhù zhāo zháo zhe zhuó 业 业 ㄨˋ ㄠ 业 业 ㄠˊ ˙ㄜ 业ㄨㄛˊ	著	著	作品，寫作，顯明 works, write books, famous 作品，写作，显明	著名(zhù míng) renowned 名著(míng zhù) famous works
zhù 业 ㄨˋ	鑄	铸	熔冶金製造器物 cast 熔冶金制造器物	鑄成大錯(zhù chéng dà cuò) 铸成大错 to blunder 鑄幣(zhù bì) 铸币 coin
zhuā 业 ㄨㄚ	抓	抓	搔，用手拿取東西 ，把握 scratch, grab, hold 搔，用手拿取东西 ，把握	抓癢(zhuā yǎng) 抓痒 scratch where it itches 抓賭(zhuā dǔ) 抓赌 crack down on gambling
zhuǎ 业 ㄨㄚˇ	爪	爪	手，腳的指甲 claw, paw 手，脚的指甲	雞爪(jī zhuǎ) 鸡爪 chicken feet
zhuān 业 ㄨㄢ	專	专	集中精力做一件事 singleminded, specialize in	專心(zhuān xīn) 专心 concentrate on 專利(zhuān lì) 专利 patent

zhuān ㄓㄨㄢ	磚	砖	用粘土燒製成的方塊建築材料 brick 用粘土烧制成的方块建筑材料	磚塊(zhuān kuài) 砖块 brick 磚瓦(zhuān wǎ) 砖瓦 brick and tile
zhuǎn ㄓㄨㄢˇ	轉	转	繞圈子走 revolve, rotate 绕圈子走	轉動(zhuǎn dòng) 转动 roll 公轉(gōng zhuǎn) 公转 revolve
zhuàn ㄓㄨㄢˋ	賺	赚	設法獲得 gain 设法获得	賺錢(zhuàn qián) 赚钱 make money 賺取(zhuàn qǔ) 赚取 obtain
zhuàn ㄓㄨㄢˋ	撰	撰	寫書或文章 write article 写书或文章	撰文(zhuàn wén) write article 杜撰(dù zhuàn) fabrication
zhuāng ㄓㄨㄤ	莊	庄	村子，商店 village, shop	村莊(cūn zhuāng) 村庄 village 地下錢莊(dì xià qián zhuāng) 地下钱庄 underground bank
zhuāng ㄓㄨㄤ	妝	妆	婦女修飾容貌 put on makeup 妇女修饰容貌	化妝(huà zhuāng) 化妆 put on makeup 卸妝(xiè zhuāng) 卸妆 remove makeup
zhuāng ㄓㄨㄤ	裝	装	衣服，打扮，做假 dress, dress up, pretend	服裝(fú zhuāng) 服装 garment 裝病(zhuāng bìng) 装病 feign illness
zhuàng ㄓㄨㄤˋ	壯	壮	健碩，強大 stout, strong 健硕，强大	健壯(jiàn zhuàng) 健壮 stout 壯丁(zhuàng dīng) 壮丁 able-bodied man
zhuàng ㄓㄨㄤˋ	幢	幢	用於房屋的量詞 classifier for building 用于房屋的量词	一幢樓(yí zhuàng lóu) 一幢楼 a building

zhuàng ㄓ ㄨ ㄤ	狀	状	外形，情況，文件 shape, condition, certificate 外形，情况，文件	形狀(xíng zhuàng) 形狀 shape 狀況(zhuàng kuàng) 状况 condition
zhuàng ㄓ ㄨ ㄤ	撞	撞	打，東西相碰 strike, collide 打，东西相碰	碰撞(pèng zhuàng) collide 撞球(zhuàng qiú) billiard
zhuī ㄓ ㄨ ㄟ	椎	椎	脊柱骨 vertebra	脊椎(jí zhuī) vertebra
zhuī ㄓ ㄨ ㄟ	錐	锥	鑽孔的尖銳工具 awl 钻孔的尖锐工具	錐子(zhuī zi) 锥子 awl 錐形(zhuī xíng) 锥形 cone-shaped
zhuī ㄓ ㄨ ㄟ	追	追	從後面趕上去，跟 著 pursue, follow 从后面赶上去，跟 著	追趕(zhuī gǎn) 追赶 chase after 追隨(zhuī suí) 追随 follow
zhuì ㄓ ㄨ ㄟ	墜	坠	掉落，往下沈 fall down, sink	墜落(zhuì luò) 坠落 crash 墜子(zhuì zi) 坠子 pendant
zhuì ㄓ ㄨ ㄟ	惴	惴	恐慌 anxious and fearful	惴惴不安(zhuì zhuì bù ān) anxious and fearful
zhuì ㄓ ㄨ ㄟ	贅	赘	多餘的 extraneous 多余的	累贅(lěi zhuì) 累赘 burden

zhǔn ㄓ ㄨˇ ㄣ	準	准	根據，正確 standard, exact 根据，正确	標準(biāo zhǔn) 标准 standard 準確(zhǔn què) 准确 precise
zhǔn ㄓ ㄨˇ ㄣ	准	准	允許，同意，將成 爲正式的 allow, agree, would-be 允许，同意，将成 为正式的	批准(pī zhǔn) approve 准新娘(zhǔn xīn niáng) bride-to-be
zhuō ㄓ ㄨ ㄛ	捉	捉	逮捕，握住，戲弄 arrest, grasp, tease 逮捕，握住，戏弄	捕捉(bǔ zhuō) catch 捉弄(zhuō nòng) tease, make fun of
zhuō zhuó ㄓ ㄓ ㄨ ㄨˊ ㄛ ㄛ	拙	拙	笨 clumsy	笨拙(bèn zhuó) clumsy 拙作(zhuó zuò) my work
zhuō ㄓ ㄨ ㄛ	桌	桌	一種台面上可以放 東西的日常家具 table, desk 一种台面上可以放 东西的日常家具	書桌(shū zhuō) 书桌 desk 餐桌(cān zhuō) dining table
zhuó ㄓ ㄨˊ ㄛ	濁	浊	水不清，不乾淨 muddy, dirty 水不清，不干净	污濁(wū zhuó) 污浊 dirty 混濁(hún zhuó) 混浊 muddy
zhuó ㄓ ㄨˊ ㄛ	茁	茁	植物才生長出來的 樣子grow sturdily like a young plant 植物才生长出来的 样子	茁壯(zhuó zhuàng) 茁壮 robust 茁長(zhuó zhǎng) 茁长 robust growth
zhuó ㄓ ㄨˊ ㄛ	灼	灼	燒，明亮 to burn, bright 烧，明亮	灼傷(zhuó shāng) 灼伤 injury from burn 灼見(zhuó jiàn) 灼见 great insight

zhuó ㄓ ㄨ ㄛ	鐲	镯	套在手腕上的環形 裝飾品 bracelet 套在手腕上的环形 装饰品	手鐲(shǒu zhuó) 手镯 bracelet
zhuó ㄓ ㄨ ㄛ	卓	卓	高而直，不平凡 tall and straight, extraordinary 高而直，不平凡	卓越(zhuó yuè) outstanding 卓見(zhuó jiàn) 卓见 great vision
zhuó ㄓ ㄨ ㄛ	焯	焯	光明，明顯 bright, conspicuous 光明，明显	焯見(zhuó jiàn) 焯见 great insight
zhuó ㄓ ㄨ ㄛ	酌	酌	斟酒，考慮 drink wine, consider 斟酒，考虑	小酌(xiǎo zhuó) a little drink 酌量(zhuó liàng) at one's discretion
zhuó ㄓ ㄨ ㄛ	琢	琢	雕刻玉石使成器物 ，精益求精 to carve jade, seek perfection 雕刻玉石使成器物 ，精益求精	琢磨(zhuó mó) carve and polish
zhuó ㄓ ㄨ ㄛ	啄	啄	鳥類用嘴叩擊並夾 住東西 to peck 鸟类用嘴叩击并夹 住东西	啄木鳥(zhuó mù niǎo) 啄木鸟 woodpecker 啄米(zhuó mǐ) peck at a grain of rice
zhuó zhāo zháo zhe zhù ㄓ ㄓ ㄨ ㄠ ㄛ ㄓ ㄓ ㄠ ㄜ ㄓ ㄨ	著	著	挨上，附上 come close to, apply 挨上，附上	著陸(zhuó lù) 著陆 to land 著重(zhuó zhòng) emphasize
zī ㄗ	資	资	財物，費用，經歷 capital, expenses, experience 财物，费用，经历	資本(zī běn) 资本 capital 工資(gōng zī) 工资 wage 資產(zī chǎn) 资产 asset
zī ㄗ	滋	滋	生出，味道 give rise to, taste	滋養(zī yǎng) 滋养 nourish 滋味(zī wèi) taste

zī ㄗ	諮	咨	詢問 inquire 询问	諮詢(zī xún)咨询 to consult 諮商(zī shāng)咨商 discuss with
zī ㄗ	姿	姿	容貌，樣子 the looks, posture 容貌，样子	姿勢(zī shì)姿势 posture 低姿態(dī zī tài)低姿态 a low profile
zī ㄗ	茲	兹	這，現在 this, hereby 这，现在	茲事(zī shì) this matter
zǐ zi ㄗˇ˙ㄗ	子	子	兒子，對人的稱呼 son, you 儿子，对人的称呼	子孫(zǐ sūn)子孙 posterity 子女(zǐ nǚ) children 兒子(ér zi)儿子 son 桌子(zhuō zi) table 帽子(mào zi) hat
zǐ ㄗˇ	仔	仔	幼小的，周密 young animals or fowls, careful 幼小的，周密	仔細(zǐ xì)仔细 detail oriented
zǐ ㄗˇ	籽	籽	植物的種子 seeds of plants 植物的种子	菜籽(cài zǐ) vegetable seed 稻籽(dào zǐ) rice seed
zǐ ㄗˇ	梓	梓	落葉喬木，木材可 製器物；把木頭刻 成印書的版 catalpa, print block 落叶乔木，木材可 制器物；把木头刻 成印书的版	桑梓(sāng zǐ) one's native place 付梓(fù zǐ) send to the press
zǐ ㄗˇ	紫	紫	藍色和紅色調成的 顏色 purple 蓝色和红色调成的 颜色	紫色(zǐ sè) purple color 紫外線(zǐ wài xiàn) 紫外线 ultraviolet ray

zì ㄗ、	自	自	本人，當然的，從 oneself, natural, from 本人，当然的，从	自己(zì jǐ) oneself 自私(zì sī) selfish
zì ㄗ、	字	字	記錄語言的符號， 人的別號 written word, alias 记录语言的符号， 人的别号	字典(zì diǎn) dictionary 文字(wén zì) written word
zì ㄗ、	漬	渍	浸泡，污染的痕跡 soak in, stains 浸泡，污染的痕迹	油漬(yóu zì) 油渍 oil stain 漬水(zì shuǐ) 渍水 waterlogging
zōng ㄗㄨㄥ	宗	宗	祖先，同一家族， 目的 ancestor, of the same clan, goal	祖宗(zǔ zōng) ancestor 宗旨(zōng zhǐ) goal, purpose
zōng ㄗㄨㄥ	棕	棕	常綠喬木，葉作掌 狀分裂，樹幹圓直 palm tree 常绿乔木，叶作掌 状分裂，树干圆直	棕色(zōng sè) light brown 棕櫚樹(zōng lǘ shù) 棕榈树 palm tree
zōng ㄗㄨㄥ	綜	综	對事物或現象進行 分析，歸納整理 analyze and summarize 对事物或现象进行 分析，归纳整理	綜合(zōng hé) 综合 roundup
zōng ㄗㄨㄥ	鬃	鬃	豬等獸類頸上的長 毛 bristles 猪等兽类颈上的长 毛	鬃毛(zōng máo) bristles 豬鬃(zhū zōng) 猪鬃 pig's bristles
zōng ㄗㄨㄥ	蹤	踪	腳印，事物痕跡， 追隨 footprint, trace, follow 脚印，事物痕迹， 追随	行蹤(xíng zōng) 行踪 whereabouts 跟蹤(gēn zōng) 跟踪 to tail somebody

zǒng ㄗ ㄨˇ ㄥ	總	总	全部的，經常 entire, always 全部的，经常	總是(zǒng shì) 总是 always 總數(zǒng shù) 总数 sum total
zòng ㄗ ㄨˋ ㄥ	縱	纵	釋放，放任，即使 release, let drift, even if 释放，放任，即使	縱使(zòng shǐ) 纵使 even if 縱容(zòng róng) 纵容 abet
zòng ㄗ ㄨˋ ㄥ	粽	粽	用糯米等外包竹葉 或荷葉的角glutinous rice dumpling 用糯米等外包竹叶 或荷叶的角	粽子(zòng zi) glutinous rice dumpling
zōu ㄗ ㄡ	鄒	邹	姓氏 Chinese surname	
zǒu ㄗ ㄡˇ	走	走	步行，前往，離開 walk, to head for, leave 步行，前往，离开	走私(zǒu sī) smuggle 走路(zǒu lù) walk
zòu ㄗ ㄡˋ	奏	奏	音樂高低的拍子， 吹彈樂器 rhythm, play music 音乐高低的拍子， 吹弹乐器	節奏(jié zòu) 节奏 rhythm 演奏(yǎn zòu) play music
zòu ㄗ ㄡˋ	揍	揍	毆打 beat up 殴打	揍人(zòu rén) beat someone up 挨揍(ái zòu) get beaten
zòu ㄗ ㄡˋ	驟	骤	忽然，快速的 suddenly, swiftly	驟然(zòu rán) 骤然 suddenly 驟雨(zòu yǔ) 骤雨 sudden rain

zū ㄗ ㄨ	租	租	房子，田地或東西借給人用所收的代價　rent 房子，田地或东西借给人用所收的代价	房租(fáng zū) house rent 出租(chū zū) put up for rent
zú ㄗ ㄨˊ	足	足	人體，動物下肢，不缺乏，充滿 lower limb, enough, full of 人体，动物下肢，不缺乏，充满	足夠(zú gòu) 足够 sufficient 足球(zú qiú) soccer
zú ㄗ ㄨˊ	族	族	有血統關係的親屬、人種　clan 有血统关系的亲属、人种	種族(zhǒng zú) 种族 race 民族(mín zú) nation
zú ㄗ ㄨˊ	卒	卒	兵士，差役，死亡 soldier, attendant, die	獄卒(yù zú) 狱卒 prison guard 病卒(bìng zú) die of illness
zǔ ㄗ ㄨˇ	祖	祖	父母的父母，創始人，先人 grandparents, forefathers, founder 父母的父母，创始人，先人	祖父(zǔ fù) grandfather 祖先(zǔ xiān) ancestors
zǔ ㄗ ㄨˇ	組	组	分類單位，聯合 a group, to organize 分类单位，联合	組織(zǔ zhī) 组织 organization 重組(chóng zǔ) 重组 reorganize
zǔ ㄗ ㄨˇ	阻	阻	隔斷不通，擋住 disconnect, obstruct 隔断不通，挡住	阻礙(zǔ ài) 阻碍 obstruct 交通阻塞(jiāo tōng zǔ sè) traffic jam
zuān zuàn ㄗ ㄗ ㄨ ㄨˋ ㄢ ㄢ	鑽	钻	穿孔，深入研究，穿孔的器具　drill hole, study, a drill 穿孔，深入研究，穿孔的器具	鑽洞(zuān dòng) 钻洞 drill hole 鑽研(zuān yán) 钻研 assiduous research

zuǎn ㄗㄨㄢˇ	纂	纂	搜集並整理材料 collate 搜集并整理材料	編纂(biān zuǎn)编纂 compile
zuàn zuān ㄗ ㄗ ㄨ ㄨ ㄢ ㄢ	鑽	钻	金剛石，可做裝飾品，或用來切割玻璃 diamond 金刚石，可做装饰品，或用来切割玻璃	鑽石(zuàn shí) 钻石 diamond 鑽戒(zuàn jiè) 钻戒 diamond ring
zuàn ㄗㄨㄢˋ	賺	赚	因買賣或工作取得的利益 earning 因买卖或工作取得的利益	賺錢(zuàn qián) 赚钱 make money 穩賺(wěn zuàn) 稳赚 guarantee profit
zuǐ ㄗㄨㄟˇ	嘴	嘴	吃東西的器官；器具尖形的出口 mouth, nozzle 吃东西的器官；器具尖形的出口	嘴唇(zuǐ chún) lips 嘴巴(zuǐ ba) mouth
zuì ㄗㄨㄟˋ	最	最	極，無比的 extremely, incomparable 极，无比的	最好(zuì hǎo) the best 最大(zuì dà) the biggest
zuì ㄗㄨㄟˋ	罪	罪	犯法的行為，過失 crime, sin 犯法的行为，过失	犯罪(fàn zuì) commit crime 罪犯(zuì fàn) a criminal
zuì ㄗㄨㄟˋ	醉	醉	喝酒過度而神志不清，沈浸於 drunk, be steeped in 喝酒过度而神志不清，沈浸于	酒醉(jiǔ zuì) drunk 醉心於(zuì xīn yú) entirely absorbed in
zūn ㄗㄨㄣ	尊	尊	稱呼別人的父親，敬重，高貴 your father, respect, noble 称呼别人的父亲，敬重，高贵	尊敬(zūn jìng) respect 令尊(lìng zūn) your father

zūn ㄗㄨㄣ	遵	遵	依照，奉行 in accordance with, comform with	遵守(zūn shǒu) abide by (the rules) 遵照(zūn zhào) conform with
zūn ㄗㄨㄣ	鱒	鳟	銀白色魚類，夏天 到河的上游產卵， 秋冬初回到海裏 trout 银白色鱼类，夏天 到河的上游产卵， 秋冬初回到海里	鱒魚(zūn yú) 鳟鱼 trout
zuó ㄗㄨㄛˊ	昨	昨	過去，前一天 the past, yesterday 过去，前一天	昨日(zuó rì) yesterday
zuǒ ㄗㄨㄛˇ	左	左	"右"的相反，違 背 left, violate "右"的相反，违 背	左右(zuǒ yòu) left and right, about 左傾(zuǒ qǐng) 左倾 leftist
zuǒ ㄗㄨㄛˇ	佐	佐	幫助，輔助 help, assist 帮助，辅助	輔佐(fǔ zuǒ) 辅佐 assist 佐餐(zuǒ cān) taken with meal
zuò ㄗㄨㄛˋ	作	作	做成，進行，優美 的詩歌，文章 make into, carry out, works 做成，进行，优美 的诗歌，文章	作品(zuò pǐn) works 作戰(zuò zhàn) 作战 in a battle
zuò ㄗㄨㄛˋ	坐	坐	臀部休息在地上或 椅子上，搭乘 sit, ride a vehicle 臀部休息在地上或 椅子上，搭乘	坐下(zuò xià) sit down 坐車(zuò chē) 坐车 ride a car
zuò ㄗㄨㄛˋ	做	做	進行工作，舉行， 假裝 do work, hold, feign 进行工作，举行， 假装	做工(zuò gōng) to work 做主(zuò zhǔ) be the decision maker

zuò ㄗㄨˋㄛ	怍	怍	慚愧 feel ashamed 慚愧	愧怍(kuì zuò) feel ashamed
zuò ㄗㄨˋㄛ	座	座	坐位 seat	座位(zuò wèi) seat 滿座(mǎn zuò) 滿座 a full house

INDEX

Bold-faced page number denotes
the most commonly usage
粗體字頁碼表示最常見用法

-1-

10 (ten), **275**
11 (eleven), 90, 275
12 (twelve), 275
13 (thirteen), 275
14 (fourteen), 275
15 (fifteen), 154, 275
16 (sixteen), 275
17 (seventeen), 275
18 (eighteen), 275
19 (nineteen), 275
20 (twenty), 275
30 (thirty), 275
40 (forty), 275
50 (fifty), 275
60 (sixty), 201, 275
70 (seventy), 275
80 (eighty), 275
90 (ninety), 275
100 (one hundred), 6
1,000 (one thousand), 239
10,000 (ten thousand), 317
1,000,000 (one million), 6
10,000,000 (ten million), 239
100,000,000 (one hundred million), 369

-A-

a, 1, 2, 3, 4, 6, 8, 10, 12, 13, 15, 16
abandon, 228, 268
abbreviate, 272
abbreviation, 93, 103
abdicate, 254
abdomen, 55, 70, 72
abduct, 85
abet, 289, 423
ability, 17, 169, 178, 210
able-bodied man, 51, 417
abnormal, 115, 297
abolish, 64, 237
abominable, 327
aborigines, 310
abortion, 57
aboveboard, 167
abroad, 243
absentminded, 101, 108
absolutely, 148
absolve, 269
absorb, 250, 269, 328
abstain, 237
abstinence, 394
absurd, 203, 236, 300
abundance, 71, 72, 161
abundant, 16, 63, **66**, 254, 273, 372, 382
abuse, 164, **216**, 259
abyss, 384
accent, 241
accept, 56, 111, **133**, **279**
accident, 113, 276, 382
acclaim, 95
accommodate, 91, 127
accompany, 7, 67, **222**
accomplish, 27, 316

according to, 3, **146**, 258, 354, 359, **367**
accountant, 158
accounting, 158
accumulate, 114, **167**, 390
ace, 317, 381
achieve, 41, 305
achievement, 15, 115
acids, 241
acne, 222
acquiesce, 205
acre, 206
acrobatics, 389
act, 7, 111, 207, 261, 280, 300, 360
activity, 112, 330
actor, 384
actress, 160
acupuncture, 142, 401
acute, 37
add, 120, 304, 393
addicted, 373
addiction, 226, 373
addition, 120, 178
address, 26, 132, 408
adjust, 133
administration, 405
administrative, 16
admire, 140, **207**, 223, 245, 322, **337**, 362
admit, 68, 372
admonition, 77, 135
adopt, 17
adore, 30
adult, 41
adulteress, 229
adultery, 122, 229
advance, 49, 138
advantage, 23, 26, 171, 276, 377
advice, 178, 252, 411
advocate, 24
affirm, 253
again, 30, 72, 184, 261, **379**, **389**
agate, 189, **209**
age, 79, 118, 177, 189, 190, 211, 293, 316
agent, 302
aggression, 245
aggressor, 156
agile, 134, 171, 178, 202
agony, 143
agree, 216, 256, 350, 387, 390, 419
agreeable, 367
agreement, 1, 52, 238, 385
agriculture, 214
aid, 385
air, 33, 148, 331, 338
air force, 148
air raid, 331
air-conditioning, 168
airplane, 63, 114
air-raid shelter, 94
alcohol, 142
alcoholic, 350
alert, 304
alienate, 385
alike, 63
alimony, 266
alive, 272
all, 25, 53, 59, 61, 78, 97, 111, 112, 133, 134, **140**, 145, 164, 169, 180,

229, 241, 244, 258, 288, 291, 329, 414
all day long, 140
alley, 101, 184, 338
alliance, 197
allied, 197
alligator, 59
allocate, 15
almond, 255
almost, **336**
alms, 16, 274
already, 120, 368
also, 59, **365**, 369, 377
altar, 298
although, 292
aluminum, 185
always, **23**, 86, **339**, 423
ambassador, 275
ambition, 347, 366
ambush, 68
amend, 73
amendment, 52
amnesty, 269
amuse, 53
analyze, 14, 187, 232, 328, 422
anatomy, 135, 232
ancestor, 120, 334, 422
ancestral grave, 65
ancestral temple, 36
anchor, 193
ancient, 42, 52, 70, 77, **83**, 89, 91, 98, 118, 165, 277, 278, 307, 322, 324, 356, 368
ancient times, 42, 70, 83
anecdote, 371
anemia, 229
anesthesia, 189
anger, 66, 215, 388
angle, 131
angling, 50
angry, 25, **66**, 209, **215**, 237
animal, 33, **53**, 272
animal husbandry, 350
annex, 15, 138, 312
annihilate, 123, 132
anniversary, 118, 412
announce, 272, 383
annoyed, 217
anonymous, 211
answer, 41, 198
ant, 368
antagonistic, 47
antiquated, 142
antler, 183, 257
ants, 190
anus, 75
anxious, 41
apartment, 383
ape, 385
apologize, **9**, 241, 408
appeal, 382
appear, 97, 182, 336
appearance, **14**, 142, 194, 257, 339
appendix, 72
apple, 230
appoint, 183, 229, 256, 321
appointment, 229, 385
appreciate, 344
apprehensions, 106
approach, **138**, 153, 176, 181, 338
appropriate, 43, 238, 387

433

mule, 188
multinational, 157
multiplication, 27
multiply, 10, 27
multitude, 118, 253
mumble, 310
munch, 131
mundane, 158, 184, 375
mural, 13
murder, 90, 263, 347
murdered, 90, 382
muscle, 114, 258
museum, 86
mushroom, 83, 149
music, 166, 198, 250, **371**, 386, 423
mustard, 135
mute, 357
mutual, 103, 337, 415
my, 324
mysterious, 271, 351
mystery, 4, 198
myth, 271

-N-

nagging, 187, 295
nail, 51, 121
naked, 188
name, 1, 52, 62, 70, 91, 92, 95, 105, 138, 144, 188, 189, **202**, 208, 239, 245, 277, 282, 289, 322, 324, **346**, 371, 412
namelist, 42
nanny, 206
napkin, 408
narcotics, 54
narrate, 283, 291, 350
narrow, 142, 182, 333, 395
narrowminded, 147
nasal, 304
nasopharynx, 358
nasty, 321
nation, 89, 188, 197, 424
national defense, 62
national emblem, 109
national flag, 235
national martyr, 267
nationality, 89, 117
natural, 233, 304, 422
naturalization, 87
naughty, 225
nauseating, 58, 217
navel, 235
navigate, 93
navy, 148
near, 138, 176, 306
neck, 16, 79, 140, 339
necklace, 339
needle, 33, 155, 401
negative, 371
neglect, 42, 191
negligence, 101
neighbor, 176
neighborhood, 62
neon, 210
nephew, 272, 407
nepotism, 253
nerves, 43
nervous, 137, 234, 397
nest, 24, 324
nestling, 32
net, 187, 318, 398
network, 188, 318

New Year, 43, **211**, 331, **344**, 384
news, 58, 90, 237, 323, 328, 355, 371
newsletter, 355
newspaper, 13, 408
next, 78, 119, 333
nickname, 95
niece, 272, 407
night, 25, 207, 270, 316, 340, 366, 413
night soil, 22
nightmare, 197
nine, 142
no, 16, 21, 63, 68, 194, 237, 284, 322, 325, 406
noble, 100, 267, 425
noisy, 25, 103, 209, 254, 351, 392
nonsense, 88, 101, 332
noodle, 200, 305
normal, 357, 405
north, 10, 287, 320
North Pole, 10, 116
nose, 11, 213, 232, 346
nostril, 11, 155
not, 2, 3, 9, **16**, 41, 43, 63, 64, 68, 84, 94, 95, 108, 110, 111, 134, 137, 155, 171, 172, 191, 196, 204, 209, 227, 239, 246, 247, 249, 256, 262, 268, 274, 278, 281, 287, 289, 318, 322, 325, 327, 328, 331, 333, 335, 340, 342, 346, 349, 364, 365, 385, 389, 398
not only, 43, 137
notebook, 16
notice, 243
notorious, 117
noun, 36
nourish, 420
November, 386
now, 36, 81, 120, 136, 237, 258
nowadays, 136
nozzle, 425
nuclear, 96
nude, 188
numb, 12, 189, 206
number, 6, 48, 84, **95**, 173, 189, 234, 239, 274, **283**, 288, 366
numbness, 12, 206
numerous, 65, 97, 271
nun, 210
nunnery, 2
nurse, 150
nursery, 233, 313
nurture, 69, 382

-O-

oath, 277, 351
oatmeal, 190
obese, 411
obesity, 221
obituary, 72
objective, 46, 154
oblivion, 358
obscene, 321, 372
obscure, 358
observe, 53, 85, 127, 277
obsessed, 198, 226
obstacle, 398
obstinate, 214, 128
obstruct, 2, 44, 78, 163, 209, 424
obtain, 113, 124, 165, 205, 215, 375, 417

obvious, 336
occasional, 402
occupation, 93, 366, **407**
occupy, 5, 19, 146, 396
occur, 196, 272, 400
ocean, 192, 317, 362
October, 386
odd, 283
ode, 217
odor, 262, 322
of course, 162
offend, 194
offender, 167
offensive, 80, 300
offer, 70, 120, 146, 313, 337
offerings, 81
office, 6, 144, 181, 282, 294, 306, 321, 356, 378
official, 25, 47, 68, 85, 106, 170, 175, 184, 276, 327, 399, 407
oil, 140, 378, 394, 422
ointment, 68
old, 83, 92, 142, 165, 190, 231, 234, 259, 290, 316, 324, 350, 365
olive, 74, 164
Olympic Games, 4
omen, 89, 400, 403
omit, 182, 368
on, 5, 8, 19, 71, 77, 85, 152, 405
on fire, 65, 175, 237
once, 43, 143
oncoming, 374
one, 3, 6, 7, 9, 14, 16, 20, 24, 28, 39, 46, 48, 55, 56, 60, 71, 78, 90, 91, 101, 118, 134, 140, 146, 158, 183, 190, 191, 198, 200, 201, 213, 214, 215, 218, 227, 229, 230, 232, 239, 242, 245, 278, 279, 280, 282, 301, 315, 323, 331, 342, 346, 355, 362, 364, 366, 367, 380, 381, 383, 398, 400, 412, 415, 420, 421
oneself, 65, 66, 117, 170, 204, 346, 402, 422
one-sided, 227
only, 43, 137, 320, **408**
ooze, 271
open, 21, 23, 90, 103, 113, **150**, 167, 175, 190, 224, 225, 236, 244, 288, 289, 308, 313, 314, 334, 397, 403
openminded, 165
opera, 138
operate, 122
operation, 44
ophthalmology, 360
opinion, 99, 125, 274, 369, 371, 379, 380
opponent, 55
opportunity, 114, 327, 332, 382
opposite, 61
oppression, 356
or, 3, 49, 52, 55, 56, 65, 68, 73, 112, 127, 132, 152, 153, 156, 159, 184, 205, 215, 236, 260, 275, 278, 281, 296, 335, 339, 340, 351, 365, 393, 395, 421
oral, 65, 72
orally, 65
orange, 27, 144
orbit, 87
orchid, 163

441

order, 13, 21, 37, 65, 95, 135, 175, 178, **203**, 235, 275, 305, 306, 350, 354, 399, 409, 412
ordinary, 61, 226, 230, 233, 284, 411
organ, 16, 85, 238
organization, 277, 405, 424
organize, 82, 424
origami, 400
origin, 11, 369
original, 291, 384, 411
oriole, 168, 373
ornament, 107, 222, 277
orphan, 32, 82
osmanthus, 88
ostrich, 313
other, 36, 52, 59, 103, 178, 235, 244, 296
otter, 296
outbreak, 209
outdated, 142
outdoor, 103
outline, 75, 187
out-of-the-way, 226
outside, 14, 130, 315
outsider, 315
outstanding, 348, 420
oval, 313
ovary, 186
overaged, 24
over-ambitious, 327
overcoat, 302
overdraft, 309
overflow, 191
overhaul, 61
overindulgence, 211
overseas, 243
overstate, 157
overthrow, 72, 311
overturn, 48, 61, 72
overworked, 39
ovulate, 186
owe, 71, 241, 268
owl, 193
owner, 49
ox, 131, 206
oxidize, 362
oxygen, 362
oyster, 93, 206

-P-
package, 8
paddy, 45, 198, 204
page, 66, 366
pagoda, 296
pain, 10, 92, 157, 302
painful, 32, 302, 309
paint, 234, 310
painting, 69
pair, 285
palace, 12, 42, 49, 80, 108
palanquin, 132
pallid, 39
palm, 184, 397, 422
palpitate, 119, 223
pampered, 130
pan, 185, 301
panda, 193, 347
panic, 107
panicking, 107
panting, 33
papaya, 206

paper, 9, 14, 24, 64, 264, 408
parachute, 129, 261
paragraph, 55
paralyzed, 298
parcel, 89
pardon, 283
parenthesis, 102
Paris, 168
park, 80
parrot, **326**, 374
part, **16**, 20, 52, 144, 172, 252, 262, 268, 316, 329, 362
partial, 227
participate, 18
particle, 5, 169, 209
partner, 112, 342
partridge, 83
party, 44, 126, 360, 369
pass, 13, 33, 86, 89, 139, 220, 251, 278, 290, 308, 309
pass away, 251, 278
passenger, 27
passion, 255
passionate, 255
passport, 103
past, 20, 83, 108, 251, 269, 278, 293, 318, 328, 341, 368, 380, 413, 426
paste, 14, 76, 102, 128, 210
pastor, 206
pastry, 76
patent, 416
path, 140, 235
patience, 209
patricide, 278
patrol, 188, 354
pause, 56
pavilion, 78, 307
paw, 347, 416
pawn, 44, 233
pay, 6, 63, **70**, 81, 129, 132, 154, 179, 208, 222, 284, 286, 338, 416
payment, 70, 132, 154, 237, 286, 376
pea, 2, **53**, 95, 121, 199, 213, 297, 316, 360
peace, 2, 95, 199, 213, 297, 360
peaceful, 2, 305
peach, 302
peacock, 253
peak, 66, 122, 318
peak season, 318
peanut, 153, 198
pear, 168
pearl, 153, 414
peasant, 214
peck, 420
peculiar, 87, 328
pedantic, 379
peddle, 53, 62
peddler, 62
peek, 159
peel, 15, 275, 340
peer, 306
peerage, 148
pellet, 43, 169
pen, 12, 406
penalty, 345
pencil, 12, 42, 239, 340
pendant, 418
penetrate, 33
penguin, 237

peninsula, 44
pension, 351, 362
people, 17, 18, 21, 50, 54, 71, 82, 83, 92, 94, 98, 103, 105, 112, 117, 118, 131, 187, 202, 243, 284, 318
pepper, 130
percent, 5
percentage, 6
perception, 74, 148, 346
perch, 234
perform, 261, 360
performer, 33
perfume, 337
period, 55
perk, 244
permeate, 198, 271
permit, 350, 380, 387
perpetrator, 400
perplexed, 180
perseverance, 98, 370
persevere, 98
persimmon, 276
person, 11, 46, 49, 51, 52, 94, 96, 104, 115, 116, 132, 149, 157, 158, 164, 165, 196, 200, 205, 221, 232, 259, 264, 308, 309, 318, 319, 320, 327, 332, 338, **340**, 342, 369, 375, 397, 401, 413
personality, 78, 255, 347
persuade, 110, 286
perverted, 85, 170
pessimistic, 10
pester, 21, 142
pestilence, 323, 370
pestle, 33
petal, 8
petroleum, 274, 378
petulant, 231
pharmaceutical, 119
phenomenon, 218
Philippines, 63
philosophy, 400
phoenix, 68, 107
photo, 188
photocopy, 375
photography, 269
phrase, 36
physically, 39
physician, 202, 367, 383
piano, 75, 127, 245
pick, 17, 124, 218, 301
pickpocket, 5, 218
picky, 303
picture, 14, 107
piecemeal, 177, 293
pierce, 33, 36
pig, 163, 258, 312, 321, **414**, 422
pigeon, 77, 83, 142
pigment, 291
pile, 38, 51, 55, 114
pill, 42, 199
pillar, 416
pillow, 402
pimp, 9
pin, 14, 21, 313
pinch, 213
pine, 289
pineapple, 16, 68, 168
pingpong, 220
pipe, 37, 86
pirates, 324
pistil, 259

總 筆 畫 查 字 表

部首	筆畫		
1 畫			
一	一	367	
乙	乙	369	
2 畫			
一	七	234	
	丁	51	
丿	乃	208	
乙	九	142	
亅	了	166	
二	二	59	
人	人	255	
入	入	259	
八	八	5	
几	几	114	
刀	刀	44	
	刁	50	
力	力	167	
十	十	274	
又	又	379	

3 畫		
一	下	333
	三	261
	丈	398
	上	267
、	丸	316
丿	久	142
	么	363
乙	乞	236
	也	365
二	于	379
亠	亡	317
几	凡	61
刀	刃	255
勹	勺	267
十	千	239

又	叉	20
口	口	156
土	土	310
士	士	275
夕	夕	329
大	大	41
女	女	215
子	子	421
	孑	134
寸	寸	39
小	小	340
山	山	265
巛	川	33
工	工	80
己	己	117
	已	368
巾	巾	136
干	干	74
弓	弓	80
手	才	17

4 畫		
一	丑	31
	丏	73
	不	16
丨	中	411,412
、	丹	42
丿	之	405
亅	予	380
二	互	103
	斤	306
	井	140
	五	326
人	仆	232
	介	135
	今	136
	仇	31

什	271,274	
仁	255	
仍	256	
儿 元	384	
允	387	
八 六	180	
公	80	
入 內	210	
凵 凶	347	
刀 切	244	
分	65	
勹 勾	81	
勿	327	
匀	387	
匕 化	104	
十 升	272	
午	326	
又 及	116	
友	378	
反	61	
大 太	297	
天	304	
夫	68	
子 孔	155	
小 少	268	
尢 尤	377	
尸 尺	29	
屮 屯	312	
幺 幻	106	
弓 引	372	
心 心	344	
戈 戈	77	
戶 戶	103	
手 手	279	
扎	394	
支 支	406	

文 文	323	
斗 斗	53	
斤 斤	136	
方 方	62	
日 日	256	
月 月	386	
木 木	206	
欠 欠	241	
止 止	408	
歹 歹	41	
比 比	12	
毛 毛	193	
氏 氏	277	
水 水	286	
火 火	112	
爪 爪	416	
父 父	71	
片 片	227	
牙 牙	356	
牛 牛	214	
犬 犬	252	
玉 王	317	

5 畫		
一 丙	15	
且	244	
丘	248	
世	276	
二 井	140	
、 主	415	
丿 乎	101	
乏	60	
人 付	70	
代	42	
他	296	
令	178	
仙	334	

仗	398	
仕	276	
仔	421	
以	368	
几 兄	347	
充	30	
冂 冉	254	
冊	19	
冫 冬	52	
凵 凹	3	
凸	309	
出	31	
刀 刊	150	
力 功	79	
加	120	
勹 包	8	
匆	37	
匕 北	10	
十 半	7	
卉	110	
人 仟	239	
卜 卡	150	
占	396	
厶 去	251	
口 叨	50	
叭	44	
叩	156	
叫	132	
叮	51	
可	154	
古	83	
另	178	
台	297	
句	146	
只	408	
召	399	

451

部	字	頁	部	字	頁	部	字	頁	部	字	頁	部	字	頁
艸	芒	192		併	15		呇	143	子	孟	197	戶	房	62
見	見	125		佩	223		周	412		孤	82		戾	170
見	見	125		佻	305		呸	222		季	119		所	294
艮	良	173		來	162		咆	221	宀	定	52	手	承	27
艸	芒	192		佬	166		呵	95		官	85		拔	5
見	見	125		例	170		呼	101		宙	413		抱	9
角	角	131		供	81		咐	72		宗	422		拌	7
言	言	359		佳	121		呢	209, 210		宜	367		拍	219
谷	谷	83		佼	131		咀	144	小	尚	266		抛	221
豆	豆	53		侏	414		呻	270	尸	居	136		拼	229
貝	貝	11		使	275		味	322		居	142		披	225
赤	赤	29		侍	277	口	固	84		屈	249		抹	204
走	走	423		依	367	土	坡	231	山	岡	75		捆	206
足	足	424	儿	兔	311		坪	230		岸	3		抵	47
身	身	270		兒	59		坦	299		岩	359		抬	297
車	車	25	入	兩	173		垃	162	山	岳	386		拖	313
辛	辛	344	八	典	49		塔	296	巾	帕	218		拓	314
辰	辰	25		具	145		坷	154		帖	306		拉	162
辵	迢	237		其	235		坤	160	干	幸	346		拐	85
	巡	354	凵	函	91	夕	夜	366	广	府	70		拘	143
	迅	354	刀	券	252	大	奔	11		底	47		拒	145
	迁	379		到	45		奉	67		店	49		招	399
邑	邦	8		刮	84		奈	208	廴	延	358		拙	419
	那	208		刻	154		奇	235	弓	弧	102		折	21
	邪	342		制	409		奄	358	彳	征	404		抽	30
	邢	345		刷	284	女	妻	234		往	318		押	356
里	里	169		刺	36		妾	245	心	忿	66	攴	放	63
阜	防	62	十	協	342		委	321		念	212	斤	斧	70
	阮	259		卓	420		妹	195		忽	101	方	於	379
8 畫				卒	424		姆	206		忠	411	日	昆	160
丿	乖	85	己	巷	338		妮	210	心	怕	218		昏	111
乙	乳	258	卜	卦	85		妳	211		怦	223		昌	22
亅	事	276	卩	卷	147		姑	82		怪	85		昇	272
二	些	341	又	取	250		姊	135		怯	245		昂	3
二	亞	357		受	279		姐	135		性	347		易	370
亠	京	138		叔	281		姓	346		怍	427		旺	318
	享	338	口	命	203		始	275		怡	367		明	202
人	佰	6		和	95&93		姍	266	戈	或	112	月	朋	223

455

部首	字	頁
	恤	351
	恃	277
戶	扁	13
手	拜	6
手	拼	229
	挑	305
	拱	81
	拷	152
	指	408
	拯	404
	持	28
	拾	274
	拭	278
	拴	285
	按	3
	挖	315
攴	故	83
	政	405
方	施	274
旡	既	120
日	星	345
	春	35
	是	278
	昧	196
	昨	426
	映	375
木	某	205
	柏	6
	柄	15
	東	124
	柒	234
	查	20
	柔	257
	染	254
	柳	179
	柑	74
	枴	85
	柯	153
	枯	156
	枷	121
	架	122
	柱	416
	柿	276
	柚	378
止	歪	315
歹	殆	42
	殃	361
殳	段	55
气	氟	68
水	派	219
	洞	53
	流	179
	洛	188
	活	112
	洪	99
	津	137
	洗	331
	洽	238
	洵	347
	洲	412
	洋	362
火	為	321
	炭	299
	炳	15
	炬	145
	炫	352
	炸	394,393
牛	牲	272
犬	狠	97
	狡	131
	狩	280
玉	玻	16
	玲	177
	珍	401
	珊	265
甘	甚	271
田	界	136
	畏	322
疒	疤	5
	疫	370
白	皇	108
	皆	133
皿	盃	10
	盆	223
	盅	411
	盈	374
目	盼	220
	眉	195
	眈	56
	盾	56
	看	150, 151
	相	339,337
	省	272,346
矛	矜	137
石	砍	151
	砌	238
	砂	264
	研	359
示	祈	235
内	禹	381
禾	秒	201
	科	153
	秋	248
穴	突	310
	穿	33
竹	竿	74
糸	紅	99
	紀	118
	紂	413
	紉	256
	約	385
缶	缸	75
羊	美	195
羽	羿	369
而	耐	209
	耍	284
耳	耶	365
肉	胞	8
	胚	222
	胖	221
	胎	296
	胡	101
肉	背	10
	胃	413
	胄	321
艸	茅	193
	茂	193
	苗	200
	范	61
	苔	297
	苟	81
	苛	153
	苦	157
	茁	419
	若	260
	英	373
虍	虐	216
虫	虹	99
行	衍	360
衣	衫	265
西	要	364
言	訃	72
	訂	52
	計	118
	負	71
貝	貞	402
走	赴	71
	赳	142
足	趴	218
車	軌	87
	軍	148
辵	迫	231
	迪	47
	迢	305
	述	283
邑	郎	164
	郊	130
酉	酋	249
里	重	30,411
門	悶	285
阜	陌	204
	陋	182
	降	338
	限	336
面	面	200
革	革	78
韋	韋	320
韭	韭	142
音	音	371
頁	頁	366
風	風	66
飛	飛	63
食	食	274
首	首	279
香	香	337

10 畫

部首	字	頁
丿	乘	27
人	倍	10
	們	196
	俸	68
	倒	45
	倘	300
	倪	210
	倆	173
	倫	187

	個	78	土	埋	190		徑	140	
	候	101		埃	1		徐	349	
	借	136	夂	夏	334	心	恭	80	
	俱	145	大	套	302	心	恐	155	
	倔	148		奚	329		息	328	
	倦	147	女	婷	229		恥	29	
	倩	241		娩	200		恕	283	
	修	348		娘	212		恩	59	
	值	406		姬	115		恙	363	
	倉	18		娟	146		悍	92	
	俺	2		婆	294		悔	109	
	倚	368		娥	58		悄	242	
	倭	324		娛	380		悚	289	
儿	党	44	子	孫	294		悟	327	
八	兼	123	宀	宮	80		悅	386	
冖	冥	203		害	90	戶	扇	266	
	冤	384		家	121	手	拿	208	
冫	凋	50		宵	340		拳	252	
	凍	53		容	257		捕	16	
	凌	178		宰	389		挺	307	
刀	剮	15		宴	360		捏	213	
	剖	232	寸	射	269		挪	216	
	剔	303	尸	屜	115		捆	160	
	剛	75		屑	343		捐	146	
匸	匪	64		展	396		挾	342	
厂	原	384	山	峰	66		振	402	
又	叟	290		島	44		捉	419	
口	唐	300		峻	149		挫	40	
口	哪	208		峭	244		挨	1	
	哥	77		峽	333	攴	效	341	
	哭	156	工	差	20,21	斗	料	175	
	哼	98	巾	席	330	方	旁	221	
	哮	341		師	273		旅	185	
	哲	400	广	庭	307	日	晃	108	
	哨	268		庫	157		晉	138	
	唆	294		座	427		時	274	
	員	384	弓	弱	260		晏	360	
口	圉	233	彳	徒	310		書	280	

月	朗	165		涉	269
	朕	403		浴	382
	朔	287	火	烙	166
木	桃	302		烈	175
	栗	170		烤	152
	桌	419		烘	98
	桑	262		烊	363
	案	2	鳥	鳥	212
	格	78	父	爹	51
	根	79	牛	特	302
	桂	88	犬	狼	165
	核	96		狹	333
	桓	105	玉	班	6
	栖	234		珮	222
	校	341&133		琉	179
	桐	349		珠	414
	桎	410	瓦	瓶	230
	株	414	田	畔	220
	梳	281		畝	206
	栓	285		留	179
	栽	389		畜	350,33
	桅	319	广	病	15
歹	殉	355		疲	225
	殊	281		疽	43
殳	殷	371		疼	302
气	氦	91		疾	117
	氣	237		症	404
	氧	362	皮	皰	222
水	泰	297	皿	益	370
	浮	69	目	眠	199
	涅	213		眩	352
	涂	310		眨	394
	浪	165		眞	401
	海	90	矢	矩	144
	浩	94	石	破	231
	涓	146		砲	222
	消	340		砸	389
	浙	401	示	祝	415

	得	45		採	17	水	淡	43	
	徙	331		措	40		淘	301	
	從	37		掃	262		添	304	
	御	383		掩	360		涙	167	
心	您	213	反	敗6, 敝12			淋	177	
	患	106		敏	202		涼	173	
	悉	329		教	133		淪	187	
	悠	377		救	143		涵	91	
	惉	49		啓	236		淮	104	
	惕	304		敘350, 教3			混	112	
	惣	101	斗	斜	342		淨	141	
	悸	119	斤	斬	396		淺	240	
	悽	234	方	旋	352		清	247	
	情	247		族	424		淅	328	
	惜	329	日	晝	413		涎	335	
	悵	23		晨	26		深	270	
	悴	39		晤	327		淑	280	
	惟	320		晚	316		涯	357	
	惋	317		曹	19		液	366	
	惆	318	月	望	318		淹	357	
戈	戚	234	木	梵	62		淫	372	
手	排	219		棄	237		淤	379	
	捧	224		梆	8		淵	384	
	掏	301		梅	195	火	烹	223	
	探	300		梯	303		烽	67	
	推	311		條	305		焊	93	
	捻	212		桶	308		鹵	182	
	掛	84		梨	168	爻	爽	286	
	接	133		梁	173	牛	牽	237	
	捷	134		桿	74	犬	猛	197	
	掘	148		梗	79		猙	403	
	捲	146		械	344		猖	22	
	掐	238		梓	421		猜	17	
	掀	334		梭	294	玄	率	285	
	掙	403	欠	欲	253	王	理	169	
	捨	268	殳	殺	263		球	249	
	授	279	毛	毫	94		現	336	

瓦	瓶	230		粗	37
	瓷	36	糸	累	167
甘	甜	304		紮	393
生	產	22		絆7, 統308	
田	畢	12		細	332
	略	187		終	410
	異	370		紳	270
疋	疏	281		組	424
疒	痕	97	缶	缽	16
	痙	251	羊	羞	348
	痤	252	羽	習	330
	痔410, 疵35		耳	聊	174
	瘂	368		聆	178
白	皎	132	肉	脖	16
皿	盉	159		脯	232
	盒	96		脫	313
	盛	273		脣	35
目	眷	147	舟	船	33
	眾	411	艸	莫	204
	眺	306		莓	195
	眶	159		莽	192
	眼	360		莉170荷96	
示	票	228		英	121
	祭	120		莖	139
	祥	338		莒	144
禾	移	368		莊	417
穴	窕	306		莘	271
立	竟	140		莎	264
	章	397	虍	處	33
竹	笨	11	虫	蛋	43
	符	69		蚶	91
	笛	47		蚯	248
	第	48		蛆	250
	笠	170		蛀	416
	答	297		蛇	268
米	粘	395	行	術	283
	粒	169	衣	被	10

袍 221	都 53,54	十 博 16	尊 425	揚 362
袖 348	邑 郭 89	厂 厥 148	尢 就 143	握 325
袋 42	酉 酗 350	口 單 42	山 嵐 163	援 385
袈 120	里 野 366	喬 243	巾 帽 194	攴 敦 56
見 覓 198	金 釣 50	喜 331	幄 325,幅69	敢74, 敵23
規 87	釧 34	啼 302	幺 幾 117	散 262
言 訪 63	門 閉 12	唾 314	广 廊 164	文 斑 7
訣 147	阜 陪 222	喇 162	廄 143	斤 斯 288
許 350	陶 301	喝 95	廂 337	日 普 233
設 269	陵 178	喉 100	廁 19	晶 140
訟 290	陸 183	喊 92	彡 彭 224	景 140
訝 357	陷 336	嗦 420	彳 復 71	晴 247
豆 豉 83	陳 26	喚 105	徨 107	晰 330
豕 豚 312	陰 371	善 266	循 354	智 409
貝 貧 229	佳 雀 253	喪 262	心 悲 10	暑 282
販 62	雨 雪 353	喧 351	悶 196	日 最 425
貪 298	頁 頂 52	喘 33	惑 113	替 304
貫 86	頃 247	哟 375	惠 111	曾 393,20
貨 112	魚 魚 380	喂 321	惡 327	月 期 235
責 392	鳥 鳥 212	喻 382	惰 57	朝 24
赤 赦 269	鹿 鹿 183	口 圍 319	惱 209	木 棒 8
足 趾 408	麥 麥 190	土 報,堡 9	慨 150	棚 224
車 軟 259	麻 麻 189	壺 102	惶 107	棉 199
辶 逢 67	**12 畫**	堤 303	惻 20	棟 53
逗 53	人 傘 261	堪 151	愕 58	棺 86
透 309	備 10	場 23	愉 379	棍 88
途 310	傅 71	大 奠 49	手 掌 397	棵 153
通 308	傀 160	女 媒 194	描 200	棘 117
連 171	傢 121	媚 196	提 302	椒 130
逑 87	傑 134	婷 307	揮 108	樓 234
逍 340	日 最 425	婿 350	換 105	棋 236
這 401	几 凱 150	媛 384	揭 133	植 407
逐 415	刀 割 77	屢 184	揀 124	棧 396
逞 28	創 34	广 寐 195	插 20	椎 418
逝 278	剩 273	富 71	捶 35	棄 391
造 392	力 勞 165	寒 92	揉 258	棕 422
速 292	勛 353	寓 382	搓 423	森 263
邑 部 16	勝 272	寸 尋 354	揹 367	椅 369

461

傷	266	干 幹	74	暉	108	煤	195	禁	138
催	38	广 廉	172	暇	333	煩	61	内 禽	246
傲	3	虜	334, 264	暄	351	煉	173	萬	317
傭	376	廈	280	暗	3	煥	106	禾 稚	409
刂 剿	132	弋 弒	278	暈	387	煌	108	稠	30
力 募	207	殳 彀	153	會	109	煙	358	竹 筷	158
勤	246	彳 徬	221	木 楓	67	父 爺	365	節	134
勢	276	微	319	榔	365	犬 猾	104	米 粵	386
匚 匯	111	心 愛	2	楷	150	獅	273	糸 綁	8
口 嗎	189	感	74	極	116	猿	385	經	139
嗆	242	想	338	楚	32	玉 瑙	209	絹	147
嗅	348	愁	31	椰	365	瑚	102	网 置	409
嗤	28	惹	255	業	366	瑕	330	罩	400
嗜	278	慈	36	楊	362	瑞	259	署	282
嗓	262	意	371	欠 歇	342	田 當	43	罪	425
嗚	325	愚	379	止 歲	293	疒 瘁	12	羊 群	253
嗡	324	愈	382	殳 殿	49	痰	299	羨	337
囗 圍	384	愧	160	毀	109	麻	189	耳 聘	229
圓	384	慌	107	毛 毽	126	皿 盟	197	聖	272
塌	296	慎	271	水 滂	220	盞	396	聿 肆	288
塘	300	慍	388	滅	201	目 睦	207	肅	292
塔	296	手 搏	16	滇	304	督	54	肉 腦	209
填	304	手 搬	7	滔	301	睪	76	腳	131
塗	310	搭	41	溺	211	睫	134	腺	337
塊	158	搗	45	溜	178	睛	139	腥	345
塞	261	搪	300	溝	81	睜	403	腫	411
塑	292	搞	76	滑	104	矢 矮	2	腸	23
塢	327	搶	242	溪	329	石 碑	10	白 舅	143
士 壺	102	捶	35	渲	322	碰	224	與	381
大 奧	4	搓	39	準	419	碉	50	舟 艇	307
女 媽	189	搜	290	溶	257	磁	36	艸 葡	232
嫉	117	損	294	溫	322	碌	184	董	52
嫁	132	搖	364	源	384	碎	293	落	188
媳	331	搗	45	火 煎	123	碗	317	葛	78
嫌	335	攴 敬	141	煦	351	示 祿	184	葵	160
嫂	263	斤 新	344	照	399	福	69	葫	101
山 嵩	289	日 暖	25	煞	264	裸	188	葷	111

部首	字	頁	部首	字	頁	部首	字	頁	部首	字	頁	字	頁
	葬	391		路	183	革	靶	5	士	壽	280	摸	204, 搏 16
	葱	37		跟	79		靴	353	夕	夢	197	摟	181
	葉	366		跪	88	頁	頒	6, 頓 56		夥	112	搯	400
虍	虜	183		跨	157		頌	290	大	奪	56	摘	394
	號	95		跡	115		頑	316	女	嫖	223	摔	284
虫	蜂	67	身	躲	57		預	382		嫡	47	摧	38
	蜇	400		較	133	食	飽	9, 飾 277		嫡	47	敲	242
	蛻	312	車	軾	278		飼	289		嫩	210	幹	74
	蛾	58		載	390	馬	馱	313	宀	寞	205	旗	235
	蜈	326	辰	農	214		馴	354		寧	213	暝	203
衣	補	16	辵	逼	11		馳	29		寥	174	暨	120
	衰	284		遍	14	鳥	鳩	142		寡	84	暢	24
	裊	213		達	41		鼎	52		寢	246	榜	8
	裙	253		道	45	鼓	鼓	83		寨	395	榴	179
	裝	417		過	89	鼠	鼠	282		察	20	構	82
	裟	264		遐	333		**14 畫**			實	274	榾	75
	裕	382		遏	59	人	僕	232	寸	對	55	槐	105
角	解	135		遊	377		僚	175	尸	屢	184	槍	241
言	該	73		達	320		僥	131	山	嶇	250	榨	394
	詭	88		逾	380		催	83	巾	幣	12	槌	35
	誇	157		遇	382		僑	243		慢	191	榮	256
	話	104		運	387		像	339		幕	207	歌	78
	誅	109	酉	酪	202		僧	263		幗	89	歎	241
	詮	251		酬	31	几	兢	139	广	廖	175	漂	228
	詳	338	采	釉	378	刀	劃	104		廓	161	漠	205
	詢	354	金	鈾	378	厂	厭	360	廿	弊	13	滿	191
	誅	414		鈴	177	口	嘆	299	彡	彰	397	漫	191
	誠	28		鉛	239		嘉	121	彳	徹	25	滴	46
	詩	273		鉗	240		嘗	23	心	態	297	滌	47
	試	278	阜	隔	78		嗽	291		慇	372	漏	182
	詣	371		隙	332		嘔	220		慢	191	滾	88
豕	豢	106	佳	雋	149	囗	圖	310		慟	309	漢	92
貝	賈	122		雅	357		團	311		慣	86	滸	103
	賄	111	雨	雹	9	土	墓	207		慚	18	滬	103
	資	420		電	49		墊	49		慷	151	漸	126
	賊	393		雷	166		境	141	戈	慘	18	漆	234
足	跳	306		零	177		塵	26		截	134	漩	352
			青	靖	141		墅	284	手	搬	228	滯	410

廚 32	暮 207	皿 盤 219	膠 129	賣 190
廝 288	暫 390	目 瞇 198	膝 330	賢 335
弓 彈 43	木 標 14	瞑 203	舌 舖 233	質 407
彡 影 375	橫 98	瞌 153	艸 蓬 224	賞 267
彳 德 46	樂 386	瞎 332	蔓 192	走 趟 301
徵 404	樓 181	石 磅 8	蔑 201	趣 251
心 慕 207	樟 397	磐 220	蔣 128	石 碰 224
慶 247	樞 281	磊 167	蔗 401	足 踏 296
憂 377	樣 362	磕 153	蔬 281	踢 302
慮 185	欠 歎 299	確 253	蔡 18	踐 126
慧 110	歐 217	磋 39	蔭 371	踩 17
慫 289	殤 217	禾 稻 45	虫 蝙 13	身 躺 301
慰 322	殳 毆 217	稿 76	蝠 69	車 輛 174
慾 382	毅 370	稽 115	蝶 51	輪 187
憫 202	水 漿 128	稷 120	蝸 324	輝 108
憤 66	潑 231	稼 122	蝴 102	辵 遮 400
憐 172	潘 219	穴 窮 248	蝗 107	遭 391
憬 140	漂 299	窯 364	蝦 332	適 278
憔 243	潢 107	竹 篇 227	行 衝 30	遨 3
憧 30	潔 134	範 61	衣 褐 96	邑 鄧 46
手 摯 204	澆 129	箭 127	言 誕 43	鄰 176
摰 410	澗 125	箱 337	談 298	鄭 405
撥 15	潛 240	米 糊 102	調 305	酉 醉 425
播 15	潮 24	糸 編 13	諒 174	醋 38
撲 232	潤 260	緬 200	論 187	醯 357
撫 69	火 熟 279	締 48	課 154	金 鋪 233
撈 165	熱 255	緞 55	請 247	鋒 67
撩 174	熬 3	練 172	諸 414	鋁 185
撬 244	熨 387	緘 124	諂 22	銬 152
撰 417	大 獎 128	線 336	誰 270	銷 339
撞 418	玉 瑩 374	緯 320	誼 371	鋤 32
撐 27	璃 168	緣 385	諛 380	銳 259
撕 288	广 瘤 179	网 罷 6	豆 豎 284	門 閭 184
撒 261	瘠 116	罵 189	豌 316	閱 386
攵 敷 68	瘡 34	羽 翩 227	豕 豬 414	雨 霆 307
敵 47	瘦 280	肉 膜 204	貝 賠 222	震 403
數 283	瘟 323	膚 68	賭 54	非 靠 153
日 暴 9	皮 皺 413	膛 300	賤 126	革 鞏 80

石	礎	33	金	鎊8, 鎮403		瓊	248	金	鏡	141	犬	獻	337
示	禮	169		鎔	256	爪	辦	8	門	關	85	玉	瓏	180
禾	穡	111		鎚	34	田	疆	128	隹	難	209	广	癱	404
穴	竅	244		鎖	295	日	曠	196		離	168		癢	362
竹	簡	125	隹	雞	114	石	礙	2	雨	霧	327	石	礪	170
	簫	340		雛	32	示	禱	44	非	靡	198	石	礫	171
米	糧	173		雙	285	禾	穫	113	音	韻	387		礦	159
糸	繡	348		雜	389		穩	323	頁	顛	48	穴	竇	54
	織	405	革	鞭	13	竹	簿	16		類	167	立	競	141
	繞	255	頁	題	302		簾	172		願	385	竹	籃	163
羽	翻	61		顏	359		簽	239	食	饅	191		籍	117
	翹	244	食	餾	180	糸	繪	110	馬	騙	227		籌	31
耳	職	407		餿	290		繳	132		驚	327	米	糯	216
肉	臍	235	馬	騎	236		繭	124	髟	鬍	102	糸	辮	14
艸	舊	142	魚	鯉	169		繫	331	魚	鯨	138		纂	425
	藐	201, 藍163	髟	鬆	289		繩	272	鳥	鵬	224		繼	119
	藉	135	鬼	魏	322	网	羅	187		鵲	253	羽	耀	365
	藏	18,391	門	閡	332	肉	臘	162		鶉	326	舟	艦	125
	薩	261	魚	鱟	264	艸	藤	302	鹿	麗	169	艸	蘋	230
虫	蟬	22	黑	點	333		藕	217		麓	184		蘆	182
	蟲	30		**19 畫**			藝	369		麒	236		蘇	291
襾	覆	72	土	壟	181		藥	364		**20 畫**		虫	蠔	93
角	觴	267		壞	105	虫	蟹	344	力	勸	252	見	覺	132,148
言	謾	192	广	龐	221	虫	蟻	368	口	嚼	131	言	譬	226
	謬	203		廬	182		蠅	372		嚷	254		警	140
	謹	137	心	懲	27	衣	襟	137		嚴	358		議	369
豆	豐	66		懶	164	言	譜	233	土	壤	254		譯	370
貝	贅	418		懷	104		識	114		壞	105	貝	贍	266
足	蹦	11	手	攀	219		證	405	女	嫿	286		贏	375
	蹟	115		攏	181		識	274	子	孽	213	衣	襪	315
	蹤	422	日	曝	233	貝	贊	390	心	懸	351	采	釋	278
	麼	38		曠	159		贈	393		懺	22	金	鐘	410
身	軀	250	水	瀟	340	足	蹺	242		懷	104	耳	聞	323
車	轉	417	火	爆	10		蹧	32	手	攔	163	風	飄	227
辵	邃	293		爍	287	車	轎	132	日	曦	330	食	饑	114
酉	醬	129	犬	獸	280	辛	辭	36	月	朧	180		饒	254
	醫	367		獺	296	辵	邊	13	水	瀾	163	香	馨	344
里	釐	168	玉	璽	331		遲	162	火	爐	182	馬	騰	302

469

簡體繁體對照表

二畫

簡	繁	頁
厂	廠	23
儿	兒	59
几	幾	117
了	瞭	175

三畫

簡	繁	頁
干	乾	73
干	幹	74
亏	虧	160
万	萬	317
与	與	381
千	韆	239
亿	億	369
个	個	78
广	廣	87
门	門	196
卫	衛	322
飞	飛	63
习	習	330
马	馬	189
乡	鄉	337
食	食	274

四畫

【一】

簡	繁	頁
丰	豐	66
开	開	150
无	無	325
韦	韋	320
专	專	416
云	雲	387
艺	藝	369
厅	廳	306
历	歷	170
区	區	249
车	車	25

【丨】

冈	岡	75
贝	貝	11
见	見	125

【丿】

气	氣	237
长	長	397
仆	僕	232
风	風	66
币	幣	12
仅	僅	137
凤	鳳	68
乌	烏	212

【丶】

闩	閂	285
为	爲	320
斗	鬥	54
忆	憶	369
订	訂	52
计	計	118
讣	訃	72
认	認	256

【乛】

丑	醜	31
队	隊	56
办	辦	7
邓	鄧	46
劝	勸	252
双	雙	285
书	書	280

五畫

【一】

簡	繁	頁
击	擊	114
扑	撲	232
节	節	134
术	術	283
龙	龍	180
厉	厲	170
灭	滅	201
东	東	52

【丨】

卢	盧	182
业	業	366
旧	舊	142
帅	帥	285
归	歸	87
叶	葉	366
号	號	94
电	電	49
只	隻	406
叹	嘆	299
叹	歎	299

【丿】

们	們	196
仪	儀	367
丛	叢	37
尔	爾	59
乐	樂	166
鸟	鳥	212
务	務	327

【丶】

闪	閃	266
兰	蘭	163
汇	匯	111
头	頭	309
汉	漢	92
宁	寧	213
讧	訌	99
讨	討	302
写	寫	343
让	讓	254
礼	禮	169
讪	訕	266
讫	訖	237
训	訓	354

六畫

【一】

簡	繁	頁
动	動	53
执	執	407
巩	鞏	80
扩	擴	161
扫	掃	262
扬	揚	362
场	場	23
亚	亞	357
朴	樸	233
机	機	114
权	權	251
过	過	89
协	協	342
压	壓	356
厌	厭	360
库	庫	157
页	頁	366
夸	誇	157
夺	奪	57
达	達	41
轨	軌	87
划	劃	104
迈	邁	190
毕	畢	12

【丨】

贞	貞	402
师	師	273
当	當	43,44
尘	塵	26
吁	籲	382
吓	嚇	334
虫	蟲	30
团	團	311
吗	嗎	189
屿	嶼	381
岁	歲	293
岂	豈	236
则	則	392
刚	剛	75
网	網	318

【丿】

迁	遷	239
伟	偉	320
传	傳	33
优	優	377
伤	傷	266
价	價	122
伦	倫	187
华	華	103
伪	僞	320
向	嚮	338
后	後	100
会	會	109
杀	殺	263
众	眾	411
爷	爺	365
伞	傘	261
创	創	34
杂	雜	389
负	負	71

【丶】

壮	壯	417
冲	衝	30
冲	沖	30
妆	妝	417
庄	莊	417
庆	慶	247
刘	劉	179
齐	齊	235
产	產	22
闭	閉	12
问	問	324
闯	闖	34
关	關	85
灯	燈	46
汤	湯	300
兴	興	345
兴	興	347
讲	講	128
讶	訝	357
许	許	350
论	論	187
讼	訟	290
讽	諷	67
农	農	214
设	設	269
访	訪	63
诀	訣	147
寻	尋	354
尽	盡	138
尽	儘	137
异	異	370
导	導	44
孙	孫	294
阵	陣	402
阳	陽	362
阴	陰	371
妇	婦	71
妈	媽	189
戏	戲	331
观	觀	85
欢	歡	105
买	買	190
红	紅	99
纣	紂	413
驮	馱	313
纤	纖	334
驯	馴	354
级	級	116
纪	紀	118
驰	馳	29
纫	紉	256

七畫

【一】

簡	繁	頁
寿	壽	280
麦	麥	190
玛	瑪	189
进	進	138
远	遠	385
违	違	320
韧	韌	256
运	運	387
坛	壇	298
搏	搏	428
坏	壞	105
扰	擾	255
坝	壩	5
贡	貢	81
折	摺	400
抢	搶	242
坟	墳	65
护	護	103
壳	殼	153
块	塊	158
声	聲	272
报	報	9
拟	擬	211
严	嚴	358
芦	蘆	182
劳	勞	165
苏	蘇	291
极	極	116
杨	楊	360
两	兩	173
丽	麗	169
医	醫	367
励	勵	171
还	還	90
还	還	105
歼	殲	123
来	來	162
连	連	171

【丨】

卤	鹵	182
坚	堅	123
时	時	274
县	縣	336
里	裏	169
园	園	384
旷	曠	159
围	圍	319
吨	噸	56
邮	郵	378
员	員	384
听	聽	306
呛	嗆	242
鸣	鳴	325
财	財	17
岖	嶇	250
岗	崗	75
帐	帳	398
岚	嵐	163

【丿】

针	針	401
钉	釘	51
体	體	303
佣	傭	376
彻	徹	25
馀	餘	380
邻	鄰	176
肠	腸	23
龟	龜	87
犹	猶	377
鸠	鳩	142
条	條	305
岛	島	44

简	繁	简	繁	简	繁	简	繁	简	繁	简	繁	简	繁
邹	鄒423	坠	墜418	矿	礦159	舍	捨268	诠	詮251	标	標14	选	選352
饨	飩312	劲	勁138	码	碼189	觅	覓198	诡	詭88	栈	棧396	适	適278
饪	飪255	鸡	雞114	厕	廁19	贪	貪298	询	詢354	栋	棟53	种	種411
饭	飯61	驱	驅250	奋	奮66	贫	貧229	谐	諧342	栏	欄163	复	復71
饮	飲372	纯	純35	态	態297	肤	膚68	该	該73	树	樹283	复	複72
系	係331	纱	紗263	垄	壟181	肿	腫411	详	詳338	砖	磚417	覆	覆72
系	繫331	纲	綱75	轰	轟98	胀	脹398	【乛】		面	麵200	贷	貸42
【丶】		纳	納208	顷	頃247	肮	骯3	隶	隸170	牵	牽239	顺	順286
冻	凍53	纵	縱423	转	轉417	胁	脅343	录	錄183	鸥	鷗217	伧	傖124
状	狀418	纶	綸187	斩	斬396	鱼	魚380	弥	彌198	残	殘18	剑	劍126
亩	畝206	纷	紛65	轮	輪187	备	備10	驾	駕122	轴	軸413	须	須349
库	庫157	纸	紙408	软	軟259	饰	飾277	参	參18	轻	輕246	胧	朧186
弃	棄237	纹	紋323	【丨】		饱	飽7	艰	艱123	鸦	鴉356	胜	勝272
疗	療175	纺	紡63	齿	齒29	饲	飼289	线	線336	【丨】		鸨	鴇9
应	應373	驴	驢184	虏	虜183	【丶】		绅	紳270	战	戰396	狭	狹333
这	這401	纽	紐214	肾	腎271	变	變14	细	細332	点	點48	狮	獅273
闲	閑335	八畫		贤	賢335	庞	龐221	驶	駛275	临	臨176	独	獨54
间	間123	【一】		昙	曇299	庙	廟201	驸	駙72	览	覽164	狱	獄382
闷	悶196	杰	傑134	国	國89	疟	瘧216	终	終410	竖	豎284	贸	貿194
灿	燦18	环	環105	畅	暢24	疡	瘍362	织	織405	尝	嘗23	饵	餌59
灶	灶392	责	責392	鸣	鳴203	剂	劑119	驻	駐416	呕	嘔217	饶	饒254
沦	淪187	现	現336	咛	嚀213	废	廢64	绊	絆7	哑	啞357	蚀	蝕275
沟	溝81	规	規87	罗	羅187	闹	鬧209	驼	駝313	显	顯336	饷	餉338
沪	滬103	拢	攏181	帜	幟408	卷	捲146	经	經139	晓	曉341	饼	餅15
怄	慪217	拣	揀124	岭	嶺178	单	單42	贯	貫86	贵	貴88	【丶】	
怀	懷104	担	擔42	凯	凱150	炉	爐182	九畫		虾	蝦332	恋	戀186
忧	憂377	顶	頂52	败	敗6	浅	淺240	【一】		蚁	蟻368	弯	彎316
怅	悵23	拥	擁376	贬	貶13	泻	瀉343	帮	幫8	蚂	螞190	孪	孿186
灾	災389	势	勢276	贮	貯13	泼	潑231	珑	瓏180	虽	雖292	将	將127
穷	窮248	拦	攔163	图	圖310	泽	澤393	项	項339	骂	罵189	奖	獎128
证	證405	拧	擰213	购	購82	怜	憐172	赵	趙400	勋	勛353	疮	瘡34
评	評230	拨	撥15	【丿】		学	學353	挂	掛84	哗	嘩103	疯	瘋67
补	補16	择	擇393	钓	釣50	宝	寶9	挡	擋44	响	響338	亲	親245
识	識274	苹	蘋230	钗	釵21	审	審271	垫	墊49	峡	峽332	闺	閨87
诈	詐394	范	範61	制	製409	帘	簾172	挤	擠118	罚	罰60	闻	聞323
诉	訴291	柜	櫃88	叠	疊51	实	實274	挥	揮108	贴	貼306	闽	閩202
诊	診402	板	闆7	刮	颳84	诔	誄414	莱	萊121	【丿】		闾	閭184
诏	詔399	松	鬆289	侠	俠332	试	試278	带	帶42	钙	鈣73	阁	閣78
译	譯370	枪	槍241	侥	僥131	诙	詼109	茧	繭124	钞	鈔24	阂	閡96
【乛】		枫	楓67	侦	偵402	诚	誠28	荟	薈110	钟	鐘410	养	養362
灵	靈178	构	構82	凭	憑230	衬	襯26	荡	蕩44	钢	鋼75	姜	薑127
层	層20	丧	喪262	侨	僑243	视	視277	荣	榮256	钥	鑰365	类	類167
张	張397	画	畫104	货	貨112	诛	誅414	荤	葷111	钦	欽245	娄	婁181
际	際119	枣	棗391	质	質407	诞	誕43	胡	鬍102	钧	鈞149	总	總423
陆	陸183	卖	賣190	征	徵404	诟	詬82	荫	蔭371	毡	氈395	炼	煉173
陈	陳26	郁	鬱382	径	徑140			药	藥364	气	氣237	烁	爍287

漢語拼音發音法

	聲母 (Initials)			韻母(Finals)	
ㄅ	b (o)	spy	ㄚ	a	father
ㄆ	p (o)	pie	ㄛ	o	saw
ㄇ	m (o)	may	ㄜ	e	error
ㄈ	f (o)	fair	ㄝ	ê	yet
ㄉ	d (e)	style	ㄧ	i	see
ㄊ	t (e)	tie	ㄨ	u	super
ㄋ	n (e)	night	ㄩ	ü	French tu
ㄌ	l (e)	light			
ㄍ	g (e)	sky	ㄞ	ai	eye
ㄎ	k (e)	kite	ㄟ	ei	eight
			ㄠ	ao	how
ㄏ	h (e)	German nach	ㄡ	ou	soul
ㄐ	j (i)	jeep	ㄢ	an	can
ㄑㄧ	q (i)	cheap	ㄣ	en	women
ㄒ	x (i)	between s and sh	ㄤ	ang	German Gang
ㄓ	zh (i)	judge	ㄥ	eng	lung
ㄔ	ch (i)	church	ㄨㄥ	ong	German jung
ㄕ	sh (i)	shirt	ㄧㄚ	ia	Asia
ㄖ	r (i)	leisure	ㄧㄝ	ie	yes
ㄗ	z (i)	friends	ㄧㄠ	iao	yowl
ㄘ	c (i)	hats	ㄧㄡ	iu	you
ㄙ	s (i)	say	ㄧㄢ	ian	yen
	y (i)	yea	ㄧㄣ	in	in
	w (u)	way	ㄧㄤ	iang	young
			ㄧㄥ	ing	sing
			ㄩㄥ	iong	German jünger
			ㄨㄚ	ua	wander
			ㄨㄛ	uo	wall
			ㄨㄞ	uai	wide
			ㄨㄟ	ui	we
			ㄨㄢ	uan	one
			ㄨㄣ	un	went
			ㄨㄤ	uang	oo + ang
					ü + eh
				üe	ü + an
				üan	German grün
				ün	

漢語拼音文法和規則

一、聲調符號一(一聲)ˊ(二聲)ˇ(三聲)ˋ(四聲)

(1a) 標在音節的主要母音上，輕聲不標。媽ma，麻ma，馬ma，罵ma，嗎ma。

(1b) i和u和其他韻母一起時，聲調符號總是標在第二母音上。

	一聲	二聲	三聲	四聲	輕聲
例如	huāng荒	liáng糧	luǎn卵	piàn片	ne呢

(1c) i和u同時在一起時，標音符號總是標在後面一個上，如giu，標在u上，Shui標在i上面。

> 如果漢語拼音母音多於一個母音，標音以a e i o u為順序，如xian。但是除了iu和iong
> 如giǔ標在u上，xióng熊（標在o上）

二、 ㄓ　　ㄔ　　ㄕ　　ㄖ　　ㄗ　　ㄘ　　ㄙ
　　　zh　　ch　　sh　　r　　z　　c　　s

單獨使用後面必須加"i"。而拼成zhi, chi, shi, ri, zi, ci, si參看發音對照表拼音欄。

三、 i前面沒有聲母時改i成ㄚ。　　　　　　u前面沒有聲母時，改u成w。

一	i→yi	衣(yi)
一ㄚ	ia→ya	鴨(ya)
一ㄝ	ie→ye	耶(ye)
一ㄠ	iao→yao	腰(yao)
一ㄡ	iu→you	優(you)
一ㄢ	ian→yan	煙(yan)
一ㄣ	in→yin	陰(yin)
一ㄤ	iang→yang	央(yang)
一ㄥ	ing→ying	英(ying)
ㄩㄥ	iong→yong	雍(yong)

ㄨ	ua→wa	蛙(wa)
ㄨㄛ	uo→wo	窩(wo)
ㄨㄞ	uai→wai	歪(wai)
ㄨㄟ	ui→wei	威(wei)
ㄨㄢ	uan→wan	彎(wan)
ㄨㄣ	un→wen	溫(wen)
ㄨㄤ	uang→wang	王(wang)
ㄨㄥ	ong→weng	翁(weng)

四、儿(er)在韻尾的時候寫成r，例如「兒童」értóng，但是「這兒」「花兒」拼音是(zhèr)(huār)。

五、ü前面沒有聲母的時候寫成yu。省去兩點

例yu(迂)，yuē約，yuán鴛，yūn暈

六、ü和聲母j, q, x拼的時候，寫成ju(居)，qu(區)，xu(虛)，ü上兩點都略成u。

但是和l和n拼音時，寫成nü(女)和lü(綠)。

七、iou, uei, uen前面再加聲母時，寫成iu(一ㄡ), ui(ㄨㄟ), un(ㄨㄣ) 例如niu(牛), gui(規), lun(論)。

八、a, o, e連接在其他音節後面，如果音節的界限發生混淆，用隔音符號(ˊ)隔開，例pi'ao(皮襖)。

1. 拼音字母順序：A至Z表
   Pin Yin Alphabetical order = The A-Z Word List
   填入空格按字母順序
   Fill in the blank according to the alphabetical order
   _ b _ d _ f g _ _j _ _ _ _o p q_ _ _ _u v w_ _ _z

2. 將拼音按字母順序排列
   Put the Pin-Yin in alphabetical order.

Wo	Yi	Peng	ni	wei	weng
ta	pen	Yen			

   1____   2____   3____   4___   5___   6___
   7____   8____   9____

3. 請將標音聲調順序排列
   Put the Pin-Yin sound in order.

   Ex.   má   mà   mǎ   mā
              ①mā   ②má   ③mǎ   ④mà

              tā   tǎ   tà   tá
              1_____   2_____   3_____   4____

中文註解練習 (Chinese Explanation Practice)

4. 第五頁，連連看正確的註解
   On page 5. Look at the explanation column meaning, match the correct meaning.

   1. 八   a. 抽起
   2. 疤   b. 七加一得到的數目字
   3. 拔   c. 射擊的目標
   4. 把   d. 父親
   5. 靶   e. 傷口癒後留下的痕跡
   6. 爸   f. 握

中文舉例練習(Chinese Example Practice)

5. 第五頁，舉例連連看

On page 5, look at the example column, match the correct example.

1. 八	a. 拔河
2. 疤	b. 靶場
3. 拔	c. 八面玲瓏
4. 把	d. 疤痕
5. 靶	e. 爸爸
6. 爸	f. 把持

英文註解練習(English Explanation Practice)

6. 第一頁，連連看英文註解

On page one, look at the English Explanation column, match the word with the correct meaning.

1. 哀	a. dust
2. 埃	b. cancer
3. 挨	c. sorrow
4. 癌	d. friendly
5. 藹	e. suffer

注音拼音練習(Phonetical Symbol/Pin Yin Practice)

7. 第一頁，連連看拼音注音

On page 1, look at phonetical symbol/Pin Yin column. Match with the correct word.

1. 阿	a. ai ㄞ
2. 哀	b. a ㄚ
3. 藹	c. ai ㄞˊ
4. 挨	d. ai ㄞˇ

英文舉例練習(English Example Translation Practice)

8. 第五頁，舉例欄，連連看英文註解

On page 5, look at the example column, match the correct meaning.

1. 拔河	a. shooting range
2. 靶場	b. very sociable
3. 八面玲瓏	c. tug of war
4. 爸爸	d. control
5. 把持	e. dad

拼音練習 (Pin Yin Practice)

9. 第五頁，舉例欄，連連看拼音

On page 5, look at the example column match the correct Pin Yin.

1. 拔河
2. 靶場
3. 八面玲瓏
4. 疤痕
5. 爸爸
6. 把持

a. bá chí
b. bà ba
c. bā hén
d. bǎ chǎng
e. bā miàn líng lóng
f. bá hé

拼音練習 (Pin Yin Practice)

10. 第五頁，圈出正確的拼音

Look at page 5, circle the correct Pin Yin.

Ex. 八   (bā)   bà
1. 疤   bā   bà
2. 拔   bā   bá
3. 把   bǎ   bā
4. 爸   bà   bǎ
5. 霸   bà   bā

注音練習　Phonetical Symbol Practice

11. 第五頁，圈出正確的注音

Look at page 5, circle the correct phonetical symbol.

Ex. 八   (ㄅㄚ)   ㄅㄚˋ
1. 疤   ㄅㄚ   ㄅㄚˋ
2. 拔   ㄅㄚ   ㄅㄚˊ
3. 把   ㄅㄚˇ   ㄅㄚ
4. 爸   ㄅㄚˋ   ㄅㄚˇ
5. 霸   ㄅㄚ   ㄅㄚˋ

總筆劃查字表練習
Total Stroke Table Practice

12. 總筆劃查字表第六頁，寫出下列字的筆劃、部首和頁數。
Look at "The Total Stroke Table Practice" page 6 write the following word's total stroke, root and page.

部首	繁體字	筆劃	頁數
例 Example　　人	倍	10	196
目	相	9	339 337
	看		
	是		
	要		
	洗		
	春		
	們		

注音拼音查字對照表練習
Phonetical Symbol / Pin Yin Table Practice

13. 看注音拼音對照表填入空格Look at phonetical symbol/Pin Yin table practice fill in the page.

Phonetical Symbol	Pin Yin	Page
Ex.　　ㄅ	b	5
ㄋ		
ㄏ		
ㄍ		
ㄉ		
ㄚ		
ㄣ		
ㄠ		

1. 拼音字母順序：A至Z表
Pin Yin Alphabetical order = The A-Z Word List
填入空格按字母順序
Fill in the blank according to the alphabetical order
a b c d e f g h i j k l m n o p q r s t u v w x y z

2. 拼音按字母順序排列
Put the Pin-Yin in alphabetical order.
Wo   Yi   Peng   ni   wei   weng
ta   pen   Yen
1 ni 2 pen 3 peng 4 ta 5 wei 6 weng
7 wo 8 Yen 9 Yi

3. 請將樣音聲調順序排列
Put the Pin-Yin sound in order.

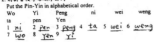

Ex.   má   mà   má   mǎ
①má   ②má   ③mǎ   ④mà

1 tǎ 2 tá 3 tǎ 4 tà

4. 第五頁，連連看正確的註解
On page 5. Look at the explanation column meaning, match the correct meaning.

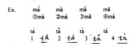

1. 八   a. 抽起
2. 疤   b. 七加一得到的數目字
3. 拔   c. 射擊的目標
4. 把   d. 父親
5. 靶   e. 傷口癒後留下的痕跡
6. 爸   f. 握

5. 第五頁，舉例連連看
On page 5, look at the example column, match the correct example.

1. 八   a. 拔河
2. 疤   b. 靶場
3. 拔   c. 八面玲瓏
4. 把   d. 疤痕
5. 靶   e. 爸爸
6. 爸   f. 把持

6. 第一頁，連連看英文註解
On page one, look at the English Explanation column, match the word with the correct meaning.

1. 哀   a. dust
2. 埃   b. cancer
3. 挨   c. sorrow
4. 癌   d. friendly
5. 藹   e. suffer

7. 第一頁，連連看拼音注音
On page 1, look at phonetical symbol/Pin Yin column. Match with the correct word.

1. 哀   a. ai 所
2. 哀   b. a Y
3. 藹   c. ai 所ˇ
4. 挨   d. ai 所ˋ

8. 第五頁，舉例欄，連連看英文註解
On page 5, look at the example column, match the correct meaning.

1. 拔河   a. shooting range
2. 靶場   b. very sociable
3. 八面玲瓏   c. tug of war
4. 爸爸   d. control
5. 把持   e. dad

9. 第五頁，舉例欄，連連看拼音
On page 5, look at the example column match the correct Pin Yin.

1. 拔河   a. bá chi
2. 靶場   b. bǎ ba
3. 八面玲瓏   c. bǐ hén
4. 疤痕   d. bǎ cháng
5. 爸爸   e. bā mián líng lóng
6. 把持   f. bá hé

10. 第五頁，圈出正確的拼音
Look at page 5, circle the correct Pin Yin.
Ex. 八   bā bà
1. 疤   bā bà
2. 拔   bá bá
3. 把   bǎ bá
4. 爸   bǎ bà
5. 靶   bǎ bā

11. 第五頁，圈出正確的注音
Look at page 5, circle the correct phonetical symbol.
Ex. 八   ㄅㄚ ㄅㄚˋ
1. 疤   ㄅㄚ ㄅㄚˊ
2. 拔   ㄅㄚˊ ㄅㄚˋ
3. 把   ㄅㄚ ㄅㄚˇ
4. 爸   ㄅㄚ ㄅㄚˋ
5. 靶   ㄅㄚˇ ㄅㄚˋ

12. 總筆劃查字表第六頁，寫出下列字的筆劃、部首和頁數。
Look at "The Total Stroke Table Practice" page 6 write the following word's total stroke, root and page.

部首	繁體字	筆劃	頁數
例 Example 人	俏	10	196
目	相	9	339 337
日	春	9	150 & 151
日	是	9	278
雨	雪	9	284
水	洗	9	331
日	春	9	35
人	們	10	10

13. 看注音拼音對照表填入空格Look at phonetical symbol/Pin Yin table practice fill in the page.

Phonetical Symbol	Pin Yin	Page
Ex. ㄅ	b	5
ㄋ	n	208
ㄏ	h	90
ㄍ	g	73
ㄉ	d	41
ㄚ	a	1
ㄣ	en	59
ㄠ	ao	3

字典練習

Sample

注 音				
ㄓ ㄧ ㄨ ㄣ				
頁 數 Page				
拼 音 PinYin				

注音	ㄅ ㄚˋ	ㄇ ㄚ	ㄇ ㄚˊ	ㄉ ㄚˋ
頁數	5,6	189	189	41
拼音	bà	mā	mǎ	dà

字典練習

頁數 Page	正體字 Traditional	注音 Phonic	筆劃 Stroke	中文註解 Chinese Explanation	英文註解 English Explanation	造詞 Make a phrase 注音 Pinyin	英文解釋 English Meaning
340	小	ㄒㄧㄠˇ	3	"大"的相反，壞人，年紀輕	Small Mean	小人 ㄒㄧㄠˇ ㄖㄣˊ Xiao Ren	A mean person

1 畫

一 yī ・ 丨 gǔn ・ 丶 zhǔ ・ 丿 piě ・ 乙 yǐ ・ 亅 jué

2 畫

二 èr ・ 亠 tóu ・ 人 rén ・ 儿 rén ・ 入 rù ・ 八 bā ・ 冂 jiōng ・ 冖 mì ・ 冫 bīng ・ 几 jī ・ 凵 kǎn ・ 刀 dāo ・ 力 lì ・ 勹 bāo ・ 匕 bǐ ・ 匚 fāng ・ 匸 xì ・ 十 shí ・ 卜 bǔ ・ 卩 jié ・ 厂 hǎn ・ 厶 sī ・ 又 yòu

3 畫

口 kǒu ・ 囗 wéi ・ 土 tǔ ・ 士 shì ・ 夂 suī ・ 夕 xī ・ 大 dà ・ 女 nǚ ・ 子 zǐ ・ 宀 mián ・ 寸 cùn ・ 小 xiǎo ・ 尢 wāng ・ 尸 shī ・ 屮 chè ・ 山 shān ・ 巛 chuān ・ 工 gōng ・ 己 jǐ ・ 巾 jīn ・ 干 gān ・ 幺 yāo ・ 广 yǎn ・ 廴 yǐn ・ 廾 gǒng ・ 弋 yì ・ 弓 gōng ・ 彐 jì ・ 彡 shān ・ 彳 chì

4 畫

心 xīn ・ 戈 gē ・ 戶 hù ・ 手 shǒu ・ 支 zhī ・ 攴 pū ・ 文 wén ・ 斗 dǒu ・ 斤 jīn ・ 方 fāng ・ 无 wú ・ 日 rì ・ 曰 yuē ・ 月 yuè ・ 木 mù ・ 欠 qiàn ・ 止 zhǐ ・ 歹 dǎi ・ 殳 shū ・ 毋 wú ・ 比 bǐ ・ 毛 máo ・ 氏 shì ・ 气 qì ・ 水 shuǐ ・ 火 huǒ ・ 爪 zhǎo ・ 父 fù ・ 爻 yáo ・ 爿 qiáng ・ 片 piàn ・ 牙 yá ・ 牛 niú ・ 犬 quǎn

5 畫

玄 xuán ・ 玉 yù ・ 瓜 guā ・ 瓦 wǎ ・ 甘 gān ・ 生 shēng ・ 用 yòng ・ 田 tián ・ 疋 pǐ ・ 疒 chuáng ・ 癶 bō ・ 白 bái ・ 皮 pí ・ 皿 mǐn ・ 目 mù ・ 矛 máo ・ 矢 shǐ ・ 石 shí ・ 示 shì ・ 禸 róu ・ 禾 hé ・ 穴 xué ・ 立 lì

6 畫

竹 zhú ・ 米 mǐ ・ 糸 mì ・ 缶 fǒu ・ 网 wǎng ・ 羊 yáng ・ 羽 yǔ ・ 老 lǎo ・ 而 ér ・ 耒 lěi ・ 耳 ěr ・ 聿 yù ・ 肉 ròu ・ 臣 chén ・ 自 zì ・ 至 zhì ・ 臼 jiù ・ 舌 shé ・ 舛 chuǎn ・ 舟 zhōu ・ 艮 gèn ・ 色 sè ・ 艸 cǎo ・ 虍 hū ・ 虫 huǐ ・ 血 xiě ・ 行 xíng ・ 衣 yī ・ 襾 yà

7 畫

見 jiàn ・ 角 jiǎo ・ 言 yán ・ 谷 gǔ ・ 豆 dòu ・ 豕 shǐ ・ 豸 zhì ・ 貝 bèi ・ 赤 chì ・ 走 zǒu ・ 足 zú ・ 身 shēn ・ 車 chē ・ 辛 xīn ・ 辰 chén ・ 辵 chuò ・ 邑 yì ・ 酉 yǒu ・ 釆 biàn ・ 里 lǐ

8 畫

金 jīn ・ 長 cháng ・ 門 mén ・ 阜 fù ・ 隶 dài ・ 隹 zhuī ・ 雨 yǔ ・ 青 qīng ・ 非 fēi

9 畫

面 miàn ・ 革 gé ・ 韋 wéi ・ 韭 jiǔ ・ 音 yīn ・ 頁 yè ・ 風 fēng ・ 飛 fēi ・ 食 shí ・ 首 shǒu ・ 香 xiāng

10 畫

馬 mǎ ・ 骨 gǔ ・ 高 gāo ・ 髟 biāo ・ 鬥 dòu ・ 鬯 chàng ・ 鬲 gé ・ 鬼 guǐ

11 畫

魚 yú ・ 鳥 niǎo ・ 鹵 lǔ ・ 鹿 lù ・ 麥 mài ・ 麻 má

12 畫

黃 huáng ・ 黍 shǔ ・ 黑 hēi ・ 黹 zhǐ

13 畫

黽 mǐn ・ 鼎 dǐng ・ 鼓 gǔ ・ 鼠 shǔ

14 畫

鼻 bí ・ 齊 qí

15 畫

齒 chǐ

16 畫

龍 lóng ・ 龜 guī

17 畫

龠 yuè

注音拼音查字對照表　　Pronounciation Guide

注音符號	漢語拼音	頁數	注音符號	拼音	頁數	注音符號	漢語拼音	頁數	Pinyin	English Equivalient
ㄅ	b	5	ㄙ	si / s	261	一ㄞ	yai		a	as in father
									ai	eye
ㄆ	p	218	ㄚ	a	1	一ㄠ	yao / iao	364	b	Bob
									c	hats
ㄇ	m	189	ㄛ	o	217	一ㄡ	you / iu	377	d	dog
ㄈ	f	60	ㄜ	e	58	一ㄢ	yan / ian	357	e	error
									en	women
ㄉ	d	41	ㄝ			一ㄣ	yin / in	373	f	fair
ㄊ	t	296	ㄞ	ai	1	一ㄤ	yang / iang	361	g	girl
									h	hunt
ㄋ	n	208	ㄟ	ei		一ㄥ	ying / ing	375	I	see
									iu	you
ㄌ	l	162	ㄠ	ao	3	ㄨㄚ	wa / ua	315	j	jeep
ㄍ	g	73	ㄡ	ou	217	ㄨㄛ	wo / uo	325	k	kite
									l	life
ㄎ	k	150	ㄢ	an	2	ㄨㄞ	wai / uai	315	m	may
ㄏ	h	90	ㄣ	en	59	ㄨㄟ	wei / ui	319	n	night
ㄐ	j	114	ㄤ	ang	3	ㄨㄢ	wan / uan	316	o	note
									ou	soul
ㄑ	q	234	ㄥ	eng		ㄨㄣ	wen / un	322	p	pie
ㄒ	x	328	ㄦ	er	59	ㄨㄤ	wang / uang	317	q	cheap
									r	leisure
ㄓ	zhi / zh	405 / 393	一	yi / y,i	367	ㄨㄥ	weng / ong	324	s	say
									sh	shoe
ㄔ	chi / ch	20	ㄨ	wu / w,u,	315	ㄩㄝ	yue / ue	386	shi	shirt
ㄕ	shi / sh	263	ㄩ	yu / u	379	ㄩㄢ	yuan / uan	384	t	tie
									u	super
ㄖ	ri / r	254	一ㄚ	ya / ia	356	ㄩㄣ	yun / un	387	ua	wander
ㄗ	zi / z	389	一ㄛ	yo / io	375	ㄩㄥ	yong / iong	375	w	way
									x	sheet
ㄘ	ci / c	17	一ㄝ	ye / ie	365				y	young
									z	zero
									zh	judge

主　　編/黃敦柔，蘇發興

出版日期/2008 年 6 月第一刷

美國地區郵購辦法：
　　利用匯票訂購，書價加掛號郵資共計美金　　　　元。

　　匯票抬頭：J&R Co.
　　通訊地址：13729 Capistrano Rd.,
　　　　　　　La Mirada, CA 90638
　　或者
　　匯票抬頭：Saw Associates LLC
　　通訊地址：1712 Chattanooga Ct.,
　　　　　　　Claremont CA 91711

　　電子郵件信箱：pinyin@verizon.net
　　　　　　　　　francis@sawllc.net

國際統一書號/ISBN 978-0-615-19698-5

ORDER FORM

J&R CO.

13729 Capistrano Rd.,
La Mirada, CA 90638
Email: pinyin@verizon.net

Note: The *Practical Chinese/English and English/Chinese Dictionary* is $ _____ each. For orders of 5 books and less, please add $4.00 per book to cover shipping and handling charges as well as taxes. Shipping charges are 9% for orders of 6 to 50 books and 8% for orders of over 50 books, plus applicable sales taxes. Alaska, Hawaii and international customers are charged 25% for shipping and handling. UPS will be used unless the customer specifically requests otherwise.

Purchase Order Number	Date:
Bill To Address:	**Ship To Address:** (if different from "Bill to Address")

□ Adult School □ High School	
□ Jr or Middle School □ Elementary School	
School (Institution)	
Name	
Title	
Address	
City	State Zip
Telephone	
Authorized Signature	

Title	Qty	Price	Total
Subtotal			
Sales tax (CA residents only)			
Shipping & Handling			
Grand Total			

* Please make check payable to *J&R Co.*